QUINE

ARGUMENTS OF THE PHILOSOPHERS

The purpose of this series is to provide a contemporary assessment and history of the entire course of philosophical thought. Each book contains a detailed, critical introduction to the work of a philosopher or school of major influence and significance.

Also available in the series:

* AQUINAS
Eleonore Stump

* DESCARTES
Margaret D. Wilson

* HEGEL
M.J. Inwood

* HUME
Barry Stroud

KANT
Ralph C.S. Walker

KIERKEGAARD
Alastair Hannay

* LOCKE
Michael Ayers

* MALEBRANCHE
Andrew Pyle

* KARL MARX
Allen Wood

* MERLEAU-PONTY
Stephen Priest

* NIETZSCHE
Richard Schacht

* PLATO
Justin Gosling

* PLOTINUS
Lloyd P. Gerson

* ROUSSEAU
Timothy O'Hagan

* THE PRESOCRATIC
PHILOSOPHERS
Jonathan Barnes

* SANTAYANA
Timothy L.S. Sprigge

* THE SCEPTICS
R.J. Hankinson

* WITTGENSTEIN,
2nd edition
Robert Fogelin

* also available in paperback

QUINE

Peter Hylton

NEW YORK AND LONDON

FOR SALLY

First published 2007
by Routledge
270 Madison Ave, New York, NY 10016

Simultaneously published in the UK
by Routledge
2 Park Square, Milton Park, Abingdon, Oxon OX14 4RN

Routledge is an imprint of the Taylor & Francis Group, an informa business

© 2007 Peter Hylton

Typeset in Garamond by
Taylor & Francis Books
Printed and bound in Great Britain by
Antony Rowe Ltd, Chippenham, Wiltshire

British Library Cataloguing in Publication Data
A catalogue record for this book is available from the British Library

Library of Congress Cataloging-in-Publication Data
A catalog record for this book has been requested

ISBN 10: 0-415-06398-1
ISBN 13: 978-0-415-06398-2

CONTENTS

CONTENTS

ACKNOWLEDGEMENTS

I wish to record my gratitude to all who have assisted and encouraged me in the writing of this book. First among them is Andrew Lugg. For the last five or six years, as I have written and rewritten, he has been my intellectual companion and chief interlocutor, always ready to discuss difficulties of understanding or of exposition. He has subjected my drafts to a careful, sympathetic, yet critical reading, from which I have greatly benefitted. I owe a crucial debt also to Tom Ricketts; a number of conversations with him over the years have decisively influenced the book. I am indebted to the publisher's readers, especially to Dagfinn Føllesdal whose comments led me to rethink one section completely. Others who have read and commented on parts of the book in preparation include Walter Edelberg, Juliet Floyd, Bob Fogelin, Warren Goldfarb, Bill Hart, Gary Kemp, Matt Moore, Sally Sedgwick, and Rogério Severo. I may well have omitted some who ought to be on this list; I can only beg their forgiveness.

I am indebted in a rather different way to Sean Morris, who prepared the index for the book, and to Bill Hart (again) who first introduced me to Ted Honderich, then editor of the series in which the book appears.

I have received generous institutional support. I gratefully acknowledge the UIC Institute for the Humanities, the NEH, and the ACLS; also the UIC College of Liberal Arts and Sciences, under successive deans. Without the time free from teaching which those institutions made possible, this book would, at best, have taken much longer. The UIC department of philosophy has provided a supportive and encouraging environment; Bill Hart was its Chair for almost the entire period during which the book was written and I owe him (yet again) particular thanks.

ABBREVIATIONS

To reduce clutter, I use abbreviations for works which are referred to repeatedly in the text. I divide them into three categories: books by Quine, essays by Quine, and volumes of essays about Quine which contain responses or comments by Quine. Detailed references may be found in the Bibliography.

Books by Quine

FLPV	*From a Logical Point of View*
FSS	*From Stimulus to Science*
OR	*Ontological Relativity and Other Essays*
PL	*Philosophy of Logic*
PT	*Pursuit of Truth*
RR	*Roots of Reference*
TT	*Theories and Things*
WO	*Word and Object*
WP	*Ways of Paradox*

Essays by Quine

C&LT	"Carnap and Logical Truth", in *WP*
EC	"Empirical Content", in *TT*
EESW	"Empirically Equivalent Systems of the World"
EN	"Epistemology Naturalized", in *OR*
FM	"Facts of the Matter"
MSLT	"Mr. Strawson on Logical Truth", in *WP*
MVD	"Mind and Verbal Dispositions"
NLWM	"Naturalism, or Living within One's Means"
NNK	"The Nature of Natural Knowledge"
SLS	"The Scope and Language of Science", in *WP*
TDE	"Two Dogmas of Empiricism", in *FLPV*

TDR   "Two Dogmas in Retrospect"
TPT   "Things and Their Place in Theories", in *TT*
WPB?   "What Price Bivalence?", in *TT*
WPO?   "Whither Physical Objects?"

Collections of essays about Quine, with replies or comments by Quine

B&G   Barrett and Gibson, eds, *Perspectives on Quine*
D&H   Davidson and Hintikka, eds, *Words and Objections*
H&S   Hahn and Schilpp, eds, *The Philosophy of W. V. Quine* (2nd edn)
L&S   Leonardi and Santabrogio, eds, *On Quine*
O&K   Orenstein and Kotatko, eds, *Knowledge, Language and Logic*

INTRODUCTION

The subject of this book is the philosophy of W. V. Quine (1908–2000). In it, I attempt a unified, sympathetic, and comprehensive treatment of his philosophical thought. I proceed, for the most part, thematically rather than chronologically. I do not discuss his technical work in logic and set-theory, except very briefly. The details of that work seem to me to be largely independent of his philosophical work. This is not to deny all contact between the two. The spirit in which the technical work is done is recognizably the same as that which pervades his philosophical thought. In particular, Quine's technical work places great emphasis on precision, clarity, and simplicity, sometimes to the exclusion of other factors which some have thought important. The idea that our theories should be reformulated so as to maximize theoretical virtues of this kind also plays a major role in his philosophical work. But this sort of relation between the two did not seem to me to justify the space that would be required to explain his technical work in any detail. I was also concerned to keep the book as broadly accessible as possible. To that end, I draw on very little logic that I do not explain; the uses of the logic that I do explain are fairly elementary, and even they can be skipped without great loss.

Quine is surely among the best known analytic philosophers of the second half of the twentieth century. For all his fame, however, I think that his view is not generally very well understood. I also think that his philosophy as a whole is underestimated. That is an odd thing to say about the thought of so widely celebrated a philosopher, but as I have worked on his texts, and on this book, I have come to think that his philosophy is far more powerful than is generally recognized. A large part of the reason for this power is that he is an immensely systematic thinker. Many commentators have not sufficiently appreciated the extent to which his views hang together to form a coherent whole.[1] His thought is wide-ranging; within the realm of theoretical philosophy (as opposed to practical philosophy, or value theory) he has

1

something to say on almost every topic that has engaged analytic philosophers since Frege. But anyone who approaches Quine's work primarily interested in one of those topics—the status of second-order logic, say, or scepticism about the external world—is likely to miss the larger Quinean picture and thus also to miss the power of his thought. And examined in isolation, Quine's views on a particular topic may seem under-motivated or even arbitrary. Because Quine's philosophy is systematic, I mostly do not treat it chronologically. Rather than considering first this work and then that, I discuss the philosophy more or less as a single whole. There are, of course, changes of mind and shifts of emphasis over time within his thought, and I note these when they are relevant to my discussion. But these changes are for the most part on points of detail, or anyway for fairly detailed reasons, not because of any change of heart. So I found it best to treat all his philosophical works as expressions of the same view, albeit one that became clearer to him over time.

Where can one begin the explanation of a philosophical view at once so systematic and so wide-ranging? At the heart of Quine's system is his naturalism, his rejection of any form of knowledge other than our ordinary knowledge manifested in common sense and in science. (Quine does not see these as different in kind; scientific knowledge, in his view, develops as we strive to improve upon common sense.) Taken broadly, as the claim that the methods and techniques of natural science are the source of knowledge about the world, naturalism is widely accepted. But what is the status of the naturalistic claim itself? Quine insists that it too must be based on science. (He simply accepts whatever circularity there is here.) This is a revolutionary step. Quine denies that there is a distinctively philosophical standpoint—which might, for example, allow philosophical reflection to prescribe standards to science as a whole. For him, naturalism is "the recognition that it is within science itself, and not in some prior philosophy, that reality is to be identified and described" (*TT*, p. 21). The philosopher, therefore, reflects on science from within science. There is no theory of knowledge distinct from science.

This step is revolutionary because of the implications that Quine draws from it. He takes it to imply that the theory of knowledge—indeed philosophy as a whole—has no standards which transcend those of our most successful science; there is no external standpoint from which we can question that science. He thus also takes it to imply that philosophy itself is subject to the standards of clarity, of evidence, and of justification which are most explicitly displayed, and most successfully implemented, in that science.

Quine sticks to this view with great consistency and rigour; it sometimes seems, indeed, as if he finds it wholly obvious and does not appreciate how different it is from that of most philosophers. One result is that even when he phrases a question using the same form of words as others—in talking about how we can have knowledge of the external world, for example—it is far from clear that we should really take him to be addressing "the same problem". His understanding of what is at stake, and of what would count as a solution, is quite novel; his work thus amounts to a reconceiving of the problems of philosophy. (Hence his work might be cited against the idea that philosophy consists of attempts to solve eternal and unchanging problems, and in favour of the idea that the problems are historically conditioned.[2])

Quine's assumptions are thus very different from those of most philosophers; often he simply takes them for granted, without even articulating them. This fact is no doubt another reason that his work is widely misunderstood. It also explains why it is hard to compare Quine's views with those of other philosophers in a way that is useful; all too often there is simply a missing of minds. So I have largely refrained from such comparisons, except that I often found it useful to relate Quine's views to those of Carnap, who is the philosopher who most directly influenced Quine. (The divergence of Quine's assumptions from those of most philosophers is also one reason that the most revealing statements of his view very often occur in his replies to those who have written about his work, as if it is only when confronted with misunderstandings that he sees the need to be fully explicit.)

What we have said about Quine's naturalism raises many questions. Most obviously, perhaps: what counts as "science", and why should it be accorded a privileged position? Also, more generally, it raises questions about what naturalism comes to in Quine's hands and what its rationale is. Answering such questions requires that we draw on various aspects of Quine's thought. As with any truly systematic philosopher, one may have the sense that there is no point at which an exposition can begin: whatever one wants to say first only really makes sense in the light of the view as a whole. I have resolved this problem, as best I can, by beginning with a chapter that explains Quine's naturalism and, in the process, explores its place in his thought and some of its ramifications. Given the centrality of naturalism to Quine's philosophy, this chapter is also an overview of Quine's philosophical view as a whole; it thus serves to orient the reader for the rest of the book.

In the last section of the first chapter, I argue that Quine's naturalism leaves him with two tasks. One is to outline an account of human cognition within the constraints of what he would count as a purely naturalistic framework. Since the seventeenth century, when our modern conception of natural science developed, philosophers have faced the question whether the human mind is susceptible of treatment which is scientific in the sense in which Galileo's physics or (paradigmatically) Newton's physics is scientific. Quine gives an unequivocally affirmative answer, and by very rigorous standards of what counts as scientific. The first task is simply to make it plausible that this answer is correct, that there is an account of this kind to be given. The other task facing Quine is to spell out the naturalistic framework, to show just what constraints it should be taken to impose, what justifies them, and how our knowledge is to be fitted into those constraints. I call his attempts to carry out these tasks "the epistemological project" and "the metaphysical project" respectively.[3] (These labels are further explained in Chapter 1 and in the rest of the book.) There are, of course, points of contact between the details of each project. There is also a very general question about the relation between them. In the bulk of the book, however, they are for the most part considered separately—the epistemological project in Chapters 4 through 7, the metaphysical project most centrally in Chapters 9 through 13.

Quine is often thought of as primarily a negative philosopher, chiefly concerned to deny this and to reject that. That seems to me a mistake—a mistake that arises from a failure to appreciate how systematic a thinker he is. Both the epistemological project and the metaphysical project are constructive rather than negative. In the end, indeed, I think they are aspects of the single constructive project of articulating and defending a thoroughgoing naturalistic view of the world. Quine's negative remarks are only defensible—or even properly comprehensible—in the context of his positive aims. His notorious "rejection of the concept of meaning", for example, must be seen in the context of his attempt to show that we have no need for such a concept because we can manage without taking it for granted—that we can give an account of (what he takes to be) the phenomena of language-use in (what he takes to be) purely naturalistic terms. His strongest argument against the concept is simply that we have no need for it.

The account of the book two paragraphs back leaves three chapters unmentioned. Chapter 2 deals with Quine's intellectual background. It includes brief discussions of his early intellectual life and of his work on logic but the bulk of the chapter is spent on the work of Rudolf Carnap, who is, as already mentioned, the philosopher who most directly influenced Quine. The subject of Chapter 3 is Quine's view about the distinction between the analytic and the synthetic. The wider issue under consideration, however, is the way in which Quine differs from Carnap; this difference is

often seen as based on their differences over the analytic–synthetic distinction. That issue is an important one, but, from the point of view of Quine's
constructive projects, it functions primarily as preparatory work, clearing
the ground. Chapter 8 discusses the vexed issue of the indeterminacy of
translation. Various questions arise here: exactly how the thesis is to be
understood; whether it is, as some have claimed, quite evidently absurd, or
incoherent; and what arguments can be brought for and against it. All these
issues are discussed in the chapter. I also discuss the significance of the
indeterminacy thesis; I argue that its role within Quine's thought is quite
minor. Indeterminacy is perhaps Quine's best known—most notorious—
idea, and has provoked a vast body of literature, but I do not see it as
playing any kind of central role in his thought.

The conclusion of the book, finally, takes up the question of the relation
between the two projects, and how they amount to aspects of a single
overarching philosophical project. I also briefly discuss the criteria of success
for this project, and various ways in which one might disagree with
Quine—not on this or that point of detail, but with the Quinean project as
a whole.

1

OVERVIEW

Quine's naturalism

The purpose of this chapter is to set out some fundamental points of Quine's philosophy, to orient us and guide us in what follows. We begin with a very compressed and abstract summary, and then enlarge and qualify as we go.

I Fundamentals

Quine's philosophical concern is with human knowledge, and with the most general features of the world that we attempt to know. (He finds the word "knowledge" unacceptably vague, but it will do to get us going.) He has no particular philosophical interest in ethics, or the nature of a just society, or the nature of art; indeed he does not seem to see those matters as falling within his purview at all.[1] His most explicit writing on ethics is chiefly a speculation on how moral values might be inculcated in human beings as they mature.[2] His work is thus, in one way, narrow in scope. In another way, however, it is perhaps broader than one might expect, especially as compared with that of Rudolf Carnap, the philosopher who most directly influenced him. Carnap wholly rejects the idea that philosophy gives us knowledge of the world. He suggests that the first-order activity of finding out about the world is a matter for the scientist; the philosopher's activity is higher-order, dealing with understanding first-order knowledge, organizing it, systematizing it, and so on. Quine, by contrast, *is* concerned with the most general features of the world. This is not because he thinks that there is some special philosophical way of knowing which gives us a priori insight into the world; he is no more inclined to that view than is Carnap. It is, rather, because he rejects the distinction between the first-order and the second-order. On his account, organizing and systematizing a body of knowledge, finding the best notation in which to phrase it, understanding its basis, removing apparent difficulties in it—activities of this sort are

6

themselves first-order contributions to that body of knowledge, and thus tell us something about the world: "The quest of a simplest, clearest pattern of canonical notation is not to be distinguished from a quest of ultimate categories, a limning of the most general traits of reality". (*WO*, p. 161).

Quine's fundamental philosophical doctrine is what he calls *naturalism*. He explains the doctrine as "the recognition that it is within science itself, and not in some prior philosophy, that reality is to be identified and described" (*TT*, p. 21). Let us take the idea piecemeal. One crucial point is that, in considering human knowledge, philosophers have no vantage point, no method, no stance, which is different in kind from that of the knowledge which is their subject. The importance of this idea to Quine is such that it is found in the words with which he begins *Word and Object*, his first philosophical monograph, and in the words with which he ends that book. After the dedication, to Carnap, the book begins with an epigraph taken from Neurath: "We are like sailors who must rebuild their boat on the open sea, without ever being able to put into dock and reconstruct it from the best components".[3] The final paragraph of the book starts like this:

> The philosopher's task differs from the others' ... in detail, but in no such drastic way as those suppose who imagine for the philosopher a vantage point outside the conceptual scheme he takes in charge. There is no such cosmic exile. He cannot study and revise the fundamental conceptual scheme of science and common sense without having some conceptual scheme, whether the same or another no less in need of philosophical scrutiny, in which to work. He can scrutinize and improve the system from within, appealing to coherence and simplicity, but this is the theoretician's method generally.
>
> (*WO*, pp. 275–76)

The philosopher thus works from within, beginning in the middle of things (see "Reply to Roth", H&S, p. 461). This idea, however, is as yet too vague to take us very far. Where are we when we are "in the middle of things"? Given Quine's concerns, it is clear that we are in the middle of our system of *knowledge*. (And the philosopher's work is intended as a contribution to that system.) It is human cognitive or theoretical activity that is Quine's focus, not human culture in general. How this demarcation is to be made—how the cognitive is to be distinguished from other aspects of culture—is something we shall have to discuss. In other ways, too, we need to see something about how Quine understands our system of knowledge before we can see what it comes to to say that the philosopher is always

7

working within that system. So making Quine's starting point explicit will require substantive Quinean doctrine. (So perhaps any linear account of his philosophy will distort it: still, we must do what we can.)

Quine's naturalism, the view that "it is within science ... that reality is to be identified and described", may seem to place too much weight on science: why should we accept that science, rather than our ordinary knowledge, is what tells us about the world? Two points help here. The first is largely a point of usage. In a late work, Quine says that he uses the word "science" broadly; he explicitly includes psychology, economics, sociology, and history under that heading (see *FSS*, p. 49).[4] The second point is more obviously substantive. He holds that science is continuous with common sense, with everyday knowledge. All (putative) knowledge is in the same very general line of business. Where common sense and science appear to compete, it is not because they have different concerns or different standards of evidence; it is, rather, because unreflective common sense has not yet absorbed an improvement made by science. Quine's sketch of the business of knowledge gives some basis for this idea. It is not, however, an idea that receives very detailed articulation and defence in his work, perhaps because it always seemed to him obvious. It is, nevertheless, a crucial part of his overall view. (The idea that all knowledge is in the same line of work may be what justifies Quine's broad use of the term "science", just noted.)

Quine thus holds that science is our most successful attempt at knowledge. Hence philosophy, as part of our knowledge which aims, of course, to be successful, will aspire to scientific standards. It will not rely uncritically on terms simply because they are in ordinary use; it will, rather, use standards of clarity and explanatoriness which are drawn from the more successful sciences. A small example of this sort of thing, already noted in passing, is Quine's criticism of the term "knowledge". He finds the word vague, because it is unclear just how strong the evidence must be for something, and how certain we must be of it, to count it as knowledge. The word, he says, is "useful and unobjectionable in the vernacular where we acquiesce in vagueness, but unsuited to technical use because of lacking a precise boundary." ("Relativism and Absolutism", p. 295.) Quine himself sometimes uses the word in contexts where precision is not at issue (we will continue to do the same); at other times he speaks instead of "our system of the world" or simply "our theory". By giving up on the term for "technical use" he avoids such problems as whether I can really *know* something if I could be wrong.

Quine's insistence on the continuity of science and common sense is helpfully thought of as an aspect of a more general doctrine: the *seamlessness* of knowledge. There are no fundamental differences of kind within it. In particular, Quine denies that it splits into the a priori and the a posteriori. This point is of particular importance with regard to the guiding idea that philosophy seeks to understand our theory from within. One might claim to accept that idea and still go on to say that philosophy draws particularly on one part or aspect of that theory, namely the a priori part, and that this fact accounts for its difference from empirical subjects. Such is not Quine's view: he does not think there is an a priori part which can be drawn upon.

Quine's denial of a distinction between the a priori and the a posteriori is closely connected with his attitude towards the analytic–synthetic distinction. It is still widely held that he denies any such distinction. This is incorrect; he accepts a version of the distinction, but not a version which will do serious philosophical work. (His denial of the a priori is his rejection of the idea that there is serious philosophical work of this kind that needs doing.) Quine's rejection of a serious analytic–synthetic distinction is integral to his disagreement with Carnap, and occurs relatively early in his philosophical career. Quine's position here draws on his general outlook, and on his fundamental assumptions. Only when we have at least a preliminary understanding of those assumptions shall we be in a position to understand his attitude towards analyticity. (That gives one reason for our beginning with this overview chapter, rather than by launching into the dispute between Carnap and Quine over analyticity.)

Quine's rejection of a philosophically useful distinction between the analytic and the synthetic is also connected with his attitude towards meaning, and the uses that philosophers have made of that idea. One astute commentator puts Quine's attitude towards meaning at the very heart of his philosophy as a whole.[5] It is indeed central to his negative views, including his argument against Carnap's analytic–synthetic distinction. As I have already implied, however, his position here rests on his more general, and more positive, views. (We will return to this point towards the end of the chapter.)

Quine, as we said, rejects the distinction between the a priori and the a posteriori. This is not to say that he cannot accept any distinctions at all among the various things that we take ourselves to know. My knowledge that there is a table in front of me; my knowledge that my name is "Peter Hylton"; a physicist's knowledge of the latest theory; a mathematician's knowledge of a theorem that she has just proved—surely these are very different sorts of things, known in very different ways. Quine's view can, I think, leave room for these differences, but explaining them is not a major concern of his. (The chief exception is the difference between observational knowledge—that embodied in what he calls observation sentences—and other kinds.) Three points are worth making briefly. First, Quine thinks that all kinds of knowledge fall under the same very general account. The account is so general that one might think that it ruled out nothing; crucially, however, it does rule out most versions (at least) of a priori knowledge. Second, while Quine can accept that there are differences, he denies that there is a single clear distinction, such as is held by advocates of the distinction between the a priori and the a posteriori. Finally, Quine's thought is for the most part exceedingly abstract. While there are differences among various kinds of knowledge, none of these differences (with the exception noted above) seem to him important at the level of abstraction at which he is working. For the most part, Quine sees things from a very lofty perspective indeed; from that perspective, the sorts of differences with which we began this paragraph seem to him relatively minor.

So far we have been outlining Quine's fundamental concern and doctrines, largely in abstraction from discussion of particular texts. As an illustration, and as a way of beginning to elaborate and to raise further questions, we shall consider some passages from "The Scope and Language of Science" (SLS). The essay starts with the following striking paragraph:

> I am physical object sitting in a physical world. Some of the forces of this physical world impinge on my surface. Light rays strike my retinas; molecules bombard my eardrums and fingertips. I strike back, emanating concentric airwaves. These waves take the form of a torrent of discourse about tables, people, molecules, light rays, retinas, prime numbers, infinite classes, joy and sorrow, good and evil.
>
> (SLS, *WP*, p. 228)

Here we have the basic picture which Quine always presupposes; we shall frequently revert to it in what follows.

The passage is not intended as autobiographical; Quine's situation as he describes it is clearly meant to typify what is philosophically most significant about the human situation generally. (In this respect the paragraph resembles the *Meditations* of Descartes; in other respects the contrast is striking.) Let us grant the *truth* of Quine's claim here; still we might wonder about its relevance. Why should a statement of these facts be thought to be a starting point for philosophy? If this is a place to begin philosophy, how is that subject being conceived? How is Quine thinking of its aims, its method, its point?

Some matters are familiar from our first few pages. Quine clearly feels free to use our theory of the world; he makes no attempt to begin with absolute certainty, or with the a priori, or with what is in some sense *given* to him at the outset of his cognitive endeavours. This alone marks a drastic break from the procedure of many philosophers. Even granted that point, however, we can ask: why does he draw upon *that* part of our theory, and why described in this way, using something like the vocabulary of physics? Of the indefinitely many truths about the human condition, why does he begin with *these*? As we have already said, Quine's concern is with the theoretical or cognitive aspects of our lives. He takes it that our knowledge is embodied in language; hence the emphasis on the concentric airwaves that we emit.[6] The emphasis on the physical forces which impinge on his surface is also explained by his focus on cognitive activity; this point is perhaps less straightforward, and we shall return to it in the next section. Before doing so, however, we shall briefly consider the issue of the *vocabulary* that Quine adopts.

Quine assimilates philosophy to our knowledge in general, and he sees that knowledge as seamless. Science, in his view, is continuous with common sense. They are in the same line of business; science is simply the more self-conscious and more successful end of the spectrum. So philosophy, as we have said, should aspire to something like the standards of clarity and explanatoriness found in the most successful sciences; Quine, indeed, seems to suggest that higher standards may be appropriate:

> the scientist can enhance objectivity and diminish the interference of language, by his very choice of language. And we [i.e. we philosophers], concerned to distill the essence of scientific discourse, can profitably purify the language of science beyond what might reasonably be urged upon the practicing scientist.
>
> (*WP*, p. 235)

To get a more precise idea of what Quine takes to be the appropriate vocabulary to use, when we are concerned to maximize clarity and objectivity, we need to await the results of that part of philosophy which is concerned to "purify the language of science".

Much of the vocabulary which is in general philosophical use does not meet Quine's standards. He rejects it as insufficiently clear; an account couched in those terms will not advance our understanding. Quine, by his own account, is an empiricist, so one might think that he would take the notion of experience as absolutely fundamental. But not so:

> Experience, really, like meaning and thought and belief, is a worthy object of philosophical and scientific clarification and analysis, and, like all those it is ill-suited for use as an instrument of philosophical clarification and analysis.
>
> (*TT*, p. 185)

A little earlier, commenting just on thought and belief, he suggests an alternative to those ideas, closer to what is observable:

> For instruments of philosophical and scientific clarification and analysis I have looked rather in the foreground, finding sentences ... and dispositions to assent. Sentences are observable, and dispositions to assent are fairly accessible through observable symptoms. Linking observables to observables, these and others, and conjecturing causal connections, we might then seek a partial understanding, basically neurological, of what is loosely called thought or belief.
>
> (*TT*, p. 184)

Quine thus criticizes terms which most philosophers take for granted and use both for posing philosophical problems and for attempting to resolve them. By his standards, many such terms simply are not sufficiently clear and precise to be used in that way.

Quine's attitude here is complicated. He does not claim that terms such as "means" or "understands" are senseless, nor does he argue that they should be wholly banished from the language. In contexts in which there is no reason to insist on high standards of clarity and precision, such terms are unobjectionable. Moreover Quine himself sometimes uses such terms, for more or less rhetorical purposes or when full precision is not at issue. (We shall follow him in this.) But he rejects the idea that familiar ways of describing things, just because they are in general use, must be accepted as clear enough to use for "philosophical and scientific" purposes. The problems that he takes seriously are those that can be formulated using terms which *do* meet his standards of clarity; other (supposed) problems he is willing to dismiss.

II Stimulations and science

How does language come to be about the world? Or, more or less equivalently, what is the relation between language and the reality that it is supposedly about? Quine interprets this question in his own terms, as a scientific question, and gives it a clear answer: language comes to be about the world in virtue of its relations to sensory stimulation. That is why in the opening paragraph of "The Scope and Language of Science" Quine emphasizes the physical forces which impinge on his sensory surfaces, and the noises that he emits. Physical forces impinging on appropriate parts of the body give rise to stimulations of the sensory nerves; emitted noises are about the world in virtue of their relations to such stimulations. The principle is straightforward enough, although the details, as we shall see, are exceedingly complicated.

Why do sensory stimulations play this role? Quine holds that the only source of our knowledge of the world around us is energy impinging on our sensory surfaces and stimulating our sensory nerves. It is for this reason that sensory stimulation is central to his views about cognition. The relation of noises to sensory stimulations is central to cognition because the sensory stimulations I receive at any given moment are themselves correlated with the way the world around me is at that moment. The crucial fact here is that the world affects me only through such stimulations. How do we know this? It is a matter of plain fact, which science teaches us. Here we have a crucial illustration of Quine's naturalism. It is, Quine says, "a finding of natural science itself ... that our information about the world comes only through impacts on our sensory receptors" (*PT*, p. 19; see also SLS, *WP*, p. 229). He takes acceptance of this fact as definitive of empiricism, and he is in this sense as thorough-going an empiricist as he could be.

The claim that our utterances are about the world in virtue of their relation to stimulations of our sensory surfaces may seem quite implausible. A few of our remarks may be correlated with concurrent stimulations in fairly reliable ways: banalities about the weather, for example, at least if uttered out of doors. But for most utterances the idea of such a correlation seems preposterous. Consider the assertion that the Battle of Hastings was fought in 1066, or that the ratio between the diameter of a circle and its circumference is approximately 3.141, or that the common cold is caused by a virus—these claims, like most of what we take ourselves to know, do not concern the immediate circumstances. Utterances of sentences of this sort typically have no interesting correlation at all with concurrent stimulation. Quine is, of course, fully aware of this point. His view here depends upon the idea that our (putative) knowledge forms a highly interconnected system. Some sentences, which he calls *observation sentences*, are directly correlated with sensory stimulations. (They are not, however, *about* sensory stimulation.) Other sentences are not directly correlated with stimulations, but are connected with observation sentences, in some cases quite indirectly. The connection may be, for example, that our coming to accept some observation sentences—to be willing to utter them, or to accept them when they are uttered by another—makes us more or less likely to accept a given non-observation sentence.

As we consider increasingly abstract aspects of knowledge, it may become increasingly difficult to say exactly what observation sentences are at stake. Much of our knowledge—certainly all of logic and mathematics, the more abstract and general parts of physics, and philosophy itself—is more plausibly thought of as bringing order and system to the whole, rather than as being more directly connected with sensory stimulations. Quine, however, denies that there is a sharp line to be drawn here. Our body of knowledge as a whole is connected with sensory stimulations, and the sentences which serve to systematize that knowledge get their point, and their claim to be part of our knowledge, from that fact. So they still count as being related to sensory stimulations, although in a more or less indirect fashion. They thus count as being about the world, and potentially as part of our knowledge.

The claim that there are sentences which are related to sensory stimulations but are not directly correlated with them is often known as *holism*, and it plays an important role in Quine's thought. It is worth stressing, then, that on his account it is not a mysterious doctrine of obscure provenance. It is rather a matter of ordinary fact.

The idea that the sentences which are a potential part of our knowledge are those which are in some way connected with sensory stimulation is, for Quine, something like a definition of (putative) knowledge. There is a difficulty to note here. Quine speaks, "oddly perhaps", as he admits, of "the prediction of stimulation" (*PT*, p. 2). This is indeed odd, to the point of being misleading. He does *not* mean that what our theories in general predict are things of the form: "At time *t* subject *A* will undergo such-and-such stimulations". The point is perhaps better put in terms of predictions of observation sentences, which *are* directly correlated with sensory stimulation.

Now we can say how Quine understands the idea of *cognitive* language: it is the hallmark of the cognitive that it issues in predictions of observation sentences, or at least plays some sort of role in such predictions. We might say: a sentence counts as cognitive if it is a necessary element in a significant body of sentences which, taken as a whole, issues in predictions of observation sentences and is answerable to the success of those predictions. Because of the vagueness of "significant" this is not a useable criterion of the cognitive; nor does Quine take it to be so (see Chapter 7, section II). But Quine does take the prediction of observation sentences to be something like a *definition* of science in his broad sense:

> when I cite predictions [of observation sentences] as the checkpoints of science ... I see it as defining a particular language game, in Wittgenstein's phrase: the language game of science, in contrast to other good language games such as fiction and poetry. *A sentence's claim to scientific status rests on what it contributes to a theory whose checkpoints are in prediction.*
>
> (*PT*, p. 20; emphasis added)

14

We have noted that Quine denies any principled distinction in kind between common sense attempts at knowledge and scientific versions of the same. Science is "refined common sense" ("Posits and Reality", *WP*, p. 253). Now we can better understand the basis for this assimilation. Stating the matter very generally and abstractly, all (actual and putative) knowledge has the same standards of success—the prediction of observation sentences. What we call "science" does better at prediction than does common sense knowledge, but it does better by the same standards as those used by the layperson:

> Science is not a substitute for common sense but an extension of it. The quest for knowledge is properly an effort simply to broaden and deepen the knowledge which the man in the street already enjoys, in moderation, in relation to the commonplace things around him.
>
> (SLS, *WP*, p. 229)

And again:

> science is itself a continuation of common sense. The scientist is indistinguishable from the common man in his sense of evidence, except that the scientist is more careful. This increased care is not a revision of evidential standards, but only the more patient and systematic collection and use of what anyone would deem to be evidence.
>
> (SLS, *WP*, p. 233)

Quine's characterization of science, in his broad sense, is justified by the fundamental fact that it is only through the impact of energy on our sensory surfaces, and consequent stimulations of our sensory nerves, that we find out anything about the world. Here we have a perfect illustration of Quine's general method: working from within our system of knowledge to shed light upon it. The "fundamental fact" is put forward as itself a well confirmed item of science in the broad sense. It is something that we know in a perfectly ordinary way, both by low-level empirical trials and, more abstractly, by inference from independently well confirmed theories (of neurophysiology and psychology, perhaps). And this, Quine takes it, is what justifies the central idea of empiricism. It is then by reference to this idea that we are to understand our system of the world—the very system which we drew on to tell us that it is by sensory experience that we find out about the world.

We can gain further insight into Quine's general view of knowledge by emphasizing that he sees it as a biological phenomenon. The opening sentences of *From Stimulus to Science* read like this: "We and other animals notice what goes on around us. This helps us by suggesting what we might expect and even prevent, and thus fosters survival". (p. 1). This is a conception of knowledge as an adaptive mechanism, fostering the survival of the individual and of the species. Quine explicitly compares human knowledge with the knowledge of other animals:

> An animal's innate similarity standards are a rudimentary instrument for prediction, and then learning is a progressive refinement of that instrument, making for more dependable prediction. In man, and most conspicuously in recent centuries, this refinement has consisted in the development of a vast and bewildering growth of conceptual or linguistic apparatus, the whole of natural science. *Biologically, still, it is like the animal's learning about cats and owls; it is a learned improvement over simple induction by innate similarity standards. It makes for more and better prediction.*
>
> (NNK, p. 71; emphasis added)

This point reinforces the connection between knowledge and sensory stimulation. The anticipation and control of future sensory stimulations have obvious survival value.

To put the point another way: a body of sentences which made no contact at all with sensory stimulation could be dismissed as a mere game, with no implications beyond itself; there would be no reason to think of it as telling us anything about the world, or even as attempting to do so. There would be no reason to think of such sentences as conveying putative knowledge, or as being true or false. But it would not be possible to dismiss what we take to be our ordinary knowledge in the same way. My very survival depends on my knowing which things to eat and which not, on my staying away from cliff edges and fierce animals, on my crossing busy roads with some care, and so on. In these ways and others, some parts, at least, of our ordinary elementary knowledge must be taken seriously if we are to survive. It cannot be dismissed. So we are inevitably in the business of gathering knowledge; the attempt to do it as well as we can results in advanced science. No doubt our survival depends on many factors other than knowledge—our ability to cooperate with others, for example. But ordinary elementary knowledge is indispensable here too; without it we would not even know that there are others around us with whom we may cooperate. Knowledge is not all that there is to human life and human survival, but it is both indispensable and fundamental.

Having said this much, however, we must qualify. The links between knowledge, survival value, and the prediction of stimulations hold only at the most general level. The biological origins of our theorizing about the world may be that it enhances survival value. But once the enterprise gets going it takes on a life of its own, independent of its origin. Much of our knowledge has no readily conceivable survival value, and is none the worse for it: questions of cosmology, or of remote prehistory, are likely examples. Once we have in place a conception of the world as enduring through time, questions about the remote past and future will arise, and their answers will count as putative knowledge, even if they have no conceivable survival value. Similarly, perhaps, we have very general methods of solving mathematical questions, and generating new ones; we may have adopted those methods because of their useable applications, but they will then lead to further questions with no thought of application (see Chapter 3, section V, below). Quine is not saying that survival value is or should be the main goal of science. Science may have originated in the struggle to survive, but by now it is a long way from its origins. For science as it exists (now and at least throughout historical times), understanding is a major goal (*PT*, p. 2). No doubt the curiosity that makes understanding a goal of science itself has, or had, survival value, as leading to the growth of knowledge and predictive power. But curiosity, the drive to understand the world, has also taken on a life of its own, independent of its survival value. (In this it is no different from other biological drives.) Again, there is no reason to infer from Quine's view that the progress of science is bound to enhance the prospects for human survival. As he says: "Traits that were developed by natural selection have been known to prove lethal ... " (NNK, p. 72).

A few paragraphs back we held up Quine's use of the idea that our information about the world came only from stimulations as a paradigm of his naturalism, of his method of working from within. Some, however, might hold it up rather as an example of circularity. We could put the point made earlier by saying: for Quine, a system of beliefs which successfully predicts sensory experience counts as *knowledge*, as telling us about the world, because we know that it is through sensory experience, and only through sensory experience, that we know anything at all about the world. From the point of view of more traditional philosophy, however, this answer begs the question completely. How do we know that it is through sensory experience that we know anything at all about the world? Quine's answer is that we know this in the same very general way in which we know anything else: it is part of a system of beliefs which successfully predicts sensory experience. But what was in question was precisely whether having that status is really sufficient to make something count as knowledge.

Another way to make this point is to raise a version of scepticism: is it not conceivable that our system of belief should succeed completely in its predictions, yet still fail to tell us the truth about the world? It is striking that Quine has no sympathy at all for this kind of scepticism. He states it and dismisses it in a single short paragraph:

> Our scientific theory can indeed go wrong, and precisely in the familiar way: through failure of predicted observation. But what if, happily and unbeknownst, we have achieved a theory that is conformable to every possible observation, past and future? In what sense could the world then be said to deviate from what the theory claims? *Clearly in none.* ... Our overall scientific theory demands of the world only that it be so structured as to assure the sequences of stimulations that our theory gives us to expect.
>
> (TT, p. 22; emphasis added)

There is no alternative to working from within some conceptual scheme— our own, since we know no better. So there is no sense to the idea of some wholly extra-theoretical reality with which our theory could be compared and perhaps found wanting. Our theory must be judged primarily by its ability to make correct predictions, even though the connection between prediction and truth is itself a theoretical matter. So we can ask no more of our theory of the world than that it enables us to make successful predictions (and do so in the clearest and simplest fashion). For Quine there is no notion of "the world" or "reality" which is sufficiently robust to give sense to the idea that we might have a theory which was correct in all its predictions, but still wrong about the world. This issue is connected with the question of realism, which we take up immediately.

III Realism, instrumentalism, pragmatism

We have been emphasizing the role of sensory stimulation in Quine's view of knowledge. This emphasis may give rise to the idea that Quine cannot really take the things that our knowledge professes to tell us about as *real*. If our knowledge is no more than a means of predicting stimulation, why should we take the things it purports to tell us about as really existing? It is not hard to find passages which reinforce this idea. The first paragraph of "Things and Their Place in Theories", for example, reads like this:

> Our talk of external things, our very notion of things, is *just a conceptual apparatus* that helps us to foresee and control the triggering of our sensory receptors in the light of previous triggering of our sensory receptors. The triggering, first and last, is all that we have to go on.
>
> (TT, p. 1; emphasis added)

Again, Quine frequently speaks of objects—the ordinary familiar objects which he says he counts as real—as *posits*; this may, again, suggest that he does not take such objects as being fully real and independent of us. In spite of these suggestions, however, Quine insists he is a realist about ordinary objects, and the objects of which the scientists inform us; indeed he describes his view as "robust realism" (*TT*, p. 21). How, and in what sense, can he be a realist?

Let us begin by contrasting his view with one non-realist position. Passages such as those just quoted might seem to put forward a view sometimes known as *instrumentalism* (also called *fictionalism*). According to that view, scientific theories are simply instruments for making predictions, and the (apparent) entities named in such theories, electrons and neutrons and what not, are not *real* entities at all. We accept them as a sort of useful fiction, because doing so enables us to make predictions successfully, but we do not claim that they really exist; they are posited simply for their instrumental value. According to some versions of the view, the same applies also to ordinary entities of common sense knowledge, tables and trees, mountains and (other) people. Now Quine's view has something in common with instrumentalism, as we shall see. But there is also a crucial difference. Instrumentalism presupposes a contrast between two kinds of (alleged) entities: one held to be real, and another held to be no more than useful fictions. Useful for what? For enabling us to attain knowledge about the real entities. On one version, fictional entities are postulated by scientific theories to help us attain knowledge of ordinary physical objects, which are counted as real. On another version, the entities of science and ordinary physical objects are both to be thought of as fictions, postulated in order to facilitate real entities which are supposed to be given to us in experience. In either case, the contrast is what gives the view its anti-realist character: entities of one class do not measure up to the standard of reality set by entities of some other class, and are characterized as being simply posits which are useful for obtaining knowledge of the real.

Quine is no instrumentalist; for him there is no contrast. One cannot hold that stimulations of our sensory surfaces are real and that physical objects are mere fictions. Sensory surfaces *are* physical objects; sensory stimulations are physical events on a par with any other. This fact indicates the importance of Quine's naturalistic approach to knowledge, which begins by taking for granted the physical world and our knowledge of it. Another way to make the point is to say that for Quine there is no knowledge which is *given*, in wholly presuppositionless extra-theoretical fashion. The occurrence of stimulations is independent of theory, but we do not know about them independent of theory; they can hardly be thought to be more real than the entities presupposed by the rest of our theory.

With no basis for a contrast, it is merely perverse to withhold the word "real" from ordinary things. Indeed to do so threatens to leave the word without sense:

> We cannot significantly question the reality of the external world, or deny that there is evidence of external objects in the testimony of our senses; for, to do so is simply to dissociate the terms "reality" and "evidence" from the very applications which originally did most to invest those terms with whatever intelligibility they may have for us.
>
> (SLS, *WP*, p. 229)

This does not imply that we cannot come to reject the claims of things we were brought up to accept. Reflection upon our "conceptual apparatus" might lead us to realize that we do better overall by discarding some entities that we formerly accepted. (Witches and ghosts and Santa Claus fall under this sort of censure; likewise perhaps space, conceived as absolutely independent of time.) This is simply replacing one set of ideas by another with the same fundamental status. We still have "a conceptual bridge of our own making" (TPT, *TT*, p. 2); we simply have a better bridge.

What Quine leaves no room for, however, is the idea that ordinary objects have a second-rate status, not because they are elements in an *inferior* conceptual scheme but simply because they are elements in a conceptual scheme at all. Quine rejects the idea that for philosophical purposes there is a standard of reality wholly different from that employed in distinguishing, say, a real pool of water up ahead from a mere mirage. There is no superordinate standard of reality; there is no knowledge of objects independent of our ordinary conceptual scheme—no wholly extra-theoretic given, no a priori intuition, "no first philosophy prior to natural science" ("Five Milestones of Empiricism", *TT*, p. 67). There is only "ordinary knowledge", and what that ordinary knowledge may lead to by a process of internal development. There are no objects which are *given* in a stronger sense than are the familiar objects of everyday life; there are no standards of reality higher or better than that of being an element in an efficient conceptual apparatus; there are no "philosophical purposes" which are independent of the very general and abstract scientific and philosophical purpose of establishing the best conceptual apparatus, that is, the best theory for predicting and making sense of sensory stimulation.

These points show up in Quine's use, or mis-use, of the word "posit". In the ordinary sense, the positing of a kind of object is the act of some one person or small group of people at a particular time; electrons, for example, were posited in the late nineteenth century in order to account for certain observed phenomena. But Quine applies the word also to ordinary medium-sized objects, which were certainly not posited in this sense; no one decided that certain data were more easily accounted for if we supposed that there are rocks and trees, say. The reason for this broad use of the word is that he holds that both ordinary objects and the objects of advanced science have the same very general kind of status—at least each shares the features that Quine thinks most important. The existence of each is presupposed by a theory which is a human invention; since we accept the relevant portion of each theory we accept the objects as real. Hence, as Quine memorably says,

> To call a posit a posit is not to patronize it. ... Everything to which we concede existence is a posit from the standpoint of a description of the theory-building process, and simultaneously real from the standpoint of the theory that is being built. Nor let us look down on the standpoint of the theory as make-believe; for we can never do better than occupy the standpoint of some theory or other, the best we can muster at the time.
>
> (WO, p. 22)

Or, as one might put it, it's posits all the way down.

Posits are real "from the standpoint of the theory"; we accept the objects because we accept the theory. It is natural to hear this as qualifying the sense in which posits are real, to hear "real from the standpoint of the theory" as less than fully real. This implication, however, is not what Quine intends. On his usage there is no such implication, because he distorts the ordinary usage of the word "theory" here in ways analogous to those in which he distorts that of the word "posit". In ordinary usage we often contrast theory with fact; "just a theory" often has the same somewhat derogatory overtones as "just a posit". But Quine departs from ordinary usage on this point. For him, the idea of a wholly neutral standpoint, which one could occupy at least for the purposes of pure inquiry, is a myth.[7] We are always working from within, always, in Quinean terminology, committed to a theory. "Theoretical", there-fore, does not describe a kind of knowledge which is in some way second-rate, because, again, there is no contrasting kind of superior knowledge: "we can never do better than occupy the standpoint of some theory or other".

There is a final point worth making on the basis of the passage quoted above. Quine distinguishes two standpoints: "the standpoint of a description of the theory-building process" and "the standpoint of the theory that is being built". (Sometimes we will call them simply the epistemological and the ontological.) He writes now from one standpoint and now from the other, saying things which might appear to point in rather different directions. He sees no conflict, however. In his view, acknowledging that our knowledge is a human artefact is compatible with accepting the objects it tells us about as fully real. Given that our knowledge is our own creation, we can of course study how it is created; indeed this study is a vital part of his philosophy. When Quine is in this way concerned with "the theory-building process" he is nonetheless taking for granted "the theory that is being built", with its fully realistic attitude towards light rays, nerve endings, human beings, sensory nerves, and what have you. This is the way in which Quine's naturalism is revolutionary: he denies that there is a distinctively philosophical standpoint from which we can reflect on knowledge. To the contrary, our study of human knowledge takes place within the theory that it studies and presupposes the reality of the entities mentioned in that theory. On Quine's account, then, remarks to the effect that our knowledge is "just a conceptual apparatus" do not conflict with realism.

The epistemological standpoint thus presupposes the ontological standpoint: our explanation of how we come by our theory of the world is itself part of that theory. In a different sense, however, epistemology contains ontology, for it is a study of how we come to know that very theory. Thus we have the "reciprocal containment" of epistemology and science:

> The old epistemology aspired to contain, in a sense, natural science; it would construct it somehow from sense-data. Epistemology in its new setting, conversely, is contained in natural science, as a chapter of psychology. But the old containment remains valid too, in its way. We are studying how the human subject of our study posits bodies and projects his physics from his data, and we appreciate that our position in the world is just like his. Our very epistemological enterprise, therefore, and the psychology wherein it is a component chapter, and the whole of natural science wherein psychology is a component book—all of this is our own construction or projection from stimulations. ... There is thus reciprocal containment, though in different senses; epistemology in natural science, and natural science in epistemology.
>
> (EN, *OR*, p. 83)

In doing epistemology we draw on our theory of the world; our possession of the very theory that we draw upon, however, is to be examined and explained by the epistemological enterprise.

One conclusion from all of this might be put by saying that Quine is willing to accord reality to whatever is required by a theory that works sufficiently well. Putting it this way is reminiscent of pragmatism, and it is worth emphasizing differences as well as similarities here. Quine is unlike the pragmatists in that he makes a clear distinction between the cognitive and the non-cognitive, between what is good for human beings by way of the prediction of sensory experiences and what is good for them in other ways. Only the former, in his view, counts as science, and should be thought of as (putatively) true, as telling us how things are; only the former is his concern. Within the realm of the cognitive, however, Quine's attitude is akin to that of the pragmatists. He does not take a pragmatic attitude towards the whole of human experience (in the broad sense); he is not willing to use the word "true" of everything that contributes to human flourishing. Within the realm of the cognitive, however, his attitude is, in a broad sense, pragmatic.

IV "Our theory"

Quine often speaks of "our theory" or "our system of the world"; similarly, he sometimes talks of "our science" or (more rarely) of "our knowledge". Almost all his philosophical work concerns "our theory", in one way or another. Yet the idea is perhaps less straightforward than it might seem.

An important preliminary point is that Quine takes our theory to be, or to be embodied in, language. For "scientific and philosophical purposes", he thinks of it as a set of sentences.

> What sort of thing is a scientific theory? It is an idea, one might naturally say, or a complex of ideas. But the most practical way of coming to grips with ideas, and usually the only way, is by way of the words that express them. What to look for in the way of theories, then, are the sentences that express them.
>
> (*TT*, p. 24; see also *RR*, section 9)

Clearly Quine is here opposed to the view that knowledge should be treated as a matter of ideas, or of propositions (thought of as, roughly, the meanings of sentences). As we shall see, he argues that talk of ideas or propositions is too vague and loose, and too remote from the evidence, to have a place in a genuinely scientific account of knowledge. Words and sentences, or our uses of them, are, by contrast, open to public view and to scientific study.

Quine's view here is also to be distinguished from the idea that knowledge is fundamentally a matter of states of the brain, which are poorly represented in language. (See, for example, Paul M. Churchland, "Eliminative Materialism and the Propositional Attitudes".) Quine does not explicitly consider this kind of view. He would be in sympathy with its scientific motivation but would still, I think, hold that knowledge should be treated as a matter of language. First, he thinks of our knowledge as something public: not merely "public in principle" as states of the brain are, but actually accessible, with no particular devices or stratagem. Much of the survival value of knowledge comes from the fact that it is *ours*, it is shared, and was so from its earliest inception. Second, he takes all knowledge to be of the same fundamental kind. A sophisticated scientific theory is embodied or expressed in words (and mathematical symbols); any alternative is almost unimaginable.[8] Since this sort of knowledge is to be thought of as linguistic, *all* knowledge must be thought of as linguistic, unless we are to accept sharp differences in kind. (Quine's attitude here may also in part be a sign of the continuity of his thought with that of his predecessors, most obviously Carnap, who placed enormous emphasis on language.)

Quine takes it, then, that our theory of the world is embodied in language. Let us make three further points about how he conceives it. First, in ordinary usage, "theory" is often contrasted with "fact"; for Quine, as we have seen, there is no such contrast. As we emphasized in discussing Quine's realism, he holds that all of our knowledge is in some sense theoretical. None simply embodies the result of unmediated contact with reality; all has the same sort of status, and differences within it are differences of degree and not of kind. In some contexts, for some purposes, it may be useful to separate what is known with some confidence as the facts of the case, and contrast that with more or less speculative theories of some matter, but this does not correspond to any fundamental or general distinction.

Second, in the ordinary use of the word "theory" there are many theories—the Theory of General Relativity, the Theory of Evolution, and so on. Quine sometimes uses the word this way, but he also often speaks of "our theory" to mean the aggregate of all that we know or take ourselves to know. The various parts of our knowledge overlap and interlock; apart from anything else, they all employ logic, and most employ mathematics. This is a long way from their forming a single integrated whole. The idea of such a whole, of the unity of knowledge in any strong interpretation, functions for Quine as a regulative ideal; it is not an established fact, and not a requirement of our having knowledge at all, but it is something towards which we should strive. It is, after all, a single world that we attempt to know. In *Word and Object* he says:

> knowledge develops in a multiplicity of theories, each with its
> limited utility. . . . These theories overlap very considerably, in their

so-called logical laws and in much else, but that they add up to an integrated and consistent whole is only a worthy ideal and hap- pily not a prerequisite of scientific progress. ... let the reconci- liations proceed; each step advances our understanding of the world.

(p. 251)

Thirty-five years later, he is perhaps more explicit:

Naturalism itself is noncommital on this question of the unity of science. Naturalism just sees it as a question within science itself, albeit a question more remote from observational checkpoints than the most speculative questions of the hard and soft sciences ordi- narily so called.

Naturalism can still respect the drive, on the part of some of us, for a unified all-purpose ontology. The drive is typical of the sci- entific temper, and of a piece with the drive for simplicity that shapes scientific hypotheses generally.

(NLWM, p. 260)

A final point about "our theory" focuses on the first word of the phrase. Who are we who hold this theory? The answer is not a straightforwardly statistical one—Quine's conception of our theory of the world is not, that is to say, based on an imagined survey of all fully functioning human beings. What Quine means by "our theory" is something like: the best knowledge, on all subjects, currently available. "Best" here is to be understood in terms of the prediction of sensory experience, and also factors such as clarity and simplicity. This is a normative rather than a statistical conception: *our* theory of the world is not in fact held by any single person (it's too exten- sive and too complex), let alone by each of us. To that extent, it is an idealization, but one that remains in contact with actual human practice. One point of contact is that each element in our theory is known to some among us; it is not simply the ultimate truth about the world, which we do not yet possess. A second point of contact is that our theory of the world, in Quine's sense, is what the rudimentary knowledge that we share aspires to be. To speak less metaphorically, Quine's view is that all knowledge, even the most rudimentary, is answerable to certain standards of success, and that the most sophisticated form of knowledge—"our theory", the sum total of what is accepted by the experts in each subject-area—is the best knowledge available *by those same standards*. The fundamental point here is the con- tinuity of low-level common sense knowledge with the most advanced sci- entific knowledge.

25

V Tasks for philosophy

Given the general picture that we have sketched, what is there for the Quinean philosopher to do? He has one task which faces any systematic philosopher: to articulate his general picture, and to defend it against what he sees as its most important competitors. Here an important role is played by the work of Carnap and by Quine's break with Carnap, most obviously over the distinction between the analytic and the synthetic. Accordingly, Chapters 2 and 3 will sketch the relevant parts of Carnap's thought and Quine's arguments against it. Quine's concerns, however, are not primarily negative; the positive, constructive, side of his work is of much greater importance to him. (Though this is less widely appreciated than is the negative side of his thought.) As indicated in the Introduction, we shall, over-schematizing, no doubt, distinguish two aspects here. The first is epistemological, in a very broad sense of that word: it concerns our relation to the world. It thus encompasses issues having to do with both meaning— what is it for our language to be about the world?—and knowledge—how do we come to have beliefs which are, for the most part, correct?[9] Quine often approaches these questions through the genetic question, how knowledge and language could be acquired. This range of issues is our primary concern in Chapters 4 to 7. The second aspect is the analogue of ontology, or of metaphysics more generally.[10] Its method is the regimentation and reformulation of our theory, but its ultimate concern is with the nature of the world. This will be the focus of Chapters 8 to 13. The remainder of this chapter will enlarge on these two positive tasks.

In his last two or three decades, Quine came to approach epistemology chiefly through the genetic project of explaining how a child might acquire knowledge and a language in which that knowledge can be expressed. Why is this genetic question of any philosophical relevance? Consider again the picture set out in the opening paragraph of "The Scope and Language of Science", discussed in section I, above. That picture immediately raises questions about the possibility of meaning and of knowledge. Physical forces bombard the subject, giving rise to stimulations of his sensory nerves. By way of striking back, the subject emanates concentric airwaves. Some of these emanations take the form of meaningful speech. Some of the meaningful speech purports to convey information about the world, and is thus a candidate, at least, for being part of our theory of the world. But what is it for concentric airwaves, noises, to "take the form of" meaningful speech? What is it for some of them to be about objects in the world? What is it for some of them to be true or false of the world? How does it come about that the human animal, given certain stimulations, emits noises which have these characteristics?

We have already indicated the very general form of Quine's answer to these and other related questions: some of our noises achieve the relevant status in virtue of their relations to stimulations of our sensory nerves. The attempt to make out this answer, however, raises further questions. What are the relevant sorts of relations? Is it really plausible that these relations between noises and stimulations are all that there is to language and to knowledge? If each of us has only his or her own stimulations to go on, what even gives us the idea of a shared objective world which we can talk about? Given that stimulations are not shared, how do we come to share a language? What sorts of relations to sensory stimulations make some linguistic item worth including in our theory? How do we get from one to the other? How, to echo the title of Quine's last book, do we get from stimulus to science?

These are not conventional philosophical questions; they are examples of the way in which Quine reconceives the problems of philosophy. To address them, he considers, in a more or less speculative way, how the human child, subject to various stimulations of its sensory nerves, could come to acquire our theory of the world. Our knowledge is embodied in language, and Quine holds that an acquisition of the one goes hand-in-hand with an acquisition of the other. Hence he considers how elementary cognitive or theoretical language could be acquired. On Quine's account, the child makes primitive vocal responses to stimulation, being encouraged in some responses and discouraged in others; the full repertoire of sophisticated language gradually emerges as this process continues. Quine is concerned to show that it is possible to give a naturalistic account of this process, one that does not take for granted ideas such as meaning and understanding. (As suggested in the Introduction, Quine's strongest argument against such ideas is simply that they are unnecessary.)

By seeing how cognitive language is acquired, Quine holds, we will also see what it consists in. The genetic project will thus show us what there is to the meaning of cognitive language, and to the knowledge which is embodied in that language. In particular, it will enable us "to see whatever there is to see about the evidence relation, the relation borne by theory to the observations that support it." (RR, pp. 3–4.) Relations to observation sentences, and thus to stimulations, constitute the evidence for theory; to become a master of the language, the learner must come to use it in accordance with those same relations. "[T]he evidential relation", Quine says, "is virtually enacted . . . in the learning" (NNK, pp. 74–75).

Quine also considers epistemological issues independent of the genetic project—in particular, how, in the finished product of science, evidence relates to theory. This approach is much less important, in his mature

27

thought, than is the genetic approach. Still, it raises some issues that we need to take into account, and we shall discuss these in Chapter 7.

I turn now to the second of the two aspects that I distinguished. Much of Quine's work is concerned with what the world is like in its most general feature; this is what I speak of as Quinean metaphysics, or Quine's analogue of metaphysics. Ontology—what there is in the world—is a particular focus of his. (Quine freely uses the word "ontology" but not "metaphysics"; his concerns, however, clearly go beyond the ontological, so I adopt the more general word on his behalf, as it were. In the later decades of his working life he places less emphasis on ontology, conceived narrowly, as distinct from metaphysics.) The method of Quinean metaphysics is, primarily, the clarification and simplification of our theory of the world; our theory as thus clarified tells us what it is that we are really committed to believing, and hence what the world is really like—at least as far as we know it at the moment. As this description makes clear, Quine does not claim that there is a metaphysical source of knowledge (a priori insight, say), distinct from what the sciences rely upon; metaphysics on his account is not a rival to the sciences, and does not offer to tell us the real truth on matters about which science offers mere appearance or partial truth. On the other hand, Quine holds that philosophy really is in the business of contributing to knowledge. He does not think of it as a second-order activity, distinct from the genuine cognitive work of the sciences. Clarifying, simplifying, and reorganizing are first-order scientific activities, undertaken in the sciences as well as by philosophers. Transformation of a theory to simplify it may be no less of a scientific achievement, no less a genuine advance in knowledge, than is transformation of a theory in order to account for new observations.

A particular concern of Quine's, here as in his more obviously epistemological work, is the relation of evidence to theory. Ideally, our theory, as simplified and reorganized, *implies* its evidence, or the sentences in which evidence is embodied. But what does the notion of implication come to here? A ready answer is provided by modern logic, a system to which Quine himself has contributed a great deal, primarily by way of clarification; in particular, Quine claims, it is first-order logic with identity to which we should look for an understanding of implication relations. (The idea of first-order logic will be explained in Chapter 10; see especially sections I and III.) But if the methods of logic are to be directly applicable to our theory of the world then that theory must be adapted to the limited syntax of logic; this adaptation will require significant reorganization. The use of logic requires "preparatory operations, in applied logic, whereby sentences of ordinary language are fitted to logical forms by interpretation and paraphrase" (MSLT, *WP*, p. 142). This sort of preparatory work, on a large scale, is the reformulation required for Quine's metaphysical enterprise. The reformulation aims at making theory safe for the application of logic. Such reorganization has further benefits; the clarity and perspicuity of the syntax of logic contributes to the clarity of the theory as formulated in that syntax. Quine makes considerable claims for the insight that can be achieved by reformulating knowledge in the syntax of logic: "the motivation of the Procrustean treatment of ordinary language at the hands of the logicians has been ... that of achieving theoretical insights comparable to those which Arabic notation and algebra made possible" (MSLT, *WP*, p. 149).

Much of what I am counting as Quine's metaphysical work thus consists in considering how our theory can best be reformulated in the notation of logic ("canonical notation", Quine often calls it). An obvious and important example here is the fact that English is full of expressions which function grammatically as singular terms, but which the logician will (rightly) not accept as the names of objects. A favourite example of Quine's is the word "sake", as it occurs in the phrases "for the sake of ... " or "for so-and-so's sake". Fitting our theory into the framework of first-order logic puts a premium on ontological decisions. Because first-order logic deals with generalizations over objects, it must be clear exactly what objects there are, what expressions are to be taken as referring to objects. (This is, no doubt, part of the reason for Quine's emphasis on the genesis of referential language in his epistemological enterprise.) From Quine's point of view, it is an advantage of the syntax of logic that it sets out a clear and definite criterion for the ontological commitments of a theory formulated in that syntax, thereby enabling us to clarify the idea of ontology.

Quine takes his reformulation of our system of the world as itself an integral part of our coming to know the world better. If the best reformulation available requires that we accept one sort of entity as real, and reject another (alleged) sort as not really existing, then we have made progress in determining what there is in the world. In Quine's view, this is not different in principle from the physicist's attempts at a better theory, one which perhaps accepts entities of one kind but rejects (alleged) entities of another kind. (See again the final paragraph of *Word and Object*, quoted near the beginning of this chapter.)

A normative tone has crept into our sketch of Quinean philosophy: we have been speaking of how our theory of the world can *best* be reformulated, and so on. What can this sort of talk mean for the Quinean? It cannot be a matter of imposing upon our knowledge standards drawn from elsewhere. Since it is our total knowledge that is in question, there is no "elsewhere". (This is one way of understanding Quine's naturalism.) The standards by which the philosopher seeks to organize and clarify the system of our knowledge are not external to that system. This does not, however, imply that the standards to which our knowledge already conforms must be the correct ones, so that the philosopher can only stand back and approve of what is in place. We might have reason to think that certain standards are the best available, perhaps because paradigmatic cases of our knowledge employ those standards, or perhaps for more abstract theoretical reasons; and it might turn out that some of our supposed knowledge in fact does not conform to those standards. Then there would be philosophical investigations and decisions to be made—to see whether more of our knowledge could be brought to conform to the desired standards, or whether the standards could be modified without significant loss. The appropriate standards are those which will best enable the system of our knowledge as a whole to do what we want of it; the claim that such-and-such are the appropriate standards to use is to be justified in the same very general way as any other claim to knowledge.

Finally, on this matter, let us attempt to deflect one kind of misunderstanding of Quine's project of reformulating our system of knowledge. He does not think that the "simplest, clearest overall pattern of canonical notation" is the only meaningful language. Nor does he think it is the language that we ought to speak. His is not a programme of language-reform, either for the language of the marketplace or even for the language of the laboratory. He cheerfully accepts that his canonical notation might not be learnable as a first language (see, for example, SLS, *WP*, p. 236). Further, in a section of *Word and Object* revealingly titled "The Double Standard", Quine suggests "a bifurcation in canonical notation", with different standards corresponding to different purposes. The most austere is the one to use if we are "limning the true and ultimate structure of reality" (*WO*, p. 221) or "venturing to formulate the fundamental laws of a branch of science" (op. cit.). For purposes of this sort, we philosophers can, as already noted, "profitably purify the language of science beyond what might reasonably be urged upon the practicing scientist" (SLS, *WP*, p. 235; quoted in context p. 11, above). Different standards may apply if we have different aims—if, for example, we aim merely "to dissolve verbal perplexities or facilitate logical deductions" (*WO*, p. 221). Quine suggests "a grading of austerity", depending on the task in hand. His attention, however, is usually focused on the most fundamental aim, and thus on what he takes to be the clearest and most rigorous version of canonical notation.

We have sketched two general sorts of enterprises which, on Quine's view, confront the philosopher. Now we face a rather different sort of question.

What is the status of philosophy itself? Where does it fit into our system of the world? We have indicated that Quine holds that the philosophical examination of our science is itself part of that science; but it is perhaps not clear how he can hold this. Although he occasionally draws on the results of experimental science, Quine's own work is clearly the product of the study, the seminar room, and the library, not of the laboratory. Yet Quinean philosophy cannot claim to be known a priori. Its justification, by its own lights, must be that it contributes in some way, no doubt very indirectly, to our overall system of theory of the world. As we have seen, Quine makes it clear that he regards understanding, as well as prediction, as a major aim of science. Knowledge may have originated in a concern with prediction, but clearly it has by now far outstripped its origins. The point of philosophy is the understanding that it brings, rather than its direct role in the prediction of sensory experience. That much is true on Quine's account of the discipline, as on almost anyone's. Still, for Quine, we cannot say of philosophy that it is justified because it brings us understanding unless that understanding is connected in some way (however remote and vague) with prediction.

Quite generally, Quine holds that some claims may count as parts of our theory although their connection with prediction is very loose indeed:

> We believe many things because they fit in smoothly by analogy, or they symmetrize and simplify the overall design. Surely much history and social science is of this sort, and some hard science. Moreover, such acceptations are not idle fancy; their proliferation generates, every here and there, a hypothesis that can indeed be tested. Surely this is the major source of testable hypotheses and the growth of science.
> (NLWM, p. 256)

Philosophy surely gets its claim to be part of our knowledge in this general sort of way, by its ability to facilitate, clarify, and systematize our overarching theory of the world, to explain what that system is based upon and how it is possible; that is where its contribution to the scientific enterprise lies. It reflects in various ways on our system of knowledge, seeking to understand it, to defend it against certain very general sorts of criticisms, to deflect useless or needlessly confusing questions. It shows how that system can best be organized and clarified so as to reveal its structure—and thereby the structure of the world that we take ourselves to know. At the same time, however, it is part of the overarching theory which it reflects upon and attempts to clarify: our philosophical endeavours are the varied results of our reflecting on that theory from within.

31

2

QUINE'S PHILOSOPHICAL BACKGROUND

Beginnings; logic; Carnap

No philosopher had greater influence on Quine than Rudolf Carnap. While in Europe on a traveling fellowship in 1932–33, Quine spent six weeks in Prague, attending Carnap's lectures, visiting him frequently for lengthy discussions, and reading *Logische Syntax der Sprache* "as it issued from Ina Carnap's typewriter" (H&S, p. 12). In a tribute that he gave soon after Carnap's death in 1970, Quine says:

> Carnap was my greatest teacher. . . . I was very much his disciple for six years. In later years his views went on evolving and so did mine, in divergent ways. But even where we disagreed he was still setting the theme; *the line of my thought was largely determined by problems that I felt his view presented.*
>
> ("Homage to Rudolf Carnap", *WP*, p. 41; emphasis added)

These are extraordinarily strong words, and there is other evidence to the same effect. In the opening sentence of an essay written twenty years before the tribute, he says: "no one has influenced my philosophical thought more than Carnap" (*WP*, p. 203); in another essay written twenty years after the tribute Quine speaks of his early lectures on Carnap as "abjectly sequacious";[1] and he dedicated *Word and Object*, his first philosophical monograph, to Carnap. Our main concern in this chapter will, accordingly, be with the work of Carnap—or, at least, with those aspects of Carnap's work which are of most direct relevance to understanding Quine. The discussion of Carnap, or Carnap as he influenced Quine, will occupy the last three sections of the chapter; the first section will consider earlier influences on Quine's philosophy; it will also very briefly discuss his work in logic and something of the influence that logic had on him.

I Early forays, logic, logicism

Quine's initial interests in philosophy seem to have been sparked by his reading, among other things, Poe's "Eureka" and William James's *Pragmatism*; by his own account, this early reading left little trace.[2] When he began his undergraduate career, at Oberlin in 1926, philosophy was one of the subjects he considered, along with mathematics and classics, as an area of concentration. The issue was settled by news of Bertrand Russell and of a subject which combined mathematics with philosophy. He majored in mathematics, and wrote a thesis on "mathematical philosophy". Working towards the thesis involved a large amount of independent reading of late nineteenth- and early twentieth-century logic, and philosophy that draws on logic. He claims to have read, among other things, Venn, Peano, Couturat, Russell's *Principles of Mathematics*, and, astonishingly, half of the three volumes of Whitehead and Russell's *Principia Mathematica* (H&S, p. 8; we shall return to logic in a couple of pages). His veneration of Russell also led him to read *Our Knowledge of the External World*; *Philosophy*; and *Introduction to Mathematical Philosophy* (as well as some of Russell's more popular works). These books, he says, "whetted my appetite for cosmic understanding" (op. cit., p. 7).

A result of Quine's decision to concentrate on mathematics was that his formal study of philosophy, as distinct from logic, was not extensive. As an undergraduate he took two survey courses in the subject, which evidently made little impression.[3] For graduate school he chose the philosophy department at Harvard, largely because Whitehead, co-author of *Principia Mathematica*, was teaching there (though not teaching logic; his interests had shifted considerably in the twenty years since *Principia*). At Harvard he spent only two years on his doctorate. The first was spent preparing for the department's comprehensive examinations and taking courses (including C. I. Lewis's famous course on Kant). One may well imagine that the haste required to do both of these things in one year would have left Quine little time for real philosophical reflection, and less for the development of even inchoate views of his own. His second year in graduate school was devoted to the rapid completion of a dissertation devoted to *Principia Mathematica*.

Quine thus began his career with little background in philosophy. He does not seem to have done much systematic work to fill the gaps. With the notable exceptions of Russell and, especially, Carnap, he is not, in his early work, either reacting against or building upon the work of others. His references to the work of other philosophers are not always signs of any real knowledge or thought about such work. (Perhaps most strikingly: "Two Dogmas" contains references both to Duhem and to Pragmatism. These have given rise to some scholarly discussion about Quine's debts to the one or the other; later writings of Quine's, however, make it clear that there are no such debts.)[4] Many philosophers start out by rejecting some elements in the thought of their predecessors, and base their positive views on this reaction. In a way this is true of Quine too, for his disagreement with Carnap was indeed important to the course of his development. But his philosophy shows no sign of serious critical engagement with thinkers more distant in doctrine and approach. He is not out to refute Kant and Hegel, as Russell was at the beginning of the twentieth century; he is not out to find a basis on which to dismiss German metaphysics, as Carnap was in the 1920s. This is not to say that Quine would have any sympathy with Kant, or Hegel, or Heidegger; the point is, rather, that those were not battles that he felt a need to fight.

Russell is the one philosopher whom we know Quine took seriously before his encounter with Carnap. There are certainly areas of overlap between the views of Russell and those of the mature Quine. It is impossible to say whether these indicate Russell's influence on Quine or are signs of their being like-minded. But Quine would surely have absorbed at least a general idea of what Russell himself calls "scientific method in philosophy".[5] We may think of this, vaguely enough, as the idea of a philosophy which is focused on knowledge, which takes the natural sciences as paradigmatic of knowledge, which sees itself as in some sense scientific, and which sees the primary philosophical task as that of analysing knowledge. The idea of *analysis* as it is used here is inseparably bound up with modern logic, the logic of Frege and Russell. For Russell himself, logic became the essential tool and method of philosophy. By the use of this method, he claimed, philosophy was to be finally set on a scientific path, and to achieve definite results:

> the study of logic becomes the central study in philosophy: it gives the method of research in philosophy, just as mathematics gives the method of research in physics. And as physics, which from Plato to the Renaissance was as unprogressive, dim, and superstitious as philosophy, became a science through Galileo's fresh observation of facts and subsequent mathematical manipulation, so philosophy in our own day is becoming scientific through the simultaneous acquisition of new facts and logical methods.
> (*Our Knowledge of the External World*, p. 243)

Quine's work on logic is thus important as fitting in with a certain rather general conception of philosophy. But this barely begins to capture the significance of the role that it played in his development, or the significance that it has in his mature thought. This second topic will be examined later (see especially Chapter 10). As for the first: we have already seen that his doctoral dissertation at Harvard put forward modifications to the system of logic presented in Russell and Whitehead's *Principia Mathematica*.[6] This fact is of great importance to Quine's development, and in more than one way.

Principia Mathematica is presented as being in service of the thesis that has come to be known as *logicism*: the view that mathematics is reducible to logic. The idea of logic employed here requires discussion. (So does the idea of reduction, but we shall come to that.) What Whitehead and Russell put forward as logic is, strictly speaking, a theory of what they call "propositional functions". From a technical point of view, however, the crucial fact about this theory is that it enables them to achieve the effect of a powerful form of set-theory.[7] (As for propositional functions, we shall return to them in two or three pages.) So the technical achievement of *Principia Mathematica*, which is of considerable significance for Quine's work, can perhaps best be seen as the reduction of mathematics to set-theory. Certainly that is how Quine himself came to see it, and the reduction is important for his later views.

How can mathematics be reduced to set-theory? We shall give a brief and very compressed outline.[8] To begin with, it is important that nineteenth-century mathematicians had shown that the whole of mathematics can be reduced, with the aid of some elementary set-theory, to arithmetic, i.e. the theory of the natural numbers (zero, one, two, three, and so on). So the problem becomes one of understanding arithmetic in terms of set-theory—giving a set-theoretic understanding of the natural numbers and relations among them. The key to the solution is that we can explain, in purely logical terms, what it is for two sets to have the same number of members. (That is: we can explain this idea without appealing to the idea of number, or to any distinctively mathematical notions.) We define two sets as having the same number of members just in case there is an appropriate kind of relation between them. (It is what mathematicians call a one-to-one relation, but this idea can be defined without use of the idea of one, or any other number.)

In the Frege-Russell definition of number, a number is then defined as a set of all sets which have, in this sense, the same number of members as one another. (The number two, for example, is identified with the set of all two-membered sets, where having two members can, again, be defined without appeal to distinctively mathematical ideas.) These sets—sets of like-numbered sets—form a sequence which will play the role of the numbers. An important fact is that other definitions of numbers in terms of sets are also available—that is, there are other sequences of sets, infinitely many, in fact, which will also play the role of the numbers. (The best known of these is due to von Neumann.) What is it for sets to "play the role of" numbers? We can define all the terms of arithmetic—natural number, successor, zero, plus, times, and other arithmetical operations—in set-theoretic terms. Every arithmetical statement can be translated, via these definitions, into a statement which uses only the terms of set-theory and logic. Crucially, when a *truth* of arithmetic is translated in this fashion we obtain a truth of set-theory. (This is crucial because it is the criterion of acceptability for our definitions of the arithmetical terms.)

The definitions enable us to do arithmetic (in effect) without needing to assume that there are any numbers, over and above the sets we are already assuming. The definitions thus constitute an *ontological reduction*: they enable us to reduce an ontology containing both sets and numbers to one which does not contain numbers (except insofar as we construe certain sets as being numbers). The use of set-theory to do arithmetic would no doubt be too prolix, and too awkward, to be feasible in practice. Still, the theoretical possibility of doing so may still be taken to show that our use of (ordinary) arithmetic does not require us to accept that there are numbers, over and above sets; the appearance of there being numbers, independent of sets, can be treated as a mere notational artefact introduced for convenience and brevity but not requiring us to accept that there really are numbers. In the next section we shall see Carnap employ something like this same idea of reduction; we shall discuss Quine's use of the idea in detail in Chapter 9.

To say that the technical achievement of *Principia Mathematica* impressed Quine would be an understatement. "This is the book that has meant the most to me", he says.[9] But he found reason to dislike the philosophical underpinnings supplied in the introduction, and the theory of propositional functions which was used to define the notation of set-theory in terms of which the technical work was carried out. Reminiscing about his first encounter with the book, he calls it "My new love, in the platonic sense". He continues like this:

> I was taken with the clear, clean incisiveness of its formulas. But this was not true of its long introduction to volume 1, nor of some of the explanatory patches of prose that were interspersed. ... In those pages and passages the distinction between sign and object, or use and mention, was badly blurred. Partly in consequence, there was vague recourse to intensional properties or ideas. ... These ill-conceived mentalistic notions paraded as the philosophical foundations

for the clean-cut classes, truth-functions, and quantification that would have been better as a starting point in their own right.

(TDR, p. 265)

This passage indicates strongly held attitudes that remained unchanged throughout Quine's working life. Predominant is love of a certain kind of clarity for which logic sets the standards and, at its best, affords us a paradigm. Going along with that is the abhorrence of the enemies of that clarity: mentalism, the reliance on unexplained mental ideas, among which Quine would include meaning; use-mention confusion, i.e. confusion of linguistic expressions with the non-linguistic entities for which they stand; and intensionality, i.e. the failure of extensionality (an idea that will be explained in Chapter 11, below). Also notable is the suspicion that these vices are all somehow connected. In his philosophical writings, Quine consistently argues against mentalism and intensionality. He places great emphasis on the role of clarity, simplicity, economy, convenience, and elegance in scientific theories quite generally. His work in logic no doubt reinforced his sense of their importance, and played a role in setting his standards.

Logic, understood broadly as including set-theory, occupied most of Quine's intellectual efforts from his senior thesis at Oberlin until well after his return from a war-time stint in the US Navy. Much of his effort was directed at clarifying and simplifying the work of others. In the words of one noted commentator: "He weaned the infant [field of mathematical logic] from its ontological and notational excesses, bathed it in clarity, and clothed it in elegance".[10] In particular, much of Quine's work was devoted to clarifying and simplifying the murky foundations of the magnificent edifice that is *Principia Mathematica*, and modifying the theory of that book in one way or another. This trend begins as early as his doctoral dissertation. The explicit concern of that work is with generalizing one aspect of *Principia Mathematica*. Along the way, however, Quine also revised and clarified the basis of the system, resolving confusions and, in particular, imposing extensionality. Looking back on the matter, Quine found this clarificatory achievement by far the most significant:[11]

In retrospect the touted generalization was unimpressive. ... What is rather to be commended in the dissertation is its cleaning up of *Principia*. It resolved confusions of use and mention of expressions. Propositional functions, in the sense of attributes, ceased to be confused either with open sentences or with the names of attributes.

37

In later years Quine developed two systems of set-theory, each of which is in some sense an offshoot of the type theory of *Principia*. By his own account, the systems had a pedagogical motive. He had courses in mathematical logic to teach: "[i]t was with a view to these courses that I tried to settle on the sanest comprehensive system of ... logic and set theory" (H&S, p. 17). Each system proved to have significant drawbacks, and neither is widely used. The first of the two is New Foundations (NF), first put forward in a 1937 essay, "New Foundations for Mathematical Logic". The provenance of the second, known as ML, is more complex. In 1940 Quine published *Mathematical Logic*, which contains a system which turned out to be inconsistent. A series of repair jobs culminated in a modification by Hao Wang, which in 1951 was set forth in the revised edition of the book; this is the system which is now known as ML.

It is striking that, in developing these systems, Quine pays little or no attention to what set-theorists, for the most part, regard as the "intuitive concept of set". He sees two developments in set-theory as taking that subject beyond the reach of intuition: first, Cantor's discovery of higher infinities; second, Russell's discovery of the class paradox, and various attempts to evade it. Hence we find ourselves, in set-theory, "making deliberate choices and setting them forth unaccompanied by any attempts at justification other than in terms of elegance and convenience" (C&LT, WP, p. 117). Accordingly, Quine's concern in set-theory is with "syntactic exploration". (Ullian attributes this phrase to Dreben; see p. 584 of the essay cited in note 10, above. See that essay also for further discussion of Quine's NF and ML.)

II Carnap: the *Aufbau* project and its failure

The rest of this chapter will, as indicated, be chiefly devoted to the work of Carnap.[12] Speaking very schematically, we may say that the Carnap who influenced Quine was fundamentally anti-metaphysical and empiricist, holding that knowledge is based in sense-experience. This at once gives rise to three questions. First, how exactly is our knowledge related to sense-experience? Second, what of Carnap's own claims, including his empiricism itself? Presumably this is not a metaphysical thesis, but then what is its status? Third, what are we to say about the possibility of knowledge which does not appear to depend on sense-experience—most obviously, our knowledge of logic and mathematics? These three questions roughly correspond to the three parts of our discussion. The first will focus chiefly on Carnap's *Der logische Aufbau der Welt* (although published in 1928 this book was largely written several years earlier, as Carnap himself says in the preface to the second edition). The book was a major influence on Quine, both positively and negatively: both the ideal of an understanding of knowledge that the book holds out and also the way the project fails are very important for Quine's views on epistemology; we shall discuss it in section II of this chapter. The second part of our discussion of Carnap, in section III, will consider Carnap's way of disposing of metaphysics, drawing largely on his essay "Empiricism, Semantics and Ontology". The anti-metaphysical argument there presupposes a distinction between the analytic and the synthetic, which is also central to Carnap's attempt to account for knowledge which appears to be independent of sense-experience in a way consistent with empiricism (and which, in particular, does not accept a category of *synthetic* a priori knowledge). Carnap attempts to deploy the idea of analyticity to account for such knowledge. (Analyticity thus takes on the role that was played by the synthetic a priori in neo-Kantian thought.) The distinction between the analytic and the synthetic became the battleground in Quine's disagreement with Carnap; Carnap's attempts to explain that distinction will be the subject of the fourth and final section of this chapter.

In the *Aufbau*, Carnap set out to demonstrate that all concepts can be understood in terms of relations among immediately given experiences. The project makes heavy use of logic, including set-theory, to build an elaborate structure on the basic relation of *Remembered Similarity* (Rs) holding among such experiences. If it had succeeded it would have shown that all the concepts employed in knowledge can be defined in terms of the position that they occupy within that elaborate structure. The *Aufbau* can thus be seen as the culmination of one line of empiricist thought: that which hopes to understand all our genuine knowledge in sensory terms. The idea of exploiting modern logic to accomplish this task was first adumbrated by Russell in the years immediately before the First World War; the *Aufbau* attempts to carry it out in detail.[13]

Carnap follows the findings of *Gestalt* psychology in his understanding of the constitution of what is immediately given in experience. He thinks of immediate experience not as made up of discrete experiences of particular homogeneous sensory items, e.g. "this red patch", or even "this [possibly complex] visual sensation", but rather as the whole of a given moment's experience, involving all sense modalities. Each basic element in Carnap's construction is the total experience of one moment; the *Rs* relation holds among such elements. The most detailed parts of the book are then devoted to getting from there to the sorts of statements that others, such as Russell, might have taken as the starting point in the first place—to particular sensory items, such as a red patch given in visual sensation.

The project of the *Aufbau*, then, is to show that all concepts employed in knowledge are reducible, via logic and set-theory, to relations within immediate experience, as Carnap conceives it. The idea of a *reduction* is crucial here; it is essentially the same as the idea discussed in the previous section. In section 2 of the *Aufbau*, Carnap says: "An object (or concept) is said to be *reducible* to one or more other objects if all statements about it can be transformed into statements about these other objects". To give a reduction of a concept is thus to give a method of re-writing every statement in which an expression for that concept occurs into statements in which it does not occur: reduction is elimination. In later writings Carnap came to use the word "reduction" for a weaker relation: a theoretical sentence was said to be reduced to observational sentences when a method was given whereby the latter might be used to justify the former, with no elimination in prospect. (See, in particular, "Testability and Meaning".) The *Aufbau* project, by contrast, requires reduction in the strict sense, the sense in which reduction is elimination. (When I speak simply of "reduction" in what follows it is this strict sense that I mean.)

Carnap says that his aim in the *Aufbau* is to show how a reduction of our scientific and ordinary knowledge to immediate experience could proceed. What he actually does, however, is not adequate even as a sketch of that project. The relevant sections here are 126 and 127 (they present essentially the same material, but in different ways). The construction to this point has proceeded on a solipsistic or "autopsychological" basis.[14] Carnap has constructed the subjective impressions of colour, i.e. he has constructed the colours within the realm of experience, the autopsychological. (Because he begins with total momentary experience, getting to this point requires great labour and ingenuity.) Sections 126 and 127 are crucial precisely because they are to be the first step outside the autopsychological, the first step beyond the purely solipsistic basis to something intersubjectively valid. In particular, these sections are supposed to show us how to assign the colours we have constructed to points of four-dimensional objective space-time. One can think of this step as the definition (or reduction) of the concept "is at", where this tells you which colour is at which point in space and time.

What is wanted is thus a reduction of sentences of the form "Colour c is at point x, y, z, t, in (objective) space-time". The project of the book requires that this should be a reduction (in the strict sense): it should tell us how to *eliminate* such sentences, by providing for each such sentence a translation which makes reference purely to (subjective) immediate experience.

But in fact Carnap does not offer anything like an eliminative definition. What he gives us is, rather, a list of *desiderata* together with the instruction to satisfy them all as much as possible (while noting that it will be impossible to satisfy them all completely). But this is not a definition, not a reduction, in the sense of a recipe for elimination; instructions for using a concept are not the same as a way of eliminating that concept without loss.

Carnap thus offers no reduction (in the sense of elimination) of the crucial predicate "is at". It is, furthermore, very implausible to suppose that what he does offer could be converted into an eliminative definition, at least if we require that such a definition would apply to future experience as well as to past experience. Two obstacles are notable. First, he offers a list of *desiderata*, virtues to be achieved by the assignment of colours to objective space-time points. The satisfaction of each of these is a matter of degree, but Carnap gives no indication of how much more satisfaction of one should be traded off against how much less satisfaction of another. This suggests that the instruction to maximize the satisfaction of these *desiderata* will not in general produce a unique result. One assignment may do better at satisfying some *desiderata* while another does better at satisfying others. In such a case, Carnap's instructions do not suggest a definite answer as to which assignment is to be preferred.

Second, and more important, the assignment of colours to space-time points that Carnap has in mind are just that: the assignment of colours (in the plural) to space-time points (in the plural). In other words, the assignment does not proceed sentence by sentence, or point by point, first telling us how to make an assignment to one space-time point, then moving on to the next, and so on. Rather, Carnap's *desiderata* deal with a complete assignment all at once. The assignment is *holistic*, not atomistic: we have no way of judging two different assignments to a single point if they are taken in isolation from the total assignments of which each is a part. It is only complete assignments that can be compared and judged.

The need to deal with complete assignments here seems to be unavoidable, for reasons which are worth dwelling on. Suppose I have a visual experience, say, and wonder whether it justifies me in asserting "Colour c is at space-time point x, y, z, t"; in other words, I wonder whether I should take the experience as telling me something about the objective world, or as an hallucination. It may be impossible to make that judgment by considering the one experience in isolation. I will dismiss the experience as an hallucination if, roughly, it does not fit into the objective world which I am (supposedly) constructing from my experiences. I realize that the object I seem to see was not there a moment ago; I move closer and there is nothing there, and so on: in the light of these earlier and later experiences I judge that the experience was hallucinatory. That judgment, however, could not have been made on the basis of the one experience alone. So the individual sentence saying that such-and-such a colour is at such-and-such a point of objective space-time cannot be evaluated in isolation from others. Thus in Carnap's system, and in any plausible variation of it, assignments of colours to points will not proceed one-by-one; it is only the total assignment that can be judged.

The holism of the assignment of sensory qualities to objective points of space and time strongly suggests, at least, that no eliminative definition of "is at" can be given. The fact that Carnap does not put forward such a definition seems to be inevitable, not a mere failing of his. It is only the total assignment that can be judged; but there never is a completed total assignment. New sensory experience is occurring constantly, giving rise to new assignments of qualities to space-time points. Earlier assignments may need to be revised to accommodate these new assignments. As new experience occurs, it may lead us to change our minds about what aspects of earlier experience we should take as indicating objective features of the world. A *definition* of "is at" would put an arbitrary end to this process. As Quine puts it, commenting on the failure of the *Aufbau* at just this point:

> The worst obstacle seems to be that the assigning of sense qualities to public place-times has to be kept open to revision in the light of later experience, and so cannot be reduced to definition. The empiricist's regard for experience thus impedes the very program of reducing the world to experience.
>
> ("Russell's Ontological Development", *TT*, pp. 84–85)

I have discussed the project of Carnap's *Aufbau* in some detail because I think that both the general idea of the project, and way in which it fails, are of great importance for understanding Quine. Let us begin with the failure of the project. What this indicates, at least to Quine, is a certain looseness of fit between experience and theory; this is an idea which has had a pervasive influence on his thought. More specifically, two fundamental, and closely related, Quinean doctrines can be seen at work in the way in which the *Aufbau* fails.

The first such doctrine is Quine's holism, the claim that "our statements about the external world face the tribunal of sense experience not individually but only as a corporate body" (TDE, *FLPV*, p. 41). As we saw, holism lies behind what Quine takes to be the central reason for the failure of the *Aufbau* project; Quine himself explicitly makes the connection both in "Two Dogmas" (see especially pp. 38–41) and in "Epistemology Naturalized" (pp. 76–79). The second Quinean doctrine which can be seen at work in the failure of the *Aufbau* programme is the underdetermination of theory by evidence: that the evidence we have does not pick out a uniquely best theory. Given the looseness and vagueness of Carnap's *desiderata* for the use of "is at", why should we suppose that there will in general be a uniquely best way of satisfying them? And if there is not, then a given set of experiences does not determine a single uniquely best account of the objective world: the "evidence" fails to determine the "theory".

Quine's doctrines of holism and of the underdetermination of theory by evidence can thus be linked to the failure of Carnap's *Aufbau* project. This fact suggests that these doctrines may apply not just to advanced scientific theories but to the very beginnings of knowledge. Carnap's project, after all, does not fail because of its inability to account for sophisticated forms of knowledge, but rather because of its failure to account for the simplest and most elementary forms of objective knowledge.

So far we have dwelt on Quine's response to the failure of the project. But there is a more positive influence as well. Many of Quine's remarks suggest that if (*per impossibile*) it had succeeded it would have shown how our claims to knowledge depend on sensory experience. At one point Quine compares his own epistemological project with that of the *Aufbau*, and even indicates some detailed resemblances. (See especially *FSS*, pp. 10–13, 17; see also Chapter 4, section I, and Chapter 5, section I, below.) Quine, moreover, takes the *Aufbau*, and the work of the Vienna Circle more generally, to embody the idea that linguistic meaning depends on its relation to experience; this is a view that in some sense he clearly endorses. Thus he says: "[t]he Vienna Circle espoused a verification theory of meaning but did not take it seriously enough." (EN, *OR*, p. 80.) The lack of seriousness that he sees here is that the Vienna Circle did not realize how large a difference holism makes to their view. Quine takes holism to show that the idea of verification—or of evidence more broadly—does not, in general, apply to sentences taken one-by-one; this is a crucial change, one which in Quine's hands threatens to undermine the notion of meaning. (This is a point to which we shall return; see section I of Chapter 3.)

III Disposing of metaphysics: language-relativity, tolerance, and conventionalism

Carnap's instinct always was to eliminate philosophical problems: rather than advancing philosophical doctrines, he attempted to dissolve the questions or problems which they might answer. The method which came to predominate in his work is a form of linguistic conventionalism. He argued that what may appear to be substantive metaphysical disputes, with right answers if we could but find them, are really nothing more than questions about language; and that which language one uses is a matter of choice, a practical decision not a theoretical matter.

An important example here is the issue of the reality of the external world, whether there is a world of physical objects which exists independent of experience. Schlick, Reichenbach, and other philosophers to whom Carnap was generally sympathetic had claimed that realism is indispensable for science, and should therefore be accepted. Carnap, however, claims that what science requires is not the acceptance of a *doctrine* of realism, but merely that we speak a certain kind of language. He argues, moreover, that, beyond the choice of language, there simply *is* no intelligible metaphysical thesis of realism to accept or reject. Thus in his "Autobiography" he says:

> The general view that many sentences of traditional metaphysics are pseudo-sentences was held by most members of the Vienna Circle. ... I maintained from the beginning the view that a characterization as pseudo-sentences must also be applied to the thesis of realism, concerning the reality of the external world, and to the counter theses. ... I maintained that what was needed for science was merely the acceptance of a realistic language, but that the thesis of the reality of the external world was an empty addition to the system of science.
>
> ("Autobiography", p. 46)

Thus for Carnap there is no metaphysical claim of realism to be right or wrong about: there is merely the choice of a realist or non-realist language. If our interest is in doing science, we will perhaps be well advised to choose a realist language; but this does not mean that it is the *correct* language, or that there is a philosophical doctrine of realism which is true. It means only that a certain kind of language is the most convenient for a given purpose; our using it expresses a practical decision. Similar remarks apply also to empiricism: for Carnap, at least by the 1930s, it cannot be seen as a *doctrine*. Rather, it is a preference for one kind of language over others.

This method of disposing of philosophical problems is attractive: very often it is hard to find anything substantial at stake in a philosophical dispute, and the point does seem to be a merely verbal disagreement. But the idea that what is at stake is a question of the choice of a language does not by itself imply that the dispute is not a substantive one. The realist and idealist may speak different languages. Yet the realist, say, may insist that her language is the correct one, and correct because there really are objects of such-and-such a kind. Then the same dispute threatens to arise over again. What blocks that kind of move is Carnap's insistence that there is no right and wrong about the choice of language, that such a choice is a matter of convention—a matter for free decision rather than philosophical argument. This is what Carnap calls the Principle of Tolerance:

> It is not our business to set up prohibitions, but to arrive at conventions. . . .
>
> *In logic, there are no morals.* Everyone is at liberty to build up his own logic, i.e. his own form of language, as he wishes. All that is required of him is that, if he wishes to discuss it, he must state his methods clearly, and give syntactical rules instead of philosophical arguments.
>
> (*Logical Syntax of Language*, pp. 51–52;
> emphasis in the original)

What justifies the Principle of Tolerance? For Carnap, language, and in particular logic, play a constitutive role in knowledge: only once a logic and a language are in place is knowledge possible. Only then is a rational dispute, or rational agreement, possible. It follows that the choice of language and logic, and questions which turn on that choice, cannot themselves be matters for such dispute: with no logic in place, there will be no agreed methods which might settle such a question. Hence it will be a pseudo-question, something that looks like a genuine question with a right or wrong answer, but in fact is not. (This point is explicit in "Empiricism, Semantics and Ontology"; see p. 219.) This is Carnap's diagnosis of the intractable disputes which fill the history of philosophy. His response is to say that questions of language-choice are not matters of right and wrong, not theoretical questions at all, but practical questions. About the issue of realism, raised a page or two back, he says:

> Those who raise the question of the reality of the thing world itself have perhaps in mind not a theoretical question as their formulation seems to suggest, but rather a practical question, a matter of practical decision concerning the structure of our language. We have to make a decision whether or not to accept and use the forms of expression in the framework in question.
>
> ("Empiricism, Semantics and Ontology", p. 206)

According to the Principle of Tolerance, the choice of language thus is a practical matter, to be made on the basis of pragmatic criteria such as efficiency and convenience. Once we have chosen a language and a logic, rational disputes become possible: there are standards to which we can appeal to settle questions, and there is a right and a wrong to what we say. The choice of a language is also a choice of methods and rules for settling questions that can be raised within the language: for example, whether one thing counts as evidence for another is for Carnap a matter of whether one sentence confirms another, and this is a matter which may vary with the choice of language. A given language will have its own rules, which give us something fixed to which we can appeal in settling disputes. As long as we are both speaking the same language, the rules of the language provide a neutral court of appeal; if we are speaking different languages then there is, of course, no genuine dispute at all. The choice of a language, by contrast, is not a matter for theoretical justification at all, for without a language and its rules the notion of theoretical justification has no application. Notions of confirmation, justification, and evidence are thus internal to a given language, and so are language-relative.

The concepts of truth, fact, reality, and objectivity are also language-relative, in Carnap's view. The judgment whether or not a thing is real makes sense only within a language and by the standards of that language: there is no concept of reality which can be abstracted and taken as language-neutral. As Carnap says: "To be real in the scientific sense means to be an element of the system; hence this concept cannot be meaningfully applied to the system itself". ("Empiricism, Semantics and Ontology", p. 207.) So the decision to accept a realistic language, say, "must not be interpreted as if it meant [the] acceptance of a *belief* in the reality of the thing world; there is no such belief or assertion or assumption, because it is not a theoretical question" (op. cit., p. 208). Such a decision is "not of a cognitive nature" (ibid.).

The choice of a language, as Carnap sees it, may thus be compared with the choice of a set of rules for a game. Once that choice is made, we can appeal to the rules to settle our disputes; but if the dispute is about which rules to adopt we have no such recourse. This makes the two sorts of disputes different in kind. If we are playing bridge, say, then it is an objective, factual matter which card wins a given trick; but if three people want to play bridge while a fourth insists upon poker, then the issue between them is of quite a different kind. While the bridge players may accuse the poker player of having depraved tastes, they can scarcely hold that she believes something *false* in the same sense as that in which she would if she thought, say, that a contract of seven spades at bridge could be fulfilled by making twelve tricks. Similarly, according to Carnap, if there is a disagreement within a language we have the rules of that language to which we may appeal in settling the dispute; whereas if we disagree about which language to use there are no such rules, and no factual matter to be right or wrong about. We may prefer one language to another, but there is no rational basis on which we can say that those who hold the opposite opinion are mistaken. Hence, Carnap concludes, we should be tolerant rather than dogmatic about the choice of language, but not about the choice of a theory once the language is fixed.[15]

Carnap thus distinguishes two sorts of questions. Internal questions arise within a language, and presuppose a certain framework. These are the ordinary questions of science and of common sense; such questions may be very difficult, but they are not completely intractable in the way that philosophical questions threaten to be. External questions, by contrast, are about choice of language, and hence are not matters of right and wrong at all. There are no intractable questions of a special "philosophical" kind; appearances to the contrary are illusory, and arise from our treating external questions as if they were internal, and had right or wrong answers.

Implicit here is a picture of what we might call "language-relative rationality". A rational dispute is one in which each party articulates the rules of the language that he or she is using. Providing we are both using the same language, we can then appeal to the rules as a wholly neutral court of appeal. They will not settle all our disputes, but they will tell us how evidence bears on the disputed question, thus making the dispute tractable (though not necessarily conclusively settleable). The process of articulating the rules of the language may also show that we are not using the same language. In that case we have to recognize two points. First, there can be no dispute at all unless one of us adopts the language of the other, or each agrees to use a third language; while we are speaking different languages we are simply talking past each other, and no rational disagreement is possible. Second, the choice of language is a matter for tolerance. Since a dispute about that matter would have no rules of language to appeal to, it would not be a rational disagreement; rather than engaging in a futile and anarchic dispute, we should simply recognize that choice of language is a matter of free choice, not subject to criticism by others.

Carnap wields the internal/external distinction to defuse philosophical and ontological questions. One crucial presupposition here is the idea that there is a sharp distinction between questions that arise within a language and questions about choice of language—so that if two people assert different and apparently contradictory things, there must be a definite fact as to whether they are speaking the same language and actually contradicting one another (a substantive disagreement), or whether they are speaking different languages (a merely verbal disagreement). For Carnap a language is a precise object, with definite rules; his criterion of philosophical good faith is that one make the rules of one's language explicit. A second crucial presupposition is that questions of choice of language are different in kind, and to be settled in a different sort of way, from questions that arise within a language. The former are matters of choice, of convention; the latter are matters of (language-relative) fact. Here Carnap's position relies on the Principle of Tolerance.

IV The analytic–synthetic distinction

As the previous section indicates, Carnap's work relies on the idea of the rules of language and on the Principle of Tolerance. Insofar as our cognitive endeavours approach the ideal, we are at any given moment speaking a definite language with definite rules. (We "give syntactical rules instead of philosophical arguments"; *Logical Syntax of Language*, p. 52, quoted above, p. 45) In accordance with the Principle of Tolerance, the language is freely chosen; once we have chosen it, however, we are bound by its rules until we make another choice. The rules of the language, and the sentences which follow from them, thus have a status distinct from the other things that can be said within the language. So it follows from fundamental features of Carnap's thought that some sentences of a language follow from the rules of the language, and that those sentences have a special status, significantly different from that of other sentences of the language; these are the *analytic* sentences of the language.[16] The analytic sentences are to be those which are constitutive of the language. This view relies on the idea of implicit definition: the meaning of the terms of the language is given by the stipulation that such-and-such sentences using those terms are to be true, while such-and-such other sentences using those terms are to be false. The truth (falsehood) of the relevant sentences thus follows immediately from the meanings of the relevant terms.

Analyticity is of quite general and fundamental importance for Carnap's thought. It was to be a partial explication of the traditional philosophical notions of a priori knowledge and necessary truth. To assume those notions as basic, as given, is in Carnap's view to become mired in metaphysics; analyticity was to replace what is useful and correct in those ideas while avoiding their metaphysical implications. Analyticity was thus to be a clear and precise idea, acceptable even to the most scrupulous of empiricists, which would play something of the philosophical role of the old metaphysical ideas.

A central issue here is the status of logic and mathematics. These are, paradigmatically, subjects that seem to be a priori and necessary, and to defy empiricist explanation. Carnap's conception of analyticity promises a solution to this difficulty. In constructing a language, I lay down what rules I please; the only question is whether the language so constructed is useful, and this is settled by investigating its properties. Thus some mathematics can simply be built into the language, as it were, by constructing a language in which those mathematical statements follow from rules of that language. A certain amount of mathematics then becomes analytic for that language, in the sense that one only counts as a speaker of that language if one accepts that part of mathematics. The theorems of mathematics are thus not genuine statements, the truth of which requires some explanation. They are, rather, simply consequences of the rules of our language. Thus, Carnap says: "It became possible for the first time to combine the basis tenet of empiricism with a satisfactory explanation of the nature of logic and mathematics" ("Autobiography", p. 47). Fundamental to the empiricism of the Vienna Circle is the idea that all knowledge is based on sense-experience. Logic and mathematics might appear as exceptions; if they are analytic, however, then they do not count as knowledge in the relevant sense. They do not themselves make any claims about the world; they simply follow from our means of representing the world. For some languages, fundamental statements of the natural sciences—setting out the basic properties of space and time, say—may also count as analytic.

For Carnap, the conception of analyticity that we have sketched also plays a crucial role in a central task of philosophy, explicating the language of science. Analysing a language, on his account, requires a notion of logic and logical form, and logic is to be analytic. An analysis will specify which sentences of the language are analytic, presumably by specifying the syntactical and semantical rules from which the analytic sentences follow; these sentences are definitions of the concepts involved, and will have a status different from that of the other sentences of the theory. This enterprise is continuous with that involved in showing that works of metaphysics do *not* contain significant questions: in each case we analyse the language in order to identify and clarify just what questions (if any) are at stake.

This description of the positive philosophical task might make it seem as if philosophy is an empirical discipline: the philosopher examines the language of the scientists, in something of the same spirit as a linguistic anthropologist examining the language of a culturally remote people. This is not, however, how Carnap sees the matter: for him it is unquestioned that philosophy is in no sense an empirical discipline. He therefore distinguishes pure syntax and semantics from descriptive syntax and semantics. On the descriptive side, we do indeed study an actual language as it is spoken; this is an empirical subject. Pure syntax and semantics, by contrast, involve setting up artificial languages by means of syntactical and semantical rules; the language is then investigated by drawing consequences from the rules set up. What sort of languages we find it worthwhile to set up will of course be guided by the sorts of languages that we think are actually useful in science, but the results of our investigations into the languages we have set up are not answerable to science or to actual language-use or to anything empirical: they are analytic. Carnap compares this situation with that of the application of mathematics. A mathematician may carry out certain investigations with an eye to their being useful in physics, or some other empirical science, but the results of the mathematical work are independent of any possible application. For Carnap the investigations of the philosopher into forms of language are analogous.

Carnap also distinguishes special syntax and semantics from general syntax and semantics. Special syntax and semantics are familiar: they are the syntax and semantics of a particular language. (If it is an actual language, we have descriptive syntax and semantics; if it is an artificial language, we have pure syntax and semantics). General syntax and semantics, by contrast, are intended to be the construction of semantical and syntactic categories that apply to any language. The importance of this distinction for our purposes will emerge in Chapter 3, section II.

3

THE ANALYTIC–SYNTHETIC
DISTINCTION

The last chapter indicated the pivotal role that the analytic–synthetic distinction plays in Carnap's thought. The distinction is essential to Carnap's method of disposing of metaphysics, and to his way of accounting for logic and mathematics within the constraints of empiricism. It is also essential to his positive project of clarifying the language of science, for he takes distinguishing the analytic sentences of a language from its synthetic sentences to be a crucial part of this clarificatory activity. It is not surprising, then, that the general differences between Quine and Carnap come to a head in their disagreement over analyticity.

Carnap is, of course, not the only philosopher to have used the notion of analyticity to bear a substantial philosophical burden. Quine's attack is, accordingly, not narrowly focused on Carnap. In particular, he may have had C. I. Lewis more or less implicitly in mind; Lewis's version of analyticity, more explicitly than Carnap's, is understood in terms of meaning, mentalistically conceived.[1] In any case, the idea of "truth in virtue of meaning" or "truth by definition" is common enough for Quine to think he needs to argue against it. For these reasons, section I is primarily concerned with the idea of meaning and definition. This issue is framed by Quine's empirical attitude towards meaning. This, in turn, is an instance of his quite general insistence that concepts must meet scientific and empirical standards if they are to be suitable for "philosophical and scientific" purposes (*TT*, p. 184; quoted in context Chapter 1, section I, above).

Quine thus insists that the idea of meaning cannot simply be taken for granted and used as a philosophical tool; it is available for philosophical use only to the extent that we are able to make empirical sense of it. He also argues, of course, that we cannot make full empirical sense of the idea. (Holism plays a crucial role here, as we shall see.) Although Carnap does not usually appeal to the idea of meaning to justify his use of analyticity, he does do so in some of his replies to Quine. In those contexts he also appeals to the idea of translation to argue that the idea of meaning can be empirically grounded; this point is also briefly discussed in the section. (I do not think that Quine's views on meaning bear the main burden of his opposition to the philosophical use of the analytic–synthetic distinction; for this reason a detailed discussion of his views about translation is postponed until Chapter 8, below.)

The negative point—Quine's opposition to the idea that a notion of meaning can simply be taken for granted and used for philosophical purposes—is underpinned by a positive one. As we have already remarked, his strongest argument against the idea of meaning, taken for granted as an explanatory idea, is that we simply do not need it. This point is central to an understanding of Quine's views here. He claims that we can give an account of cognitive language which is purely naturalistic in character, and makes no appeal to an unreconstructed notion of meaning; much of his work is aimed at substantiating that claim. This is what I have called Quine's genetic project; it is the primary subject of Chapters 4–6, below. It is also relevant that Quine thinks that we can also manage without such a notion of meaning in accounting for translation, for philosophical analysis, and for belief-reports. These are matters that we shall come to in Chapters 8, 9, and 13, respectively.

In section II Carnap's views are the centre of our attention. In particular, the section discusses Carnap's idea that for clarity about analyticity we must consider artificial languages, not natural languages. Quine disagrees on this point; understanding his reasons will shed light on his views on analyticity more generally. One specific issue taken up in this section is the contrast, mentioned at the end of the previous chapter, between giving a definition for a particular language (a definition in special syntax or semantics) and giving a definition applicable to any language (general syntax or semantics). Another is the contrast that Quine draws between synonymy on the one hand and significance, or meaningfulness, on the other; the latter idea, he holds, is clearer than the former.

Quine's attitude towards the analytic–synthetic distinction is less straightforward than it sometimes appears to be. Some of Quine's writings from the early 1950s encourage the idea that he wholly rejects anything that might be called a version of the analytic–synthetic distinction. This is especially true of "Two Dogmas of Empiricism"; the wide currency of that essay is no doubt responsible for the impression that Quine totally rejects any version of the distinction. But even in that essay he leaves some room for a distinction to which he gives the name, and by the time of *Roots of Reference* (1974) he is explicitly endorsing one. (Whether it is worthy of the name is another question, but not an important one.) He does, however, reject any version of analyticity which could be used to do significant philosophical work, including explaining such notions as meaning or necessity. In particular, he rejects the idea that there is a defensible distinction *which will play the role that Carnap allotted it.*

One issue here is the *scope* of analyticity. For Carnap's purposes, it is essential that mathematics be analytic (at least enough mathematics to enable us to do physics); also that the framework propositions of natural science should have that status. But no version of analyticity acceptable to Quine will have those statements within its scope. Section III considers what sort of understanding of analyticity is acceptable to Quine and also the scope of that notion of analyticity. Section IV deals with a more complex Quinean objection to Carnap's use of the idea of analyticity. Quine takes it for granted that, in order to play the role that Carnap allots to it, the analytic-synthetic distinction would have to mark a clear and important *epistemological* difference; he holds that no defensible version of the distinction has that kind of epistemological significance. What underlies this claim, in turn, is a view of the epistemological implications of holism, which leads Quine to reject the Principle of Tolerance. Their disagreement over this principle is fundamental; it is the fulcrum on which their differences more generally turn.

Quine denies that the status of logic and mathematics can be explained by claiming that they are analytic. As in the case of meaning, his position here is not a purely negative one. As important as any specific argument against Carnapian analyticity is the fact that Quine thinks it is unnecessary. As we shall see in section V, he argues that what he takes to be the phenomena which have led philosophers to think of logic and mathematics as a priori can be accounted for in other ways.[2] He also reconceives the project of philosophical analysis, so that it too does not involve analyticity. (See Chapter 9, below.) Quine's holism, and his denial of the Principle of Tolerance, are central to his way of managing without Carnap's notion of analyticity, as well as to his rejection of that idea.

I Doubts about meanings

Quine holds that our concepts must be shown to be scientifically respectable before they are available for philosophical use. And he argues that the concept of meaning fails the test. The issue here is sometimes framed as having to do with the idea of meanings as *entities*; some of Quine's critics take it that what he objects to in philosophical talk about meaning is the reification, treating meanings as *things*. (See, for example, Alston, "Quine on Meaning".)

Quine's objection against meanings as entities, however, is not that there is something in general wrong with reification, or with abstract objects. It has to do, rather, with his insistence that it is not legitimate to suppose that there are entities of a given kind unless we have clear identity-criteria for the alleged entities; we must be able to make clear sense of the questions where one such entity leaves off and another begins, when two descriptions are descriptions of the same entity, and so on.[3] In the case of meanings, questions of identity-criteria reduce to the question of sameness of meaning, or *synonymy*. If we had a clear and objective sense for the notion of synonymy, we would thus have identity-criteria for meanings. In that case Quine would be content to accept meanings as entities; as he has remarked on more than one occasion, we could construe meanings as sets of synonymous expressions. (See, for example, Quine's reply to Alston in H&S.) Sets of synonymous expressions, however, would be of no comfort to most of Quine's critics. They would have no explanatory value. In particular, they would not enable us to explain synonymy, since they would themselves be defined in terms of synonymy. (In section VI of Chapter 8 we shall consider closely related points in greater detail.)

What Quine objects to is the uncritical postulation of meanings as entities at the outset of inquiry. More broadly, he objects to what he calls *mentalism*—an uncritical view of the mind and its powers in general. So he objects to the idea that meanings are mental entities, and that our understanding of language, and hence our use of it, can be explained in terms of our somehow "grasping" or "having in mind" such entities. In Quine's view, this gets it backwards. For the purposes of serious philosophical and scientific inquiry, we must begin with what is public and open to empirical investigation, and so with the *use* of language, not with the alleged mental underpinnings of that use. Understanding a language consists, very roughly, in being able to use it in appropriate ways (and respond appropriately to its use by others, and so on). If we were to make clear sense of synonymy, in this way, then we could define meanings, as indicated. But even then, meanings would not play anything like the role that the mentalistic philosopher wants. For Quine, then, meaning will in any case not be an explanatory notion; it may be something that the philosopher tries to explain, but it will not itself be the terminus of explanation: "Meaning ... is a worthy object of philosophical and scientific clarification and analysis, and ... it is ill-suited for use as an instrument of philosophical and scientific clarification and analysis." (*TT*, p. 185.)

Uncritical postulation of meanings is encouraged by the tendency to look upon meaning as a single undifferentiated notion. Such a view results in the following sort of anti-Quinean argument: either there *are* meanings, in which case we can define synonymy as identity of meaning, and analyticity as truth in virtue of meaning; or there are no meanings, in which case Quine must think—quite absurdly—that no one ever means anything by what they say, and so on.[4] This argument assumes that, since some of our utterances are meaningful, there must therefore be meanings which those utterances *have* (whatever exactly that comes to); and that these meanings are not mere sets of synonymous expressions, but entities fitted for more robust roles, including that of grounding a notion of truth in virtue of meaning.

Quine completely rejects this kind of argument. He distinguishes the various uses we have for the idea of meaning, or the various contexts in which the word occurs. One such context is synonymy, or sameness of meaning. Another is significance, or having a meaning.[5] Part of the point of separating these issues is that they may not all have the same status. We may be able to give a clear general account of significance, but not of synonymy. (Indeed, Quine thinks that something like this is correct; we shall briefly discuss his views on significance in section II below.) In that case we may be misled: if we phrase significance as "having a meaning" we may think that the (relative) clarity of this idea demonstrates that there are meanings which words have, and hence that sameness of meaning must make clear general sense. Quine is concerned to resist this inference. His doubts about synonymy are not intended to imply that it is, absurdly, in doubt whether any word or phrase ever has a meaning.

Of these contexts for the word "meaning", synonymy is the one that comes in for the most sustained attention in Quine's attempts to cast doubt on analyticity. The reason for this is that it is synonymy which matters if our aim is to define analyticity in terms of meaning. Certainly we can go the other way around. Given the notion of analyticity, at least on most under- standings of it, we can define what it is for two expressions to mean the same. Two predicates, *A* and *B*, mean the same just in case "All *A*s are *B*s and vice versa" is not merely true but analytic; if *A* and *B* are sentences, the relevant statement is "*A* if and only if *B*"; if they are singular terms, it is "*A* is [identical to] *B*". Understanding analyticity in terms of synonymy (the reverse direction) is less straightforward. For special cases where the sentence has one of the three forms just mentioned ("All *A*s are *B*s and vice versa"; or "*A* if and only if *B*"; or "*A* is [identical to] *B*") we can say that the sentence is analytic just in case *A* and *B* are synonymous. Or if we accept that the truths of logic are analytic, then we can say that a truth in general is ana- lytic if it can be derived from a logical truth by replacing some expressions by synonymous expressions. (This method takes for granted the idea of logical truth—as Quine does in section 1 of "Two Dogmas of Empiricism", for the purposes of argument, in order to focus attention on the idea of synonymy.) So a clear understanding of synonymy would give us at least a good start on a definition of analyticity. Synonymy is thus a primary target of Quine's, as he attempts to call into question the uncritical acceptance of analyticity.

Quine, as we have emphasized, is not willing simply to assume the notions of meaning or synonymy at the outset. Furthermore, he doubts that clear sense can, in general, be made of those ideas. Crucial to this last issue is a point that we touched on in section II of the previous chapter: Quine holds that the cognitive meaning of a sentence, insofar as we can make sense of that idea, can be more or less equated with the evidence for that sentence. Underlying this view is Quine's empiricism, in particular his claim that all our knowledge of the world is acquired through stimulation of our sensory nerves. As we saw in Chapter 1, Quine puts great emphasis on the fact that "our information about the world comes only through impacts on our sensory receptors" (PT, p. 19). For him, this is fundamental to empiricism. Part of what he takes it to involve, as we also saw, is that our language—our sounds, marks or gestures—are cognitively meaningful only insofar as they are in some way related to stimulations of our sensory nerves. Only such relations to stimulation give us reason to take noises as embodying information about the world. Quine elaborates on the point by alluding to the learning of language:

> The sort of meaning that is basic ... to the learning of one's own language, is necessarily empirical and nothing more. A child learns his first words and sentences by hearing and using them in the presence of appropriate stimuli. These must be external stimuli, for they must act both on the child and on the speaker from whom he is learning.
>
> (EN, *OR*, p. 81)

What one learns, at the outset of language-acquisition, is to use or to accept sentences in response to appropriate stimuli. Since the stimuli correspond, more or less, to external circumstances, what one learns is what circumstances justify the assertion of the sentence. (Our next three chapters will discuss Quine's views on the learning of language in greater detail.)

Does all of this mean that Quine advocates a verificationist theory of meaning? A passage in "Epistemology Naturalized", quoted in section II of the previous chapter, seems to suggest that he does. He approvingly cites the Vienna Circle's advocacy of "a verification theory of meaning" and Pierce's view that "the meaning of a sentence turns purely on what would count as evidence for its truth" (*OR*, p. 80). But this appearance is misleading. Quine's emphasis on the link between meaning and evidence in fact leads him to deny that we can, in general, make clear sense of the idea of the meaning of a sentence. The crucial point here is holism.

Given the link between meaning and evidence, how are we to think of the meaning of a sentence? One answer is in terms of Carnap's *Aufbau* programme of radical reduction, discussed in the last chapter. That programme sought to translate each sentence into sensory (and set-theoretic) terms; in Quine's view, it foundered on holism. Quine holds that almost all sentences have no implications for experience when they are taken in isolation from others. Hence, he claims, there is in general no such thing as the evidence which counts for or against an individual sentence, taken in isolation. (For some sentences there may be but *in general* there is not.) As he puts it, a typical statement "has no fund of experiential implications it can call its own" (EN, *OR*, p. 79). Evidence bears on larger or smaller chunks of theory, usually made up of more than a single sentence; it is only such chunks that have "experiential implications". A body of sentences taken together may make claims on experience, but it may be impossible to parcel those claims out among the individual sentences. Attempts to make clear sense of the evidence which bears on a single sentence run into difficulty because it may depend on what other sentences are taken for granted, as given.

This is a very abstract way of thinking about the relation between evidence and the more theoretical sentences which we accept. It is, one might say, a logician's way of thinking about the matter. Theory implies evidence. (As we shall see, making this idea precise requires that theory be regimented; see Chapter 9, section II, below.) Suppose we have a sentence which is borne out by observation and is implied by a set of theoretical sentences, and not by any smaller subset. Then that fact, presumably, lends some degree of credibility to the theoretical sentences in the set. But this way of thinking about the matter does not by itself distinguish one theoretical sentence in the set from another. Quine does not deny that there are distinctions here. In particular, working scientists will not (except perhaps in the rarest of cases) think of all the sentences in the set as equally answerable to the evidence, as equally gaining credibility if the observations go one way and losing it if they go the other way. Our scientists, that is to say, will most likely think of the observation as a test of just one, or perhaps two or three, of the theoretical sentences, with the others being taken for granted as background; they will not treat the observation as bearing equally on all the theoretical sentences in the set. Other distinctions can perhaps also be made among those sentences. But from Quine's very abstract perspective, if all the sentences in a given set are needed to imply a given observational sentence, then the observation bears on all those sentences.

Quine equates cognitive meaning with evidence. Given the holistic view of evidence indicated in the previous paragraph, it follows that there may in general be no such thing as the cognitive meaning of an individual sentence, taken in isolation from others. Equally, if we consider two sentences in isolation from their settings, there may not in general be an answer to the question whether they make the same claim upon reality, or whether they are synonymous; the answer may depend on what other sentences are being taken for granted.

The ideas of meaning and synonymy are connected with the idea of translation. In his reply to Quine's "Carnap and Logical Truth" and in his essay "Meaning and Synonymy in Natural Languages", Carnap sets out to defend the use of intensional concepts, including synonymy and analyticity, by giving "empirical, behavioristic criteria for them".[6] He argues the point in terms of translation, claiming that we can give objective behavioural criteria for the correctness of a translation, and that this suffices to legitimate the use of intensional concepts. He considers a linguist who knows nothing of the language she studies; the linguist simply studies the behaviour of its users. Carnap thinks it uncontroversial that the linguist could arrive at an extensional translation, i.e. a translation which says what objects the terms of the language apply to, and what objects the predicates of that language are true of. (The idea *is* controversial: Quine disagrees, as we shall see in Chapter 8.) Carnap then turns to what he takes to be the difficult question, that of the application of intensional concepts to the language. Two terms may have the same extension, i.e. apply to the same objects, yet have different intensions. Carnap's example is *Einhorn* (unicorn) and *Kobold* (goblin); since neither is true of any objects, they do not differ extensionally, yet clearly there is a difference in meaning. What criteria could the linguist use to capture such a difference? Carnap's answer is that with no actual objects to point to the linguist will use pictures, or present her native informant with imagined situations, and ask about the applicability of the word in that kind of situation. He says: "The tests concerning intensions are independent of questions of existence. The man on the street is well able to understand and to answer questions about assumed situations". ("Meaning and Synonymy in Natural Languages", p. 240).

Carnap thinks that he is meeting Quine on ground that the latter would find fully acceptable—taking understanding a language as having "a certain system of interconnected dispositions for linguistic response" ("Meaning and

Synonymy in Natural Languages", p. 242), and producing behavioural criteria for the notions of synonymy and analyticity. Quine would not, however, accept Carnap's technique of questioning a native informant about imaginary situations as being a satisfactory empirical clarification of the notion of meaning in general. There is no reason to think that a method which works in some easy cases—such as the *Einhorn/Kobold* case—can be relied upon to give us empirical criteria for unique translations in general. Quine, indeed, suggests that empirical criteria do *not* in general suffice to determine a unique translation of one language into another; this is his famous, or infamous, thesis of the indeterminacy of translation, which is the subject of Chapter 8.[7] Some commentators have seen this thesis as crucial to the disagreement between Quine and Carnap over analyticity, and thus to the differences between their views quite generally.[8] It should be clear from what I have already said that I do not agree. I take the issues to be discussed in sections III and IV below, to put forward more fundamental reasons for Quine's disagreement with Carnap.

It is notable that Quine, in some of his last works, describes the indeterminacy thesis as a "conjecture". (See H&S, p. 728.) This suggests that the appropriate attitude for a Quinean to have towards the objectivity of translation, and thus also perhaps towards the question whether there is a defensible notion of sentence-meaning, is agnosticism. (Some possible reasons for Quine's late view, and for agnosticism, will be discussed in Chapter 8, section IV.) But agnosticism here very much favours Quine's general position about meaning. If agnosticism is a tenable position at all then we cannot simply take a notion of meaning for granted. If the issue remains unsettled then the notion of meaning is not available. To be justified in using an idea such as meaning in our scientific and philosophical endeavours we must have positive assurance that it makes sufficiently clear sense; it is not enough that it is uncertain that it does not.

Finally, in this section, let us consider the idea that we can clarify the notion of synonymy, and thence perhaps that of analyticity, by appeal to the idea of a definition. Dictionaries are full of definitions, but Quine insists that this fact sheds no theoretical light on the notion of synonymy: even if the lexicographer constructs a dictionary entry in the belief that it records a synonymy, still the content of this belief, what synonymy is, is not thereby clarified (see TDE, *FLPV*, p. 24). It may, nevertheless, seem as if Quine is making a substantial concession here: that there is a notion of synonymy, and one that we in fact know how to apply, even if we have no good theoretical account of it. Except perhaps for the purposes of argument, however, I think there is no real concession. The reason is a significant one. Should we in fact think of the lexicographer's task as being the recording of synonymies? From a Quinean point of view, such a description is loaded, and alternatives are available. We could say: the lexicographer's task is simply to explain the correct use of each word. The explanation presupposes a reader who has a general familiarity with the use of the language, or at least the simpler parts of it, and it is intended to enable the reader to understand and use the given word. Thus a dictionary might give examples of correct uses of the given word, and explanations which will help the reader to catch on to the correct use in general. But it is a further step—and one which the existence of dictionaries does not impel us to take—to say that the uses and the explanations singled out to help the reader have any special status. There are many correct uses of a given word, many true sentences in which the word is used. Some of these will prove more effective than others when we are instructing the uninitiated in the use of the word: that does not, however, imply, or even suggest, that those sentences have a status which is different from that of others, or that their truth is to be explained in a different way. The existence of dictionaries does not prove that there are synonymies in the relevant sense: true sentences whose status is in some way different from that of other truths. (See *PT*, pp. 56–57, and *FSS*, p. 83, where Quine makes essentially this point.)

II Artificial languages

To this point we have been discussing the ideas of meaning, synonymy, and analyticity, and Quine's criticisms of them, as they apply to ordinary language. In the context of Carnap's work, however, it is natural to suggest that this is the reason for the apparent unclarity of these ideas: that we can only make clear sense of those ideas in the context of an artificial language.[9] Quine, however, holds that invoking artificial languages is simply irrelevant to the issue at stake between himself and Carnap.

As we indicated at the end of the last chapter, the project of defining analyticity for artificial languages can be understood in either of two ways: we can attempt to give a definition in special syntax or semantics or in general syntax or semantics. The first, and weaker, idea is that we take a particular language and simply specify the class of its analytic sentences. If we call the language L_0, say, then what we have defined is "analytic in L_0"; explicitly, at least, we have said nothing at all about analyticity in any other language. The stronger idea, on the other hand, is that of a definition which applies not only to a particular language but more generally. It would give us an understanding of analyticity independent of any particular language—a definition of "analytic in L" for *variable* "L". We could apply that definition to any language (at least any artificial language, or perhaps any artificial language of a certain form), and use it to pick out the analytic sentences of that language. This would be a definition in general syntax or semantics.

Can we give a definition of analyticity in *general* syntax or semantics? Carnap's most sustained attempt to do so is in *The Logical Syntax of Language*. His attempt there is limited to the truths of logic and mathematics, rather than the more inclusive class of all analytic truths; the attempt, and Quine's response, are nonetheless of considerable interest. Carnap claims to pick out the class of logico-mathematical truths by means of the specifiability of that class in purely syntactic terms. His idea here is that a sentence should count as analytic if we can show that it is true just by talking about the language, rather than by talking about the world. But much depends, it turns out, on exactly what resources you permit yourself for "talking about the language". The use of the word "syntax" might suggest that we are talking purely about marks and sequences of marks, and ascribing to them only properties definable in such terms. But the notion of mathematical truth cannot be captured in this sort of way; if we stick to the narrow sense of "syntax", mathematical truth is not a syntactic notion. This is shown by Gödel's celebrated proof of the incompleteness of any formalized theory of arithmetic. (See "On Formally Undecidable Propositions of *Principia Mathematica* and Related Systems".)

Carnap's definition avoids this problem by including the truths of logic and mathematics in the meta-language, i.e. they are among the resources that he takes for granted in talking about the object-language (the language for which logico-mathematical truth is being defined). So what he shows is essentially that logico-mathematical truth is definable for his language *if* we allow ourselves a meta-language which includes all of that truth. (In fact the meta-language must contain a more powerful theory of mathematics than does the object-language.) As Quine points out, however, truth in any subject is definable in the same sort of way, if we allow ourselves sufficient resources in the meta-language: if the meta-language contains all the truths of physics, for example, then we can define "being a truth of physics" for the object-language. In short, what Carnap shows to hold of mathematics and logic actually holds for any subject: "No special trait of logic and mathematics has been singled out after all". (C&LT, *WP*, p. 125.)

The incompleteness of any formalized theory of arithmetic thus blocks Carnap's attempt to give a definition in general syntax even of logico-mathematical truth, much less of the broader class of analytic truths. Nor does Carnap's later adoption of semantics, rather than syntax, help. In section 16 of Carnap's *Introduction to Semantics*, the matter is presented as an open problem. (See p. 84 of that work; Carnap here is concerned with the definition of the concept "L-true", but this is more or less just a technical term for analyticity.) The suggestions that Carnap makes for solving the problem, however, indicate that he envisages no solution which would play a serious philosophical role. One suggestion is, in effect, that for a language which contains the notion of necessity, we can simply identify the analytic truths of that language with the necessary truths of that language. As we saw, however, the notion of analyticity was introduced in part precisely to avoid appeal to an unexplained notion of necessity, so this tactic threatens to undermine the very rationale for that notion. The second suggestion is that if we presuppose that the meta-language contains the notion of analyticity then we may be able to use the meta-language to define that notion in any given object-language. But clearly the presupposition here—that the meta-language already contains the notion of analyticity or something equivalent—means that the definition will not answer any of the philosophical questions about that notion.

Carnap's attempts to give a general definition of analyticity are unsuccessful, and for reasons that make it unlikely that anything of the kind can succeed, at least for languages rich enough to capture mathematics. Carnap can, however, define analytic-in-L in special syntax or semantics, i.e. for a particular artificial language, L. What is the significance of such a definition? Carnap takes it for granted that we have at least a vague, rough and intuitive notion of what it is for a sentence to be analytic, or true in virtue of meaning, that there is "an inexact concept already in current use" ("Reply to TDE", p. 430). We give a precise replacement for the inexact concept, in a given language, by saying that for that language exactly *these* sentences are the analytic ones. What we have accomplished is what Carnap calls an *explication*, a precise version of a vague concept; in doing so we have answered doubts about that concept, insofar as those doubts arise from its excessive vagueness. For Carnap, giving such explications is paradigmatic of the philosopher's task.

In "Two Dogmas", Quine writes as if he is unwilling to accept that we have any intuitive notion of truth in virtue of meaning at all. In that case, Carnap's explication of analyticity accomplishes nothing. All that it does is to pick out a class of sentences of the given language and apply to them the label "analytic", a label whose significance is in doubt. As Quine puts it, referring to a postulated language L_0:

> Obviously any number of classes K, M, N, etc. of statements of L_0
> can be specified for various purposes or for none; what does it mean

to say that K, as against M, N, etc., is the class of the "analytic"
statements of L_0?

(*FLPV*, p. 33)

Unless we already know what we are trying to define, a definition of analytic-in-L for a particular language L accomplishes nothing. Similar remarks
apply also to attempts to define analyticity in terms of semantical rules,
meaning postulates, and other concepts from the technical apparatus in
terms of which Carnap defines and discusses artificial languages. Quine's
point is the same: if we do not have a *general* concept of semantical rules then
it does not help to be told that the analytic sentences are those which follow
from the semantical rules of a language. A definition of analyticity for one
particular language—in special syntax or semantics—accomplishes nothing,
unless we already understand what it is that is being defined; and this is a
point that Quine does not concede.

Further light may be cast on this complaint of Quine's if we compare
analyticity (and the related idea of synonymy) with significance, or meaningfulness. Quine's claim is that significance, or meaningfulness, makes
clearer sense than synonymy. The crucial distinction is that we can give, in
rough terms, a language-neutral criterion of what we are trying to do when
we give rules which demarcate the significant sequences of a given language;
along with that, we have an idea of the role of the distinction between the
meaningful and the meaningless in the actual use of language. In "The
Problem of Meaning in Linguistics", Quine indicates what this criterion is:
"What are wanted as significant sequences include not just those uttered but
also those which *could* be uttered without reactions suggesting bizarreness of
idiom". ("Meaning in Linguistics", *FLPV*, p. 53.) (Where "[o]ur basis for
saying what 'could' be generally consists ... in what *is* plus *simplicity* of the
laws whereby we describe and extrapolate what is." Ibid., emphasis in the
original.) This gives us a rough understanding of significance in terms of
the actual use of the language, and thus an understanding of the notion
which is not tied to any particular language. We have an understanding of
meaningful-in-L where L is conceived of as a variable ranging over all languages. Quine's claim is that Carnap offers us nothing comparable in the
case of analyticity or synonymy; he does not offer us an understanding of
analytic-in-L for *variable* L.

In "Two Dogmas" it thus seems to be Quine's position that we have no
general understanding at all of the notion of analyticity, and for that reason
Carnap's definitions of analytic-in-L for this or that language, L, are of no
use. In later works Quine seems to take a somewhat different view. In *Word*

and Object he acknowledges that we have "analyticity intuitions" (p. 67; cf. also pp. 56f.).[10] In *Roots of Reference*, as we shall see, he actually offers his own definition of analyticity. Is there a change of mind here? Certainly there is a shift of emphasis, but perhaps it is to be explained by the polemical aims of "Two Dogmas". Quine's intent there is to attack the idea of analyticity, not to see how much can be made of it. So perhaps the point there is simply that Carnap has not done enough to show that there is a clear intuitive idea of analyticity which his definitions make precise. Some encouragement for this reading comes from the fact that even in "Two Dogmas" Quine does not rule out the possibility that some sort of understanding of analyticity may be available:

> Appeal to hypothetical languages of an artificially simple kind could conceivably be useful in clarifying analyticity, if the mental or behavioural or cultural factors relevant to analyticity—whatever they may be—were somehow sketched into the simplified model.
>
> (TDE, *FLPV*, p. 36)

The idea of the "mental or behavioural or cultural factors relevant to analyticity", however, takes us away from artificial languages, and to consideration of the actual use of a language.

In Quine's view we can only hope to clarify the idea of analyticity by considering the actual use of the language—just how we understand the idea of meaningfulness in terms of actual language use. It is only in this way that we can hope to find any sort of understanding of analyticity for languages in general. And it is by considering this kind of approach that we can evaluate the philosophical significance of a defensible notion of analyticity; this will be our task in sections III and IV below.

From Quine's point of view, then, invoking artificial languages in the definition of analyticity, with no reference to their actual or hypothetical use, is irrelevant. Why should Carnap have thought otherwise? Quine suggests a reason. In setting up an artificial language, we have to proceed by laying down semantical rules or in some similar way specifying the language. It is easy to think that what we have thereby done is to specify some sentences whose truth is constitutive of the language, i.e. that we have specified the analytic sentences of the language, as those which follow from the rules of the language. Quine, however, argues that this is a confusion.

Suppose we lay down the rules for an artificial language, in Carnapian fashion. If we imagine people actually using a language which we have specified, what is the status of the rules in the imagined situation? It is tempting to reply that they are the rules of the language, and so must have some special status, so that when we imagine people using the language we must imagine that *they* treat the sentences which follow from the rules in a different fashion from that in which they treat other sentences of the language. In Quine's view, however, this reply involves a confusion of levels (see C&LT, WP, section VIII). If I devise an artificial language and imagine its use, I may describe how people would use it. The rules then have a special status in my description, since they are the means that I use to convey to you what language I am imagining those people to be speaking. But it does not follow from that that the rules have any special role or status in the imagined situation. (Just as the examples of correct usage that the lexicographer uses to explain the correct use need have no special status, except that they are particularly useful in enabling a learner to catch on to the use of a word.) While I may use linguistic rules to convey what language I am imagining, the rules are simply a narrative device. They are a means by which I tell a story; to say that they also have a role in the story being told is to take a further step, one that is by no means justified simply by the fact that we use rules to set up an artificial language. For Carnap, who never doubted that there is a distinction between the analytic and the synthetic, it is natural to think that the appeal to artificial languages can clarify that distinction. Quine's point, however, is that if one doubts the distinction, then the existence of artificial languages will not answer the doubt.

III Quinean analyticity and the issue of scope

Our concern in this section is with the sense that *can* be made of the notion of analyticity, given Quine's assumptions, and also with the question of the scope of the analytic, on that kind of understanding of it. Much of the intuitive appeal of the idea of analyticity comes from thinking about it as truth in virtue of meaning. Quine, as we have emphasized, rejects the idea that we can approach meaning by beginning with the assumption that meanings are mental items; this is the view that he deplores as mentalism. His starting point, in thinking about meaning, is the *use* of language. In particular, since his focus is always on the cognitive or theoretical language in which our knowledge is embodied, his focus is on the assertion of sentences, both the assertions actually made and those that *would* be made under various specifiable circumstances.[11] In an essay written in 1935, he says: "in point of *meaning* ... a word may be said to be determined to whatever extent the truth or falsehood of its contexts is determined" ("Truth by Convention", WP, p. 89). He reiterates the point later; in "Carnap and

Logical Truth" he says: "Any acceptable evidence of usage or meaning of words must reside surely in the observable circumstances under which the words are uttered ... or in the affirmation and denial of sentences in which the words occur." (C&LT, *WP*, pp. 113–14.)

For the cognitive meaning of a word, then, we look to the sentences in which it occurs, and the truth-value of each sentence, or the way the truth-value of those sentences varies with variations in the observable circumstances. But then the question is: *which* of the sentences in which a word occurs must be determined in order to determine its meaning? Without some reason to discriminate, we have no reason to treat one sentence as more definitive of a word's meaning than any other. But then no true sentence in which the word appears would have any better claim to be analytic than any other such sentence; no useful analytic–synthetic distinction can be erected on that basis.[12] If we are to obtain any reasonable version of the distinction on this sort of basis, we must be able to discriminate, and say that the truth of some contexts is constitutive of the meaning of a given word, and the truth of others is not. Then sentences of the first kind will count as true in virtue of the meaning of that word.

What sort of thing might give us reason to discriminate among contexts? If mastery of a small number of a word's uses gave one mastery of its use as a whole, then there would be reason to say that those uses, those contexts, constituted its meaning. And clearly this holds in some cases. A child who otherwise has a fair degree of linguistic sophistication but does not know the word "bachelor" can be given a mastery of that word all at once, at a single stroke, by being told that bachelors are unmarried men. This fact gives us every reason to say that "bachelor" *means* unmarried man, and that the sentence "All bachelors are unmarried" is analytic—a point which Quine explicitly accepts (see e.g. *WO*, section 12; also TDR, p. 270).

Quine's position here is similar to that defended by Putnam in "The Analytic and the Synthetic", perhaps the most insightful of the early responses to "Two Dogmas". Putnam interprets Quine in "Two Dogmas" as straightforwardly denying that there is any distinction between the analytic and the synthetic. As against the view he attributes to Quine, Putnam argues that some distinction of that kind must be accepted. More importantly, however, he argues that a tenable version of the distinction will not in fact do any epistemological work because all analytic truths are trivial and uninteresting. Certain concepts, Putnam points out, are single-criterion concepts: the only criterion for being a bachelor is being an unmarried man; the only criterion for being a vixen is being a female fox, and so on. These are the concepts which give rise to analytic statements. In such cases we have only one criterion for the application of the concept, and we have reason to think that this situation will not change (though as Putnam points out we can *imagine* its changing). For this reason a statement such as "All vixens are female foxes" has, as Putnam says, "little or no systematic import. . . . there could hardly be *theoretical* reasons for accepting or rejecting it." (P. 68; emphasis in the original.)

On Putnam's account, all analytic sentences will thus be trivial (or at least trivially obtainable from trivial sentences). Interesting concepts are not single-criterion concepts; they have multiple criteria for their application. Interesting scientific concepts, in particular, are what Putnam calls "law-cluster concepts": their identity is given not by a single criterion of application but rather by a multitude of laws and inferences into which they enter. To separate these laws into the analytic and the synthetic would be misleading, for epistemologically they are all on a par: even if some are called "definitions", still all are in fact accepted because of the acceptability of the overall theory, and if a revision in the theory is necessary then any one may be abandoned or modified. No theoretically interesting sentence is analytic. In *Word and Object*, Quine cites Putnam's essay (then at press) approvingly, saying that it "offers an illuminating account of the synonymy intuition. . . . My account fits with his. . . ." (P. 57.)

Can we give a criterion of analyticity along the lines suggested by Putnam's discussion? Such a criterion would presumably say that where the whole use of a word can be conveyed by a single (short) sentence, we have reason to say that that sentence embodies the meaning of the word, and is analytic. The difficulty here, however, is that a sentence which will convey the whole use of a word to one person may not do so to another: it depends on one's preparation. So Quine's criterion for analyticity refers us to how language is in fact learnt. He counts a sentence as analytic *for a speaker* if that speaker learnt the truth of the sentence in coming to understand it. Socializing the criterion, he defines analyticity *tout court* like this: "a sentence is analytic if *everybody* learns that it is true by learning its words" (*RR*, p. 79; emphasis in the original). How far will such an understanding of analyticity take us? An initial answer is: not far. "All bachelors are unmarried" and "Vixens are female foxes" will probably count, but sentences of serious interest will not, for the reasons suggested by Putnam. All of the sentences that count as analytic by this criterion, it seems, will be quite trivial. But in fact Quine, at least in some of his later writings, takes a somewhat more extensive view of the matter. He counts certain inference-patterns as analytic, and argues that we should count as analytic "all truths deducible from analytic ones by analytic steps" (*TDR*, p. 270). Sentences trivially obtainable from trivial sentences may not themselves be trivial. Quine claims that on this understanding of the matter all the (first-order) logical truths will count as analytic; we might still come to repudiate the law of the excluded middle, say, but our doing so would involve a change of meaning.

There is, however, no prospect of arguing on the same or a similar basis for the analyticity of mathematics as a whole. Quine insists that mathematics as a whole is *not* deducible by obvious steps from obvious truths (see C&LT, WP, p. 111). For a scientifically minded philosopher, mathematics is the central and most important kind of knowledge that is usually classified as a priori. An account of analyticity which does not extend to mathematics will not perform the crucial function of the traditional conception of the a priori.

Quine's sense of analyticity does share some other characteristics with traditional conceptions of the a priori. Sentences which are in that sense analytic are known by virtue of understanding the meanings of their words, so that one learns them in learning the language; one would be wholly at a loss to say what experience was relevant to their truth. Quine's notion of analyticity perhaps even functions as an explanation of certain sorts of knowledge: if I am asked how I know that Wednesday comes after Tuesday the best I will be able to do is to say that that's what the words mean— which is a way of saying that "Wednesday comes after Tuesday" is true in virtue of meaning, or analytic. Still, a conception of the a priori based on Quine's definition of analyticity is unlike the traditional one in ways which leave it without a significant philosophical role to play, both because of its limited scope and because of its limited epistemological significance, which we shall get to in the next section.

IV An epistemological distinction?

We now turn to what Quine came to think of as the crucial issue concerning the analytic–synthetic distinction: the epistemological significance of the distinction, however exactly we construe it. In a work published in 1986, he wrote: "I now perceive that the philosophically important question about analyticity and the linguistic doctrine of logical truth is *not* how to explicate them; it is the question rather of their relevance to epistemology" (H&S, p. 207; emphasis in the original). His considered view is that even where we can make sense of the distinction, it does not have the epistemological significance which would be required for Carnap's use of it to be legitimate.

Analyticity in Carnap's philosophy is not an absolute notion; it is language-relative. An analytic sentence is immune to revision *provided that* there is no change of language. We may cease to accept a sentence which up to that point we had counted as analytic, or we may come to accept a sentence whose negation we had, up to that point, counted as analytic. Carnap counts such cases as changes of language; a change of mind about a synthetic sentence, by contrast, is a change of belief or of theory within a language.

The issue of the epistemological significance of the analytic–synthetic distinction can thus be raised by asking: what *epistemological* difference is there between a change of mind which involves an analytic sentence and one which involves a synthetic sentence? Is there a clear and systematic difference in the way the two kinds of revision are to be justified? At least in some of his writings, Carnap seems to offer an answer to exactly this question.[13]

Let us speak of an *internal revision* when we have a revision involving a synthetic sentence (and thus no change of language); and of an *external revision* when an analytic sentence (and therefore also a change of language) is involved. Given Carnap's view, one might think that there must be a clear epistemological distinction here. In the former case, there is a question of the correctness of the revision, and of its justification, of the evidence that can be brought to bear for or against making it; in the latter case, by contrast, there is no question of justification or of evidence, at least not in anything like the same sense; nor is there a question of correctness.

What is the distinction based on? For Carnap, the concepts of truth, of justification and of evidence are language-relative; to speak of a sentence as true or as justified presupposes a particular language, a framework which gives sense to those concepts. So an internal revision can be evaluated as correct or incorrect, or as more or less justified; because no change of language is involved, we have those concepts to draw on. But an external revision is another matter. Here the question is precisely one of shifting from one language to another. Since no language is presupposed, there is no notion of justification in terms of which the change can be evaluated.[14] Evaluating such a revision is, therefore, not a matter of deciding on its correctness, or even whether it is justified (not, at least, in the sense in which a synthetic sentence may be justified). We do not have a theoretical question but rather the "practical problem" of the suitability of a given language for this or that purpose ("Empiricism, Semantics and Ontology", p. 209). What is at stake is not truth but expedience: "The acceptance [of a new language] cannot be judged as being either true or false because it is not an assertion. It can be judged as being more or less expedient, fruitful, conducive to the aim for which the language is intended". (Op. cit., p. 214.)

Quine seeks to cast doubt on this alleged epistemological distinction from both sides. On the one hand, he insists, with Carnap, that factors such as simplicity, convenience, and fruitfulness—considerations of expedience, we might call them—play an ineliminable role in settling Carnap's external questions, i.e. choice of language. On the other hand, he argues that those same kinds of factors are crucial to what Carnap takes to be internal questions. The upshot, of course, is that there is no clear epistemological difference between the two sorts of questions; they are to be settled in the same sorts of ways.[15]

The controversial point is Quine's claim that what Carnap counts as internal questions are to be settled by the same sort of considerations of expedience which Carnap holds are used to settle external questions. The holism of the evidential relation is crucial here. It does not, for the most part, hold between individual sentences and experience; it holds, rather, between theories, sets of interrelated sentences, and experience. Some simple statements—that there is now a table in front of me, for example—may be more or less directly related to sensory stimulations. For sentences in general, however, this simple picture is misleading. In general, the relation of a sentence to sensory stimulation is mediated by other sentences. So we cannot maintain that for each (synthetic) sentence the rules of our language determine a limited range of experiences whose occurrence or non-occurrence settles the acceptability of the sentence. In evaluating a proposed internal revision we may have to take into account the impact of the change on the theory as a whole. This sort of holistic justification is far too complex a matter to be settled by any predetermined rules. The question to ask is not: do the rules of our language, together with our experience, tell us to make this change? But rather: does making the change result in a theory which, taken as a whole, is better? In giving an answer, we will appeal to such broad and vague factors as simplicity and fruitfulness; these are just the sort of factors which Carnap thinks should be used to settle external questions.

Quine also insists that the very same factors play a role also in change of language, i.e. in Carnap's external questions. This second point is not controversial but it is essential. Quine is not merely arguing that simplicity, convenience, and similar factors must play a role in a Carnapian account of the evidential relation holding within our scientific language. He is, rather, arguing that there is no epistemological difference between the supposedly internal and the supposedly external:

Carnap, Lewis, and others take a pragmatic stand on the question of choosing between language forms, scientific frameworks; but their pragmatism leaves off at the imagined boundary between the analytic and the synthetic. In repudiating such a boundary I espouse a more thorough pragmatism.

(TDE, FLPV, p. 46)

The emphasis here is not on the nature of the "pragmatic" factors (he is "merely taking Carnap's word and handing it back to him", TDR, p. 272; see Chapter 2, note 4, above). It is, rather, on the fact that it is *the same* factors playing a role on each side of the supposed boundary between the internal and the external, the analytic and the synthetic.

Quine insists that our language does not in fact have rules which set up the sort of tight relation between theory and evidence which Carnap had sought. Carnap's attempts to formulate such a "confirmation relation" quickly proved inadequate for all but the most artificial cases of knowledge. As Quine says in "Two Dogmas": "I am impressed ... with how baffling the problem has always been of arriving at any explicit theory of the empirical confirmation of a synthetic statement." (*FLPV*, pp. 41–42.) It is important here that Quine is talking about synthetic statements quite generally. If we presuppose a background theory, then in some cases we can make sense of a tight relation of justification. Quine speaks of "prefabricated examples of black and white balls in an urn". There are more interesting cases in which, given a background theory, we can say to what extent one statement is justified by others. (The inheritance of dominant or recessive traits is an example.) But the justification relation here depends on the background theory. When we cease to take that theory for granted we have to ask about its justification, and here there is no prospect of a similarly precise and tight relation to evidence. We have no reason to expect a rule-governed notion of justification for statements in general.

Quine is not simply arguing from the failure of Carnap and others to produce a plausible theory of confirmation. His view is that the holism that underlies that failure will block any attempt along the same lines. The evidential relation does not, in general, hold between experience and individual sentences, but rather between experience and theories, more or less sizeable groups of sentences. We cannot in general think of an individual sentence, considered apart from its containing theory, as being confirmed or disconfirmed by experience at all. What must be evaluated is in general a part of our theory larger than a single sentence. Since the parts of our theory interlock, it is in principle the theory as a whole that is evaluated.[16] Stopping short of that extreme, we need at least a large enough fragment of theory to have observational consequences, which most individual sentences do not, and to include all uses of the given sentence. How large a body of theory must be considered here will vary from sentence to sentence, with observation sentences at one end of the spectrum and logic, which runs throughout our theory, at the other. The success of the total theory, or of some fragment, is for Quine a matter of its expedience, of its working better than any other that we have. The acceptability of a given sentence lies in its contribution to a larger or smaller fragment of the overall theory, and in the success of that theory. So if we want to say something of a wholly general nature, the best we can do is to say that a sentence is to be accepted if it is part of a theory which, taken as a whole, enables us to cope with sensory experience better than any rival.

In general, then, a sentence is to be evaluated not by its individual relation to experience, but rather by its contribution to a larger or smaller fragment of theory which, taken as a whole, is related to experience. It is the theory as a whole which is, ultimately, what is evaluated, and the criteria are, crucially, of the same sort that we use to evaluate supposedly external revisions. The change from Newtonian mechanics to Einsteinian mechanics is, by Carnapian standards, an external revision. Yet as this example shows, some choices of language are more efficient than others, more conducive to the construction of successful and fruitful theories; clearly the physicists had compelling reasons to make the change. Nor would Carnap disagree with this point. What he would disagree with is that these "methodological considerations" make the choice a matter of theoretical correctness, in the same sense as a choice of theory within a language. But Quine claims that holism shows that considerations of that sort are what we go on in the case of Carnap's internal revisions, as well as in the case of external revisions. In short, he claims that holism shows that there is no epistemological difference between the two kinds of revision.

What is at issue between Quine and Carnap here is the Principle of Tolerance. We can see that principle as based on the following train of thought: there is no language-neutral sense of justification; hence justification is language-relative; hence the choice of language itself cannot be a matter requiring justification; hence we should be tolerant about choice of language. Quine's contrary position can be summarized by saying that holism shows that it is, in the end, whole theories that must be evaluated; the crucial evaluative question is whether a given theory, taken as a whole, enables us to cope with sensory experience better than any rival; but this test, on Quine's account, is *not* language-relative; hence it can be applied equally to choice of language and to choice of theory within a language. As Quine puts it in a relatively early essay: "the purpose of concepts and language is efficacy in communication and prediction. Such is the ultimate duty of language, science, and philosophy, and it is in relation to that duty that a conceptual scheme has finally to be appraised". ("Identity, Ostension, and Hypostasis", *FLPV*, p. 79.) Hence even if we can make a sharp distinction between choice of language and choice of theory within a language—between Carnap's external revisions and his internal revisions—we have no more reason to be tolerant in the one case than we do in the other.

Let us bring this discussion to bear on what Quine, in "Carnap and Logical Truth", takes to be the strongest candidates for creating analytic truths: legislative postulation and definition. A legislative postulate is not a selection from a number of already accepted truths, for the purpose of axiomatization, say. It is, rather, an assertion made as part of a new theory (which may be a modification of an old one). Quine argues that nothing analogous to this is to be found in many areas where Carnap had claimed that there are analytic truths, but he does think that something of the sort sometimes takes place—most obviously, perhaps, in set-theory (see C&LT, WP, p. 117). Legislative definitions, analogously, are stipulative: unlike cases of discursive definition, in which a lexicographer sets out to capture existing uses, these are cases in which a new expression is introduced by means of an explicit definition.

A sentence which is the result of legislative postulate or definition looks very much like a Carnapian analytic truth; they are truths by convention in a more or less literal sense of convention. (Though, as Quine points out, in the case of definition we need elementary logic to get truths out of the definition.) Does the existence of such truths undermine Quine's general position? The crucial claim in this regard is that the way in which such truths are introduced does not give them an enduring epistemological status which is different from that of other accepted truths. The fact that a given sentence was introduced as a definition does not affect the way in which evidence is subsequently brought to bear on it. Conventionality, Quine says, "is a passing trait, significant at the moving front of science but useless in classifying sentences behind the lines. It is a trait of events and not of sentences". (C&LT, WP, p. 119.) Discovering that a certain sentence was originally introduced as a postulate or a definition tells us nothing at all about the way in which evidence now bears on it. Seen very abstractly, evidence bears on all sentences in the same way: for any sentence, the reason to accept it is that it is part of a theory which, taken as a whole, enables us to deal with experience better than does any rival theory.

Quine's view here is a reversal of Carnap's view that conventionality is imposed upon the actual language of science by the philosopher's activity of clarification and explication. On Carnap's picture, sentences whose status is at first unclear later become classified as conventional (analytic) truths or empirical (synthetic) truths. For Quine, it is almost the opposite: to classify a sentence as true by convention is at most an historical speculation about the way in which it came to be accepted; it says nothing about the way in which evidence now bears on it, what justifies our accepting it or what would justify our ceasing to accept it. Even in those cases where we can make sense of the idea of truth by convention, it refers to the way in which a sentence was introduced into our theory, not to its subsequent epistemological status. It is simply irrelevant to the present epistemological status of those sentences to which it applies; the notion thus marks no significant epistemological distinction.

The point of our discussion in this section is that even if one begins by granting Carnap's distinctions between choice of language and choice of theory, and thus also between analytic sentences and synthetic sentences, still the latter distinction does not mark a clear *epistemological* difference. The sorts of considerations that might lead us to change from one language to another are not in principle different from the sorts of considerations that might lead us to make a change from one theory within a language to another theory within the same language: in each case the most we can say, generally and in the abstract, without detailed examination of the particular case, is that the new theory is more successful in its predictions, or simpler, or more elegant, or more fruitful, than the old—whether the new theory is within the same language or involves adopting a new language. Hence there is no epistemological cleavage between the analytic and the synthetic, or between change of language and change of theory within a language. Indeed the very distinction between language and theory ceases to be fundamental, for a language is no longer conceived of as a neutral framework. As we shall see further, one has to agree with others in a range of substantive judgments in order to count as speaking the same language as them. Hence Quine tends to use the terms "language" and "theory" interchangeably in some contexts—though not in all, since speakers of the same language can clearly hold different theories. (See Quine's "Reply to Chomsky", especially section 5.)

V The putatively a priori

In Quine's view, Carnap needs the analytic–synthetic distinction primarily to account for knowledge which appears to be a priori rather than empirical—most obviously, our knowledge of logic and of mathematics. As we have emphasized, he does not merely reject Carnap's use of analyticity; he claims that that use is redundant, because we can manage without it. He claims, that is to say, that we can account for putatively a priori truths—in particular, for logic and mathematics—without invoking Carnapian analyticity and without assuming any notion of the a priori. We simply have no need for the Carnapian idea, nor for the more overtly metaphysical conceptions of the a priori that it was meant to replace.

Quine argues that the only general account that we can give of justification is that we have reason to accept a sentence if it is part of a theory which, taken as a whole, enables us to deal with sensory experience better than any other that we have. But this criterion applies not only to those sentences which Carnap counted as synthetic but also to those he counted as analytic. There is thus a single criterion for all knowledge, the supposedly analytic and the supposedly synthetic alike. In this way, we can account for those phenomena which led philosophers to invoke the idea of the a priori.

The underlying point here is that of the previous section: Quine argues that Carnap's "internal" questions and his "external" questions are answered in the same very general sort of way. Carnap thinks that (supposedly) external questions are to be answered by considerations of expedience; Quine claims that those same sorts of considerations operate also in our answers to (supposedly) internal questions. The same sorts of factors operate everywhere; for that reason we cannot use the role of those factors to mark the distinction that Carnap wants—between set-theory, say, and natural science. Consider again the role of legislative postulation, or convention, in set-theory. Quine acknowledges that role, but goes on to argue that it does not distinguish set-theory from what Carnap would take to be the empirical sciences:

> What seemed to smack of convention in set theory ... was "deliberate choice, set forth unaccompanied by any attempt at justification other than in terms of elegance and convenience"; and to what theoretical hypothesis of natural science might not this same character be attributed? For surely the justification of any theoretical hypothesis can ... consist in no more than the elegance and convenience which the hypothesis brings to the containing body of laws and data.
>
> (C&LT, WP, p. 121)

We cannot deny a role for considerations of expedience in what Carnap thought of as synthetic questions; hence we can no longer mark a sharp distinction between them and the questions which Carnap held to be analytic.

Quine thus denies a sharp epistemological difference between set-theory and the empirical sciences. At first sight this may seem implausible. It may be true that simplicity and convenience play a role in each sort of theory, but is there not a crucial difference? In the case of the empirical sciences, records of observations are among the sentences of a theory that the scientist aims to form into a coherent, elegant and convenient whole. In the case of set-theory, so one might think, this is not so. It might seem that here we have a clear epistemological distinction between the subjects, to which the similarity of their appeals to simplicity and convenience is quite irrelevant; and that Carnap's notion of analyticity, whatever its troubles, was to account for exactly this difference. Quine, however, denies that there is any sharp difference here:

> The situation may seem to be saved, for ordinary hypotheses in natural science, by there being some indirect but eventual confrontation with empirical data. However, this confrontation can be remote; and, conversely, some such remote confrontation with experience may be claimed even for pure mathematics and elementary logic. The semblance of a difference in this respect is largely due to overemphasis on departmental boundaries.
>
> (*WP*, p. 121)

Quine is not committed to the view that the working scientist takes all aspects of his or her theory to be equally vulnerable to disconfirmation. The biologist who uses statistics does not take that subject as being up for consideration at all; in such a case, the mathematics functions as unquestioned background. It is important, also, that for the most part we do not have alternative theories of mathematics. From Quine's very abstract point of view, however, these facts are not crucial. The way our biologist proceeds is understandable, and justifiable, but does not indicate a difference in kind between mathematics and other subjects.

Holism thus does not merely cast doubt on the notion of analyticity; it casts doubt on the distinction between the a priori and the empirical which that notion was supposed to explicate. (See C&LT, *WP*, p. 122.) Some supposedly empirical claims are related to experience only very indirectly, via much other theorizing. These sorts of theoretical claims, at least, are epistemologically on a par with the supposedly a priori claims of logic, set-theory and mathematics. In each case, a given claim taken by itself has no consequences for experience; in each case, however, the given claim is an integral part of a more general theory which, taken as a whole, does have such consequences. Logic and mathematics are thus not wholly free-standing theories, independent from the rest of our knowledge. They are, rather, integrated with our knowledge as a whole. The ultimate justification of those subjects lies in their role within our wider system of beliefs; but this is true also, to a greater or lesser extent, of much of our supposedly synthetic knowledge. Quine is thus not advocating the sort of view often attributed to J. S. Mill, that our knowledge of the truths of arithmetic, say, is directly based on observation, in the same sort of way in which my knowledge of the truth of "There is a desk in front of me" is directly based on observation (see *PL*, p. 100). His view is, rather, that this fairly direct relation to observation is the exception rather than the rule even for synthetic sentences. A better picture of the relation of empirical sentences in general to observation, a picture which takes holism fully into account, extends also to the supposedly a priori. He thus urges "a kinship" between logic and mathematics and "the most general and systematic aspects of natural science, farthest from observation" (ibid.). He continues:

> Mathematics and logic are supported by observation only in the indirect way that those aspects of natural science are supported by observation; namely, as participating in an organized whole which, way up at its empirical edges, squares with observation. *I am concerned to urge the empirical character of logic and mathematics no more than the unempirical character of theoretical physics; it is rather their kinship that I am urging, and a doctrine of gradualism.*
>
> (ibid.; emphasis added)

How does this Quinean view enable us to explain what appear to be the distinctive features of logic and mathematics? It is sometimes said, perhaps vaguely but not implausibly, that the falsehood of a simple truth of arithmetic or logic is *inconceivable*, that we simply cannot imagine what it would be like for it to be false. A related point is that we do not in fact reject the laws of logic or arithmetic, even where we seem to have counter-examples. We do occasionally run into cases of rabbits in a cage, or books on a shelf, or what-have-you, which do not seem to add up as the laws of arithmetic indicate they should; such cases do not, however, make us doubt arithmetic. We do not *in fact* ever question the laws of arithmetic on this kind of basis.

Quine thinks that our attitude here can be explained, and justified, by the extreme generality of logic and mathematics: they are very widely applied; in the case of logic, universally applied. We use logic (more or less implicitly) in every branch of knowledge, in every part of our overall theory of the world. Wherever truth is at stake, logic is applicable. The more elementary parts of mathematics, at least, are almost as widely applicable.[17]

Wherever we have objects distinguishable from one another we can count them, and wherever we can count we can apply arithmetic. This generality means that a change in a law of logic, say, would have consequences for every branch and aspect of our knowledge. Logic plays a crucial role throughout our theory of the world. (At least it does so in the regimented theory that is Quine's ideal; see Chapter 8, below.) So changing our logic would be tantamount to tearing up our whole theory of the world and starting again. It is not to be wondered that we find such a thing inconceivable; if that is what the falsehood of a law of logic would mean, then that too will seem inconceivable. For the same reason we are almost certain never to do it—and for good reason.[18] The disruption to our total system of knowledge would be so great that it is hardly likely that any resulting theoretical gains could justify such a move. While we cannot say that it could never happen, we can say that the magnitude of the disruption which would be involved justifies a sort of regulative principle: always try to describe and explain any situation in a way that does not violate the laws of logic. Quine speaks in this context of a "maxim of minimum mutilation" (see *PL*, pp. 7, 86, 100). The point, roughly, is that any given gain in simplicity or efficiency of the system as a whole should be achieved with as little change as possible from the current system. This maxim will militate against changes to logic, for those will require changes everywhere.

Quine appeals to exactly the sorts of factors we have been discussing to explain why logic and mathematics are often thought of as sharply distinct from other branches of knowledge, and why, in particular, they are taken to be a priori and necessary:

> [The vocabulary of mathematics and logic] pervades all branches of science, and consequently their truths and techniques are consequential in all branches of science. This is what had led people to emphasize the boundary that marks pure logic and mathematics off from the rest of science. This is also why we are disinclined to tamper with logic and mathematics when a failure of prediction shows that there is something wrong with our system of the world. We prefer to seek an adequate revision of some more secluded corner of science, where the change would not reverberate so widely through the system.
>
> This is how I explain what Parsons points to as the inaccessibility of mathematical truth to experiment, and it is how I explain its aura of *a priori* necessity.
>
> (H&S, pp. 399f.)

Quine's view here raises a question about inapplicable mathematics. Much work is done in that subject without thought of physical application. In some cases it is very hard to see how such work could ever be applicable. What are we to make of these parts of mathematics? Why, on Quine's account, should we think of them as either true or false, as part of our knowledge? It is notable that this is a question which Quine takes seriously; he is a sufficiently thoroughgoing empiricist to think that we need a reason to think of inapplicable mathematics as a contribution to knowledge, rather than as an idle game.

The reason that Quine puts forward is that the applicable and inapplicable mathematics do not separate neatly. Speaking of the fact that "pure mathematics extravagantly exceeds the needs of application", he says:

> I see these excesses as a simplistic matter of rounding out. We have a modest example of the process already in the irrational numbers: no measurement could be too accurate to be accommodated by a rational number, but we admit the extras to simplify our computations and generalizations. Higher set theory is more of the same.
>
> (H&S, p. 400)

A slightly different way to emphasize the point is to ask: once the vocabulary of mathematics is in place, how is inapplicable mathematics to be excluded? The demarcation makes no sense in mathematical terms, and so would lead to a clumsy and unworkable theory. Speaking specifically of "the higher reaches of set theory" Quine says: "They are couched in the same vocabulary and grammar as applicable mathematics, so we cannot simply dismiss them as gibberish, unless by imposing an absurdly awkward gerrymandering of our grammar". (FSS, p. 56.)

This addresses the meaningfulness of inapplicable mathematics—why we do not dismiss it as "gibberish". But it says nothing directly about its justification. And here a more general issue arises. We do not generally justify a mathematical claim by appealing to its application. Paradigmatically, such a claim is justified by a proof from other mathematical claims which are taken as established (or simply as obvious). In the absence of proof, mathematicians may give plausibility considerations, but what is taken to make a mathematical claim plausible is, again, not its application but rather other bits of mathematics. How do these facts fit with Quine's picture of mathematics as justified holistically, by its indispensable role in our theory as a whole? There is no explicit answer to this question in Quine's work; we can, however, indicate what a Quinean answer to the question might look like.

Mathematics forms an integrated system, with statements linked one to another by methods of proof. A Quinean account of the role of mathematics in knowledge must focus on the system, and on the developing totality of mathematical methods.[19] The system as a whole is justified—is counted as part of our knowledge, rather than as an arbitrary game—because it consistently produces results which are usefully (indeed indispensably) applicable to empirical knowledge. But a particular mathematical statement is not justified by its application; it is justified by the role that it occupies in the mathematical system—in particular, whether it can be proved from others. The role that mathematics plays in our empirical knowledge, however, is the justification for counting the system as a whole as part of our knowledge. In this sort of way, we can do justice to the undeniable fact that we do not justify mathematical theorems by seeing how useful they are to other branches of knowledge; we justify them in ways internal to mathematics—by proofs. At the same time, however, we can preserve Quine's essential idea that all justification comes from participation in a system of knowledge which is empirical, i.e. makes contact with sense-experience.

4

RECONCEIVING EPISTEMOLOGY

What is the nature of epistemology, as Quine conceives it, and how are we to approach that subject? In the 1968 essay "Epistemology Naturalized", Quine sets out his view of epistemology, or its successor:

> Epistemology, or something like it, studies a natural phenomenon, viz., a physical human subject. This human subject is accorded a certain experimentally controlled input—certain patterns of irradiation in assorted frequencies, for instance—and in the fullness of time the subject delivers as output a description of the three-dimensional external world and its history. The relation between input and output is a relation that we are prompted to study for somewhat the same reasons that always prompted epistemology; namely, in order to see how evidence relates to theory, and in what ways one's theory of nature transcends any available evidence for it.
>
> (EN, *OR*, pp. 82–83)

Here we see the basic Quinean picture that we introduced in our discussion of passages from "The Scope and Language of Science" (see section I of Chapter 1, above). The putative knower is taken to be a physical object, an input–output device, subject to physical forces (input) and emitting concentric airwaves, i.e. sounds (output).

As Quine conceives of epistemology, it is thus concerned with the relation between input and output—but only with some inputs and some outputs. Not every noise that we emit is part of our cognitive language. The distinction between the relevant and the irrelevant here cannot be taken for granted. On the contrary: an integral part of the enterprise is to show what it is for some noises to amount to cognitive language, potentially true of the world. This is to be explained in terms of the systematic relation that some (but only some) of our noises have to stimulations of our sensory surfaces, or

81

to other noises, or to both. Not even all of our noises that are systematically related to stimulations are of epistemological interest: there is no doubt a relation between stimulations of my nasal passages and my sneezes, but these are of no concern to epistemology, except insofar as it is concerned to eliminate the sneeze as irrelevant.

Epistemology in this sense is concerned not only with how we can *know* anything about the world, but also with the question how we can say or believe anything—true or false—about the world at all. One aspect of what might be called Quine's philosophy of language is thus included in his epistemology, as we are using the word here. (Another aspect will concern us in Chapters 9–13.)

Quine thus seeks to explain what it is for some of our noises to amount to cognitive language, to be potentially true or false of the world. His most worked-out approach to this task proceeds by discussing how an infant might come to be capable of emitting noises which have the right sort of relation to stimulations and to other noises. It is thus a genetic project, an explanation of how the ability to use cognitive language—to emit the appropriate sorts of noises—is or might be acquired. By seeing what has to be learnt in order for the infant to acquire cognitive language, we see what cognitive language is, what it amounts to: "for language is man-made and the locutions of scientific theory have no meaning but what they acquired by our learning to use them" (NNK, p. 74). Acquisition of elementary cognitive language, on this account, goes hand-in-hand with acquisition of at least a rudimentary theory of the world. In *From Stimulus to Science* Quine describes the overall project like this:

> It is rational reconstruction of the individual's and/or the race's actual acquisition of a responsible theory of the external world. It would address the question how we, physical denizens of the physical world, can have projected our scientific theory of that whole world from our meager contacts with it: from mere impacts of rays and particles on our surfaces and a few odds and ends such as the strain of walking uphill.
>
> (p. 16)

Quine's project is to explain the acquisition of cognitive language in a way which is, by his standards, scientific and *naturalistic*. Exactly what constraints this imposes will be the subject of Chapters 9–13. (The constraints are significant; the language in which the explanation is to be given is both extensional and, in Quine's sense, physicalistic.) It is in this respect a significant departure from more traditional approaches to epistemology: in seeking to explain or account for or justify our science it draws on and presupposes that science. Quine says explicitly that he "repudiate[s] the Cartesian dream of a foundation for scientific certainty firmer than scientific method itself" (*PT*, p. 19). One familiar version of this "dream" postulates two forms of pure and certain knowledge: on the one hand, sensory experience; on the other, a priori knowledge of general principles.[1] These forms of knowledge were taken to be independent of our more mundane knowledge. That mundane knowledge was then held to be explained, and justified, insofar as it could be shown to arise from those two elements. In the case of each supposedly presuppositionless form of knowledge, Quine has doubts and criticisms which are to some extent independent of his general commitment to naturalism. The idea of sensory experience as a source of presuppositionless "given" knowledge will be our concern in section I, below. It should be clear from our discussion in the previous chapter that Quine does not think that there is an a priori source of knowledge which could play the role allotted to it by this version of the Cartesian dream. Of particular interest here is the fact that any justification of our knowledge as a whole would presumably have to appeal to some sort of principle of induction. On Quine's account, Hume showed that no such principle can be justified by experience; nor does Quine think that a priori justification will fill the gap. Hence: "The Humean predicament is the human predicament".[2] Let us dwell on this point, and on the more general issue of the naturalizing of epistemology.

The project of justifying our knowledge as a whole is liable to run into insuperable obstacles over induction. Quine cites the abandonment of justificatory hopes as part of the rationale for his naturalizing of epistemology:

> If the epistemologist's goal is validation of the grounds of empirical science, then he defeats his purpose by using psychology or other empirical science in the validation. However, *such scruples against circularity have little point once we have stopped dreaming of deducing science from observations.* If we are out simply to understand the link between observation and science, we are well advised to use any available information, including that provided by the very science whose link with observation we are seeking to understand.
>
> (EN, *OR*, p. 76; emphasis added)

If the aim were one of justification, there would be a circularity here: we would be using our science to justify that very science. If our aim is one of understanding, however, rather than of justification, then this circularity is in no way vicious.

Quinean epistemology is thus not engaged in considering the justification of our attempts at knowledge as a whole: it is not, as we might say, *globally* normative. Those who think that this is all that is really at stake in talk of the normativity of epistemology will hold that Quine's view gives up completely on normativity. If we take a less absolutist line, however, we will find, with Quine himself, that some normative elements survive. Quine takes the idea that prediction is the test of an hypothesis "as defining a particular language game ... the game of science" (*PT*, p. 20; cf. also NLWM, p. 258). The goal of knowledge is thus given; epistemology is normative because it tells how we should best act to achieve this goal:

> For me normative epistemology is a branch of engineering. It is the technology of truth-seeking, or, in a more cautiously epistemological term, prediction. Like any technology, it makes free use of whatever scientific findings may suit its purpose. It draws upon mathematics ... in scouting the gambler's fallacy. It draws on experimental psychology in exposing perceptual illusions. ... There is no question here of ultimate value, as in morals; it is a matter of efficacy for an ulterior end, truth or prediction. The normative here, as elsewhere in engineering, becomes descriptive when the terminal parameter is expressed.
>
> (H&S, p. 665)

Aeronautical engineering can be thought of as normative in one sense; it tells us how we should construct aeroplanes in order to have them fly safely, efficiently, and so on. Epistemology, for Quine, is normative in the same sort of way: it tells us how we should act so as to obtain successful theories. The examples in the passage above are mistakes which we should avoid.

Quine also thinks that there is a normative element in the thinking-up of scientific theories. "Creating good hypotheses", he says in *FSS*, "is an imaginative art, not a science. It is the art of science". (P. 49.) Like other arts it can be done more or less well, and tips on how to do it well will count as part of normative epistemology. Quine himself has from time to time identified such *desiderata*. In "Posits and Reality", for example, he distinguishes four (apart from correct prediction): simplicity, familiarity of principle, scope, and fecundity (*WP*, p. 247). In *FSS* he mentions only two: "conservatism, or the maxim of minimum mutilation" and, again, simplicity (see p. 49). His longest discussion of these matters is in a chapter of *The Web of Belief*, written jointly with J. S. Ullian. The details, however, have not been a major concern of Quine's, and we shall not go into them further.

84

There is a lot of ground to cover in this chapter. The first section discusses Quine's views on the knower's "input", or sensory evidence. Here we have a point which is important both on its own account and as an illustration of Quine's method. The second section introduces the genetic project. In some places Quine puts the project forward as an answer to (one form of) scepticism; the section follows this approach to some extent, but also emphasizes the wider significance of the project within Quine's thought. The third section further clarifies the nature of the project, while the next two enlarge upon the methods which Quine adopts in carrying it out. The sixth section considers Quine's attempts to show how ordinary ideas of meaning and understanding can, to some extent, be reconstructed in his terms.

I Input: observations, evidence, and stimulations

As we saw above, one influential approach to epistemology sees sensory experience as a certain and presuppositionless source of knowledge. Sensory evidence, thought of in that sort of way, has two aspects. On the one hand, it is supposed to consist of the epistemologically most fundamental items of our knowledge: they are known before anything else—they are *evident*—so other items of knowledge must be inferred from them. On the other hand, sensory evidence is also held to consist of immediately given data, devoid of any conceptual impositions of our own; since no interpretation is involved, there is no room for doubt. These two aspects are in tension. What is literally known first seem to be facts about other people and ordinary physical objects. Yet sentences recording such facts do not seem simply to record raw data. They involve conceptualization, and are (notoriously) open to doubt.

Some philosophers have tried to evade this difficulty by appealing to "sense data", which supposedly play both of the required roles. They are supposed to be immediately given, and to be first in the order of knowledge. Quine argues that sense data cannot be epistemologically fundamental because most, at least, of what we take ourselves to know about them depends on our already having accepted a world of physical objects. The issue is of quite general importance for Quine's thought, and we shall spend a little time considering it.

In "Posits and Reality", Quine considers an argument against the truth of our theories of molecules, and similar unobservable entities, and thus against the reality of the supposed entities. Such things, the argument goes, are merely *posits*; our theories of them may be useful for organizing and extending our knowledge of observable things but this does not show that the theories are true, or that the entities really exist.

Quine, of course, wishes to refute this argument. To do so he shows that a similar argument could be made against the reality of ordinary physical objects, and the truth of the things we say about them. The unobservable entities postulated by scientists are known only through their effects on ordinary objects, and our theory of such things is useful only to the extent that it affects our knowledge of ordinary objects. Analogously, Quine says, physical objects are known only through their effects on experience, and our theory of them is useful only to the extent that it affects our knowledge of experience (e.g. by enabling us to predict its course). But this argument, Quine claims, proves too much: "It leaves each of us . . . nothing but his own sense data. . . . It leaves each of us in the position of solipsism . . .." ("Posits and Reality", *WP*, p. 250.) Quine claims that this conclusion is incoherent:

> it vitiates the very considerations that lead to it. We cannot properly represent man as inventing a myth of physical objects to fit past and present sense data, for past ones are lost except to memory; and memory, far from being a straightforward register of past sense data, usually depends on past posits of physical objects. *The positing of physical objects must be seen not as an ex post facto systematization of data, but as a move prior to which no appreciable data would be available to systematize.*
>
> ("Posits and Reality", *WP*, p. 251; emphasis added)

Knowledge of sense data was supposed to be prior to, and independent of, any other form of knowledge. But what we really know first are mundane facts about other people and the objects around us. Sense data, after all, are a philosophical invention, even if the philosopher claims that everyone has always known them (in some sense). In "Posits and Reality", Quine does not argue the point about one's present sense data. About past sense data, however, he insists that our knowledge of them is not direct and immediate, but is mediated by concepts applicable to physical objects. Our knowledge of our past sense data depends upon our already having a language in which we can describe physical objects. Hence knowledge of sense data is not independent and autonomous in the way the sense-datum philosopher claims; it is not even potentially a foundation for empirical knowledge generally.

In *Word and Object* Quine repeats the point about our memories of sense data, but adds other arguments. He claims that much of our supposedly given knowledge of sense data in fact depends on what we know about the physical world. An important example is the idea that visual sense data are two-dimensional. We come to believe this, he insists, not by reflecting on what is immediately given but rather "by reasoning from the bidimensionality of

86

the ocular surface" (*WO*, p. 2). In this sort of way, he claims, our supposedly immediate knowledge of sense data in fact depends on "sidelong glances into natural science" (ibid.) or on "rudimentary physical science" (NNK, p. 67).

The upshot of this is that sense data have no special status for Quine. On some occasions, mostly in the 1950s, he adopts his opponents' talk of sense data, but does not treat them as epistemologically fundamental. In "Posits and Reality" he straightforwardly says: "Sense data are posits too. They are posits of psychological theory, but not, on that account, unreal". (*WP*, p. 252.) The point here is that, even if we accept the existence of sense data, they do not constitute the sort of immediate extra-theoretic given by contrast with which the posits of our theory are unreal. (Note also that Quine says that sense data are posits and "not, *on that account*, unreal"—leaving room for the view, which I take to be his, that they are unreal, not because they are posits but rather because, roughly, they are not *useful* posits, not part of a useful theory.)

It is useful to compare Quine's views on sensory evidence—as on many topics—with those of Carnap. In the late 1920s Carnap maintained that it was possible and useful to adopt something akin to a sense-datum language; whether he ever thought of such a language as wholly presuppositionless and extra-theoretical is unclear. What is clear is that by the early 1930s he urges that the question of the nature of sensory evidence is not a philosophical problem but rather a question of language-choice: choice of language determines which sentences will count as evidentially basic. And, as we saw in a different context, he holds that choice of language is not a matter of right or wrong. (See the discussion of the Principle of Tolerance in Chapter 2, section III, above.) He continues to claim that a sense-datum language is possible but, under the influence of Neurath, he prefers to use a language in which the basic sort of evidence is taken to consist in statements about observable objects. From Quine's point of view, however, this resort to language-relativity does not dispose of the problem. First, for the reasons we have just seen, he does not hold that a sense-datum language is possible unless we also have a language for physical objects; since we do not need both, there is no argument for retaining a sense-datum language. Second, he holds that Carnap's resort to observable objects as basic unduly limits epistemological inquiry. We shall enlarge on this second point.

Taking evidence to consist of statements about observable physical objects eliminates all epistemological enquiry into our knowledge about such objects. On that approach, there is no philosophical story to be told about how we come to know sentences about ordinary physical objects. Yet surely there should be some such story. Alluding to these points, Quine says: "the notion of observation is awkward to analyze. Clarification has been sought by a shift to observable objects and events. But a gulf yawns between them and our immediate input from the external world" (*PT*, p. 2). If statements about physical objects are the most basic kind of evidence, there can be no question as to how we know such sentences. But this, in Quine's view, eliminates a central question of epistemology. (We shall emphasize this point later, in a somewhat different context; see Chapter 5, section II, below.)

Quine's naturalistic approach to knowledge faces no such difficulties. He simply abandons the traditional conception of evidence. Unlike Carnap, he does not rest content with our knowledge of sentences about ordinary physical objects; he seeks something more fundamental in terms of which such knowledge can be explained. Unlike traditional philosophers, however, he does not take this "something" as itself a form of *knowledge*. He dismisses the allegedly "given". His focus is on the way in which our knowledge arises from the stimulation of our sensory receptors, on responses to those stimulations, and on observation sentences which are closely related to such responses. (Observation sentences are, roughly, those which any speaker of the language is disposed to accept or reject simply on the basis of current stimulation; we shall consider them in detail in the next chapter.) The passage quoted in the previous paragraph continues as follows:

> A gulf yawns between [observable objects and events] and our immediate input from the external world, which is rather the triggering of our sensory receptors. I have cut through all this by settling for the triggering or stimulation itself and hence speaking, oddly perhaps, of the prediction of stimulation. . . .
>
> Observation drops out as a technical notion. So does evidence, if that was observation. We can deal with the question of evidence for science without the help of "evidence" as a technical term. We can make do instead with the notion of observation sentence.
>
> (*PT*, p. 2)

We might say that what he does is to take the more or less mentalistic notion of a sense datum and physicalize it. He explicitly speaks of his notion of a global stimulus as the "physical analogue" of Carnap's *Aufbau* notion of an elementary experience (*FSS*, p. 17).

What is at stake in philosophical talk of evidence, from Quine's point of view, is the issue of how we find out about the world. Here we have a crucial example of his method, of what he means by the idea that the study of knowledge is to be naturalized. For him, epistemology is neither a matter of a priori philosophical argument nor a matter of philosophically neutral language-choice. It is, rather, to be dealt with naturalistically. So he interprets the question about the nature of evidence as the scientific question: how do we come by information about the world? We have already seen his answer: it is, he says, "a finding of natural science itself" (PT, p. 19) that we come by our information about the world by the impingement of various forms of energy on the surfaces of the body, and the consequent stimulation of our nerve endings.[3]

We thus have a crucial shift in perspective. In traditional epistemology, sensory evidence was supposed to be encapsulated in sentences which could be known without other knowledge. In the most literal sense, such sentences could be known first, before any others. But clearly sentences about impingements and stimulations do not satisfy this condition.[4] Such sentences draw on concepts from neurophysiology, and psychology; to know a particular sentence of this type would presuppose both some general information on these matters, and also a considerable amount of precise and detailed knowledge of the particular circumstances of the person whose body is in question. Such knowledge is in no sense *given*. Quine's use of the notion of stimulations is thus symptomatic of his general shift in perspective; epistemological questions are construed as "scientific questions about a species of primates" (NNK, p. 67). Accordingly, the question about evidence is not: what is given to me at the outset of my cognitive endeavours? It is, rather: how do human beings come to have knowledge of the world? Quine changes the question to which the traditional conception of evidence was meant to be an answer.

Does Quine's view give us a conception of sensory evidence which is presuppositionless and theory-independent? In one sense it does; in another, perhaps more relevant to the sense-datum theorist's concerns, it does not. The sense in which it does is that what energy impinges on the surface of one's body at a given moment, and hence what nerve endings are stimulated at that moment, is independent of the theory one holds. Human beings ten thousand years ago had their sensory receptors triggered by the impingement of energy upon them; they acquired all their information about the world on this basis. Their inability to theorize about matters in these terms does not affect the stimulations, or their role in the acquisition of knowledge. The knowledge of non-human animals too is based on stimulations of their sensory surfaces; their lack of knowledge of this fact is neither here nor there. So in the most straightforward sense it must be true that stimulations are independent of and prior to theory.

The sense-datum theorist, however, will ask how we know the facts presupposed in the previous paragraph. The concept of a stimulation is itself a theoretical concept. It is our general theory of the world itself that tells us that for the source of our information about the world we should look to the impingement of energy on the surface of our bodies, and to the consequent firings of nerve endings. We might bring out the objection by saying that *according to our theory of the world*, stimulation of our sensory surfaces is the basis on which that theory itself is known. So, the sense-datum theorist will claim, we do not have here support of the theory which is genuinely independent of the theory. In Quine's view, the sense-datum theorist is making an impossible, perhaps incoherent, demand. That demand could only be satisfied by a source of knowledge altogether different in kind from our ordinary theoretical knowledge, independent and prior, which would thus afford us a perspective from which all our ordinary knowledge could be critically evaluated. Quine derogatively calls this idea "First Philosophy", and rejects it completely. This rejection is one way of articulating his naturalism, his "recognition that it is within science itself, and not in some prior philosophy, that reality is to be identified and described." (*TT*, p. 21.)

Quine rejects the idea of any kind of extra-theoretical knowledge, free of the vicissitudes affecting the ordinary knowledge of common sense and science. Within what we take ourselves to know there is, no doubt, great variety; there is more and less secure, more and less abstract, and so on. There is, however, no knowledge of a wholly different and superior kind. He is consistent in this naturalism: he does not take even the most fundamental points of his own philosophy to be known in other than the usual sort of way. This includes even the doctrine that we know about the external world through impacts on our sensory surfaces. We might, under extreme circumstances, come to accept other methods of finding out about the world:

> Even telepathy and clairvoyance are scientific options, however moribund. It would take some extraordinary evidence to enliven them, but, if that were to happen, then empiricism itself—the crowning norm, we saw, of naturalized epistemology—would go by the board. For remember that that norm, and naturalized epistemology itself, are integral to science, and science is fallible and corrigible.
>
> (*PT*, pp. 20f.)

Our checkpoints might continue to be sensory prediction, but we "would admit extra input by telepathy or revelation" (*PT*, p. 21). Or we might "modify the game itself", change our understanding of science, by accepting checkpoints other than sensory prediction. As he adds however, "[i]t is idle to bulwark definitions against implausible contingencies" (ibid.).

For Quine, as we have said, the central fact about knowledge is that it is only through stimulation of our nerve endings that we know anything at all about the world. Such stimulations provide the only empirical constraint on our system of knowledge, the only external criterion of success. (By speaking of an *external* criterion I mean to leave room for what one might think of as internal factors: the overall simplicity of the system, for example. This use of "external" and "internal" is unrelated to Carnap's use of the same words, discussed above pp. 99–173.) This fact suggests that there may be empirical slack between evidence—even the totality of all possible evidence—and theory; this is an idea to which we shall return. (See Chapter 7, section III.)

II The genetic project

Scepticism is sometimes thought to be central to epistemology. In some places Quine seems to endorse this view and to use the idea of scepticism as a way of motivating and articulating his own epistemological views; we shall begin by following this strategy although, as we shall see, it is unclear that Quine is really motivated by sceptical concerns. Quine begins "The Nature of Natural Knowledge" like this:

> Doubt has oft been said to be the mother of philosophy. This has a true ring for those of us who look upon philosophy primarily as the theory of knowledge. For the theory of knowledge has its origin in doubt, in scepticism. Doubt is what prompts us to try to develop a theory of knowledge.
>
> (NNK, p. 67)

The matter is complicated, however, for the idea of scepticism can be understood in various ways.

Any form of scepticism that Quine can take seriously will be one that can arise within his naturalism. Quine dismisses one form of scepticism out of hand, because it does not meet this condition. This form of scepticism asks: even if what we take to be knowledge is entirely successful on its own terms, why should we accept it as telling us what the world is *really* like? (See the end of the second section of Chapter 1; also *TT*, p. 22, quoted there.) This question presupposes the idea of a standpoint wholly external to our ordinary system of beliefs, a standpoint from which we can talk about the way the world really is, and ask whether that system of beliefs is correct about the world. Quine, however, finds the idea of such a standpoint to be incoherent. We have no conception of reality other than that provided by our ordinary system of beliefs, and internally generated modifications and extensions of that system. All we can demand of our knowledge, he holds, is that it should make successful predictions; no further demand makes sense.

What form of scepticism can Quine make sense of, given his naturalist presuppositions? He begins *The Roots of Reference* with the following question:

> Given only the evidence of our senses, how do we arrive at our theory of the world? Bodies are not given in our sensations, but only inferred from them. Should we follow Berkeley and Hume in repudiating them?
>
> (p. 1)

Here a threat of scepticism seems to arise from a gap between what we ordinarily take ourselves to know and what is given in sensation. As we saw in the previous section, however, Quine rejects the conception of the sensory given which he takes Berkeley and Hume to be relying on. He does not, however, reject their question entirely; rather, he says, "the problem was real but wrongly viewed." (*RR*, p. 2.)

How are we to conceive the problem correctly? The answer depends on Quine's claim that older epistemologists' idea of sense data in fact depends on "sidelong glances into natural science" (*WO*, p. 2; see first section of this chapter). What generates the sceptical problem is, on Quine's view, what we know, in the ordinary sort of way, about the available evidence for our knowledge. Thus he says: "Berkeley was bent on deriving depth from two-dimensional data for no other reason than the physical fact that the surface of the eye is two-dimensional." (*RR*, p. 2.) Elsewhere, Quine emphasizes the fact that scepticism arises from a contrast between how things are and how they seem; the straight stick in water seems bent, the square tower appears round from a distance. So it is only in the light of a conception of the way the world is—"rudimentary physical science", again—that the sceptical question can be formulated. Reiterating the point made in the passage quoted at the start of this section, he puts the point like this: "Doubt prompts the theory of knowledge, yes; but knowledge, also, was what prompted the doubt. Scepticism is an offshoot of science." (NNK, p. 67.)

The kind of scepticism that Quine can make sense of is thus, as one might expect, internal to science. It does not seek to compare the way we take the world to be with a wholly independent conception of reality. Neither does it question the relation between our scientific knowledge and a wholly independent form of evidence, the sensory given. Rather it asks: if the evidence for our science is what our science tells us it is, how could that be the basis on which we come to know our science? This is a challenge to our system of beliefs, our science in Quine's broad sense, from within; the sceptic of this stripe is "assuming science in order to refute science" (NNK, p. 68). Quine sees this as "a straightforward argument by *reductio ad absurdum*" (ibid.). The claim is that our system of beliefs is self-refuting. We know that we are forced to rely on perception, which is fallible enough to make straight sticks appear bent when they are in water, and which misleads us about the shape of towers seen at a distance. We know that the surfaces of our eyes are two-dimensional. How, given these sorts of limitations, could we possibly come by the knowledge that we take ourselves to have? More generally, this form of scepticism holds that the means of gaining knowledge which are allowed for in our theory make it impossible to explain how we could come to have beliefs which are really about the world, much less how those beliefs could be true. In *Roots of Reference* Quine puts it like this:

> The challenge runs as follows. Science itself teaches that there is no clairvoyance; that the only information that can reach our sensory surfaces from external objects must be limited to two-dimensional optical projections and various impacts of air-waves on the eardrums and some gaseous reactions in the nasal passages and a few kindred odds and ends. How, the challenge proceeds, could one hope to find out about the external world from such meager traces? In short, if our science were true, how could we know it?
>
> (*RR*, p. 2)

This is the sceptical challenge that Quine takes seriously, and attempts to answer.

We might wonder why this is really a *sceptical* challenge. There are, after all, many phenomena that we cannot yet explain, many scientific questions that we cannot yet answer. We do not, for the most part, take these facts to challenge our knowledge in any general way; they merely show that it is still incomplete. Why is this case different? The sceptic's claim is not merely that we do not yet fully understand the relation between evidence and theory. It is, rather, that human knowledge does not fit into the scientific world-view at all; that the general conception of the world which we get from our scientific knowledge—our knowledge at its best, in Quine's view—cannot hope to account for the fact that we have that knowledge.

Consider again the basic Quinean picture. At the start of "The Scope and Language of Science" Quine speaks of himself as a physical object; physical forces impinge upon him, and he emits concentric airwaves. In the following paragraph Quine says:

> All I am or ever hope to be is due to irritations of my surface, together with such latent tendencies to response as may have been present in my original germ plasm. And all the lore of the ages is due to irritation of the surfaces of a succession of persons, together, again, with the internal initial conditions of the several individuals.
> (SLS, *WP*, pp. 228–29)

This picture is fundamental to Quine's view of our cognitive condition, and to his thought as a whole. He takes it to be exceedingly well confirmed, and to be an integral part of the scientific world-view. But how does human knowledge itself fit into that picture? An answer to this question would have to tell us what it is for the concentric airwaves which I emit to constitute knowledge. It would also have to explain how I could come to have such knowledge, or would at least leave room for such an explanation. The scientific world-view, if it is to be internally coherent, must make it possible to tell a story about what our knowledge amounts to, and how we obtain it.

Telling this story, or at least making it plausible that there is such a story to be told, would constitute not merely the defence of a particular scientific theory but something like a defence of the scientific world-view as a whole. For the claim that Quine is concerned to refute here is that human knowledge is not susceptible to scientific treatment at all: that we cannot explain knowledge, and the language in which it is embodied, and how they are acquired, without invoking methods and ideas which go in principle beyond anything drawn from our study of the natural world. The "sceptical challenge"—if we count it as such—is thus that our knowledge cannot be accounted for in ways consistent with the scientific world-view. What is at stake is whether we can give a purely scientific (naturalistic) account of the human mind, or at least of its cognitive powers. This can be phrased as a form of scepticism because a negative answer means that science cannot account for its own success, that at least insofar as it claims to be a total theory of the world it undermines itself. But clearly a philosopher does not have to have any particular concern with scepticism in order to find the question an important one.

The most obvious non-scientific ideas which one might invoke in order to account for our knowledge are the ideas of meaning and (relatedly) understanding. Quine's genetic project is an attempt to indicate how we can account for knowledge and cognitive language in purely scientific terms. So it is, among other things, an attempt to show that no such ideas need be presupposed in order to account for cognitive language. As we have remarked before, Quine's strongest argument against the idea of meaning, taken for granted as an explanatory idea, is that we simply do not need it. The genetic project is Quine's attempt to make good on this claim, to give at least a sketch of an account of cognitive language and its acquisition that does not rely on an unreconstructed notion of meaning, or on similar mentalistic notions.

To this point we have been discussing the significance of the genetic project in very general terms: it defends science against a certain kind of internal challenge; it shows that we can understand our knowledge and our language in purely scientific terms. But Quine also thinks that the project has a more narrowly epistemological significance. In particular, he claims that pursuing the project is the best way that we have to investigate the relation between evidence and theory, a task that he sees as "central to traditional epistemology" (PT, p. 19).[5] Speaking of the project ("even apart from any thought of a skeptical challenge") he says:

> Its philosophical interest is evident. If we were to get to the bottom of it, we ought to be able to see just to what extent science is man's free creation; to what extent, in Eddington's phrase, it is a put-up job. And we ought to be able to see what there is to the evidence relation, the relation borne to theory by the observations that support it.
>
> (RR, pp. 3–4)

Why does Quine think that the genetic project has epistemological implications of this sort? For a sentence of our language to count as cognitive, it must connect in some way with sentences which are answerable to sensory stimulations: some sort of relation must exist, however indirect. (The idea that some sentences are only very indirectly related to stimulations is one way of stating holism.) In order to master that language, the infant must come to use language in response to sensory stimulations. Again there must be a relation—and, Quine claims, it is the same relation in each case. For observation sentences, as we shall see, the point is more or less straightforward. They are "the link between language ... and the real world that language is about" (PT, p. 5); this link is vital both for the child's acquisition of language and for the fact that the finished theory is answerable to evidence, and thus about the world. For more sophisticated language too, Quine claims, the same parallelism holds:

95

science [is] a linguistic structure that is keyed to observation at some points. ... some of the sentences, the observation sentences, are conditioned to observable events. ... [T]he rest of language ... depends, for whatever empirical content it has, on its devious and tenuous connections with the observation sentences; and those are the same connections, nearly enough, through which one has achieved one's fluent part in that discourse. *The channels by which, having learned observation sentences, we acquire theoretical language, are the very same channels by which observation lends evidence to scientific theory.* It all stands to reason, for language is man-made and the locutions of scientific theory have no meaning but what they acquired by our learning to use them.

We see, then, a strategy for investigating the relation of evidential support, between observation and scientific theory. We can adopt a genetic approach, studying how theoretical language is learned. For the evidential relation is virtually enacted, it would seem, in the learning.

(NNK, pp. 74–75; emphasis added)

The point here is that "epistemology becomes semantics" (EN, *OR*, p. 89). In Quine's view, how evidence bears on a given sentence and what is required for the understanding of that sentence are different versions of the same question; each is best approached through a study of the learning of language. The genetic project includes both epistemology and semantics. This is not to say that we should expect the genetic project to throw much light on the way in which evidence bears on a particular theoretical sentence, at some remove from observations; the difficulty arises because such sentences relate to observation only quite indirectly. The same fact also means that there will not be a complete story about the learning of such a sentence, or about what understanding comes to in such a case. (See MVD p. 89, discussed on p. 112, below.) But the parallel between semantics and epistemology holds; Quine's claim is that the genetic strategy will do as much as can be done to shed light on the relation between evidence and theory.

III Clarification of the genetic project

Two points of clarification will occupy us in this section: first, the fact that Quine thinks that there is value even to a somewhat incomplete and speculative version of the account he seeks; second, the nature of Quine's concern with language.

The genetic project is a study of how human beings have come by the knowledge that they have. It is the question "how man works up his command of [natural science] from the limited impingements that are available to his sensory surfaces" (*RR*, p. 3). This question is interpreted as a scientific question, "a question of empirical psychology" (ibid.). Nevertheless, Quine does not think that the project can only be pursued by detailed empirical study. The question, he says, "may be pursued at one or more removes from the laboratory, at one or another level of speculativity" (ibid.). This might seem puzzling. If so, it is helpful to recall the nature of the sceptical challenge. The challenge is that the scientific world-view *cannot* account for our having the knowledge we take ourselves to have (including, of course, the knowledge embodied in that world-view itself). This challenge is met if we can show, in naturalistic terms, how we *might* have acquired our system of beliefs; how that system, understood in that way, would genuinely be about the world; and how it would stand a chance of being, at least to some extent, true of the world. Whether Quine's suggestions fully correspond to the psychological realities of the situation is, from this point of view, not crucial. His claim is that the challenge would be met by an account, in purely naturalistic terms, of how cognitive language might be acquired.

The story that Quine seeks to tell is thus explicitly speculative, aiming at plausibility, not necessarily at truth. In a response to an essay by Charles Parsons, he says that in *Roots of Reference* he "was posing a Kantian sort of question: how is reification possible?" (B&G, p. 291). A little later he elaborates:

> I was speculating on how we as a species could have got onto talking about properties in a reifying way. ... How could we have got onto that? Not how did we; it would be nice to know that too, but I was on the Kantian course.
>
> (B&G, p. 291)

The reason Quine takes it to be worthwhile to offer an avowedly speculative answer is surely that he is envisaging the sceptic as having motives of the broadest scope and generality (philosophical motives, one might say). The sceptic is challenging the scientific world-view as a whole, claiming that that world-view cannot account for the fact that we possess it. The challenge here is not simply that we do not yet have an account of how we come by our knowledge. It is, rather, that there is no possibility of such account, given the scientific world-view; hence that that world-view is wrong. If that is the nature of the challenge, then the sort of speculative account that Quine offers is a response.

Quine also holds that a more or less speculative answer, or at least a very incomplete answer, is the best that we can hope for. As we shall see, he thinks that a complete story would require a detailed knowledge of the

97

structure of the human brain, and of particular events within particular brains; such knowledge is beyond our reach now, and for the readily fore-seeable future. We may, however, know enough about the brain and its workings to be able to make it plausible that the detailed story would be more of the same, an extension of our knowledge along the same lines, rather than a complete break. He also expresses the hope that a sketchy and speculative account would provide clues for the fuller answer that neuro-physiology may eventually afford us.

The fact that a full explanation of language-use would be at the neuro-physiological level has implications which go beyond anything explicit in Quine's work. It is not only our ignorance that stands between us and a full neurophysiological account of the acquisition of language. Your brain is not my brain. The full account of how I acquired language, were such a thing possible, would be different from the full account of how you acquired language. At a fairly coarse level we could correlate the accounts: the gen-eral region of my brain particularly involved in my acquisition of some aspect of language may well be correlated with the general region of your brain involved in your acquisition of the same aspect of language. (Thus neurophysiologists speak of the Broca region of the brain, for example.) But there is no reason at all to suppose that these correlations can go beyond the level of general regions to the level of individual brain cells. Yet it is, pre-sumably, at that level (and at even finer levels) that our imagined full explanation would operate. We could encapsulate the point here by saying that on Quine's account language is social and public, whereas a full expla-nation of language would be neurophysiological, and hence individualistic and eccentric. This is an issue which will return, in various guises, both in the next section and in the next chapter.

Our second point of clarification concerns the nature of Quine's concern with language. As we have already emphasized, he thinks that the best—the most scientific—way to approach human knowledge is via its public mani-festations in language. So his concern with human knowledge, and how we come by it, is also and at the same time a concern with cognitive language and how we come by *it*. We should emphasize immediately that what cog-nitive language comes to, and how we should think about it, is not some-thing to be taken for granted at the outset. It is, rather, one of the questions to be answered by Quine's account; this is a point which will receive a good deal of attention in our subsequent discussion.

Quine's concern with language and its acquisition thus arises out of his concern with knowledge. This fact gives his discussion a very different cast from that of most linguists and psychologists who are concerned with language-acquisition. There are, after all, various aspects to language-acquisition. To make a crude distinction between two such aspects: on the one hand, learning a language requires that we learn to form grammatical sentences; on the other it requires that we learn what makes a given (assertoric) sentence true or plausible. These points cannot be wholly separate; only when we have an utterance which is at least more or less grammatical does the issue of bringing evidence to bear on it arise.[6] Yet clearly there are different aspects here, different emphases in the study of language-learning. Many linguists are chiefly concerned with the former, how the child comes to acquire speech which is, for the most part, grammatically correct, and to distinguish grammatical from non-grammatical utterances. Their emphasis is thus on the learning of grammatical constructions and transformations.

Quine's concern, by contrast, is with the *cognitive* aspects of language— what it is for utterances to be about the world, and how the capacity to make such utterances is or might be acquired. The sort of correctness that is of interest to him is epistemological rather than grammatical. How do sentences of our language come to be answerable to evidence, and hence to have a claim to cognitive content, and to being about the world? How does the child come to learn that some circumstances make it appropriate to make a given sort of sound, and others make it inappropriate? And how does this primitive learning relate to the apparently more sophisticated ways in which our adult language is held to be answerable to evidence? The two kinds of learning—the grammatical and the epistemological—are not unrelated. Still, they are on the face of it rather different matters, and Quine's concern is with the epistemological. As he puts it:

> I am interested in the flow of evidence from the triggering of the senses to the pronouncements of science; also in the rationale of reification and in the credentials of cognitive meaning. *It is these epistemological concerns, and not my incidental interest in linguistics, that motivate my speculations.*
>
> (B&G, p. 3; emphasis added)

In a related passage, he says:

> in my writings I have limited my concern with it [i.e. with "the child's acquisition of language"] to the minimum necessities of ontology, the structuring of science, and the meeting of minds regarding events in the external world: traditional concerns of philosophy.
>
> (O&K, p. 419)

IV Language, meaning, and behaviour

Many philosophers have held that the use of language is the characteristic and decisive manifestation of rational thought. Quine too, in his way, accepts "the affinity of mind and language" that is widely claimed; "but", he adds, he "want[s] to keep the relation the right side up" (MVD, p. 84). By this he means that language-use, linguistic behaviour, is primary and that thought is to be understood in terms of it. He would not deny that when we talk to one another we express and convey our ideas and thoughts. But he would insist that saying this cannot explain what is fundamental to the working of language, and does nothing to explain what it is to have thoughts or ideas in the first place. The capacity to have meaningful discursive thought, at least of any complexity, is parasitic on a mastery of language, not the other way around; "mastery of language" is in turn approached through the use of language, i.e. through behaviour. Quine speaks of this "behaviorizing of meaning" as "simply a proposal to approach semantical matters in the empirical spirit of natural science." ("Philosophical Progress in Language Theory", p. 8.)

Let us enlarge upon Quine's rejection of the notion of meaning as a tool for the investigation of language, and on his methods more generally. His animus against an unreconstructed notion of meaning is evident in this passage from "Mind and Verbal Dispositions":

> People persist ... in talking of knowing the meaning and of sameness of meaning. ... They do so because the notion of meaning is felt somehow to *explain* the understanding and equivalence of expressions. We understand expressions by knowing or grasping their meanings; and one expression serves as a translation or paraphrase of another because they mean the same. It is of course spurious explanation, mentalistic explanation at its worst. ... where the real threat lies, in talking of meaning, is in the illusion of explanation.
> (MVD, pp. 86–87; emphasis in the original)

This passage indicates very clearly the reason for Quine's rejection of many philosophical uses of the notion of meaning. It is not that people never mean anything by their words and deeds, nor that reification is in general illicit. Even the point that the identity conditions for meanings are unclear is not the crucial one—though Quine does hold that entities must have identity-criteria, and that those of meanings are not, in general, clear. The fundamental point is that the notion of meaning does not have the general explanatory power that many philosophical uses of it presuppose. By engendering an illusion of explanation, the term may prevent questions and approaches which might lead to genuine insight. The vague term "meaning" certainly includes phenomena which are real, and worthy of explanation; it is just that that term should not itself be taken for granted at the outset of our investigation.

There are many uses of the term "meaning" which are, I think, entirely unobjectionable from a Quinean point of view. Some of them are in a superficial sense explanatory. We may, for example, explain a bizarre utterance by saying that the speaker is mistaken about the meaning of one of the words she is using. Here we point to a failure of understanding as the cause of a glitch in the conversation; the remark does not embody a theory about what understanding amounts to. Quine's animus should not be seen as directed against that sort of ordinary discourse; he has no quarrel with the ordinary use of the word "meaning", within its limits. His animus is, rather, directed against the idea that the notion of meaning can play any role in explaining what it is to understand language in the first place. Where our concerns are of this fundamental sort, it will be of no help to invoke an unanalysed notion of meaning. The meaningfulness of language is not to be explained by means of such a notion. It is, rather, to be explained as a matter of the language-users' having dispositions to exhibit certain forms of behaviour, especially verbal behaviour, in certain circumstances. (Possessing knowledge in Quine's view is also a matter of having such dispositions; this is one way to think about Quine's view that knowledge and language go hand-in-hand.)

Let us see how Quine continues his methodological discussion in "Mind and Verbal Dispositions". He distinguishes "three levels of purported explanation, three levels of depth: the mental, the behavioural, and the physiological":

> The mental is the most superficial of these, scarcely deserving the name of explanation. The physiological is the deepest and most ambitious, and it is the place for causal explanations. The behavioural level, in between, is what we must settle for in our descriptions of language. ... It is here, if anywhere, that we must give our account of the understanding of an expression, and our account of the equivalence that holds between an expression and its translation or paraphrase. These things need to be explained, if at all, in behavioural terms: in terms of dispositions to gross behaviour.
>
> (MVD, p. 87)

The point is that it is only in behavioural terms that we can know what we are talking about when we use terms such as "understanding" or

101

"meaning"—or, indeed, whether we are talking about anything at all. In "Facts of the Matter" Quine puts it this way:

> Mental states do not reduce to behavior, nor are they explained by behavior. They are explained by neurology, when they are explained. But their behavioral adjuncts serve to specify them objectively. When we talk of mental states or events subject to behavioral criteria, we can rest assured that we are not just bandying words; there is a physical fact of the matter, a fact ultimately of elementary physical states.
>
> (p. 167)

(We shall return to these issues; see Chapter 12, section III below.)

Quine clearly thinks of the physiological level as unavailable for the explanation of language. Our knowledge of the brain is limited. Given the complexity of the organ, and the difficulty of knowing in detail what is going on inside a living brain, there are restrictions here which we cannot hope to escape in the foreseeable future. As we indicated in the previous section, however, there is also a different sort of reason for focusing on behaviour rather than on brains; there is the nature of the subject. Language, Quine insists, is public, shared, and learned from others.[7] What goes on in the brain is relevant only insofar as it is at least potentially manifest. Since language is learned from others, it is learned on the basis of what is publicly observable, without use of special techniques:

> In psychology one may or may not be a behaviorist, but in linguistics one has no choice. Each of us learns his language by observing other people's verbal behavior and having his own faltering verbal behavior observed and reinforced or corrected by others. ... There is nothing in linguistic meaning beyond what is to be gleaned from overt behavior in observable circumstances.
>
> (PT, pp. 37–38; see also "Philosophical Progress
in Language Theory", p. 5)

The reference to behaviourism here, and elsewhere, has encouraged the view that Quine's approach to language, perhaps even his philosophy as a whole, depends on a behaviourist approach to psychology, which is widely regarded as outmoded. I think this view is mistaken. Quine's approach to language is simply a special case of his general empiricism. Thus he makes the essentially same point as in the passage just quoted with no obviously controversial assumption beyond his empiricism:

The sort of meaning that is basic to translation, and to the learning of one's own language, is necessarily empirical meaning and nothing more. A child learns his first words and sentences by hearing and using them in the presence of appropriate stimuli. These must be external stimuli, for they must act both on the child and on the speaker from whom he is learning. Language is socially inculcated and controlled; the inculcation and control turn strictly on the keying of sentences to shared stimulation. Internal factors may vary *ad libitum* without prejudice to communication as long as the keying of language to external stimuli is undisturbed. Surely one has no choice but to be an empiricist so far as one's theory of linguistic meaning is concerned.

(EN, *OR*, p. 81)

Quine appeals to what he takes to be undeniable facts: language is learnt by infants who receive information about the world only through their sensory simulations. This is a special case of his empiricism, the idea that "our information about the world comes only through impacts on our sensory receptors" (*PT*, p. 19); it is empiricism applied to language, which is "socially inculcated and controlled". In spite of his use of the word "behaviourism", then, I do not see Quine as committed to an outmoded approach to psychology.[8] (Here we have two rather different senses of the word "behaviourism".) But there remain questions about what Quine's approach can include, and whether it can possibly be adequate for an account of language. We take up some of these questions in the next section.

V Methods of the project: dispositions

It may seem that Quine's emphasis on behaviour means that his approach is too constrained to permit any account of language. One issue here is that behaviour may seem to be simply too sparse to enable us to account for the astonishing richness of language. For example, there is the familiar fact that the number of sentences—strings of words that native speakers would accept as meaningful—far outruns the number of sentences actually uttered. Another issue arises over the idea of innate mechanisms. Such mechanisms must surely be present, and must play a vital role in the learning of language; yet it might seem unclear whether Quine's focus on behaviour leaves room for them. More vaguely, it might seem that the emphasis on behaviour does not do justice to the fact that language is shared. You and I have an understanding of English in common, but our behaviour is not the same. It is not just that your actions are yours and mine are mine; it is not at all obvious that your

103

behaviour and mine can be coordinated so as to make it clear how each amounts to the same thing—an understanding of English. These difficulties may make it seem as if we cannot hope to account for language in terms of behaviour; each is therefore liable to be taken as a reason to adopt mentalism.

The supposed difficulties are, I think, largely illusory. Quine's methods, in the study of language and its acquisition, are more liberal than his emphasis on behaviour might lead one to think. The crucial fact here is that he is concerned not only with behaviour but also with *dispositions* to behaviour: not only with the utterances that are in fact made, but also with those that *would* be made in any of various situations. One question facing us here is the legitimacy of Quine's talk of dispositions. How does he conceive of them, so that they fit into his physicalistic ontology and his generally empiricist approach to knowledge? A second question is: how does accepting dispositions help with the worries expressed in the previous paragraph? We begin with the first of these questions; this discussion will occupy the next couple of pages.

The fundamental idea of a disposition is that an object has the disposition to do X in circumstances C just in case it *would* do X if it *were* in circumstances C. As an explanation, however, this is unhelpful because of its reliance on an irredeemably counterfactual conditional. (See Chapter 13, section VII, below.) Explaining what it means to say that something would have done so-and-so under certain circumstances which never in fact came about is simply another way of saying that it has the relevant disposition. So how is the idea to be explained?

Quine takes the view that attributing a disposition to an object is really attributing to it a certain physical make-up. To call a sugar lump soluble, say, is to attribute to it whatever characteristic is in fact responsible for the dissolving of such sugar lumps as happen to end up in water. We may not know anything else about this physical characteristic. It is, nevertheless, what we are talking about when we describe something as soluble: we are talking about whatever feature of the object in fact explains the relevant behaviour—presumably a physical mechanism, an aspect of the object's physical structure. There need not be a single kind of mechanism. The term "soluble" as applied to sugar lumps might pick out one kind of structure, as applied to salt crystals quite another; it might even be that sugar lumps are in fact of two or more distinct kinds, with different sorts of structure accounting for the dissolving in each case. No matter: we can speak of a disjunction, having this sort of structure *or* this sort *or* this sort, if we please. What matters is that in describing an object in dispositional terms we are attributing to it some structural feature, known or unknown.

Ontologically, then, a disposition of an object is a physical state of it. Accepting dispositions in our scientific discourse is thus compatible with Quine's overarching physicalism. Epistemologically, too, they are acceptable. We need not be able to say, in other terms, *what* explains why the object behaves as it does (dissolving, say). It is enough that we have reason to believe that some underlying feature of it does. We attribute a disposition to an object on the basis of its superficial resemblance to other objects which have reliably manifested the disposition in the past. This sugar lump resembles all the others I have seen, so I infer that it has the same underlying physical make-up—and, in particular, that it has whatever physical features explained the dissolving of the others, so that it too, if put into warm water under favourable circumstances, would dissolve. I may be incorrect in my inference, of course; gross physical resemblance usually goes with resemblance in micro-structure, but not always. Fallibility, however, is no objection.

Under favourable conditions we can test for the presence of the disposition by bringing about the relevant circumstances. The idea of favourable conditions here is important. A sugar lump has the disposition to dissolve in water but may be put in water and not dissolve, perhaps because the water is already saturated with sugar, or too cold, or for some other reason. Dispositions come with a *ceteris paribus* clause: if an object has the disposition to do X under circumstances C then if we bring about C the object will do X *provided that* circumstances are normal. What constitutes normal circumstances here may be open-ended, difficult or even impossible to specify fully in advance. Where we have an open-ended *ceteris paribus* clause we do not have an operational definition for the disposition. In this, however, dispositional terms are no worse off than many other scientific terms, and Quine sees no reason to impose more stringent conditions upon them. Provided circumstances are favourable we have some sort of test for the presence of the disposition; that, for Quine, is enough.

We have been using the simple example of the solubility of sugar. On Quine's account, however, the same notion of a disposition applies also to human beings and their behaviour. The underlying physical state or mechanism, and the circumstances under which it is manifested, are immensely more complicated, but the basic point is the same. A disposition is the physical state of the (human) organism which would lead to its doing so-and-so if circumstances were such-and-such. Some dispositions may have "physical workings we can scarcely conjecture" (*RR*, p. 10) but this is no barrier to Quine's use of the idea. That use is not intended as explanatory; only neurophysiology will give us genuine explanations.

Quine sees language as embodied in dispositions to behaviour. Actual behaviour is the *evidence* for someone's possession of the dispositions which constitute a mastery of a given language. But the underlying reality for which it is evidence consists of *dispositions* to behaviour, and these are enduring (though changeable) states of the organism. What the language-learner witnesses is the manifestation of a disposition; what he has to acquire, however, is the disposition itself. In the previous section we distinguished the behavioural level from the physiological level in accounts of language. We can now see that the levels are linked. A behavioural account is an account in terms of dispositions to behaviour. Such dispositions are physical states of the organism (though not, in general, ones that we can specify in physical terms). So a behavioural account is also, by Quine's lights, a physicalistic account.

How does the idea that language is embodied in dispositions to behaviour, rather than merely in actual behaviour, help with the worries expressed in the first paragraph of this section? There is immediate help with one issue: the sparseness of behaviour relative to the richness of language. Actual behaviour may be relatively sparse, but dispositions to behaviour are not. There are surely sentences which have never been uttered and never will be. In the case of many, there are counterfactual circumstances under which they *would* be uttered. Even if that fails for a given sentence, there will be some circumstances such that its utterance in those circumstances would lead to a reaction, at least from some speakers of the language. The "reaction" here may also be a matter of dispositions, rather than of any immediate behavioural response. When I hear or read a sentence I may make no immediate overt response to what I hear, but still my dispositions to utter or to assent to other sentences may change.

Another worry was over innate mechanisms, which seem to be required for any account of how language is learnt. What sort of innate mechanisms can Quine accept, given his empiricism? Again, the idea of a disposition, as Quine understands it, provides a ready answer. Certain dispositions are innate. For Quine this is to say only that the organism arrives in the world with a physical make-up—a brain and nervous system, in particular—that determines its responses to the various stimulations that come its way. Other dispositions are acquired, which is to say that one way in which the organism responds to stimulations is by changes in its make-up. These in turn lead to changes in the way it will react to future stimulations, either by overt responses or by forming yet further dispositions.

We should emphasize that Quine does not grudgingly concede the need for innate mechanisms. On the contrary: "Any behaviorist account of the learning process is openly and emphatically committed to innate beginnings.

The behaviorist recognizes the indispensability, for any kind of learning, of prior biases and affinities". ("Philosophical Progress in Language Theory", pp. 5–6.) Similarly: "the behaviorist is knowingly and cheerfully up to his neck in innate mechanisms of learning readiness" ("Linguistics and Philosophy", WP, p. 57). Even the narrowest kind of behaviourism, relying exclusively on the conditioning of responses to stimuli, requires innate predispositions. Pavlov's dog, we say, is subjected to "the same stimulus" on various occasions, but there are different ringings of the bell. For learning to be possible, the dog must find one occasion on which the bell rings more similar to another occasion on which the bell rings than it does to an occasion on which the bell does not ring. Learning is only possible for an animal which innately has this kind of quality space: it finds one occasion of stimulus more similar to a second than either is to a third. Much more than this will be needed for language learning, as Quine acknowledges: "it has long been recognized that our innate endowments for language go yet further than the mere spacing of qualities" ("Philosophical Progress in Language Theory", p. 6; cf. also "Linguistics and Philosophy", WP, p. 57). In the same vein, the learning compatible with what Quine calls "behaviourism" is by no means limited to the conditioning of responses to stimuli: "this method is notoriously incapable of carrying us far in language" ("Linguistics and Philosophy", WP, p. 57).

This is not to say, however, that Quine's empiricism, or "behaviourism" in his sense, imposes no restrictions whatsoever. The idea of a disposition to do X in circumstances C is sufficiently clear only to the extent that X and C are themselves sufficiently clear. In particular, Quine requires that they be in some way accessible to observation; if they are not themselves observable, they must be terms for which we can devise observational tests. "What matters ... is just the insistence upon couching all criteria in observation terms." ("Linguistics and Philosophy", WP, p. 58.) This requirement is crucial. Without it, we could give a wholly trivial version of the idea that knowing the meaning of an expression is a dispositional state: to know the meaning of an expression is to be disposed, upon hearing that expression, to understand it, or to have the relevant idea in one's mind, or what not. Clearly statements of this sort are completely uninformative; they embody the kind of mentalism that Quine abhors. In the uninformativeness of these answers, indeed, we have an example which indicates the sort of defect he finds in mentalism quite generally.

A further issue raised at the beginning of this section was whether a behavioural approach to language can do justice to the fact that you and I understand the same language. The idea of a disposition to behaviour answers the question by providing a level of description at which it becomes evident what two speakers of the same language have in common. You and I both understand English: we have *the same ability*. But the sense in which this is so cannot be understood if we merely look at your (actual) behaviour and at mine. There will be a few sentences which we have both uttered, but the overlap between your utterances and mine will be small, relative to the wholes. There will be many more sentences which we have both heard or read, but our overt responses will, again, show only a small overlap. Nor is the appeal to neurophysiology promising here. There is no reason to think that any interesting mapping between your brain and mine can be carried out at a sufficiently fine-grained level to have explanatory power. But at the level of dispositions it becomes much clearer what it is that we have in common. Suppose, for example, you and I are both looking at well watered grass on a June day and are asked "Is it green?"; provided each of us has normal vision then each of us has the disposition to say: "Yes".[9] This kind of case may seem quite trivial but it is, as we shall see, fundamental for Quine's approach in general.

VI Approaches to language: working backwards

Quine's most sustained approach to cognitive language is the one that we have indicated: he discusses, in a more or less speculative way, how an infant might acquire cognitive language. The basis for the discussion is the sort of picture that Quine sets out at the start of "The Scope and Language of Science": the infant is bombarded by physical forces, and emits noises. What is required for emitted noises to amount to cognitive language, and how do some of the infant's noises come to acquire that character? How, on this basis, can we think of the infant as acquiring cognitive language? Answering these questions is the genetic project. It is, I think, the most important way of thinking about language, from a Quinean point of view; it will be our focus in the next two chapters.

Quine also sometimes approaches language via what he calls radical translation. He imagines an idealized linguist encountering a group of people. She is supposed to be completely ignorant of their language (and, indeed, of their culture). Over time she comes to be able to negotiate and communicate with them, and to translate their language into hers; she comes to understand their language. As Quine says explicitly, this idea is a thought-experiment.[10] Somehow, we suppose, radical translation succeeds: by observing the foreigners, our linguist comes to be able to use the alien language to do what its native speakers can do. The question is: how? An understanding of the data that our linguist has to go on, and the methods that she uses, would tell us something about what makes the utterances of those she encounters meaningful speech.

Quine's linguist already has a language, so we can suppose that she is self-conscious about method and procedure, that she begins by coming up with ways of translating the foreign language into her own, and that she explicitly forms and tests hypotheses about the language that she is trying to learn.[11] The fact that it is *translation* that she is engaged in also makes it possible to formulate the idea of the *indeterminacy of translation*: that two linguists might come up with non-equivalent translations, each equally correct. This is one of Quine's most controversial ideas, and has provoked voluminous discussion, mostly hostile; we shall return to radical translation, and to the question of its indeterminacy, in Chapter 8, below.

In both of these approaches, Quine works forwards: he begins with the situation described in non-mentalistic terms, and shows how something which might be thought to approximate an understanding of cognitive language could develop. In the case of the infant, stimulations go in and noises come out; the task is to show how some of those noises constitute cognitive language. In the scenario of radical translation, our idealized linguist again has the noises which the natives emit, and some idea of what forces are impinging on their sensory surfaces, and must work forward from there. At times, however, Quine considers language in a different way, which at least appears to be of a more conventional philosophical kind. At those moments Quine is, we might say, working backwards, beginning with something like the traditional vocabulary of meaning and understanding. His point here is a heuristic one. We should not think of him as accepting the mentalistic vocabulary as legitimate. He aims to show how, and to what extent, those notions can be approximated in terms which are acceptable to him; also to show that such an approximation will not fully justify the traditional vocabulary. These discussions can be useful, even though they use a vocabulary which is not, in the end, fully legitimate by Quine's standards.

In "Mind and Verbal Dispositions", Quine speaks explicitly of what is required for the understanding of an expression. What can that idea come to, in Quinean terms? For him, it must be something public, hence a matter of use, of behaviour. So understanding an expression is to consist in the ability to use it appropriately, and to react appropriately to its use by others, in any of an almost unlimited variety of contexts. (The great thing about language is precisely its flexibility.) So understanding, and, correlatively, meaning, consists in having dispositions to use the relevant expression. But this is too general to be very helpful. For any expression, we seem to be faced with unmanageably many dispositions; how are we to sort matters out, so as to have something more informative to say than that understanding human language consists in behaving the way that human beings behave?

Quine's focus is on the assertoric use of language, its use to make claims which are true or false. He thus focuses, in the first instance, on *sentences*, rather than on smaller units of language. He considers the *truth-conditions* of sentences, or, more accurately perhaps, the conditions under which speakers of the language will accept or reject a given sentence. These steps require some further elaboration and justification. (We must bear in mind, however, that this whole discussion is purely heuristic; we will not get genuine explanations or fully satisfactory justifications.)

The notion of a *sentence*, as used above, is not a syntactical one. It means, roughly: unit of language capable of significant assertion by itself, without linguistic context. Since our concern is with dispositions relevant to linguistic behaviour—with the use of language, and with responses to uses of language—it makes sense to focus on units of language which have an independent assertoric use. Of course something will still need to be said about other units of language, which are incapable of significant use by themselves but which combine with others to make up sentences. But that, for Quine, is a derivative matter. Sentence meaning comes first.

There are, as Quine recognizes, many uses of sentences—a "[b]ewildering variety", as he says (MVD, p. 87). After listing some of the various uses, he continues:

> Somehow we must further divide: we must find some significant central strand to extract from the tangle.
> *Truth* will do nicely. Some sentences, of course, do not have truth-values. ... Those that do may still be uttered for a variety of reasons unconnected with instruction. ... But, among these sentences, truth is a great leveller, enabling us to postpone consideration of all those troublesome excrescences. Here, then, is an adjusted standard of understanding: a man understands a sentence in so far as he knows its truth conditions. This kind of understanding stops short of humor, irony, innuendo, and other literary values, but it goes a long way. In particular it is all we can ask of an understanding of the language of science.
> (MVD, pp. 87–88; emphasis in the original)

Quine thus makes truth central to his account of language. This step is crucial, although here taken in an apparently casual way. There are two sorts of reasons offered for it. One, indicated in the last sentence of the passage, is that the sort of understanding which focuses on truth is all that we need care about when our concern is with the language of science, for the business of science is precisely the truth about the world. This presupposes that truth-conditional understanding can be isolated and treated in abstraction from the more general context of linguistic interchange. That we can indeed do this is, presumably, to be shown by Quine's discussion of language as a whole.

The second sort of reason amounts to the idea that truth-conditional understanding is the fundamental kind of understanding, from which the rest flows. Truth, Quine says, is the "central strand" in language-use as a whole (MVD, p. 87). This sort of general view goes back a long way in Quine's thought. In 1936 he says: "in point of *meaning* ... a word may be said to be determined to whatever extent the truth and falsehood of its contexts is determined" ("Truth by Convention", WP, p. 89). More than thirty-five years later he says: "First and last, in learning language, we are learning how to distribute truth-values". (RR, p. 65.) Many philosophers, especially those of a scientific orientation, have simply found it obvious that the descriptive or fact-stating function of language is primary, and that meaning of that sort is meaning enough. What reasons are there to accept this sort of view? Such reasons would presumably show that a grasp on the truth-conditions of each sentence would suffice for mastery of the language, at least when supplemented by a manageable set of further linguistic devices, which can be dealt with once we have the central notion of understanding in place. This view I take to be implicit in Quine's use of the term "troublesome excrescences" in the passage quoted a page or so back. (These sorts of devices would allow one, given a grasp of the truth-conditions of "There's ice cream", to go on to ask whether there is ice cream, to demand that there be ice cream, to wonder whether there is ice cream, and so on.) Quine says little more on the topic, however, and I shall not speculate further.

With whatever justification, Quine does see truth-conditions as central to meaning. So understanding a language is a matter of knowing the truth-conditions of its sentences. This clearly allies Quine with a trend in philosophy of language which is often traced back to Frege.[12] Unlike most who have held this sort of view, however, Quine does not see knowledge of truth-conditions as an end point of the discussion; to the contrary, his aim is an account in terms of behavioural dispositions. What does knowledge of truth-conditions come to, in such terms? For a limited class of sentences, those he calls observation sentences, Quine thinks that we can answer this question. Details will occupy the next chapter; roughly, he takes knowing the truth-conditions of an observation sentence to consist in being disposed to accept the sentence under the appropriate stimulatory conditions, and not otherwise. Accepting the sentence is in turn understood in terms of a disposition to assent when the sentence is posed as a question:

> In what behavioural disposition then does a man's knowledge of the truth-conditions of the sentence "This is red" consist? Not, certainly, in a disposition to affirm the sentence on every occasion of observing a red object, and to deny it on all other occasions; it is the disposition to assent or dissent when asked in the presence or absence of red. Query and assent, query and dissent—here is the solvent that reduces understanding to verbal dispositions.
>
> (MVD, p. 88)

The above idea applies directly only to what Quine calls these *occasion sentences*, as opposed to *standing sentences* and *eternal sentences*; I shall take a moment to explain the terminology, for it will occur in later contexts. Occasion sentences are those with truth-values which vary from occasion to occasion, depending on the circumstances in which they are uttered. Examples might be "It's hot in here!" or "I'm hungry". They contrast most sharply with *eternal sentences*, which are true or false once for all; natural laws and sentences of arithmetic, for example. There are also what Quine calls *standing sentences*; their truth-values do change but not, or not only, in response to changes in the immediate situation. Some may retain their truth-values for years, such as "Bush is President of the USA"; others vary more quickly, such as "It's Monday".[13]

Quine's picture of the relation of behavioural dispositions to understanding is clear enough for occasion sentences, perhaps, but much less clear for the others. This is because such sentences are only indirectly linked to stimulation. (This, of course, is holism.) The circumstances which make it correct to assert a standing sentence are not simply a matter of current sensory experience; they are also, or instead, a matter of its links to other sentences, which in turn are linked to other sentences, and so on. The whole structure makes contact with sensory experience here and there, but the links of a given sentence may be impossible to reconstruct. Thus Quine says: "Perhaps the very notion of understanding, as applied to single standing sentences, simply cannot be explicated in terms of behavioural dispositions. Perhaps, therefore, it is simply an untenable notion, notwithstanding our intuitive predilections". (MVD, p. 89.) Another passage does more to reveal the reasons for this:

> To trace out the meaning of an eternal sentence deep inside the theory ... we have nothing to go on but its multifarious connections within the theory and ultimately, indirectly, with the periphery [i.e.

the occasion sentences]. Each of the strands being describable only by its interrelations with others, there ceases to be any clear sense in asking the meaning of a single sentence at all.

(RR, p. 64)

Sentences beyond the observational depend for their meaning on their connections with other sentences; considering a standing sentence in isolation from others, and trying to account for *its* meaning, is an unpromising endeavour. This conclusion shows the limitations of the notion of meaning. We cannot simply help ourselves to that idea and assume that it will, somehow, be shown to have the right kinds of connections with clearer and better established aspects of our knowledge. For Quine, this conclusion thus vindicates his approach to language, by contrast with more traditional approaches which simply assume a notion of meaning.

In this section we have seen Quine working backwards from intuitive notions such as meaning and understanding to what he regards as clear ideas—in particular, dispositions to behaviour, especially verbal behaviour. In this mood he uses terms such as "meaning" and "understanding" but he is not presupposing that they make complete sense; on the contrary, the point is to ask how, and to what extent, we can make clear sense of them. Questions such as: does this really amount to *understanding*? or: is this really *meaning*? are not ones that he would take as appropriate. Such intuitive notions do not provide an independent vantage point from which the reconstructions can be assessed; Quine's purpose in invoking them is heuristic.

Quine's more fundamental approach to language sticks to clear ideas throughout—that is, it sticks to ideas which Quine takes to be scientifically and empirically respectable. It uses those ideas to give an account of cognitive language and its acquisition. Quine works forward from terms he takes to be clear. The fact that we can dispense with mentalistic terms is shown by giving an account that does not assume them at any point. More important than specific arguments or what Quine *says* about unreconstructed mentalistic terms is what he *does*, that is, the sort of account of language that he offers. Quine is not, for the most part, a therapeutic philosopher. He does not re-enact the confusion of traditional philosophical terms and assumptions until they collapse under their own weight, as Wittgenstein does in such masterful fashion. He tries, rather, to present us with a view of language and its acquisition which shows that it is an undeniably public and naturalistic matter. His response to unclarity is simply to present what he takes to be clear. This he does in the genetic project, the details of which will be the concern of the next two chapters.

113

5

THE BEGINNINGS OF COGNITIVE LANGUAGE

Shared responses to stimulation and observation sentences

How are we to approach cognitive language, without presupposing mentalistic terms? We begin, again, with Quine's naturalistic picture: the human animal is bombarded by forms of energy which lead to stimulation of its sensory nerves; it moves in various ways and emits various noises. Which of those forms of behaviour should be counted as *language*? And how does an emitted noise, or a movement, come to count as being *about the world*? Three points can be taken for granted at the outset.

First, cognitive language is in some way related to sensory simulation, or neural intake.[1] All of our information about the world is acquired from sensory stimulations. For a form of behaviour to embody or to convey information about the world, then, it must be related to such stimulations. Cognitive language must be in some way related to stimulations of our sensory surfaces; this, we might say, is what it is to be *cognitive*. So we must be able to make sense of the idea of a form of behaviour being tied to current neural intake. Making sense of this idea in the individualistic case— what it is for *my* responses to be related to *my* stimulations—may seem like a trivial matter. As we shall see, however, the matter is much more complicated than might at first appear. Quine goes to considerable lengths to show that the idea makes sense in his terms; this will be the subject of the first section of this chapter.

Second, language is *public*, "a social art" as Quine says at the beginning of the preface to *Word and Object*. We respond to sensory stimulation in all sorts of ways: brain cells fire, chemicals are released into the bloodstream, the blood pressure rises or falls, and so on. None of those responses, however, are even candidates for being part of language. Cognitive language consists of public responses to stimulation, responses which can and sometimes do affect others. We respond to each other's responses to stimulation. This has everything to do with the survival-value of language, or of more primitive systems of signals: one sparrow sees a hawk, gives a cry, and the whole flock flees. Quine's focus on language, moreover, is based on the idea that in language knowledge is embodied in a medium which is open, public, and thus scientifically tractable. This second point is in tension with the first, because stimulations are not shared; this difficulty, and Quine's resolution of it, will occupy the second section of this chapter.

A third characteristic of human language is that it is learned. This does not follow from its being public. Sparrows, we are supposing, react with a certain characteristic cry to the neural intake which typically results when they see a hawk circling overhead. Those who hear the cry but do not themselves see the hawk react to the cry more or less as they would have done to the sight of the hawk. Such a cry is clearly public (unlike the release of certain chemicals into the sparrow's bloodstream, which no doubt also characteristically accompanies the sight of the hawk). Yet it might be entirely instinctive, not acquired or learned from others of the species. Human language, by contrast, is learned, and learned not just from features of the environment in general but, in particular, from other speakers of the same language:[2] "Language is a social art which we all acquire on the evidence solely of other people's overt behavior under publicly recognizable circumstances". (OR, p. 26.) The learning of responses to stimulation is the subject of the third section of the chapter.

Our concern in the first three sections of this chapter, then, is with the idea that lies at the base of a Quinean account of cognitive language: the idea of shared, public, learned responses to current stimulation. One might suppose this idea too elementary to require any explanation. Philosophical discussions of language usually begin by taking for granted far more sophisticated ideas—reference, for example, or truth-conditions, or intention, or the communication of ideas. For Quine, by contrast, the idea of shared responses to current stimulation is itself in need of explanation in more fundamental terms—most obviously, physicalistic terms which will connect it with the fundamental fact that the human knower is a physical object in a physical world, subject to physical forces and (ideally) explicable in terms of those forces. Seeing the sort of explanation that Quine offers of this idea will help to make clearer just what he means by a *naturalistic* explanation of language, and how seriously he takes the project of offering such an explanation.

The idea of shared, public, learned responses to current stimulation is fundamental for a Quinean account of cognitive language. Yet that idea receives little discussion in Quine's work in those terms. He generally assumes that there are certain bits of language which play the role of shared responses to current stimulation: these are what he calls "observation sentences". More accurately: he assumes that the act of assenting to an observation sentence, or dissenting from it, when one hears it queried is a learned shared response to current stimulation.[3]

Quine thus takes observation sentences to be directly linked to stimulation. For this reason, they are fundamental both to his account of cognitive language—how our noises can be meaningful, how the capacity to make meaningful noises can be acquired—and to his account of how our knowledge as a whole is answerable to evidence. The two issues go hand-in-hand. Observation sentences, Quine assumes, are the point at which language is directly linked to sensory stimulations. Such stimulations are the only source of our information about the world. So other sentences are cognitively meaningful in virtue of their links to observation sentences. (Links which may be exceedingly indirect and tenuous.) Similarly, for theory to be connected with evidence is for it to be linked to sensory stimulations and this, again, is a matter of its being linked (however indirectly) to observation sentences. The point of the genetic project is to trace out these links, both of meaning and of evidence, by examining how language is or might be learned. For this account, again, observation sentences are fundamental.

The significance which we have been attributing to observation sentences is based on the idea that they (or assent to them) are simply responses to stimulation. In his later work, Quine sees that some qualification to this idea may be necessary, as we shall see. But he does not go into details and tends, in practice, to ignore the point. His discussion of shared responses to current stimulation therefore takes the form of a discussion of observation sentences. I have separated the ideas here partly for analytical purposes but partly also because I think that strictly speaking no ordinary sentences are simply responses to current stimulation, and that there are systematic and important reasons for this fact. This issue, the relation of observation sentences to responses to current stimulation, will be discussed in the fourth and fifth sections of this chapter.

I Responses to stimulation; perceptual similarity

Our interest is in the idea of responses to current stimulation. Quine takes a stimulation here as a *global stimulus*. The global stimulus which a given animal is undergoing at a given moment is "the class of all sensory receptors that were triggered at that moment; or, better, the temporally ordered class of receptors triggered during that specious present" (*FSS*, p. 17). Such episodes "may be understood simply as brief stages or temporal segments of the perceiving subject's body. . . . Thus they are global episodes, including all irrelevancies". (*RR*, p. 16.) This notion is quite consciously modelled on Carnap's elementary experiences (*Elementarerlebnisse*) in *Der logische Aufbau der Welt*. (The point is explicit at *RR*, p. 16; see also *FSS*, p. 19, where Quine speaks of his "physical mimicry of phenomenalistic epistemology".) For Quine, as for Carnap in the *Aufbau*, it is the whole sensory content of a given moment which is taken as basic. The distinctions between the relevant and the irrelevant aspects of the sensory episode are not presupposed at the outset; making such distinctions is part of the work to be done. From our point of view, however, the difference between Carnap and Quine here is as striking as the similarity. Quine's version of "the whole sensory content of a given moment" is straightforwardly physical: a listing of which nerve endings are firing, and in which order, at that time. There is no supposition at all that "sensory content" in this sense is something of which the subject is aware, or anything of that sort. Quine's thought here has affinities with Carnap's view in the *Aufbau*, but always with a physicalized version of that view.

The idea of a response to stimulation presupposes a systematic correlation of stimulations with behaviour. The idea of a correlation requires that we are talking about repeatable *types* of stimulation and of behaviour, not about particular episodes or instances. To put it more precisely, we need similarity relations among episodes of stimulation and among episodes of behaviour. Correlation here is a matter of a stimulus relevantly similar to a given one being regularly followed by behaviour relevantly similar to a given episode; the notion of relevant similarity is crucial and requires explanation.

Both for sensory stimulation and for episodes of behaviour there are similarity relations which can be defined in quite straightforward physicalistic terms. For stimulation, or neural intake, it is *receptual similarity*, a matter of the physical resemblance between one episode of stimulation and another. "Episodes are receptually similar to the degree that the total set of sensory receptors that are triggered on the one occasion approximates that triggered on the other occasion". (*RR*, p. 16.) About *behavioural similarity* Quine is less definite, but he suggests that a definition "might be sought in terms of the total set of fibres of striped muscles that are contracted or released on one occasion and on another" (*RR*, p. 21; he adds, however, "or a more functional approach might be devised").

These straightforward similarity relations are not adequate for Quine's purposes. They do not allow for any interesting correlation between stimulation and behaviour. The notion of receptual similarity, most clearly, is not what is wanted. Suppose I am driving, see a red traffic light, and slow to a halt. Now imagine the exact same situation, except the light is green and I do not slow the car. My global stimuli in the two situations have a high degree of receptal similarity: all the non-visual sensory nerves are stimulated in the same order, and most of the visual nerves too. But my behaviour in the two cases is quite different. Two different occasions on which I stop at a red traffic light, by contrast, may be receptally quite dissimilar—different ambient light, different music on the car radio, different smells in the air, and so on—but my behaviour in the one case is very similar to that in the other. Yet my stopping or not stopping at a traffic light is surely to be thought of as a response to current stimulation. The problem, intuitively put, is that two occasions which a subject perceives as being similar, and as thus calling for similar action, may be receptally very dissimilar; contrariwise, two occasions which are receptally quite similar may result in different behavioural episodes because the subject does not perceive them as relevantly similar. Nor should this surprise us. Stimuli are understood "as global, including all irrelevancies". It is precisely the irrelevancies which cause the problem here; two episodes may be receptally similar or dissimilar in virtue of the firing of nerves which make no immediate difference to the subject's behaviour. What we need is a notion of *perceptual similarity* which will screen out irrelevancies; two episodes should count as perceptually similar only if they are *relevantly* similar— roughly, similar in ways that affect the animal's behaviour in the following moments.

Two episodes should thus count as perceptually similar if they affect the animal's behaviour in the same way. This might suggest that any two episodes of stimulation which are followed by similar episodes of behaviour should count as perceptually similar. But this attempt to avoid the problem of irrelevancies falls into a problem of vacuity. It amounts to a definition of perceptual similarity simply in terms of behavioural similarity: if two episodes are behaviourally similar then the two preceding episodes of neural intake would be perceptually similar by definition. But then, as a trivial result of the definition, any two behaviourally similar episodes will be preceded by perceptually similar episodes of stimulation; so *every* behavioural episode would in the relevant sense be correlated with preceding stimulation. The notion of correlation would thus become quite vacuous, and of no use at all. The suggested definition goes wrong because what we want is to single out those episodes of behaviour which are tied only to the animal's current neural intake (rather than depending also on its current internal state). Neither receptal similarity nor behavioural similarity will do. As Quine says:

> Perceptual similarity ... should be somehow intermediate between receptual and behavioral similarity. It should be reflected in the behavioral output of the episode rather than just current input, but it should be reflected in only so much of the behavioral output as is somehow distinctive to the current input.
>
> (*RR*, p. 21)

How is the idea of perceptual similarity to be understood? Quine gives the example of an animal trained to press a lever when confronted with a circular stripe, and to refrain when confronted with four spots. Confronting the animal with a circular pattern of seven spots, we find that it presses the lever; we conclude that the pattern of seven is perceptually more similar to the circular stripe than to the four spots, for that animal at that time. It is tempting to give a mentalistic explanation here, and say that the animal acts as it does because it *perceives* the seven spots as more similar to the circle than to the four. Quine, however, finds such (alleged) explanation useless, precisely because it relies on an intuitive notion of an animal's perceiving one thing as more similar to another than it is to a third. His concern is to characterize a notion of perceptual similarity in observable—and thus behavioural—terms. He does this by taking the example the other way around. The animal's behaviour, its exhibiting the sort of responses indicated, is not explained by an independently understood fact of its finding some things perceptually similar to others. Rather, we characterize perceptual similarity for the animal by saying that it consists precisely in the animal's being disposed to act in the sorts of ways indicated in the example. The notion of perceptual similarity, thus understood, cannot be invoked to explain the animal's behaviour, for it is now characterized in terms of the events that it might be thought to explain. (Here we see something of the reason that Quine holds that a discussion of language at the behavioural level, as opposed to the neurophysiological level, is not explanatory in any deep sense; see Chapter 4, section IV above.)

In the example above, we have the animal conditioned to exhibit responses of a given type (i.e. responses behaviourally similar to one another) when confronted by things of one type, and to exhibit a different response when confronted by things of a different type. Its being "confronted" by this or that must be understood in terms of stimulations; the relation which makes such episodes into instances *of the same type* must here be *receptual* similarity.

Putting all of this together, we have a behaviouristic criterion for perceptual similarity: first to condition the animal to exhibit some response to sensory episodes which are sufficiently receptually similar to *B*, and to withhold that response from episodes which are sufficiently receptually similar to C.[4] Then we can say that A is more perceptually similar to B than it is to C just in case the animal exhibits that same response to episodes which are sufficiently receptually similar to A. (This is a criterion of perceptual similarity, but hardly a definition.)

The notion of perceptual similarity enables Quine to give an account of the idea that some parts of a global stimulus will matter more than others in explaining the behaviour of the animal. In particular, it enables him to define a notion of *salience*. Those triggerings of nerve endings which a stimulus shares with others which are perceptually similar but *not* receptually similar are the salient ones. (Recall the example of the two occasions on which I stop at a red traffic light. If the global stimuli I receive on these two occasions are indeed perceptually similar for me, then the triggerings caused by the light would be salient in each.) Inspired again by Carnap's *Aufbau*, Quine uses the idea of salience to distinguish sense modalities. The visual stimuli are those global stimuli whose salient triggerings are those of retinal receptors, and so on.

Perceptual similarity, on Quine's account, is of general and fundamental importance. It is, he says, "the basis of all expectation, all learning, all habit formation" (*FSS*, p. 19). Even the most primitive kind of learning requires that distinct episodes be grouped. A dog once burned by a fire will not approach another fire. Having been hurt in one situation, we loosely say, it avoids *that situation* in the future. But what it avoids is not, of course, the particular event; that's in the past, and so can be neither avoided nor re-created. There is something intrinsically general about this kind of learning. We learn not about a particular situation at a particular moment, but about all situations *of a certain kind*; it is perceptual similarity which gives us the relevant "kind" here.

Given the role of perceptual similarity, some standards of perceptual similarity must be innate. Such standards may change, and others may be acquired, but these changes themselves require prior similarity standards. So: "perceptual similarity cannot itself have been learned—not all of it. Some of it is innate". (*FSS*, p. 19.) This does not imply that Quine accepts that we have innate *knowledge*. Perceptual similarity is not a matter of the facts of the world but rather of reactions to them. The perceptual similarity between A and B is similarity for a given animal at a given time, and is constituted by the fact that if it were first in one situation and then in the other, it would be disposed to react in similar ways each time. There is no claim of objective similarity, which the animal—somehow—knows about ahead of time. While some standards of perceptual similarity must be innate, it is also true that such standards "change radically ... and perhaps rapidly for a while, in consequence of experience and learning" (*FSS*, p. 19).

Perceptual similarity plays the crucial role in primitive induction. Experiences of an event of one kind following an event of another kind lead us (and other animals) to expect a repetition of the pattern. It is perceptual similarity that groups events into kinds here. Expectations set up by primitive induction enable animals, human and non-human, to survive, by finding food and avoiding predators. Changes in similarity standards enable animals to do this with a greater chance of success (see NNK, p. 71). The same thing happens, more rapidly and self-consciously, in human knowledge. Revision of similarity standards is not all that there is to science, since simple induction is not our only way of knowing, but it is an essential beginning.

Perceptual similarity, as Quine understands it, is a relation among global stimuli, episodes of an animal's sensory nerves being stimulated. An animal's having a certain standard of perceptual similarity—A's being more perceptually similar to B than it is to C for that animal—is thus a matter of that animal's having a second-order disposition. The animal is disposed to respond to conditioning of a first-order disposition. Upon being conditioned to respond in a certain way to stimulations receptually similar to B, but not to stimulations receptually similar to C, it is thereafter disposed to exhibit similar responses to stimulations receptually similar to A. Perceptual similarity standards are dispositions, albeit of this complex second-order sort. (A disposition to change one's similarity standards is thus a third-order disposition.) By Quine's account, a disposition is a physical state of the organism. Hence an animal's having a given standard of perceptual similarity is its being in a given physical state; the notion is a physicalistic one.

Standards of perceptual similarity are thus a physical matter, a matter of the micro-structure of the animal's brain and nervous system. But this is not to say that we can hope to characterize them in those terms. The possibility of doing that seems remote. Such, on Quine's account, is the case with the vast majority of behavioural dispositions. The best that we can hope for in such a case, pending almost unimaginable advances in neurophysiology, is a behaviouristic criterion for possession of the disposition. And this we have for perceptual similarity. As usual for dispositions, the characterization is not a definition. For one thing, we have only a sufficient condition for having certain standards of perceptual similarity. We know how we could, at least in principle, test for them, but clearly most go untested. For another, the tests are subject to an open-ended *ceteris paribus* clause (again, this is the case with most dispositions). Internal states of the subject may inhibit a response in a given case without showing that the subject generally lacks the relevant disposition. Quine appeals at this point to very general considerations which suggest that standards of perceptual similarity are fairly stable, and change only slowly, even if on particular occasions their manifestation is blocked (see *RR*, pp. 22f.) In any case, perceptual similarity is no worse in this respect than other dispositional notions.

One of the criteria that Quine gives for being an observation sentence is that assent to it is simply a response to current stimulation, in the sense that we have been discussing. Thus he speaks of "sentences that are directly and firmly associated with our stimulations", and goes on to say:

> Each should be associated affirmatively with some range of one's stimulations and negatively with some range. The sentence should command the subject's assent or dissent outright, on the occasion of a stimulation in the appropriate range, without further investigation and independently of what he may have been engaged in at the time.
>
> (*PT*, pp. 2–3)

If a sentence meets this criterion, then any individual's occasions of assent to it and dissent from it are directly conditioned to that individual's sensory stimulation at the time. (The relevant time can be fixed at some conveniently short interval, perhaps long enough to allow for movement. Quine speaks here of the *modulus* of stimulation; see *WO*, pp. 31–32.) What unifies the various stimulation patterns which all lead to the assent to a given sentence (by a given individual) is, of course, perceptual similarity of the various occasions (for that individual).[5] A competent speaker of the language will assent to a given observation sentence when undergoing one of a number of perceptually similar stimulation patterns, and not otherwise. The point is that nothing other than current stimulation is relevant to the speaker's assent or dissent. For most sentences, even most occasion sentences, other factors—memory, background beliefs—will play a role. Not so for observation sentences: "[t]heir distinctive trait is the sufficiency of present impingements." (*RR*, p. 40; as we shall see, Quine comes to modify this view.)

II Sharing our responses

The previous section was concerned simply with the idea of a single animal's responding to sensory stimulation. But language, as we have emphasized, is shared and public. If we are to understand any parts of language as a matter of responses to current stimulation then we need to find a way of extending the previous discussion to make sense of the idea of *shared* responses. There are considerable obstacles in the way of doing so.

On the face of it, the idea of our sharing a response to stimulation or neural intake is that you should respond in one way to certain stimulations, and that I should respond in the same way, to the same stimulations. But here the idea of *the same stimulations* or *same neural intake* is being used in a way that makes no clear sense. Each of us has his or her own sensory nerves, his or her own stimulations; yours are not mine. There might be an easy way out of this problem if we had reason to suppose that all people have exactly the same pattern of sensory nerve endings, i.e. that we have homologous nerve endings. If such a homology were established, we could speak of "the same nerve ending" from person to person, meaning the one occupying exactly the same place in the pattern. But there is no reason at all to expect the relevant uniformity. In *Word and Object*, Quine does not appreciate this difficulty; he simply assumes the notion of "the same stimulation" across persons. It did not take him long, however, to see the problem. In a 1965 essay he writes: "If we construe stimulation patterns my way, we cannot equate them without supposing homology of receptors; and this is absurd ... full homology is implausible" ("Propositional Objects", *OR*, p. 157). At that point, however, and for some years thereafter, Quine offers no clear solution to the problem.

The problem here is the basis of a suggestion, most famously made by Donald Davidson, that we ought not to think of observation sentences as linked to stimulation patterns at all, or to anything approximating sensory input. Instead of looking to nerve endings, the suggestion goes, we ought to look exclusively to the objective circumstances. Contrasting his own proposal with Quine's, Davidson says:

> The alternative theory of meaning and evidence is simply that the events and objects that determine the meaning of observation sentences and yield a theory of evidence are the very events and objects that the sentences are naturally and correctly interpreted as being about.
>
> ("Meaning, Truth and Evidence", p. 72)

To see the difference, consider a child who has come to be disposed to utter "Horse!" (or "Horsie!") in the presence of horses (or pictures of horses). On Quine's account, what matters is that the child has acquired a disposition to make an utterance within a certain range when it receives a stimulation pattern within a certain range; stimulation patterns within the range will be perceptually similar to one another. On Davidson's account, by contrast, the disposition which matters for the child's understanding is one that is activated by the actual horse itself (or the actual picture). The difference is sometimes phrased as that between the use of a *proximal* stimulus (one which is close to the child's brain—stimulations of its nerve endings), and a *distal* stimulus (one that is more distant from the child). Before considering Quine's solution to the underlying problem, we shall spend a page or so on his reason for rejecting Davidson's idea.

At first sight one might think that Quine would be torn between the distal and the proximal. Davidson's distal stimulus is the most obvious way of explaining the public nature of cognitive language, the fact that it is a social artefact consisting of *shared* responses. Offsetting this advantage is the fact that the proximal stimulus—firings of sensory nerves—gives an immediate connection with the child's nervous system. That looks like a natural choice if we emphasize the idea of giving a causal account of those responses, for it connects with brain physiology which is where, Quine holds, the real explanation of these matters is to be found. So, one might think, there is pressure in each direction: the public nature of language gives us reason to move the stimulus out, into the objective world; the desire for causal explanation gives us reason to move it in, to the subject's nerve endings (or even, some have suggested, further in than that, into the subject's brain). It is, one might think, just a question of which way the balance between these two factors ends up tipping, what compromise between them turns out to work best.

This way of thinking about the matter, however, is quite misleading. Davidson's proposal amounts to the idea that we should not think of cognitive language as a matter of shared responses to stimulation at all; rather that it is a matter of responses to facts, objects, events or situations in the objective world. Such an approach may make for a simpler account of cognitive language, but only at the price of changing the subject. It is the very nature of the account—not just its methods, but its goals, the questions that it can hope to answer—that is at issue. Davidson's proposal has the child learning a public, objective, language, but it does so by simply building in publicity and objectivity from the outset. Because it takes publicly available objects as the input for language-learning, the account cannot hope to explain how language comes to be shared, or how it comes to be about the shared objective world; those matters are simply assumed at the outset. Quine's question, as we have emphasized, is how cognitive language is possible at all, what it is for our language to make claims about the world, and how we can acquire a language of this kind. I am bombarded by physical forces; in response I make noises (among other things). What is it for some of those noises to be about the world? David-son's method cannot answer this question; it simply avoids it, prevents it from arising, by building in objective reference from the start, at the lowest level of language-acquisition.

Taking matters the other way around, we might offer Quine's rejection of Davidson's proposal as further evidence that the Quinean project is indeed to be understood along the lines that we have been following. Let us look again at a passage which we have already quoted in part. After mentioning Davidson's proposal, Quine says:

> But I remain unswerved in locating stimulation at the neural input, for my interest is epistemological, however naturalized. I am inter-ested in the flow of evidence from the triggering of the senses to the pronouncements of science; also in the rationale of reification and in the credentials of cognitive meaning. It is these epistemo-logical concerns, and not my incidental interest in linguistics, that motivate my speculations. Hence, indeed, my disregard of literary or poetic aspects of translation. And thus it is that the subject's reification of rabbits and the like is for me decidedly part of the plot, not to be passed over as part of the setting.
>
> (B&G, p. 3; cf. *PT*, p. 41)

It is essentially the same point as that which we saw Quine making in reply to Carnap's idea that we should take sentences about observable physical objects as epistemologically primitive. (See Chapter 4, first section, above.) From Quine's point of view, Davidson's idea evades the most important question, which is how language comes to be about the objective world at all.

Quine thus sticks to the idea that we should take the stimulus to be proximal, not distal: cognitive language is to be understood as a matter of shared responses to stimulation patterns, not to objects. How can he do so, given the difficulty that we indicated at the start of this section? The indi-vidual is still to be thought of as responding to stimulation patterns, not to items in the objective world. But we give up any attempt to define cross-person comparisons of stimulations, and instead appeal to our capacity to project ourselves into another's "perceptual situation". (Speaking of the learning of observation sentences, Quine says: "The parent ... [notes] the child's orientation and how the scene would look from there", B&G, p. 3.) How does this help? How are we to understand the sharing of responses, if they are responses to unshared stimulations? The crucial part of the answer is a way of making sense of the idea of shared standards of perceptual similarity. Quine's method for doing this is as follows. Suppose that in a given perceptual situation you undergo one stimulation pattern, A; in the same situation I undergo a stimulation pattern, A'. In another perceptual situation, you undergo B and I undergo B'. Now if A and B are perceptually similar for you, and A' and B' are perceptually similar for me, then to that extent you and I share standards of perceptual similarity.[6] Quine phrases the idea that we mostly share our standards of perceptual similarity like this: "In general, if external events ... produce neural intakes in both of us, and yours are perceptually similar for you, mine are apt to be perceptually similar for me." ("I, You, and It", O&K, p. 2.)

Given this sharing of standards of perceptual similarity, we can also make sense of the idea of shared responses to stimulation. Given a certain stimulus you manifest a certain response and, let us suppose, any similar stimulus would have induced you to manifest a similar response. The standards of similarity here are shared, so it may be that if I were given a similar stimulus pattern I would produce a similar response. (This similarity of responses will come to the fore in the next section.) In that case, we share our responses to stimulations of the given kind. Still, I respond to my stimulation patterns, not to objective features of the world; you respond to your stimulations. If we share our responses, however, then a perceptual situation which typically causes me to have a stimulation pattern which leads to a given response will also cause you to have a stimulation pattern which leads to that response. This is what it is for two distinct individuals to share their responses to stimulation. (We shall get a somewhat less abstract view of the matter when we discuss learning, in the next section.)

It is our sharing of standards of perceptual similarity which is crucial here. But why should those standards line up in the right way? Can we explain the fact that they do, or do we have to accept it as a massive coincidence? Quine's answer to this question is, briefly, that the sharing is explained by natural selection. There is, he says, "a pre-established *harmony* of standards of perceptual similarity, independent of intersubjective likeness of receptors or sensations" ("Progress on Two Fronts", p. 160; emphasis in the original). He explains the existence of such a harmony as a special case of a more general "preestablished harmony between perceptual similarity and the environment" (op. cit., pp. 160–61), which is in turn explained in terms of natural selection ('Darwin's solvent of metaphysics', as he terms it). We and other animals have "an inductive instinct: we tend to expect perceptually similar stimulations to have sequels that are similar to each other" (op. cit., p. 161). Correct inductions tend to favour survival, so humans tend to have standards of perceptual similarity which "harmonize with trends in the environment" (ibid.). Hence, derivatively, our standards of perceptual similarity tend to harmonize with those of others.

At the end of the previous section we saw the individualistic criterion for being an observation sentence. But sentences are part of a public shared language, so there is also an intersubjective or social criterion. It is essentially that assent to an observation sentence when queried (or dissent) is a *shared* response to stimulation, in the sense that we have been discussing. So the same perceptual situations which would give rise, in one speaker, to sensory stimulations that would lead him to accept an observation sentence would also give rise, in any other speaker of the same language, to sensory stimulations that would lead that speaker to accept the same observation sentence. As we emphasized, this requires that standards of similarity line up, both for one another's utterances (for the two utterances must count as utterances of *the same* observation sentence) and for other features of the situation.

The social criterion emphasizes the fact that members of the linguistic community must share a response to stimulation for that response to count as an observation sentence. It follows from this that observation sentences are all more or less trivial, by the standards of that community. In a given perceptual situation, any two members of the community will give the same verdict on a given observation sentence. (Thus they are never in dispute; hence they are suitable to play their role in the ultimate evidence for our theories; we shall qualify this idea in section V, below.) So assent to an observation sentence must be a response to something readily detectable by the senses, and must require only those discriminations which are shared. Thus "It's cold here!" might count; for English-speakers as a whole "That's Mozart!" would not, since not all of them will recognize Mozart's music on hearing it. Another point also follows. The notion is relative to that community. "That's red!" might count if we exclude the blind and the colour-blind, but not if we include them; "That's Mozart!" will count among the *cognoscenti*. Relative to small groups sentences may function as observation sentences which do not do so more generally. "Fido!" may function as an observation sentence within a given family with a dog of that name. Within a group of highly specialized experts in some technical or scientific field there may, again, be sentences which are observation sentences, relative to that group but not relative to the wider community. Finally, here, note that a sentence may acquire or lose the status of an observation sentence over the course of generations. "That's Mozart!" might perhaps become an observation sentence, with advances in musical education. There are presumably limits to this process, based on the limits to what can be readily detected by the senses, and on limits to human sensory acuity.

The points we have been making about observation sentences, here and at the end of the previous section, can be phrased in terms of Quine's technical notion of the *stimulus meaning* of a sentence.[7] We shall dwell on this matter a little, if only to explain the terminology and to dispel possible misunderstandings. The stimulus meaning of a sentence for a given speaker is a set of stimulation patterns; more precisely, it consists of two such sets, one positive and one negative. The positive stimulus meaning of a sentence for a speaker consists of all those stimulation patterns which would lead the speaker to change her verdict on the sentence to assent: if before receiving the stimulation pattern she would either dissent from the sentence or give no verdict, and after receiving the stimulations she would assent to it, then the given stimulation pattern is part of the positive stimulus meaning of the sentence for her. The negative stimulus meaning can be defined in the same way, but interchanging "assent" and "dissent". (As we have said, we need both because there will be stimulation patterns which belong to neither.) Now we can say: for a given speaker to understand an observation sentence, all that is required is that he or she have the appropriate stimulus meaning for it. This is another way of phrasing the individualistic criterion for being an observation sentence. The social criterion is more complicated, because of the problem of cross-person comparisons of stimulations. Roughly: suppose a given stimulation pattern is in my positive stimulus meaning of a sentence. Then there is a type or a range of perceptual situations that would standardly give rise to that pattern in me. If the sentence is to be an observation sentence, then a perceptual situation of that type or in that range would standardly give rise to a stimulation pattern in you which is in your positive stimulus meaning of the same sentence.

Stimulus meaning is not meaning. Using a sentence with the appropriate stimulus meaning is not, in general, sufficient for using it correctly. This point is clear in Quine's work, although missed by some commentators. To begin with, the idea of stimulus meaning has no interesting application at all to eternal sentences, whose stimulus meaning may be empty. (If I am sufficiently firmly convinced that milk is good for young children then no stimulation pattern within the relevant time period will lead to a change of verdict; hence its positive and its negative stimulus meaning for me will both be null. But that does not, of course, mean that the sentence is meaningless for me.) Other standing sentences, too, may have stimulus meanings that are vacuous or nearly so. Even for occasion sentences, stimulus meaning will not in general be close to what is required for an understanding.

Knowing the stimulus meaning with which I use the sentence "There's a phi-losopher" will, by itself, tell you almost nothing about what it is to be a philosopher—it will not enable you to understand the sentence. I could perhaps train a child to use the sentence with a stimulus meaning which lines up with the stimulus meaning with which I use it, by showing the child pictures of all those philosophers whom I recognize on sight. But the child would not thereby come to understand the sentence. My willingness to assert the sentence, after all, will change as I learn about people I meet for the first time; one's usage must be prone to change in these ways if one is to count as understanding the sentence, but the trick I might teach to a retentive child makes no provision for any such thing. In short, correct use of the sentence cannot be taught as I imagined teaching it to the child because it is answerable to evidence other than current stimulation patterns. Its meaning is far from its stimulus meaning. For an observation sentence, by contrast, all that is required for correct use is use in response to the appropriate stimulation patterns; its meaning is its stimulus meaning. (We shall qualify this a little in section IV, below.)

III Learning

Stimulus-and-response is a familiar behaviourist model of animal learning. The animal receives a sensory stimulus, makes a response, and receives a reward, i.e. a further stimulus which it finds pleasurable. A number of epi-sodes occur in which there is a similar stimulus, a similar response, and again a reward. These episodes inculcate the disposition to make a similar response when receiving a similar stimulus. Quine's model of learning is somewhat different. He considers the whole episode—the stimulus, the response, and the reward—as a single event. This event is presumably pleasant to the animal (unless the reward is outweighed by adventitious painful events), and after a number of such episodes the animal strives to re-create a further such episode, i.e. to make the new episode as similar as possible to earlier ones (similar, of course, by the animal's standards of per-ceptual similarity). Given one element, the stimulus, the animal thus acquires the disposition to add the response, so as to increase the similarity of this episode to those which were pleasant. "Learning, thus viewed, is a matter of learning to warp the trend of episodes, by intervention of one's own muscles, in such a way as to simulate a pleasant earlier episode. To learn is to learn to have fun". (RR, p. 28.)

In the description above, both Quine's model and the other appeal to the notion of pleasure. But Quine is not willing to rest content with this idea as part of an explanation of learning. Immediately after the sentences just quoted he says: "Behaviorally the shoe is on the other foot: an episode counts as pleasant if, through whatever unidentified mechanism of nerves and hormones, it implants a drive to reproduce it". (ibid.) So he does not appeal to the idea of pleasure for a fundamental explanation of why the animal acts as it does. This does not mean that it is wholly unexplanatory to say that a dog acts in a certain way because it enjoys eating a biscuit, say. Saying that much assimilates the present sequence of events to others in which the dog has also behaved in a way that resulted in its getting a biscuit; the present events are thus explained, to some extent, by being seen as an instance of a low-level generalization. If the dog's state of enjoyment were taken as explanatory, however, then explanation would stop there. Explanation in terms of a low-level generalization about behaviour, by contrast, suggests that this generalization is to be explained in turn, presumably by embedding it in a richer theory of the dog's "nerves and hormones". (Here again we have an illustration of the idea that a behavioural account of language, or here more modestly of animal learning, will not be fully explanatory; real explanations are to be sought at the physiological level.)

In the previous section our focus was on the coincidence of standards of perceptual similarity for sensory stimulations—for input, so to speak. In cases where learning depends in part on the response of others to the learner's performance, there must also be a coincidence of similarity standards for output. Some of the learner's responses to a given kind of stimulus will bring reward, others will not. For learning to take place the learner and the teacher must also group responses in similar ways.

In order to learn, therefore, an animal must have not only the appropriate similarity standards for input, for the episodes of stimulation of its sensory nerves, but also for output, for whatever nerves and muscles are involved in that. Quine's model of learning treats these together. It is total episodes— the stimulation of all nerves and the contraction of all muscles—which are related by relations of perceptual similarity. When we have a case of one animal learning from another animal, the combination of perceptual situations plus responses must be grouped in the same way by the standards of perceptual similarity of the one and by those of the other. This must hold whether the response is witnessed from the inside, as it were, by the one who makes it, or from the outside. Various episodes in which the command "Sit!" is uttered and the dog sits must be grouped together, as perceptually similar, both by the dog, who sits, and by the owner, who sees the sittings and rewards some of them.

130

A further complication arises when, as seems to be the case with human infants learning language, the learning proceeds partly by passive observation and partly by performance.[8] On some occasions, let us say, the child sees something red and hears the sound "Red"; on others it sees the red thing and makes (its version of) that sound. These episodes must be grouped by the child as perceptually similar, although the stimulation of the nerves involved in producing the sound will be present to the child in the one case and missing in the other. If the child's learning involves selective rewarding of utterances, the adult too must group events of hearing the child's utterance of "Red" together with her own production of the same sentence. The learning and teaching of language thus requires that the various parties involved should count all or almost all of the utterances of a given word or sentence as perceptually similar to one another. I am exposed to utterances of (say) "Red!" which vary greatly in tone, pitch, volume, accent, and so on. I must perceive most of those episodes as perceptually similar to one another, as well as to episodes in which I am the one who makes the utterance. There is, however, no reason that people should not have such standards of perceptual similarity, complex though they are. If possession of language gives advantage, moreover, one can easily imagine an evolutionary explanation of how people come to possess such standards.

We have already begun to talk specifically of the learning of language. Quine often assumes a simplified model of how such learning goes. In effect, he assumes the "babbling" model (see note 8). We shall see how things work out in that scenario, and then note other possibilities. In the simplified model, we are to assume that the infant emits a noise—whether as part of random babbling or by way of imitation of what it has heard its elders utter—which stimulates the auditory nerves of one or more of its elders. At the same time, more or less, the elder's sensory nerves are also stimulated in a way that would dispose her to utter a noise which she takes to be similar to that of the infant. (This does not mean that she actually utters that noise; one disposition may be inhibited by others on a given occasion, so that no behaviour results.) She rewards the child—that is, behaves towards him in a way that disposes him to re-create a similar situation, when the opportunity presents itself. If such rewards are to be distributed in a fashion conducive to learning, the adult must act not so much when her own sensory nerves are appropriately stimulated but rather when the child's are. So learning is dependent on the adult's empathetically projecting herself into the child's perceptual situation, responding to the way things look from his perspective. We are all skilled at doing this sort of thing; as Quine says: "We have an uncanny knack for empathizing another's perceptual situation, however ignorant of the physiological or optical mechanism of his perception". (B&G, p. 4.) Learning is dependent upon our being able to do this, as well as on our having standards of perceptual similarity which line up in the right ways, both for input and for output.

It is worth pausing to dwell on these points—on the complexity involved in even the simplest kind of learning, and on the role of empathy. To begin with, the learner must have standards of perceptual similarity according to which an extremely varied class of entities count as similar; all those neural events which count as his perceiving that it is raining, say:

> Each perception that it is raining is a fleeting neural event. Two perceptions by Tom that it is raining are apt to differ, moreover, not only in time of occurrence but neurally, because there are varied indicators of rain. Tom's perceptions of its raining constitute a class of events that is perhaps too complex and heterogeneous neurally to be practically describable in neurological terms even given full knowledge of the facts. Yet there is also, we may be sure, some neural trait that unites these neural events as a class; for it was by stimulus generalization, or subjective similarity, that Tom eventually learned to make the observation sentence "It's raining" do for all of them.
>
> (PT, p. 62)

In addition, someone from whom Tom is learning the sentence must have standards of perceptual similarity which unify an even more varied class of neural events: all those neural events in the teacher which are her perceptions that Tom is currently perceiving that it is raining. Tom's perceptions are neural events in his brain; the teacher's perceptions that Tom is perceiving that it is raining are neural events in her brain. Two occasions on which Tom's teacher observes that he is perceiving rain must be perceptually similar for his teacher. Her standards of perceptual similarity thus unite certain of *Tom's* neural events, even though the events in Tom's head are hidden, and for the most part unknown. What the teacher (and the rest of us) rely on is, as Quine says, "a symptom". He comments:

> And what a remarkable sort of symptom! We detect it by empathetic observation of the subject's facial expressions and what is happening in front of him, perhaps, and we specify it by a content clause consisting of a vicarious observation sentence.
>
> (PT, p. 62)

For Tom to learn the observation sentence "It's raining", according to this model, the neural states that he is in on the various occasions when he is in the vicinity of rain must (mostly) count as similar for him; the neural states that his teacher is in when she is in the vicinity of Tom, and he is in one of his rain-perceiving neural states, must (mostly) count as similar for her. All of this for the learning of an observation sentence, almost as simple as one could imagine. It is a matter of the learner and teacher each having appropriate standards of perceptual similarity. As we emphasized in section I above, these standards are higher-order dispositions and hence states of the nervous systems of those involved. So Quine takes this account to be physicalistic through and through, although it specifies states of the brains of those involved only indirectly, as dispositions.

So far we have been assuming the simplified model of language-learning which Quine takes as paradigmatic. This is not the only kind of situation in which the first stages of language-learning can occur. Children can also learn language in circumstances which are, on the face of it, far less favourable— where no effort is made to teach them, where they are not even addressed.[9] It seems to be enough that the child should witness a sufficient amount of talk about the immediate environment.[10] These facts may require modifications of Quine's simplified picture, but not, I think, of a sort that would affect his underlying point. We no longer have a child's utterance in perceptual circumstances which the adult can perceive to be appropriate (or not), and which is therefore rewarded (or not). Instead we have adult utterances, in perceptual circumstances which the child can perceive, for the child must perceive the parts or aspects of the environment to which the adult is responding. Of the adult and child one (at least) must perceive what the other is perceiving. As Quine puts it: "Ostensive learning is fundamental, and requires observability. The child and the parent must both see red when the child learns 'red', and one of them must also see that the other sees red at the time". (RR, pp. 37–38.) If the child learns by merely witnessing adult talk, he is not responding to adult encouragement as Pavlov's dogs responded to food. Something more complicated must be postulated, perhaps a disposition to mimic adults. Again, however, there is no reason to think that this will undermine what is really at stake for Quine in his discussion of language-learning. In what follows I shall speak in terms of Quine's paradigmatic situation, in spite of its over-simplification, when it is convenient to do so.

Let us suppose that our infant is on the way towards acquiring a disposition to make a certain noise when his sensory nerves are stimulated in a certain way. (More accurately: a disposition to make a noise within a certain range of noises, all similar both by his standards and by those of the adults around him, when receiving stimulations within a certain range, perceptually similar for the child.) It may take several occasions for the disposition to become firmly rooted, at least until the child has acquired second-order dispositions to learn. In which sorts of cases should we expect repeat occurrences to be forthcoming? The adult's part in the drama, whether producing the utterance or rewarding that of the child, must be keyed to events or objects which give rise, in the child, to global stimulations which are perceptually similar for the child.[11] This will not happen in the case of all sentences. The child, let us suppose, hears the utterance "That's ridiculous!" while seeing the adult reading the morning newspaper, and hears the same utterance—one that is perceptually similar by his standards—again in the evening while seeing the adult talking on the telephone. No learning is likely to take place, for there is no reason to think that the occasions will give rise to stimulations which are perceptually similar for the child. (If learning does take place, it is likely to be extinguished subsequently, when the adult responds unfavourably to what may seem to be comments about her reading of the newspaper.) An adult comment such as "It's raining!" uttered while visibly looking out of the window, by contrast, may well enable the child to catch on to the use of the same phrase; situations in which the adult perceives rain are diverse, but not as hopelessly diverse as situations in which she finds something to be ridiculous. The sentence "That's ridiculous!" is eventually learnt, of course, but not as a response to current stimulation. Its occasions are too heterogeneous for that, and too much depends upon the internal state of the speaker.

The child's "catching on" here may initially mean: acquiring a disposition to utter the sentence under appropriate stimulatory conditions. Soon enough, however, the child will find that his random utterances grow tiresome to those around him, and are discouraged. The readiness to utter is thus replaced, in Quine's scheme, with a readiness to assent upon hearing the utterance made, in appropriate conditions, by another. What does "assent" come to here? Presumably an utterance counts as assent if it is likely to bring reward as a response to "It's raining!" in those circumstances, in which that sentence might itself bring reward, but for the tiresomeness of childish babbling. An utterance will count as dissent if it is likely to have the opposite effect. Non-verbal reactions too will play a role here, perhaps even the crucial role, but they are likely to be diffuse and hard to pin down. For his schematic purposes Quine therefore focuses on assent and dissent. It would be a mistake, however, to think that he holds that non-verbal reactions have no role to play in meaning. In discussing the evidence available to the linguist in radical translation, he says:

The relevant evidence even goes beyond speech. It includes blush-
ing, stammering, and running away. It includes native customs and
rites, and indeed any observable behaviour that one can exploit in
trying to get a clue as to how to translate language. The method of
query and assent is necessary but not sufficient.

(B&G, p. 176)

A full account here, were such a thing possible, would presumably also
include the role of non-cognitive language. There is every reason to think that
the infant's grasp on "No" is solidified by his response to injunctions rather
than to assertions, and so on. Quine's concern, however, is simply to offer a
schematic account which would make it plausible that a full account, along
purely naturalistic lines, is possible; he goes into no further detail on the
matter.

IV Observation sentences

To this point our focus has chiefly been on learned shared responses to current stimulation. Quine often suggests that observation sentences, or acts of
assenting to them, are such responses. He says of observation sentences, for
example: "Their distinctive trait is the sufficiency of present impingements"
(RR, p. 40). More important, his account of the learning of observation
sentences presupposes that what is to be learned is simply a response to
current stimulation. As Quine comes to see, however, the situation is in fact
more complicated than that; observation sentences, in their ordinary use, are
not simply responses to current stimulation. One point here is that responses to stimulation are unstructured, whereas observation sentences contain
parts—words—which occur also in other sentences. Another point is that
observation sentences are corrigible, whereas a mere response to current stimulation cannot be corrigible, since there is no sense in which it can be
correct or incorrect—any more than a sneeze can be correct or incorrect. The
two points are connected; we shall begin by focusing on the second.

Are observation sentences incorrigible? If a competent speaker of the
language sincerely affirms such a sentence, is he or she bound to be correct?
In *Word and Object* Quine gives an affirmative answer, but then immediately
qualifies it: "the philosophical doctrine of infallibility of observation sentences is sustained under our version. ... (This immunity to error is, however, like observationality itself, for us a matter of degree.)" (WO, p. 44.)
Later, in *Roots of Reference*, he is more explicit in allowing for corrigibility:
"Our definition of observation sentence speaks only of concurrence of present
witnesses, and sets no bar to subsequent retractions". (RR, p. 41.) In two

late pieces of work Quine enlarges on the point, and puts forward a criterion of observationality according to which present impingements need suffice not for the *truth* of the sentence, but rather for immediate and unreflective *assent* to the sentence, even if the assent is subsequently retracted (see "In Praise of Observation Sentences", p. 108; "I, You, and It", p. 4). These are complex issues, which occupied Quine almost to the end of his life; I shall endeavour to sort them out.

Almost all candidates for being observation sentences are fallible and corrigible. To illustrate the point, take one of Quine's own examples, "Rabbit!", uttered as a one-word sentence. There are surely situations in which it looks for all the world as if rabbits are present, yet in fact there are no rabbits around. Call such a case a *deceptive situation* for the putative observation sentence in question, meaning a public situation in which any normal speaker of the language, lacking special knowledge, is likely to give the wrong verdict on the sentence. One can imagine a wholly convincing deceptive situation for "Rabbit!", either contrived or occurring naturally. In a situation of that type, observers—at least those who are not in on the illusion—will assent to "Rabbit?" when asked; each is undergoing a stimulation pattern in his or her positive stimulus meaning for the sentence. Yet they are wrong because there are in fact no rabbits around.

Thinking about corrigibility in this way shows that it is not merely a matter of subsequent retractions; the "concurrence of present witnesses" is also undermined. Suppose we are in a deceptive situation: it looks as if there are rabbits around but in fact there are none. Suppose further that you know that the situation is deceptive, whereas I do not. (You may even have contrived it to fool me.) In that case you and I will not concur. Since we have given different verdicts while receiving the same stimulations (in the convoluted sense of "same" that is relevant), the sentence does not satisfy the social criterion for being an observation sentence. The same sort of argument can be made for almost any sentence.[12] So almost no sentences in fact satisfy that criterion. A similar argument shows that the individualistic criterion is not satisfied, even by most sentences which might appear to satisfy it. Consider two situations in which I am receiving rabbit-like stimulations; my two global stimuli may even be identical in the two cases. In the one case I know that I am in a deceptive situation, in the other I do not. I presumably have the disposition to assent to "Rabbits?" in the one case but not in the other—I would give different verdicts on the queried sentence, even though I am receiving the same global stimulus in each.[13] For many sentences deceptive situations are extremely rare. But Quine's account of language proceeds in terms of dispositions: what I would do if I were to encounter a deceptive situation for "Rabbit!" matters even if I never have encountered and never will in fact encounter one.

Most of Quine's discussions of cognitive language, of how it functions and of how it might be learnt, proceed as if observation sentences were simply responses to stimulation. That view is untenable, as Quine came to see in the last years of his working life. How large a change in his general views does this fact require? Some change is certainly needed, but I think it is relatively modest.

Let us begin with the idea of degrees of observationality. We can understand this as a matter of how often deceptive situations for a given sentence in fact occur.[14] Almost always, when it seems as if there is a horse in the offing, there is. So "There's a horse" is a highly observational sentence. Contrast "It's flimsy" (see *Roots of Reference*, p. 42). Some flimsy things just *look* flimsy, and one might initially use the sentence as if there were no more to being flimsy than looking flimsy. But it is not uncommon to find flimsy things that look sturdy, and sturdy things that look flimsy. So the sentence has a lower degree of observationality. On the spectrum of observationality, one end point would be sentences for which there are no deceptive situations at all (if there are any). It is not important, however, that there be *absolutely* observational sentences; what is required is that there be sentences which are very highly observational, and surely there are. (In some contexts I shall speak of observation sentences, without qualification, instead of speaking of very highly observational sentences.)

The degree of observationality of a sentence, understood in this way, is closely connected with the way it can be learnt. Highly observational sentences can be learnt along the lines set out in the previous section, more or less. (Not all sentences that *can* be learnt in this fashion will be. I shall sometimes speak of a sentence's being learnt *as* an observation sentence to mean that it is learnt in this fashion.) Corrigibility shows that acquiring a disposition to assent to a sentence under appropriate stimulatory conditions does not amount to full mastery of the sentence. But for highly observational sentences it will come very close. An infant who acquires such a disposition will not yet be able to use the sentence in the way that an adult can under all circumstances; he will not, in particular, respond appropriately in situations which the adult can tell are deceptive. But since the sentence is highly observational, such situations will be extremely rare. So the infant's use will in fact be very close to that of the adult; the infant has gone a long way towards learning the correct use of the sentence.

What is crucial here is the idea of *partially* learning the use of a sentence. The more highly observational the sentence is, the closer this partial learning will come to full mastery. The account of how responses to current stimulations might be learnt from others is not yet an account of how any sentence might be completely learnt. But it is an account of how the infant might go a long way towards learning the correct use of some sentences, the highly observational ones. It is entirely plausible that all of our first steps into language are matters of partial or defective learning, and that once we have learnt more our earlier usage is refined and corrected until it amounts to complete adult mastery of the sentence.

Utterances of highly observational sentences are very close to being responses to current stimulation. What distinguishes them from such responses? What more than a mere response to stimulation must the infant learn, in order to be able to use such a sentence as we do? This issue turns out to be very closely connected with what makes such sentences corrigible and, indeed, with what makes it clear that they have truth-values at all. The crucial point here is that observation sentences, in their adult use, are integrated with the rest of our theory. This is a matter of how we treat observation sentences: when we are disposed to assent to certain combinations of observation sentences we are also disposed to modify our theory as a whole. (We shall discuss this in a little more detail in Chapter 7.)

This way in which utterances of observation sentences differ from responses to stimulation is closely connected with another issue, mentioned at the start of the section. Observation sentences, unlike mere responses to stimulation, are made up of significant parts. This is also a matter of the connection of observation sentences with the rest of theory; the parts are significant because we recognize them as occurring also in other sentences. What does such "recognition" amount to? It is, at least in part, a matter of our recognizing incompatibilities, such as incompatibility of the non-observation sentence "There are no horses in this region" with the observation sentence "Horses!" And that recognition, in turn, is a matter of our being disposed to revise our theory when we are disposed to accept or reject certain observation sentences.

Observation sentences are thus integrated with the rest of our theory because we tend to revise our theories—to reject some sentences, to accept others instead—in response to our acceptances of observation sentences. But the integration works both ways. Occasionally we will revise our observation sentences in response to theory; occasionally, that is to say, we will withdraw an observation sentence if accepting it would entail unacceptable theoretical adjustments. (As Quine says: "The tail thus comes, in an extremity, to wag the dog". (WO, p. 19.)) The two tendencies are inseparable. If theories are responsive to observation sentences, then we cannot rule out ahead of time the possibility of there being circumstances under which an incompatibility is settled in favour of the theory. So the corrigibility of observation sentences is not adventitious; it is a by-product of their being integrated with theory.

These same features of observation sentences lie behind our taking them to have truth-values and to be, in their minimal way, objective claims about the world. It is hard to see how a mere response to stimulation could be an objective claim. But once we introduce the idea that the response is corrigible, and may have to be retracted, the matter is quite different. Objective claims are those that you may turn out to be mistaken about—claims that later events, or the subsequent pressure of public opinion, may lead you to revise. In "The Scope and Language of Science", Quine raises the question of why we take our language to be about a world independent of it, and of us. Part of his answer is that learning is intersubjective, so others tend to echo and applaud our earliest assertions. "The real", he says, "is the stuff that mother vouches for and calls by name" (SLS, WP, p. 232). To make the present point we might add that the real is also the stuff about which mother, and others in general, may correct you, and about which you may therefore be mistaken. It is a hard lesson to learn: your saying it does not make it so. The integration with theory which explains the corrigibility of observation sentences is thus also intrinsically connected with their having truth-values, their taking part in relations of implication, and so on. It is only in virtue of these characteristics that they count as even the first steps of cognitive language.

This discussion indicates what an infant must do in order to catch on to the full adult use of observation sentences. Having first, perhaps, begun using the sentence (or assenting to it) merely as a response to current stimulation, he must acquire the disposition to change his verdict on it in the light of new evidence. This will involve his treating it not as an unstructured whole but rather as made up of significant parts. Both steps occur when the child comes to assent to the observation sentence not only on the basis of current stimulation but also on the basis of broader theory. To begin with, this will be a more modest and low-level matter than it may sound. We might imagine that the adult says things along the lines of: "It looks like a rabbit but it is not really one" while the illusion is made clear. In that way, perhaps, the child might catch on to the use of the idiom "looks like ... but is not really", and the contrast implicit in it. Clearly, however, much more work would be needed for a full account. (Quine himself says very little that is relevant to this point; see, however, FSS, pp. 36–38, for some relevant discussion.)

I have argued that no sentences completely fulfil the criteria for being observation sentences. Some sentences are highly observational; they will come close, and will be more or less learnable as responses to stimulation. But they are integrated into wider theory; hence they have truth-values and are corrigible. Quine's account of the learning of observation sentences is for the most part an account of the learning of responses to current stimulation, so the gap between such responses and even highly observational sentences leaves a gap in his account of the learning of cognitive language. But it is a gap that can be filled along more or less Quinean lines. The upshot of these considerations is to complicate Quine's account of observation sentences but not, I think, to undermine it. We can continue to think of highly observational sentences as playing something very much like the role that Quine marks out for his observation sentences.

V The Janus-faced character of observation sentences: evidence, reference

The previous section indicates that there is a gap between an observation sentence in the mouth of the infant who is first learning language and the same sentence in the mouth of the fully competent speaker of the language. For the infant, utterance of an observation sentence, or of a verdict on the queried sentence, is a mere response to stimulation. In almost all situations the adult will give the same responses to her stimulation. (Otherwise the sentence concerned would not be an observation sentence; it would not, that is to say, be highly observational in the sense indicated in the previous section.) But for the adult the sentence is integrated with the rest of her knowledge; this implies that uttering or assenting to it is not merely a response to stimulation. She has acquired a much more complicated disposition than has the infant, one which leaves her able to take account of deceptive situations, should they occur. This description of the situation also indicates what the child has to acquire in order to achieve adult mastery of the sentence. He must begin to acquire the wider theory into which the observation sentence is integrated, and that theory must come to influence his verdict on the observation sentence under some circumstances. (The circumstances may never in fact obtain; language mastery is a matter of dispositions.)

An observation sentence in the mouth of the neophyte and the same sentence in the mouth of an adult thus differ: the latter is associated with a more complex disposition. This fact helps to explain Quine's claim that observation sentences have two aspects or are, as he also says, "Janus-faced". (See "In Praise of Observation Sentences", pp. 109ff.; and PT, pp. 6–8.) This claim occurs in the context of a discussion of the role of observation sentences as the ultimate evidence for theory. He considers the view advanced by some philosophers of science that there is no notion of observation which can serve as an independent notion of evidence for theory. (He mentions N. R. Hanson and Paul Feyerabend in this regard.) Their claim is that observation is inevitably affected by theory, that supposedly neutral observations more or less covertly draw on concepts which are part of the theory of the observers. Quine responds to this idea.

Why might it be thought that observation sentences are, as Quine says, "theory-laden"? Suppose "There's Water!" is an observation sentence. "Water" is a word which occurs elsewhere in our theory of the world, in the sentence "Water is H_2O", for example. So, one might think, the word "water" is, in its modest way, a theoretical term. But in that case, the fact that the observation sentence uses this term might be taken to show that the sentence has theoretical commitments, that it already presupposes and draws upon our theory. So then it would seem that the sentence is not neutral—"theory-free"—evidence for theory.

Quine's reply is that in one sense this is correct and in another it is not. The ambiguity arises from two ways of considering observation sentences. Considered as unanalyzed wholes (holophrastically, Quine says), they are simply responses to stimulation; considered as made up of parts (piecemeal, or analytically), however, they connect with sophisticated theory, for the words which make up the observation sentence recur in more theoretical contexts. Speaking of "primitive" observation sentences, those which are "the entering wedge in language learning", Quine says:

> They are associated as wholes to appropriate ranges of stimulation, by conditioning. Component words are there merely as component syllables, theory-free. But these words recur in theoretical contexts in the fullness of time. It is precisely this sharing of words, by observation sentences and theoretical sentences, that provides logical connections between the two kinds of sentences and makes observations relevant to scientific theory. Retrospectively those once innocent observation sentences are theory-laden indeed. An observation sentence containing no more theoretical a word than "water" will join forces with theoretical sentences containing terms as technical as "H_2O". Seen holophrastically, as conditioned to stimulatory situations, the sentence is theory-free; seen analytically, word-by-word, it is theory-laden.
>
> (*PT*, p. 7)

We ought, I think, to be puzzled by this talk of observation sentences as being theory-free when seen one way, and theory-laden when seen another. What about the observation sentence itself, independent of how it is "seen", we might ask; is that theory-laden or not? The discussion of the previous section dissolves the puzzle. Our focus should be on various uses of the sentence, not on the sentence itself. As used by the infant, otherwise quite innocent of language, assent to the observation sentence (or dissent) is a mere response to stimulation; as such it is an unstructured whole, and theory-free. (This, I suspect, is why Quine speaks of "primitive" observation sentences, "the entering wedge in language learning"; he is thinking of an observation sentence in the mouth of the neophyte.) As used by the adult, however, it contains significant parts, and is integrated into the rest of language, and so not theory-free. This dissolution of the puzzle, however, may seem to undermine the idea that observation sentences are in any real sense theory-free. The infant we are envisaging has, after all, only a partial mastery of the use of the sentence. He may make the same noise as the adult (or a noise within the same range) but he will not be disposed to accept it or reject it under precisely the same circumstances. (As used by the infant it is, we might say, a *proto-observation sentence*.) The sentence as it is used by a competent speaker of the language is *not* theory-free. We may initially accept an observation sentence, and then change our minds in the light of new evidence. In doing so we draw on theory beyond the single observation sentence itself. So the theory that we hold will, after all, affect the observation sentences that we end up affirming. Quine, in late writing, comes to accept this point. After mentioning the corrigibility of observation sentences he says: "It is the infection of observation by theory; the anti-epistemologists [Hanson, Feyerabend] have a point here". ("In Praise of Observation Sentences", p. 109; cf. "I, You and It", p. 5.)

Quine, in his late work, comes to accept that observation sentences are corrigible; hence they are not mere responses to stimulation; hence they are "theory-laden". How large is this concession? It is, I think, very limited. In the previous section I argued that Quine's view of how observation sentences are learnt requires modification but not outright rejection. They cannot be learnt simply in the way that responses to stimulation are, but the learning of such responses provides a good start on the learning of a highly observational sentence. Sentences of that sort have a use that is very close to the use that they would have if they were indeed mere responses to current stimulation. So mastery of the appropriate response can give the learner a start on learning the language; once that learning has progressed a little way he will be able to use the observation sentence as more than a mere response to stimulation. The crucial point here is that the highly observational sentences are those about which we in fact almost never change our minds. (A sentence could lose this status, but then it was built into our account from the outset that which sentences count as observational can change over time.) The same point also shows that the theory-dependence of such sentences is minimal, and will make little or no difference in practice. Those sentences which are highly observational at a given time will be those about which the rest of our theory almost never leads us to change our minds. This is simply a matter of how we have defined degrees of observationality. In principle there is more to our willingness to accept or reject such a sentence than the occurrence of the relevant sensory stimulations—but in fact the stimulations almost always determine the verdict. So Quine's position is largely vindicated: highly observational sentences can, for all practical purposes, be taken as neutral between rival theories.

We have elaborated on the distinction between observation sentences seen analytically and observation sentences seen holophrastically (or between genuine observation sentences with their full use and the infant's proto-observation sentences). As we have seen, this distinction has to do with corrigibility and with neutrality as between theories. It also connects with other issues: in particular, with grammar, which will occupy us very briefly, and with reference, which we shall dwell on for most of the rest of this section.

Seen analytically, i.e. as used by an adult, an observation sentence is made up of significant parts. (The significance of the parts derives from the fact that they occur also in other sentences.) These parts presumably are systematically arranged. Grammar gets its foothold here; observation sentences in their adult usage are made up of nouns, verbs, articles, adjectives, prepositions, and so on. Seen holophrastically, i.e. as used by the neophyte, by contrast, there is no role for such grammatical categories. We cannot build them into our account of what the language-user is exposed to. The infant is exposed to the speech of competent users, but we must not assume that this speech comes ready-segmented, and that the segments somehow come labelled "noun", "noun phrase", "verb", and so on. The speech to which the learner is exposed affects him by stimulating his auditory nerves, and distinctions within that speech can be supposed to affect him only to the extent that they are manifest in such stimulations. (This is just a special case of the general point that the environment to which the learner is exposed affects him only to the extent that it results in stimulations of his sensory nerves.) Words are, of course, repeatable items in the flow of noise, but they are not the only such items: there is something in common to the expressions "I can do it!" and "canned goods", but what is in common is not a word. It is, rather, what the linguists call a *phoneme*. We may perhaps suppose that the infant begins the learning of language with standards of perceptual similarity which group noises into phonemes. (There is a fairly involved story to be told about what goes into such grouping, and how it might occur; see section 18 of *Word and Object*, "Phonetic Norms".) But this is a long way from attributing to the child the capacity to group sounds into *words*, and further still from its grouping noun-sounds together. Any such groupings must be imposed by the language-learner, by his standards of perceptual similarity, whether innate or acquired; we cannot build them into the data which he is given.[15]

Reference is another issue to which the distinction between Quine's two aspects of observation sentences is relevant. Quine often speaks of observation sentences as being "about ordinary things" (*WO*, p. 44), as opposed to being about sense data or other extraordinary entities. This makes it seem as if observation sentences, or most of them, refer to objects. (Some, such as "It's raining", are not referential on any account.) But Quine denies that any observation sentences are referential: the major theme of *Roots of Reference* is the question how the child who has already acquired some observation sentences comes to acquire the capacity to refer to objects. And the same point is made elsewhere: in *Pursuit of Truth*, for example, Quine accounts it an advantage of beginning with observation sentences that "the nature and utility of reification could be deferred" (p. 23). But this presupposes that acquiring observation sentences is not yet acquiring the capacity to refer, hence that observation sentences are not referential, not *about* anything. The appearance of conflict here is neatly resolved by Quine's distinction. What the infant first acquires, proto-observation sentences as I have called them, are not referential; the adult versions of the same sentences, however, are.

The controversial half of this claim is the first, that observation sentences as initially acquired (proto-observation sentences) are not referential. Quine views such sentences as non-referential because he sees them as most directly linked to current neural intake, not to objects (unlike Davidson; see second section, above). The learner's receiving neural intake within a given range of perceptual similarity may well go along with his being in the presence of some familiar object (another member of the household, a favourite toy, the family dog). But Quine sees the sentence as being linked to the neural intake, not to the object; hence his view that observation sentences, as initially learned, are *not* referring expressions. But the contrast between the neural intake and the object might be doubted. The child's utterances of "Fido" (say) are, in some sense, linked to his neural intake; yet in fact the child initially acquires the disposition to utter or assent to "Fido" when it is in the presence of the dog (for in fact there will be no deceptive situations in such a case). So why deny that the utterances, even seen holophrastically, are linked also to the dog? And why not say that they refer to the dog? It is no answer to say that the child's utterance is a *sentence*, to be assessed as correct or incorrect, true or false, whereas a referring expression is assessed as succeeding in referring, or failing to refer, to an object. The idea that we should construe the infant's earliest utterances in this way, as sentences rather than names, is surely one of the points in need of justification, not something to be assumed at the outset.

There are, moreover, experiments which suggest that even very young infants, well before the stage of beginning to acquire language, see the world as in some sense made up of distinct objects. An infant is seated in front of a screen. If three objects are moved towards the screen from one side and then emerge from the other the infant shows little reaction; if three objects are moved towards the screen from one side and then only two emerge from the other side the infant reacts more strongly, in ways that have been taken to indicate surprise.[16] If pre-linguistic infants see the world as made up of objects then, one might think, there is no reason to deny that they draw on this capacity in their first steps into language, and hence no reason to deny that their earliest utterances refer to the objects around them.

In his late work Quine has reacted to this sort of case, conceding part of the critic's point, but still maintaining what is essential to his own contrary position. He distinguishes between full reification and what he calls "perceptual reification". Experiments may show that the latter is innate. This does not, however, imply that the infant is innately capable of full reification which, in Quine's view, involves the ability to make sense of identity over time, and of the difference between its being the same object again and a distinct but very similar object. As before, we have no reason to think that pre-linguistic infants can make sense of such things. How they come to be able to do so is to be studied. Let us see how Quine puts the matter:

> As Donald Campbell puts it, reification of bodies is innate in man and the other higher animals. I agree, subject to a qualifying adjective: *perceptual* reification. ... I reserve *"full* reification" and *"full* reference" for the sophisticated stage where the identity of a body from one time to another can be queried and affirmed or denied independently of exact resemblance. Such identifications depend on our elaborate theory of space, time, and unobserved trajectories of bodies between observations. Prior cognition of a recurrent body—a ball, or Mama, or Fido—is on a par with our recognition of any qualitative recurrence: warmth, thunder, a cool

breeze. So long as no sense is made of the distinction between its being the same ball and its being another like it, the reification of the ball is perceptual rather than full. A dog's recognition of a particular person is still only perceptual, insofar as it depends on smell.

(L&S, p. 350; emphases in the original)

Quine is willing to ascribe perceptual reification to the infant, but not full reification. He also accepts that perceptual reification comes naturally to us; this is a point worth elaboration.

Many of our early observation sentences are utterances which, in adult usage, are terms referring to what Quine calls *bodies*. A body "typically contrasts with its visual surroundings in color and in movement or parallax, and, typically, it is fairly chunky and compact. ... If we make contact, it resists pressure". (FSS, p. 24.)[17] The fact that children so readily learn observation sentences such as "Mama", or "Dadda", or "Fido", indicates innate standards of perceptual similarity which are, so to speak, ready-made for bodies with all their vagaries:

The similarity basis of "Mama" was rather a long story. Each view of her is a continuous patch? Not quite; there was the little matter of eclipse and parallax. Each view of her is similarly shaped? No indeed, but there is the continuity of deformation. This rather tortuous sort of similarity is the unifying principle not only of Mama but of Fido and indeed of bodies generally. For all its tortuousness, it is apparently a sort of similarity that we are innately predisposed to appreciate.

(RR, p. 54)

It is unsurprising that the child finds one presentation of red to be perceptually similar to another. It is, perhaps, more surprising that the child finds one presentation of its mother similar to another, what with her varying garbs, and her varying shapes as she changes posture or is seen from different angles. Nevertheless, the child's standards of perceptual similarity do allow him readily to catch on to words for bodies. We are, Quine says in a memorable turn of phrase, "body-minded animals"; he explains this fact "by natural selection; for body-mindedness has evident survival value in town and jungle" (RR, p. 54).

Infants thus seem to come equipped with standards of perceptual similarity adapted for bodies. These are quite complex dispositions, but Quine has no methodological qualms about attributing them to the child. The justification for doing so is that children are quick to learn such observation

146

sentences as "Mama". They also quickly learn general terms for bodies: not just "Fido" but also "dog". This learning relies upon a second-order similarity, a similarity of similarities. The learner "has to appreciate a second-order similarity between the similarity basis of 'Fido' and the similarity bases determining other enduring dogs" (*RR*, p. 56). In virtue of these predispositions, the child is engaged in perceptual reification almost from the outset. But this is not yet full reification. Perceptual reification is a matter of mere reactions to stimulations. Our original question, why Quine does not construe observation sentences as referential, is thus also the question of what separates the two kinds of reification.

The answer, as indicated in the above passage, is that full reification requires certain abilities, which go beyond anything that we have reason to attribute to the infant. Full reification, as Quine sees it, involves being able to re-identify an object across time, to make sense of its being the same object over again as opposed to a different but very similar object. A fully competent speaker of the language cannot always *answer* this question, but she can at least make sense of it. This ability requires, or goes along with, "our whole schematism of space and time and the unobserved trajectories of bodies within it" (*FSS*, p. 36). The infant's initial use of observation sentences gives us no justification to attribute to him that complicated theory. The requirements for full reification are also the requirements for reference. In talking about proto-observation sentences we are talking merely about the infant's ability to respond to neural intake (grouped, admittedly, in very complex ways). That ability suffices for proto-observation sentences, but not for reference. (We shall enlarge on these matters in the next chapter.)

On Quine's account, the relation between a referring expression and the object or objects to which it refers is not fundamental but derivative. Rather than simply assuming reference, Quine's project is directed at explaining it—explaining what it is for a term to refer, and how it comes about that we are capable of using terms in that way. On his account, reference presupposes the infant's ability to respond to stimulation—that is, to use the relevant observation sentence—but it also presupposes further abilities. What those abilities are, and how they might be acquired, are, to repeat, a large part of Quine's concern with the learning of language. For this reason he does not, as Davidson does, build the notion of reference into the fundamental account of language. On the contrary: "the subject's reification of rabbits and the like is for me decidedly part of the plot, not to be passed over as part of the setting". (B&G, p. 3; quoted in context p. 125, above.)

All the differences we have looked at between the two aspects of observation sentences have to do with the difference between an infant taking his first steps into language and a speaker who has a whole range of sophisticated linguistic capacities. The former has mastered only some responses to stimulation, proto-observation sentences. For the latter, by contrast, observation sentences are connected to theory as a whole in various ways; corrigibility, reference, and the role of observation sentences as evidence for theory all arise out of these connections. What makes the difference is whether we consider the sentence in isolation or as part of a wider theory. This dual aspect is essential to the function of observation sentences as the starting point of language and conceptualization. The learning of proto-observation sentences does not presuppose any prior conceptual or theoretical resources; they are the first steps into language. But because they can subsequently be broken down into terms that recur in higher theory, such learning is a start on learning the language as a whole, for it is this sharing of vocabulary which unites the observation sentences with the rest of the language.

Putting matters this way poses what I think is the right question for Quine: how do we—or how might we—get from a mastery of observation sentences taken in isolation to a mastery of the theory of which they are a part? An answer to this question is the natural next step in his acquisition story. The extent to which he offers an answer is mixed. To the specific issue of the corrigibility of observation sentences—how we come to be able to correct our own and others' utterances in the light of later evidence—he has almost nothing to say. At the end of section IV, above, I very briefly indicated how a Quinean account of such matters might hope to proceed. On the general issue of the links between observation sentences and theory as a whole—how the former get to act as evidence for the latter—Quine gives an account in terms of observation categoricals (which we shall discuss in the next chapter). On the question how observation categoricals might be acquired he again has almost nothing to say. He does discuss how other sentences might be accepted or rejected on the basis of observation categoricals, though the discussion is at a very general and schematic level. The issue of reference is the one that occupies most of Quine's attention: how we can get from observation sentences to a mastery of language that is clearly *about* particular entities. Quine's question is how our output—the noises that we make in response to stimulation—can be or develop into language which is about the world. This issue will occupy much of our attention in the next chapter.

6

BEYOND THE OBSERVATION
SENTENCES

Let us remind ourselves where we are. The central question of Quine's naturalized epistemology is:

> how we, physical denizens of the physical world, can have projected our scientific theory of that whole world from our meager contacts with it: from mere impacts of rays and particles on our surfaces and a few odds and ends such as the strain of walking uphill.
>
> (*FSS*, p. 16)

We are physical objects; we are subject to physical forces which give rise to stimulations of our sensory nerves (input) and we emit sounds, or marks, or gestures (output). Quine's project is to explain what it is for these emissions to be about the world, and to explain how we might come to be capable of emitting sounds (or gestures, etc.) that have this character. Very generally and abstractly, his view is that our output is about the world, and thus constitutes cognitive discourse, because of its relation to input. This is the basis of cognitive language. The relation of sensory input to linguistic output is also, on Quine's view of these matters, the relation of theory to evidence. By illuminating this relation, his project will thus, he claims, fulfil some of the aims of more traditional epistemology: "the evidential relation is virtually enacted, it would seem, in the learning" of "theoretical language" (*NNK*, pp. 74–75).

In the previous chapter, we were concerned with the very beginnings of cognitive language—responses to stimulation and, in particular, observation sentences. Relative to our basic picture of the physical object subject to physical forces, observation sentences are already a large and crucial step. Quine's discussion of them is intended to explain, in physicalistic terms, how we might come to be users of at least rudimentary cognitive language; in doing so, it is also to explain how that level of cognitive language, at least, might be answerable to sensory stimulations. Relative to the richness

149

and complexity of our cognitive language as a whole, however, observation sentences may seem to be barely a beginning. They are trivialities, banal comments on what is evident about the current scene. How does our knowledge extend beyond them? How, on the basis of a mastery of observation sentences, might we learn the language in which more sophisticated knowledge is embodied? And how does that knowledge relate to observation sentences, and thus to sensory stimulations, as it must if it is indeed to count as knowledge? How do we acquire our theory of the world? How, in particular, do we come to be able to refer to the enduring objects which make up the world? Our subject in this chapter is Quine's response to questions of this sort.

Observation sentences are not typical of language as a whole. They can be learned as responses to stimulation, as unstructured wholes. Two more specific points are also important. First, the dispositions which must be acquired in order to learn a given observation sentence are relatively straightforward; those associated with other sentences are more complex, in many cases unmanageably so. Second, the number of sentences that a child learns as observation sentences will be quite small. That sort of learning proceeds sentence-by-sentence. For sentences in general this is clearly the wrong picture; here the focus is on the learning of constructions, modes of forming sentences. The first section is primarily concerned to explore these two differences, and some of their ramifications. In particular, we shall see that Quine's ("virtual") identification of the evidential relation with the relation of input to output which is involved in learning looks much less straightforward when we are considering language beyond the observational level. For this reason, we discuss the evidential relation in the next chapter; this one is concerned only with learning. The second section will discuss various ways in which, Quine speculates, some aspects of our more advanced language might be acquired on the basis of observational language. Our focus here is on the general direction of Quine's speculations and on their point, not on details and technicalities. Of particular importance here is the fact that observation sentences as they are first learned—proto-observation sentences, we called them—are without semantically significant structure. Acquiring more advanced language, as we shall see, involves combining parts of observation sentences to form new sentences—in this sense, it requires us to see observation sentences not as unstructured wholes but as made up of semantically significant parts.

The third and fourth sections of the chapter are focused on the learning of referential language. One way of asking Quine's fundamental question about cognitive language is to say: how do these noises come to be *about* anything?

How do they come to refer to things? Our language is full of words and phrases which pick out particular objects or objects of a particular kind, or so we assume. "Quine", "the first person to run a four-minute mile", "golden retrievers", "words"—there is no end to the expressions which refer to objects in the world, or appear to. But how does this jibe with the input–output picture? What is it for some of the noises in the output to refer, to be about particular objects? And how do we come to emit noises with this character? In discussing these matters, Quine's emphasis is chiefly on learning. He is concerned to show how something recognizable as reference could arise, given the basic input–output picture. If we accept that an account of the mastery of observation sentences can be fitted onto that picture, then the question is how an infant equipped only with observation sentences might acquire the ability to refer, to take part in discourse about objects. This question has occupied a good deal of Quine's attention, and will accordingly occupy a good deal of ours. Again, however, we shall focus on the general point of Quine's discussion, and neglect many of the details.

I Extending the project: learning, evidence, and holism

Observation sentences are different from sentences in general in ways that make a difference to Quine's project and to its significance. In particular, as we have noted, sentences in general differ from observation sentences both in complexity and in number; we shall enlarge on these two points and their implications in the rest of this section.

First, an observation sentence is associated with relatively straightforward and specifiable dispositions: the disposition to assent to it under one range of perceptually similar stimulation patterns and to dissent under another. So mastery of such a sentence consists, more or less, in having those dispositions.[1] For sentences in general, by contrast, there is nothing analogous. The question is: what can the adult do with a given sentence which the pre-linguistic infant cannot? What dispositions does the infant have to acquire to learn that sentence? When a theoretically embedded sentence is in question, the answer may be unmanageably complex, because it will involve reference to other sentences which must be learnt, and they in turn to yet others, and so on. Quine's concern is still with dispositions to assent to sentences under appropriate conditions (and to dissent from them; as before, I shall sometimes speak only of assent). But now the conception of "appropriate conditions" is vastly more complex. The adult understands all sorts of other sentences, which, if accepted, may make a difference to her willingness to accept the given sentence. The "appropriate conditions" for assenting to a given sentence may now consist, partly or wholly, in one's having come to accept *other* sentences. Acceptance of a given observation sentence may be reason to accept a certain theoretical sentence *if* you already accept certain other sentences, but not if you do not, and so on. This undermines the idea that we can sensibly talk about the disposition to assent to a single sentence, taken in isolation from others.

The point here is holism: considered in isolation, the given sentence may not be linked to observation sentences at all; it may have such links only when we take it together with other sentences which are already accepted. For many sentences, even relatively close to the observational level, observations bear on them in loose, open-ended, and multifarious ways. By the same token, there is a looseness in the dispositions to assent and dissent which the competent speaker has acquired with regard to that sentence. If we cannot even specify the dispositions associated with a given sentence, we can hardly hope to say, except in the most general way, how those dispositions might be acquired.

The relation between holism and the learning of language goes both ways. Holism constrains the kind of account that Quine can give of the learning of language. But it is also true that he needs to give an account which shows how holism could arise—how a holistic language could be learnt. The looseness in the way in which observation bears on some of the sentences of a holistic language will be matched by a kind of looseness in the way that the language is learnt. Thus Quine says that the learner's progress in acquiring language "is not a continuous derivation, which, if followed backwards, would enable us to reduce scientific theory to sheer observation. It is a progress by short leaps of analogy". (NNK, pp. 78–79.) On the one hand, the leaps must be short enough for it to be plausible that the learner would be able to make them. On the other hand, they must indeed be leaps—if the language being learnt is a holistic one, there must be gaps, so to speak, where what the speaker already knows only partially determines appropriate assent and dissent. These gaps are to be filled later, as the learner assimilates more of our theory as a whole; they are to be filled in holistic fashion. Subsequent sections of this chapter will expand on this account.

Our second point at the start of this section was that observation sentences are limited in number. More precisely: the number of sentences that any given speaker acquires *as* observation sentences, more or less by direct conditioning to stimulation, is quite small. That kind of learning proceeds piecemeal, sentence-by-sentence. Sentences in general, by contrast, cannot be learned one-by-one: there are too many of them. What the infant acquires, as he matures, is not simply the ability to respond appropriately to sentences from some fixed stock. As has been widely emphasized, a competent adult has the capacity to use and to respond to any of an indefinitely large number of sentences, most of which she has never heard or seen (most of which, indeed, will never be uttered by anyone). Out beyond the observation sentences, language-learning is thus primarily not a matter of learning *sentences* at all, but rather of learning ways of forming sentences.

In Chapter 4 we contrasted Quine's interest in language-learning with that of the linguist. Linguists are often concerned with how we learn to utter sentences which are grammatically correct, and to recognize grammatical correctness or deviance on sight. Quine's concerns, by contrast, are epistemological. It is a matter of how our sentences come to make claims about the world, and how we acquire such cognitive language. The most recent point may seem to blur this contrast. If Quine is to have anything to say about the learning of language other than observation sentences (other, indeed, than sentences learned *as* observation sentences), then he must, perforce, talk not of the learning of sentences but of the learning of ways of forming sentences—and hence, at least in some sense, of the learning of grammatical constructions. And so he does, in his fashion. But his concern here remains epistemological. His interest is not in the child's developing sense of grammaticality—how the child comes to learn, say, that "The boy who ate the cake is happy" is an acceptable English sentence, whereas "The boy ate the cake who is happy" is not. His aim is, rather, to indicate how the child, having learnt relevant observation sentences, might be in a position to begin to form judgments as to the correctness of other sentences—not here meaning the grammatical correctness of a given sentence, but rather its truth, or anyway its plausibility in the given circumstances. When Quine talks of accounting for the child's acquiring the ability to use relative clauses, say, it is that sort of ability that he is talking about: the ability to use the construction to make utterances that the rest of us accept as true, or at least as plausible.

Quine's aim continues to be knowledge of the world rather than of grammar; his concern continues to be how the child comes to be able to assign correct truth-values to sentences, rather than how he comes to use them grammatically. But for sentences in general it may seem that learning to assign truth-values has little to do with learning appropriate use. For standing sentences, in particular, it may seem that assigning the correct truth-value simply has nothing to do with other aspects of the use of a sentence: it is true once for all, or false once for all, and simply knowing its truth-value has little to do with knowing how to use it.

Quine's response to this worry is that in learning a grammatical construction we learn how the truth-value of a sentence of the new kind is affected by the truth-values of other sentences. The idea of distributing truth-values continues to play a vital role. An example occurs in Quine's discussion of the learning of (eternal) predication. We shall say more about this kind of learning in the next section. The immediately relevant point is made in this comment about the relation of learning to the distribution of truth-values:

> In learning to understand and use the observation sentences, we
> depended very directly on truth-value considerations; for this
> learning consisted simply in learning the circumstances in which to
> assent to or dissent from the sentences. Coming to eternal sen
> tences, we noticed with some misgivings that this approach was no
> longer suitable, because of the fixity of the truth values. But now
> we see that the variability of truth value has withdrawn merely to a
> higher level of abstraction. A predication may be saddled with one
> truth value for all eternity; the predicational mode of composition,
> however, takes on varying truth values, yielding truth for some
> pairs of terms and falsity for others. *First and last, in learning lan*
> *guage, we are learning how to distribute truth values.* ... In learning the
> eternal predicational construction, we are learning how to judge
> whether a given pair of terms produces a true predication, true for
> good, or a false one, false for good.
>
> (RR, p. 65; emphasis added)

Quine's attention continues to be on knowledge; his interest in language and its acquisition is derivative upon a concern with the way in which knowledge is acquired. His concern with the learning of the predicational construction is, primarily, a concern with the way in which the child learns to bring evidence to bear on a sentence formed in that way.

We have been drawing out the implications of the second of the two points with which we began this section. The number of sentences with which we are concerned, beyond the observational, is indefinitely large; so our concern must be with modes of composition, rather than individual sentences; nevertheless, Quine's concern is still with epistemology, albeit at "a higher level of abstraction". It might seem, however, that the level of abstraction here is so high that there is really nothing of epistemological interest to be learnt. If Quine's genetic programme were carried out fully, or as far as possible, what would it tell us about the relation of theory to evidence? There is, I think, a lot to be learnt of a general nature. But the genetic project will shed little light on what specific evidence is relevant to a particular given sentence. The fact that a sentence is an eternal predication, say, together with what we may know about how we learn to distinguish true and false among such predications in general, falls far short of an account of what counts as evidence for and against that particular sentence. The general account of how sentences of that form are learnt may tell us something about the sort of evidence which bears on a particular such sentence, but it is certainly not the whole story.

The first of the two points that we made at the start of this section is relevant here. That point concerned the complexity of the dispositions which would have to be acquired in order to learn sentences beyond the observational. Sentences in general are correctly asserted or denied on the basis of other sentences asserted or denied, as well as on the basis of stimulations; or on the basis of the other sentences alone, with no direct role for simulations. (This, again, is a way of expressing holism.) For this reason, it may be impossible even to specify the dispositions which would have to be acquired for one to learn a given sentence. And if we do not even know which dispositions are at stake then clearly we cannot hope to say anything specific about how they are acquired. The account of the relation of theory to evidence is limited in a similar way: beyond the level of observation sentences, there may be little of a general nature that can be said about what counts as evidence for and against a sentence. Holism limits how much there is to be said about the evidence relation. If Quine is right, however, holism equally limits how much there is to be said about the learning relation. Our present considerations thus support Quine's idea that his genetic account gets part of its significance from the insight that it gives us into the relation between theory and evidence—even if that insight is less than one might have hoped for. A second moral is that we should perhaps not expect an account of the relation between theory and evidence to offer us more insight than Quine's genetic account promises. Because of holism, such an account may be the best possible.

II Language-dependent learning; more on holism

How does the infant progress beyond observation sentences? The most general answer is: by language-dependent learning. Observation sentences are the first part of language to be acquired. So Quine is concerned to show how sentences of that kind might be learnt by an infant who has not yet mastered any part of language. What changes as the infant moves beyond the observation sentences is that we are no longer restricted to instances of learning which require no previous knowledge of language. On the contrary:

we presuppose that the infant has mastered some parts of the language, and then draw on that fact to explain his learning of the next stage.

Even Quine's account of the learning of observation sentences attributes some prior language-mastery to the learner, although in a very modest way. The infant may or may not pass through a stage of uttering observation sentences whenever stimulatory circumstances warrant the utterance. Even if he does pass through that stage, he will surely very quickly find that this constant babbling of trite truths does not pay. The disposition to utter is inhibited, and largely replaced by a disposition to assent to, or dissent from, observation sentences when others utter them in an interrogative sort of way. (The child must learn what tone of voice, or other modification, makes a sentence interrogative; such learning is readily imaginable.) Along the way, the infant thus comes to master assent and dissent; this greatly facil- itates his learning. The infant hears one adult assenting to, or dissenting from, the queried sentences of another; adults appropriately express assent or dissent in response to such observation sentences as the infant spontaneously ventures; the infant's own utterances of assent and dissent in response to observation sentences meet with acceptance or rejection. In these cases the infant's learning of the observation sentence relies on his mastery of other parts of language—assent and dissent. It relies, that is to say, on his coming to be able to respond in the appropriate sort of way to adult signs of assent and dissent, and to be able to make such signs in his turn; also perhaps on his assent or dissent in response to observation sentences uttered by others. These matters may all be thought of as linguistic—although tone of voice and non-verbal reactions are likely at first to play as large a role as the words. So even the learning of most observation sentences, even the learning of them *as* observation sentences, is in a limited way language-dependent.

The idea that most observation sentences are learnt with the help of assent and dissent causes no particular problem for Quine's account. One can think of the infant as first acquiring some small number of observation sentences, and then learning assent and dissent from the way in which adults respond to his utterances, and then using this knowledge to acquire a larger stock of observation sentences. Or the ability to use and to respond to assent and dissent might be acquired along with an observation sentence. Quine suggests one possible scenario, drawing on the model of learning which we briefly discussed in the previous chapter:

> One of the child's rewarding episodes may be supposed to have included a conspicuous show of red together with the sound "red" from his own mouth, followed by the sound "yes" from the parent. In a later episode there is again the color and again the sound "red".

Such is the partial similarity of the later episode to the earlier one. There are of course incidental differences, and one of these just happens to be that the sound "red" issued from the parent this time, actually with interrogative intent. Anyway the child is moved as usual to heighten the resemblance, so he supplies another element of the earlier episode, the sound "yes". Rewarded again, he has learned to say "yes" in the presence of the color red and the sound "red". Unpleasant episodes will discourage him from saying "yes" when he hears the sound "red" in the absence of the color.

(RR, p. 47)

Our purpose here is not the details of this case, but rather the general idea: language-dependent learning of language—"learning that depends on other locutions previously learned" (RR, p. 48). Like the unalloyed learning of an observation sentence, this kind of learning depends still on the learner's standards of similarity; now, however, a greater role is played by standards of similarity among noises emitted, whether by himself or by others.

So far we have simply a case where language-dependent learning facilitates the learning of observation sentences, rather than taking us beyond them in principle. There are other similar cases. One is the learning of something analogous to truth-functions—conjunction, disjunction, and negation. One can easily imagine that once the child has learnt a few observation sentences he will also be able to learn that it is appropriate to utter one, followed by "and", followed by another in just those circumstances in which it would be appropriate to utter either one of the sentences alone (or, indeed, to utter one and then, after a brief pause, to utter the other). Disjunction and negation are analogous. As Quine points out, we should think of what is initially learnt as being what he calls a *verdict function* rather than a truth-function. A sentence may be true or false, but there are three possible verdicts on an observation sentence: assent, dissent, and abstain. Thus we have a three-valued logic, though one which fails to specify a value in every case. (Where we abstain from each of two sentences, it is unclear whether we will dissent from their conjunction or abstain from it; it depends on the content of the two sentences. Likewise in the case of disjunction: if we abstain separately from each of two sentences we may assent to their disjunction or abstain.)

Another kind of learning is what Quine calls *analogical synthesis*. He gives this example:

Having been directly conditioned to the appropriate use of "Foot" (or "This is my foot"), and "Hand" likewise, and "My foot hurts" as

157

a whole, the child might conceivably utter "My hand hurts" on an appropriate occasion, though unaided by previous experience with that actual sentence.

(WO, p. 9)

Taking matters strictly, "My hand hurts" is *not* an observation sentence; the stimulatory conditions which prompt its assent are not shared, though cuts and scrapes and bruises are visible, and may bring sympathy. (The sentence is one of those which can be learnt "as wholes by direct conditioning of them to appropriate non-verbal stimulations", so it is closely analogous to an observation sentence.) It may be that the simplest kinds of observation sentences are too one-dimensional, so to speak, to allow for substitution. But clearly we do not have to get far from them before substitution sets in. Suppose, for example, that a child who has learnt "Yellow paper!" and learnt "Blue!" then coins "Blue paper!" unaided; here we have a clear case. (How this child might have come to learn "Yellow paper!" is a question to which we shall return in the next section.) Applied to the sentence "My hand hurts", the technique may take us to sentences such as "Mama's hand hurts", which is not close to an observation sentence at all, for the child's mother may not currently be visible.

Analogical synthesis enlarges the child's stock of sentences of an elementary sort. Its significance, however, goes far beyond this fact. It is a technique that combines parts of previously learned sentences to form new sentences. Sentences treated in this way are not unstructured wholes. The technique relies on the child's being able to break the sentence down into significant parts—words, more or less—and recombine those parts in novel ways. This step is of crucial importance at every level of language, not only close to the level of observation sentences.

The same point applies also to the first learning of predication. The child who has learnt "Yellow paper!" as a single response to stimulation may then pick up the locution "The paper is yellow" at first simply as an equivalent. With a few more examples, we may imagine, the child begins to utter the longer form quite freely. So far we have nothing more than stylistic variation. But the habit that the child has thereby acquired enables it to form predications from two words which it has learnt separately. The child who has learnt "Blue!" and "Paper!" may utter "The paper is blue" without going through the "Blue paper!" stage. The child's new-found ability to form predications leads it to sentences which are importantly different from observation sentences, as we shall see.

Quine considers various other constructions, such as the "in" construction. "Mama in the garden" (or its elegant variant, "Mama is in the garden") may be learnt on the basis of the earlier learning of the relevant observation sentences. The new sentence is appropriately asserted "when the respective regions that are rendered salient by these two terms are combined in a certain pattern: the one surrounded by, or embedded in, the other" (*RR*, p. 61). With some more examples, he suggests, we come to generalize, "and end up by associating 'in' with this manner of embedment" (ibid.).

Even before the generalization, however, we have taken a step beyond observation sentences, a step towards something that is quite new in principle. Suppose the child has learnt "Mama is in the garden" in something like the manner that Quine suggests. He has learnt to assert it or assent to it when confronted by his mother in the garden, and to deny it when surveying the empty garden (a small one, let us suppose, without crannies or crevices in which a mother is likely to be concealed). Has he, then, "learnt the sentence"? To some extent, of course, he has, but only to some extent. (Here I am not concerned with the issue of the corrigibility of observation sentences; the present point is additional and more significant.) The sentence, after all, may be uttered when neither the garden nor the mother are in the child's view. The child who has learnt no more than stated above has no clue as to whether to assent, dissent, or abstain in these latter sorts of circumstances. He cannot yet do with the sentence what the adult language-user can. He is good on the most direct kind of evidence for and against the sentence (the garden, with or without his mother), but weak on less direct evidence which may weigh on one side or the other. Little by little, as he becomes increasingly wise in the ways of the world—and the ways of the particular woman concerned—he will be able to bring to bear an increasingly wide range of indirect evidence. But this bringing to bear of indirect evidence is a different matter from the learning of observation sentences and their compounds, truth-functional or predicational. It is holistic: it depends on the child's having mastered a portion of the theory of the world which extends well beyond the observation sentences. It is vague, for what may count as (indirect) evidence is likely to be impossible to delineate ahead of time.

The next stage is a general mastery of the "in" construction: the child may form compounds on the basis of his grasp of the components, with no prior experience of the whole sentence. Here the distance from direct observation is likely to be greater, and so also the reliance on vague and indirect evidence. We are still at a quite elementary level, but we begin to see, at least in broadest outline, how language may progress beyond the observational. Equally, we begin to see how holism is possible—how it might be possible to learn a language in which many sentences stand in very indirect relations to sensory experience. The child learns a few sentences as observation sentences; thus far no holism, for the child's learning of the sentences involves a mastery of what counts as evidence for and against. (Because observation sentences are corrigible this will not, strictly speaking, amount to a *full* mastery.) He then proceeds to compound and modify the expressions contained in these original sentences, thereby forming new sentences. The basis on which the child comes to do this, however, will in most cases give him only a partial grasp on the evidence which counts for or against the new sentence (in some cases, perhaps, no grasp at all). If the coinage is accepted by others as a sensible sentence, the child may be counted as understanding this sentence. Still the child may be only part of the way, at most, to being able to assent to and deny the sentence under appropriate conditions. Full ability to do this will come only as he gradually assimilates more of our general theory of the world.

We have been speaking of holism, the idea that a given sentence may be linked not merely to current stimulation but to other sentences. What does the idea of a link come to here? Quine takes as an example a case in which someone observes a greenish tint in a test-tube, and says "There was copper in it". He comments:

> Here the sentence is elicited by a non-verbal stimulus, but the stimulus depends for its efficacy upon an earlier network of associations of words with words; viz., one's learning of chemical theory. . . .
>
> The intervening theory is composed of sentences associated with one another in multifarious ways not easily reconstructed even in conjecture. There are the so-called logical connections, and the so-called causal ones; but *any such interconnections of sentences must finally be due to the conditioning of sentences as responses to sentences as stimuli.* . . . The theory as a whole—a chapter of chemistry, in this case, plus relevant adjuncts from logic and elsewhere—is a fabric of sentences variously associated to one another and to non-verbal stimuli by the mechanism of conditioned response.
>
> (*WO*, p. 11; emphasis added)

To say that a sentence is connected or linked to certain other sentences is to say that a competent user of that sentence will be more or less likely to assent to it according as she is or is not inclined to assent to those other sentences. This is, clearly, a behavioural matter; since it has to do with behavioural dispositions, it is ultimately a matter of the physical state of the organism.

Our discussion of the "in" construction gives us a new perspective on Quine's attitude towards the ideas of meaning and understanding. A child, we said, may utter a sentence employing that construction while he is only part of the way to being able to assent to it and deny it under appropriate conditions. He will gain this latter ability to a greater extent as he gradually assimilates more of our general theory of the world. Now suppose we ask: at what point in this process does the child *understand* the sentence? At what point does he grasp its meaning? For Quine, these questions make no clear sense here. Under some circumstances understanding may function in the way the questions suggest. Suppose a child (or, indeed, an adult) has absorbed a good deal of knowledge, and a good deal of the language, but, for some reason, has never come across a particular word. We tell the child the usage of the word—perhaps by giving approximate synonyms, together with extra guidance at the rough spots. By doing this we may, at a stroke, enable the child to use in competent fashion a whole range of sentences which he previously could not use. (See Chapter 3, section III above, for related discussion.) Focusing on that kind of case may make it seem as if coming to understand is like the throwing of a switch: first there is darkness, and then the scene is fully illuminated. But this is not the general case, as our example of "Mama is in the garden" indicates. The child at first responds, let us suppose, only to the most direct kind of evidence. Does he understand the sentence? Well he has part of the adult use of it, but not all. Eventually he comes to be able to use the sentence as an adult can. But the process is a gradual one, and it would be a mistake to think that there is a point at which light replaces darkness, where the switch is thrown and the child understands the sentence. It is illegitimate to insist that the question: does this child understand this sentence? always has a clear-cut yes-or-no answer. The notion of understanding simply will not bear that kind of weight. While the words "meaning" and "understanding" have their uses, they cannot be accepted for "scientific or philosophical" purposes (*TT*, pp. 184ff; quoted in context, p. 54, above).

The phenomenon that we noted in the case of "Mama is in the garden" is that the child "learns the sentence", to some extent, while lacking a full mastery of the circumstances which make assent or dissent appropriate. The child first produces the sentence on the basis of merely partial learning of its conditions of appropriate assertability. This phenomenon is surely pervasive in the learning of language. The example gives a more concrete sense of what Quine means by saying that the language-learner's progress "is not a continuous derivation. ... It is a progress rather by short leaps of analogy" (NNK, pp. 77–78). It is because language-learning in general progresses in this way that what is learnt is a holistic language, one in which evidence generally bears on a given sentence indirectly, via other sentences. (One might equally put the point the other way around, and say that because what is to be learnt is a holistic language, the learner can only master it if he proceeds by leaps rather than by derivation.) One kind of leap is exemplified in our example: we envisaged the sentence first being learnt in the garden, but then used in other contexts, where its truth or falsehood is no longer evident. This kind of thing happens constantly. "It's raining" is an observation sentence, keyed to rain here and now (or, strictly, to appropriate stimulations). "It's raining in London", said somewhere else, is not an observation sentence, and the only available evidence for it is indirect. Once the child masters idioms of time and tense, they too will give rise to similar cases: "It will rain next week" is, notoriously, not answerable to current evidence in the most straightforward kind of way, but is appropriately asserted or denied now on the basis of complex factors, requiring a good deal of rather specialized knowledge of the world.

Some of the examples above involve sentences which, if asserted to hold here and now, would be observation sentences; asserted, here and now, to hold of other places and times, they are no longer observation sentences, but answerable to vaguer and more complex forms of evidence. There are, however, many other kinds of example. One involves predication. We saw an example: "Yellow paper" may be learnt as a kind of compound of two observation sentences, and then "This paper is yellow" may be learnt as an equivalent form. That is *occasional predication*, true or false from occasion to occasion. Such a sentence is directly linked to stimulation almost in the way that an observation sentence is. *Eternal predications* are a different matter. They are true once for all, or false once for all; examples include "Snow is white" or "Fido is a dog", Grammatically they are similar: "Fido is wet" and "Fido is a dog". (The examples are Quine's; see *RR*, p. 67.) But Quine's concern is epistemology, not grammar. From that point of view, he insists, the distinction is a large one; eternal predications, because they are true or false once for all, cannot be thought of as associated with current stimulation. Learning a sentence of this sort, and the general idiom it illustrates, is not like learning an observation sentence. How can we think of such learning as coming about?

Quine envisages a child who has already mastered "Snow" and "White" as observation sentences, i.e. he has the appropriate dispositions to assent and dissent. Then, he suggests, the child's hearing the *word* "snow" may have something of the same effect on him as his seeing snow; enough of an effect, indeed, to dispose him to assent to "White?" just as seeing snow would. The child comes to be disposed to assent to "Snow is white?" because his hearing the first word disposes him to assent when he hears the second:

> The mechanism that I am suggesting is ... a transfer of conditioning. The child has been conditioned to assent to the query "White?" when snow is presented, and then this response becomes transferred from the snow stimulus to the associated verbal stimulus, the word "snow".
>
> (RR, p. 65)

The "leap" that is involved here is of a particularly interesting kind, for it is based on "the idea that the sound of a word can have somewhat the same effect as the sight of its object" (RR, p. 67). Here we have a prototype of the confusion of use and mention, of a word with the thing it designates. As Quine says: "Language is rooted in what a good scientific language eschews. ... Language is conceived in sin and science is its redemption". (RR, p. 68.)

Similar remarks apply to a further sort of predication, which will prove of particular importance in the discussion of reference in the next section. The crucial new point is that the subject, as well as the predicate, is a general term; rather than combining the singular term "Fido" with the general term "dog", we combine two general terms to get, say, "Dogs are animals". As Quine remarks, it is "really a universal categorical, 'Every a is a β'." (RR, p. 66.) As in the previous case, the learning mechanism which Quine rather speculatively postulates is based on a confusion of use with mention:

> Having learned the term "animal", the child is disposed to assent to the query "An animal?" if he surmises the presence of dogs or other animals. Then, by transfer, he comes to assent to "An animal?" on hearing the words "A dog". He assents to "A dog is an animal".
>
> (RR, p. 66)

Both in this case and in the previous one, we may imagine that the child who comes to express a number of sentences of the given kind quickly catches on to the general technique of forming such sentences. The child thus comes to learn the predicative mode of composition, in the one case, and the universal categorical, in the other.

What goes into the child's first coming to utter or assent to a sentence of one of the new kinds is far from an adequate evidential basis for the sentence. The child comes to assent to "Snow is white", we may suppose, on the basis of having seen a few instances of snow. This is, of course, far from conclusive evidence for the sentence, which is quite general in its claim. And once the child masters the general construction whereby one term is predicated of another, he may get yet further away from the basis on which the sentences he utters can be responsibly asserted. Is the child in this case to be counted as really having *learnt* the sentences concerned, as genuinely *understanding* them? As we have indicated, these are not questions which Quine accepts as clear questions, in need of definite answers. The child can do part of what the fully competent language-user can do, but not all of it. The child's initial learning is only partial, for it gives him at most a very limited grasp on the circumstances which make assent and dissent to a given sentence appropriate. Having attained this limited grasp, however, his usage is subject to encouragement and correction by others, and this surely helps the learning process. Much of what the child must go on to learn, however, may not be specific to the given sentence. The child's ability to use the sentence as adults do depends on his absorbing various more or less directly connected parts of our general theory of the world. Beyond the observation sentences, language mastery, like the evidence relation, is holistic.

I should conclude this long section by emphasizing that I have by no means attempted to give a complete account of what Quine says on language-learning beyond the observation sentences. Many other constructions and idioms come up for discussion in his work, more than can be discussed here within reasonable limits. We shall consider some of these in the course of discussing the child's acquisition of reference, but still our selection will be quite limited, and many details neglected. Our emphasis is on the principles at work, and their general significance.

III Reference

Towards the end of the last chapter, we discussed Quine's views about observation sentences and reference. As we saw there, he argues that the capacity to use observation sentences as responses to stimulation is not yet the capacity to refer in the full sense. (Reference, as I use the word, requires full reification, not merely perceptual reification.) Yet he holds that reference, speaking about objects, is "central to our conceptual scheme" (*RR*, p. 84). So a major concern of Quine's genetic story is to account for reference, and for the infant's acquisition of the capacity to refer. The preface to *Roots of Reference* begins like this:

> Relatively little mystery enshrouds the ways in which we learn to
> utter observation sentences, and to assent to them or dissent from

them when asked. Speaking of objects, however—abstract objects, physical objects, or even sensory objects—is neither so quickly achieved nor so readily accounted for.

(RR, p. ix)

It is pondering that issue, he says, which led to the book; it is that issue which will occupy us in the rest of this chapter.

Quine wants to show that the ability to use some idioms presupposes an ability to use others. To this end, he imagines a foreigner who makes a particular response when red is present and not otherwise, and asks:

> Must this response be construed as a name of the color? Might it not be, instead, a general term by which he [our imagined foreigner] denotes each whole visible red patch but no smaller parts of such patches? or a general term by which he denotes each body that shows a conspicuously red portion of the surface? or a general term by which he denotes each whole episode or specious present that flaunts red conspicuously? Under these different choices the object of reference varies. Under the one choice it is a color. Under other choices it is a patch, and a different patch from occasion to occasion. Under still other choices it is a body.
>
> (RR, p. 82)

How are we to settle what the foreigner is referring to? Only "by working up a manual of English translation for a substantial portion of the foreigner's language" (RR, p. 82). So "the reference of the foreigner's word ... is settled only by translating a good deal of the foreign linguistic apparatus" (RR, pp. 82–83). The reference of the word is determined by the way in which the foreigner's use of that word interacts with his use of other words.

The same point applies to the language-learner. Merely making the sound "rabbit" when in the presence of rabbits, or "red" when in the presence of something red, is not yet referring.

> When can a child be said to have learned to refer to the color red? Suppose he has learned to respond, on demand, in distinctive verbal ways according as red is conspicuously present or not. Can we then say that he has learned to refer to red? No. ... We can credit the child at this point with being able to *discriminate* red, to *recognize* red. We in conferring these credits do refer to the child and to the color; these references we will readily own. But to say that he refers to the color would be to impute our own ontology to him.
>
> (RR, pp. 81–82)

165

The point here is not that the child may, for all we know, have some *other* ontology. It is, rather, that having any ontology requires capacities which we have, as yet, no reason to attribute to the child. Referring is more than discriminating; it is also a matter of being able to use what Quine calls the "apparatus of reference". He offers a rough specification of this apparatus by mentioning "pronouns, copulas, plural endings", along with the distinctions between singular terms and general terms, between the copula of predication and the copula of identity (*RR*, pp. 83f.). The child gradually absorbs this apparatus, correcting his usage against that of the adults around him, until he is a full-fledged user of referential language. Such is the vague picture; Quine seeks something more precise, both about what more must be learned in order to refer and about how the child might come to learn it.

The child comes to learn various utterances which, from a sophisticated point of view, vary in how, or whether, they refer. Thus "It's chilly" and "It's raining" are not, in Quine's parlance, referential at all; "Fido" and "Mama" are singular terms; "dog" and "apple" are individuative general terms, or count terms (we speak of "an apple", "another dog"); "milk" and "apple-sauce" are not individuative ("some milk", "more apple-sauce"). In the first stage of the child's learning, however, no such distinctions are in place. All the above sentences may initially be learnt—more or less—"by direct association with appropriate stimulations" (*TT*, p. 2); they can all be learnt, more or less, *as* observation sentences. What is learned in this fashion is, to begin with, an unstructured whole, a sentence without significant parts. (What can be learned in this way can also be learned in other ways by those who have already acquired some language.) Even at this first stage there is a distinction between utterances of the first sort, which are comments on the whole of the current scene, and the others, which are "learned by association with distinctively salient portions of the scene" (*TT*, p. 6). Quine sees the latter as "perhaps a first step towards the eventual namehood of 'Fido' and 'Milk' " (*TT*, p. 7). But it is still a long way from the full-fledged capacity to refer. How does the child come to acquire that capacity?

On Quine's account it emerges by degrees. Referring requires various linguistic capacities which the child acquires; each is at first no doubt acquired imperfectly and haltingly and then gradually perfected. When all are (more or less) perfectly acquired, we have the full-fledged referrer. Quine thus aims "to devise a series of plausibly easy stages, plausibly short leaps" (*RR*, p. 101) by which a modern-day child, or early humans, beginning with a mastery of observation sentences, might come to refer to objects. As before, there will be gaps; what must be plausible is that the child, having acquired one kind of idiom, could come to acquire the next in the series. There is no implication that when a child is represented as going from one idiom to another that the second can be plausibly *inferred* from the first; if this were so, there would be no dramatic change in expressive power as the child advanced.

Predication, which we discussed in the previous section, is an essential preliminary. Once the child is uttering predications, or their prototypes, he is in a position to learn the use of individuative general terms. Such terms function rather differently from others: the words "white" and "dog" function differently in the predications "Milk is white" and "Fido is a dog". Quine states the contrast like this:

> Milk's being white comes down to the simple fact that whenever you point at milk you point to white. Fido's being a dog does not come down to the simple fact that whenever you point at Fido you point to a dog: it involves that and more. For whenever you point at Fido's head you point at a dog, and yet Fido's head does not qualify as a dog.
>
> (*TT*, pp. 4f.)

The correct use of an individuative general term is not simply a matter of responding to the presence of the relevant kind of stuff. It is also a question of learning how much dogginess counts as *a* dog, how much as part of a dog, and how much as several dogs. Here "the peculiarities of reference emerge" because "[t]o learn 'apple' it is not sufficient to learn how much of what goes on counts as apple; we must learn how much counts as *an* apple, and how much as another." (*WO*, p. 91; emphasis in the original.) Thus the idea of objects begins to emerge—the idea of *a* dog or *an* apple rather than undifferentiated dogginess and applehood.

Predication, and the mastery of individuative general terms, make up a large step towards fully referential language. A larger step, on Quine's account, is the mastery of relative clauses. In some works, indeed, Quine puts forward the relative clause as crucial not only for reference but also for the functioning of language in general: "The power and flexibility of our language is due overwhelmingly to the relative clause" ("The Variable and Its Place in Reference", p. 165). Like predication, the use of relative clauses may initially be learnt as a mere variant. Instead of "Fido is barking" we have "Fido is a thing *which is barking*"; the two are equivalent, and the second could be learned in virtue of the equivalence. Quite generally, any sentence at all, however complex, in which the name "*a*" figures can be rephrased so as to take the form "*a* is a ... ", i.e. the form of a sentence in which a predicate is ascribed to a subject. This is achieved by the use of a

167

relative clause to form a general term which encapsulates what the original sentence says about the object. Thus we can, for example, rephrase the sentence "George W. Bush's father was President of the USA and his paternal grandfather was a US Senator" as a predication about the younger Bush, employing the general term " ... is a person whose father was President of the USA and whose paternal grandfather was a US Senator".

A minor gain here is in the learning of identity. The child may learn "same dog as", "same apple as", and so on, in more or less straightforward contextual fashion. He eventually comes to detach sameness from any particular context and generalize it, applying it in contexts where he has no direct learning to go on. A likely guide here is his learning that assent to "$a = b$" and to "a is an F" justifies assent to "b is an F", with any general term in the place of "F". The learning of relative clauses brings with it a great increase in the number of general terms that can be formed. With relative clauses in place, "a is an F" can in effect be any sentence containing "a"; what is learnt is thus identity in the full sense.

So far we have considered relative clauses in contexts from which they could be eliminated. The real importance of relative clauses for reference, however, emerges from consideration of contexts in which they are ineliminable. This may happen when what Quine calls a "substantivized relative clause"—thus "person who is F", or more generally "thing which is F"—is made the subject term of a sentence. A clear case of this is the universal categorical, "Every a is a β", briefly discussed in the previous section. We may distinguish three sorts of cases. In the first, the universal categorical is eliminable, and with it the relative clause. "Every person [who is] in the room has red hair" can perhaps be rephrased as "Mary, John, and Sarah all have red hair". (Even here it might be thought we need to add a sentence of a different kind, asserting that there are no other people who are in the room. In that sentence, the universality reappears, along with a relative clause.) In a second kind of case we may be able to think of the assertion as a sort of dummy sentence: "If — is in the room then — has red hair". The claim being made is that whatever name you slot into the blank, provided it is the same each time, you will end up with a truth. Both of these kinds of cases turn on the availability of names to take the place of the relative clause in subject position, although in the second no names are specified. The third kind of case does not require that we have names for the relevant objects. (No doubt sentences of the second kind ease the way for the learning of sentences of this third kind.)

In the first kind of case above, we have combinations of sentences, such as "Mary has red hair" and "John is in the room", which on Quine's account could be used without the ability to refer. Each such sentence might be used more or less as just a response to sensory stimulation. In the second kind of case, we have something like a general method of forming such sentences— but still, in Quine's view, no requirement that they be construed as referential. But with the third kind of case we have full-blown reference. Another example will bring this out more clearly: "Any object which is found between the high-tide mark and the low-tide mark belongs to the sovereign". Or more explicitly perhaps, "If any thing is found between the high-tide mark and the low-tide mark then it belongs to the sovereign". Here it is apparent that what is said to belong to the sovereign are those things which are found in the relevant place; it is things that we are talking about. What links the two halves of the sentence, in either version, is the sameness of the object in the one half as in the other. The pronoun "it" in the second version makes this explicit: we are saying of any *object* that if *it* is found between the high-tide mark and the low-tide mark then *it*, that same object, belongs to the sovereign.

Linguistically, Quine thus sees reference as a product of the relative clause and the general or categorical assertion. These constructions "stand forth as the roots of reference" (*RR*, p. 101). Combining them, as in cases of our third kind, requires pronouns which must be construed referentially. It also requires implicit use of identity, since the two uses of the pronoun refer to *the same object*. Our second way of taking the universal categorical yields what is known as "substitutional quantification", in which a universally quantified sentence is taken as true if every name that can be substituted for the variable yields a true sentence. Our third way, however, gives reference full-blown, what is known as "objectual quantification". Here a universally quantified sentence is true if the unquantified open sentence is true of every object, whether named or unnamed. We may attain understanding of this kind of sentence via the universal categorical substitutionally interpreted; still the gap between them, from Quine's point of view, is vast. It is only with the pronoun understood objectually that we have clear-cut reference.

We have been speaking of pronouns and their varying roles; let us dwell on them a little further. Sentences such as "Fido is hungry" and "Fido is barking" might be learnt on a more or less observational basis, giving as yet no clear basis for saying that the utterer is *referring* to the family dog. (They may be uttered by an infant who lacks the capacity to refer.) Their conjunction might then be abbreviated as "Fido is hungry and *he* is barking", but here the pronoun is simply a matter of convenience; it is what Geach has famously called "a pronoun of laziness", and gives no reason to ascribe reference. (See Geach, *Reference and Generality*, pp. 151ff.) But if we generalize and say:

"When a dog gets hungry, it barks" the pronoun, in spite of its name, is not simply a matter of convenience, an abbreviation for a name. We cannot unpack this sentence into two (or three or four) others which might be learnt more or less observationally; it is ineliminably referential. Quine's speculations about relative clauses are in part an attempt to show how we might achieve this referential use of pronouns.

Quine also speculates on another way in which we might pick up on the referential use of pronouns. Here an important role is played by the idea of an *observation categorical*. We shall discuss this idea in more detail in the next chapter. For the moment it will be enough to say that observation categoricals are sentences of the form "Whenever A, B", where A and B are themselves observation sentences. "Whenever there's smoke, there's fire" might be an example. One way in which Quine sees referential language as developing is by way of what he calls *focal* observation categoricals. An observation categorical says merely that where one feature is present, another is too. Scenes containing a raven also contain something black: "Whenever there is a raven, there is black". It is a more specific claim to say that scenes containing a raven also contain a black raven: "Whenever there is a raven, there is a black raven" (see *FSS*, pp. 27–28). So far this is compatible with there being white ravens, as long as they are never seen except in the company of their black cousins. But with predication already learned, it is, Quine claims, a small step from this sort of ordinary (or *free*) observation categorical to a focal version: Whenever there is a raven, *it* is black. It is a small step, but a crucial one:

> The pronoun "it" is a vital new link between the component observation sentences. ... It posits common carriers of the two traits, ravenhood and blackness. The carriers are ravens, bodies. I see this pronominal construction as achieving objective reference.
>
> (*FSS*, p. 25)

Again, the pronoun is crucial for reference. Quite generally, indeed, Quine sees pronouns, rather than names, as crucial for reference; he sees the logician's variables as inheriting this feature of pronouns and making it clearer and more precise.

For Quine, then, objective reference is most clearly seen in the ineliminable use of pronouns or, as we shall see shortly, variables. Many philosophers reserve this role for names, or for singular terms more generally.[2] Quine's disagreement is based primarily on the fact that a sentence containing a particular singular term may be more or less correctly used just as a response to stimulation. There is nothing about the functioning of such a sentence that requires us to construe the singular term as referential. Only with the generality achieved by pronouns is there undeniable reference. Singular terms are referential, but this status depends upon the fact that they can take the place of pronouns:

> The pronoun or variable admits substitutions of constant singular terms. ... Such terms ... are then properly seen as designating objects. This is how the pronoun or variable is primary and the name parasitic. *Were it not for the irreducibly referential pronoun, or some idiom to the same effect, any distinction between designative words and others would be idle and arbitrary.* Words would still be learned by conditioning to stimulation, and sentences would still be true and false, but a notion of objects would have no place.
> ("The Variable and Its Place in Reference", p. 167; emphasis added)

It is only because of something like this use of pronouns, Quine is claiming, that our theory posits a world made up of objects at all. Pronouns or variables, moreover, have a further advantage over names. A name may or may not succeed in naming an object, but no such vagaries afflict variables: "a variable proceeds serenely on its smooth course of values, taking whatever there may be" (op. cit., p. 168).

We have been more or less equating variables with pronouns. The variables of quantification theory possess all the relevant features of pronouns. We found the relevant sort of use of pronouns in the sentence: "If anything is found between the high-tide mark and the low-tide mark then it belongs to the sovereign". This is just the sort of sentence which goes over directly and smoothly into the notation of quantifiers and variables:

$(\forall x)$ (If x is found between the high-water mark and the low-water mark then x belongs to the sovereign)

Here it is the bound variable that plays the role played by the pronoun in the English sentence.[3] We can also construe that sentence as saying: take anything you like, if it is found between the high-tide mark and the low-tide mark then it belongs to the sovereign. Here the pronoun yet more evidently prepares the way for the bound variable. In any case, it is the bound variable that Quine sees as crucial. All our earlier remarks about the referential role of pronouns apply to it. Bound variables, indeed, play the referential role with even greater clarity and forthrightness than do pronouns, if only because of the systematization that logic brings, and the avoidance of confusion with pronouns of laziness. Thus quantification is for Quine an "encapsulation of the referential apparatus"; the variable "becomes the distilled essence of ontological discourse" (*RR*, p. 100).

For these reasons, some of Quine's detailed discussion of how the capacity to refer might be acquired is carried out in terms of how the ability to use first-order logic might be acquired. Quite generally, as we have seen, Quine conceives of his task as being at some distance from psychological reality. In fact, of course, we all learn ordinary language first; the fortunate among us then have first-order logic explained to us in that language. But Quine would be happy with an account that left out ordinary language, and explained the acquisition of quantificational language directly. In *Roots of Reference* he says: "My concern with the essential psychogenesis of reference would be fulfilled in fair measure with a plausible account of how one might proceed from infancy step by step to a logically regimented language, even bypassing English". (P. 92; cf. also *FSS*, p. 31.) Quine, let us recall, is combating the idea that full cognitive language *could not* have emerged along the naturalistic lines that he favours; his response is to set out a way in which it might have done so.

IV Reference and identity

To this point we have been discussing various idioms; mastery of those idioms constitutes the capacity to refer to objects—to bodies, in particular. It is crucial here that such mastery is not just the capacity to form the relevant kinds of sentences. It is also the capacity to use them appropriately—in circumstances where others will accept the use as saying something true, or at least plausible. Mastery of individuative general terms for bodies requires an implicit grasp not only on the conditions of individuation of a given kind of body (when you have one dog, when you have two) but also on conditions for identity over time (when the dog seen at one time is the same dog as the one seen at another). This takes us decisively beyond perceptual similarity. Two distinct dogs may be as similar as you can imagine; a single dog may present quite different appearances before and after rolling in the mud. Making sense of individuation over time thus requires, as Quine says, "acquisition of our whole schematism of space and time and the unobserved trajectories of bodies within it" (*FSS*, p. 36). This schematism is presumably acquired along with the relevant linguistic competence. Complex innate predispositions no doubt play a large role here; correction of utterances may also do so. Tense is a crucial element. A child who eats enthusiastically is perhaps told: "You *were* hungry, weren't you?" He thereby learns to name his previous state; he may also gain insight into

172

the idea of that state as changing (especially as his mentor may add: "But now you're not, are you?"). Again, the child may venture claims which are corrected by drawing his attention to cross-time identities. "Barking dogs are hungry", he says, only to have an adult point to a dog refusing its food (sick or overstuffed) and say: "That dog was barking a minute ago". The issue may turn precisely on whether the dog refusing food is the same as the one recently barking, or another similar dog.—In this, and countless more or less analogous ways, we may imagine, the child gradually catches on to the idea of persistence over time, and gradually learns the very complex ways in which adults bring evidence to bear on the question whether a body seen at one time is the same as one seen at another, or merely very similar.

Full mastery of the use of referential language for bodies thus requires at least a partial and implicit grasp of the world of bodies, occupying space, enduring through time, and interacting causally. But such "grasp" itself, in turn, requires mastery of the referential idiom:

> [At an early stage of language-acquisition we] recognize Fido in his recurrences in learning the occasion sentence "Fido", just as we recognize further milk and sugar in learning "Milk" and "Sugar". Even in the absence of distinctive traits we will correctly concatenate momentary canine manifestations as stages of the same dog as long as we keep watching. After any considerable lapse of observation, however, the question of identity of unspecified dogs simply does not arise—not at the rudimentary stage of language learning. It scarcely makes sense until we are in a position to say such things as that in general if *any* dog undergoes such and such then in due course that *same* dog will behave thus and so. This sort of general talk about long-term causation becomes possible only with the advent of quantification or its equivalent, the relative clause in plural predication. Such is the dependence of individuation, in the time dimension, upon relative clauses; and it is only with full individuation that reference comes fully into its own.
>
> (*TT*, pp. 7f.; emphasis in the original)

There is no paradox here; worries about what comes first are misplaced. *Full* understanding of the world of enduring bodies requires mastery of the referential idiom; *full* mastery of that idiom requires an understanding of the ways of bodies. The child no doubt begins with very partial and defective mastery of one and uses it to attain a partial and defective mastery of the other, and then gradually uses each to improve the other until he becomes one of us.

Mastering referential language for bodies and acquiring "the scheme of enduring and recurrent physical objects" (*WO*, p. 92) will thus go hand-in-hand.

Correction of early utterances will help with each. So also will our predispositions to see the world as made up of bodies, the "body-mindedness" considered towards the end of the previous chapter. In any case, the first referring terms that we master are terms for bodies. Our earliest understanding of the idea of an object comes from our mastery of terms which apply to familiar medium-sized bodies, occupying space, lasting through time, and interacting causally with other bodies, most notably with ourselves. Such bodies are thus "the charter members of our ontology, let the subsequent elections and expulsions proceed as they may" (*RR*, p. 85); hence they are "the prime reality, the objects *par excellence*" (*RR*, p. 88). But it is important too that there may be "subsequent elections and expulsions": Quine's account of objecthood gives no reason to assume that *only* bodies can count as objects; nor does it even imply that scientific sophistication could not lead us to change our minds about the claims of bodies to be objects. We shall enlarge upon these points in Chapter 12, below.

Our earliest reference is to observable bodies, but we quickly get beyond them. We speak of unobservable objects—those too small or distant for any human observation—and of abstract objects. Quine attributes our acquisition of these capabilities to the same sort of process, of analogies and short leaps and happy confusions. We can suppose the relative term "smaller than" learned from pairs of observable objects; the same term can then be used to introduce discourse about objects too small to be observed. (See *WO*, pp. 14f. Quine also emphasizes that our understanding of terms such as "molecule" depends only in small part on such analogies; mastery of the theory in which they occur contributes more.) The idea of an object too far away to see might in fact be introduced through actual cases, where a journey reveals something. Then we can begin to talk about objects which are even further away, and so on.

As for abstract objects, Quine envisages our talk of them as beginning in sheer laziness. Rather than repeat a description, we may say: "It is true as well of ... ", or "The same holds also in this case. ... " (see *FSS*, pp. 39f.). These uses are eliminable, at the price of prolixity. We have then only to introduce a general term—"property" or "attribute"—for this "thing" which holds or is true, however, and we have the capability to make generalizations in which talk of attributes is not eliminable. We are reifying them. Quine thinks that talk of properties and attributes should be excluded from the language of science, and from our scientific ontology, but not because they are (putatively) abstract objects. He excludes them, rather, because their identity-criteria are unclear. The principle here is exactly the same as in the positing of bodies. Reification requires criteria of identity: "there is no entity without identity".[4] ("Confessions of a Confirmed Extensionalist", p. 217). For bodies, identity-conditions are provided by "the scheme of enduring and recurrent physical objects". Reification of properties is illegitimate for lack of such criteria. But such reification nevertheless plays a role in the development of legitimate discourse, for it is here that our willingness to talk about abstract entities begins. Thus the way is prepared for more scientifically acceptable talk of classes and numbers.

There are other ways in which we might begin to talk of abstract objects. We introduce words such as "square" and "blue", presumably, to talk of the shapes and colours of particular objects; the book is blue, we say, or the room is square. But such terms, as Quine remarks, "slip over into the role of a singular term remarkably easily" (*RR*, p. 101). We speak of two objects as having the same shape. Before we know it we are saying such things as "Blue is a colour" and "Square is a shape". We can perhaps treat the first of these sentences as being about the concrete object made up of all blue stuff. The second, however, definitely seems to commit us to accepting the existence of an abstract object. (Quine, to avoid confusion, would prefer the word "squareness".)

Quine traces out a path by which a child might make his way from this first postulation of abstract objects to talk of sets (see the last chapter of *Roots of Reference*). We shall not follow him in this, but will make one final comment. Abstract objects are not in space and time, and do not interact causally; one might suppose, therefore, that our knowledge of them involves some faculty beyond the five senses. So it is worth emphasizing that Quine's sketch of a way in which we might begin to talk of such objects invokes nothing mysterious. The naturalism of the genetic project does not leave off when we come to abstract entities. No one of the senses brings us into direct epistemic contact with the abstract, so it might be thought that if we are to have knowledge of them at all then there must be some non-naturalistic analogue of the senses.[5] Quine does not, of course, accept any such thing, nor does he hold that we have "direct epistemic contact" with abstract objects. The crucial point here is that abstract objects are in this way no different from others. We do not have the alleged "direct epistemic contact" with objects at all. All objects, on Quine's account, are posits; none are known immediately, none are simply *given*. It is for that reason, indeed, that there is a need for an account of how we get from the impingement of physical forces, and stimulation of our sensory nerves, to reference. On this crucial point, there is no contrast between the abstract and the concrete, which partly explains why the distinction simply is not very important for Quine. (See *WO*, p. 233.)

Before leaving the subject of reference, or reification, let us take up one further question, which will also indicate connections between this part of the book and the next. Quine insists that referential language is useful, indeed indispensable: "Whatever its faltering origins, reification proved indispensable in connecting the loose ends or raw experience to produce the beginnings of a structured system of the world". (*FSS*, p. 29.) Whence this efficacy for theory? One part of the answer is that by speaking of objects rather than merely of features of experience we can make stronger claims— more easily overthrown, and more useful if not overthrown. Thus contrast an observation categorical with its focal analogue. The latter makes a stronger and more definite claim: it is not merely that our experience always has one feature when it has another; it is that these features are to be found *in the same object*.

A second part of the answer lies in the connection that we have indicated between reification and logic. The application of logic to our system of knowledge allows us to schematize the way in which it is knitted together by inferential connections. In particular, it allows us to schematize the crucial relation between theory and evidence (the latter embodied in observation categoricals). It thereby shows how we can understand our theory as answerable to observation. The application of logic to our system of knowledge will only work out smoothly, however, if that system meets logical standards of clarity and consistency. A crucial aspect of this clarity is that it should be clear exactly what objects that system asserts to exist, and that there should be clear-cut identity-criteria for those objects. For Quine a central philosophical task is to show how our system of knowledge can be formulated so that it meets these standards, and allows for the imposition of logic. This task is distinct from the one which has occupied us over the last three chapters, but still an integral part of Quine's naturalized empiricism. Our discussion of it will occupy Chapters 9–13, below.

7

THEORY AND EVIDENCE

Quine holds that the learning relation and the evidence relation are different sides of the same coin. Much of his discussion of epistemology, especially in the later decades of his working life, proceeds in terms of the learning side—the genetic project of explaining how our theory might be acquired. This is the issue which has occupied us in the last two chapters. At other times, however, he focuses more abstractly on the question of the relation of theory to evidence. This relation can be represented, ideally and schematically, as a matter of logic: theory implies evidence. Thus he speaks of "the baffling tangle of relations between our sensory stimulation and our scientific theory of the world", but goes on to say:

> there is a segment that we can gratefully separate out and clarify without pursuing neurology, psychology, psycho-linguistics, genetics, or history. It is the part where theory is tested by prediction. It is the relation of evidential support, and its essentials can be schematized by means of little more than logical analysis.
>
> (*PT*, p. 1f.)

Our theory, Quine holds, implies its evidence. (Idealizing, we may take implication here to be a matter of first-order logic; see Chapter 10, below.) When an implied statement turns out to be true, the theory is, to some extent, vindicated. When one turns out to be false, the theory is shown to be in need of revision or replacement. A new theory, or modification of the old one, must be created which does not imply the falsehood (but which continues, as far as possible, to imply the truths implied by the old theory). This is the hypothetico-deductive method which Quine, like many other thinkers, holds to be central to our science, even in its most rudimentary stages. Various questions and difficulties arise about this picture. One difficulty is that our theory seems too untidy, too disparate in its formulations and its language, with too many background assumptions and constraints, to stand in neat relations of logical implication to statements of evidence. Quine recognizes that the account involves "a significant degree of idealization" (*PT*, p. 17). His project of regimentation is in part an attempt to show how our theory could, in principle, be reformulated so as to live up to the ideal. This project will be the subject of Chapters 9–13, below. Another issue, which is our immediate concern, is the nature of the evidence which is, in the ideal, to be implied by our theory. What sorts of statements are to play the role of evidence? One might think that the notion of evidence, in Quine's account, is to be captured or replaced by the idea of an observation sentence. Observation sentences are, more or less, directly linked to the occurrence of sensory stimulations, which are our only way of coming by information about the world. (See Chapters 4 and 5, above.) But we cannot simply replace "evidence" by "observation sentences" in our little sketch of the hypothetico-deductive method. Observation sentences are occasion sentences, true at one time and false at another. Our theory presumably consists of eternal sentences, true or false once for all. Hence there are no direct inferential relations between our theory and observation sentences.

How is this gap to be filled? Quine eventually settles on the idea of an observation categorical, which we briefly mentioned in the previous chapter. On the one hand, observation categoricals are directly answerable to observation sentences, and thus, at one remove, to the occurrence of sensory stimulations; on the other hand, they are eternal sentences, implied by a schematized and reconstructed version of our system of the world. The idea of an observation categorical is thus crucial for Quine's schematization of the relation of theory to evidence. The first section of this chapter is concerned with the evolution of this idea in Quine's thought, and with the role that it comes to play. The closely related idea of empirical content is the subject of the second.

On most accounts, including Quine's, theory implies evidence but evidence does not imply theory. This latter fact makes it natural to wonder whether more than one theory is compatible with the evidence—whether theory is, as it is said, *underdetermined* by the evidence for it. We have already encountered the idea of underdetermination in passing. (See Chapter 2, section II, above.) The thesis, and Quine's attitude towards it, turn out to be more complex than one might suppose. In section III of this chapter we shall consider how we are to understand the thesis; we shall also argue that it does not follow directly from the fact that evidence does not imply theory, or from holism. Quine also argues that the thesis, for all its plausibility, is much harder to make sense of than may appear on the surface. This issue will occupy us in the last few pages of the section.

I Evidence; observation categoricals

As indicated above, our theory does not imply occasion sentences and so, in particular, it does not imply observation sentences. I say "It's raining" on some occasion when it is. No amount of general knowledge about the weather will imply the truth of my utterance unless we—somehow—build in facts about where and when I made my banal remark. (If our theory did imply the truth of the sentence, unqualified by reference to time and place, then the theory would be refuted by the fact that on many occasions the sentence is false.) If we want the evidence for our theory to be implied by it, we cannot simply take observation sentences as embodying that evidence. But observation sentences are the parts of language most directly related to sensory stimulations—they are "the link between language, scientific or not, and the real world that language is all about" (*PT*, p. 5); so whatever kind of sentence we take as embodying the evidence for theory must have some close relation to observation sentences.

This is an issue which Quine seems to have been slow to appreciate. The essay "Epistemology Naturalized", published in 1969, makes no mention of it but says, rather, that "observation sentences are the repository of scientific evidence" (*OR*, p. 88). A couple of years later, however, he clearly understands the problem. He suggests that "we imagine for convenience of schematism that a calendar clock is in view" (*RR*, p. 129). Then a suitable dated sentence—his example is "Black rabbit on February 9 at 10:15".—is "a plain observation sentence that commands assent under any impingement pattern that happens to include among its features a glimpse of a black rabbit and a suitable glimpse of the hands of the calendar clock" (ibid.). We can accommodate place as well as time: "We have merely to imagine that a signpost is visible saying where we are". (ibid.) The strategy here is to argue that some observation sentences, those including suitable glimpses of calendar clocks and signposts, in fact *are* standing sentences, and thus suitable to be implied by the standing sentences of our theory. (The same strategy is exhibited in "The Nature of Natural Knowledge"; see pp. 75f.) The occasions on which calendar clocks and signposts are conveniently in view are, of course, greatly outnumbered by the occasions on which they are not. Hence Quine's resort to the curious idea that we *imagine* that we see such objects. Even granted that idea, however, we would need to add the claim that the clock and signpost are correct, and that is certainly a matter of theory, not of what is observed on a given occasion. (This is a point which Quine acknowledges; see NNK, pp. 75f.)

Quine quickly abandons the resort to imaginary clocks. His first attempt to replace it relies on what he calls *pegged observation sentences*. We adopt a system of spatio-temporal co-ordinates. Then the totality of pegged observation sentences can be described as follows: "Each observation sentence expressible in our language gets joined to each combination of spatio-temporal co-ordinates". (EESW, pp. 316f.) Thus we obtain an observation sentence which is "pegged" to a particular place and time. An example might be: "It's raining, in Chicago, on February 9, 2006, at 10:15". So far this looks very like the idea discussed in the previous paragraph. The crucial difference is that Quine is not supposing that sentences of this sort are observation sentences. (See EESW, p. 328, note 4; it is, of course, no more paradoxical to say that a pegged observation sentence is not an observation sentence than to say that counterfeit money is not money.) Because pegged observation sentences are not observation sentences, we do not need to worry about imaginary clocks and signposts.

Pegged observation sentences are standing sentences. They are closely related to observation sentences: a given pegged observation sentence is true just in case the observation sentence embedded in it is (or was or will be) true at the relevant place and time. Most theories, however, will not imply any pegged observation sentence. As Quine says: "Typically a theory will descend to particulars only conditionally upon other particulars, assumed as boundary conditions". (EESW, p. 317.) His solution assumes that the boundary conditions can themselves be phrased in the form of a conjunction of pegged observation sentences. Our theory may then be taken to imply a conditional, the antecedent of which is that conjunction and the consequent of which is our original pegged observation sentence. This kind of conditional is what Quine calls an *observation conditional*. For a time he took sentences of this sort as the crucial link in the chain between evidence and theory, as being both implied by theory and answerable to observation: "the relation of theory to observation", he says, is that "the theory implies observation conditionals" (EESW, p. 318).

In a later discussion, in "Empirical Content", Quine finds problems with his idea of an observation conditional. One is that the time and place referred to in the antecedent of the conditional may be distant from that referred to in the consequent. (Indeed, the sentences conjoined in the antecedent may themselves refer to various times and places.) In that case, the observer must rely on memory, on notes, on testimony, and so forth. Such reliance is justified by theory rather than by (current) observation. If theory

180

is to be judged by the observation conditionals that it implies, it is clearly undesirable that those conditionals should themselves contain theoretical presuppositions. As a solution to this problem, Quine suggests that we consider only conditionals in which the antecedent and the consequent are pegged to the same place and time. But we still face "the problem of determining places and times on an observational basis" (EC, *TT*, p. 26). This is clearly a theoretical matter which, again, is intruding in what should be purely observational. Quine's solution to this problem draws on his solution to the previous one. The same place and time is now assumed to be under discussion in the antecedent as in the consequent. If our theory implies the connection between antecedent and consequent for one place and time then it presumably does so for all. (Since standing sentences are true or false for all places and times.) Hence we do not need to specify places and times: we can simply take the generality, that the connection holds for all places and times, as fundamental.

We thus obtain Quine's notion of an *observation categorical*. If X and Y are observation sentences, then the sentence saying that whenever X is true Y is also true—"Whenever X, Y"—is an observation categorical. ("Whenever Y, X" is also an observation categorical, but a different one.) Observation categoricals are not to be thought of as constructed by generalizing over situations, and saying, for example: all situations in which *this* is true are situations in which *that* is true, or by generalizing in similar fashion over places and times, or anything else. On Quine's account the observation categoricals are prior to such generalizations. So an observation categorical is "an irreducible generality ... to the effect that the circumstances described in the one observation sentence are invariably accompanied by those described in the other". (*PT*, p. 10.)

Quine's late work leaves no doubt as to the importance that he attributes to observation categoricals. In a passage from the 1990s, he summarizes his epistemological project like this:

> The business of naturalized epistemology, for me, is an improved understanding of the chains of causation and implication that connect the bombardment of our surfaces, at the one extreme, with our scientific output at the other.
>
> (L&S, p. 349)

The beginnings of the chain are familiar from the previous two chapters:

> The first link is causal: The bombardment of the exteroceptors causes a neural intake. The next link connects the neural intake

with language. Observation sentences become associated with perceptually similar neural intakes, at first by conditioning.

(ibid.)

The step beyond that is where observation categoricals are invoked:

> The next link in the causal and logical chain from the external world to our theory thereof is, as I see it, the observation categorical: a standing sentence of the form "Whenever this, that" whose two components are observation sentences. Being a standing sentence, rather than an occasion sentence, it can be linked to scientific theory by logical implication. The empirical test of a chunk of theory consists in first deducing an observation categorical. ...
>
> This I see as *the essential connection between neural intake and scientific output.*

(ibid.; emphasis added)

Quine does not claim to know how observation categoricals might be learnt. (See *FSS*, p. 25. There is, however, some overlap between observation categoricals and eternal predications, such as "Fido is a dog"; he does speculate about how the latter might be learnt, as we saw in the second section of the previous chapter.) According to Quine's schematic account, our remote ancestors somehow picked up the capacity to form observation categoricals from observation sentences, and each of us picked it up in turn. However it happened, it was a momentous step. For one thing, observation categoricals are themselves a beginning of a theory of the world: they are "our first faltering scientific laws" (*FSS*, p. 25), and each is "a miniature scientific theory" (*FSS*, p. 26). This is a crucial step beyond observation sentences. The survival value both of ape cries and of human observation sentences, Quine says, "is vicarious observation: we learn about what only someone else can see" (*FSS*, p. 25). "Observation categoricals", he says,

> bring us much more. They bring us vicarious habituation, vicarious induction. One gets the benefit of generalized expectations built up over the years by some veteran observer or even by that veteran's own informant long dead. Observation categoricals can be handed down.

(ibid.)

Human beings have, of course, a far greater number and variety of observation sentences than apes or birds have of their cries and calls. Still, on Quine's account what we have at that level is of the same kind as what

182

the birds and the apes have. The difference in principle comes with standing sentences—observation categoricals. The simplest of such sentences embody habits of induction, which may have been learnt through painful experience. Thus embodied, the habits can be passed from generation to generation.

An observation categorical is tested by finding, or contriving, relevant situations. It claims that whenever one given observation sentence is true, a particular other one is also true. So we examine situations in which the first one is true, to see whether the second is also true in each of them. There is a striking asymmetry here. Suppose we examine a number of situations in which the first observation sentence is true and find that the second observation sentence is indeed true in each of them. We are encouraged, no doubt. Perhaps we feel free to use the observation categorical, and the inferential step that it licenses, in our thinking about the world. But what we have is evidently short of a proof, or even of a very convincing reason. Whereas if we find a situation in which the first observation sentence is true and the second is false, then we may be sure, just from that one case, that the observation categorical is false. (Unless, indeed, we take the observation categorical to be so securely known, on other grounds, that we change our minds about one or both of the observation sentences.) As Quine puts it: "observation serves only to refute a theory and not to support it" (*PT*, p. 12); we have no choice but to accept that even the best supported observation categoricals may simply turn out to be false. Here is one of the roots of Quine's fallibilism. Observation categoricals are links in the chain by which evidence bears on theories quite generally. Their fallibility thus infects the whole system. Once more advanced theory is in place it may mitigate the asymmetry. We may have theoretical reasons to accept a given observation categorical. In that case a few favourable instances may make us extremely confident of it; an apparent counter-instance may even be dismissed as observational error. But no general argument against fallibilism is possible on this sort of basis, for the advanced theory which bears indirectly on the given observation categorical is itself fallible, being based on other observation categoricals which are themselves fallible.

In Quine's schematic account, observation categoricals provide the route by which more advanced theory comes into contact with stimulations of our sensory surfaces. If utterances which are not themselves observation sentences or observation categoricals count as cognitive, as putative parts of our theory, it is because of their relation to observation categoricals. What is the relevant relation here? We accept or reject theoretical sentences on the basis of a prior acceptance or rejection of observation categoricals. The general idea of what it is to accept or reject a sentence on the basis of others is the one we saw in *Word and Object*; it is "finally ... due to the conditioning of sentences as responses to sentences as stimuli" (*WO*, p. 11; discussed in the second section of the previous chapter). Presumably we are to imagine a child skilled in rejecting and (more problematic) accepting observation categoricals under circumstances which his elders deem to be appropriate. Then the child learns, somehow, that assent to a certain range of observation categoricals makes it appropriate—acceptable to his elders—to assent to a certain utterance (not itself an observation sentence or categorical). Or something more complicated of that general sort takes place. The complex disposition which we are imagining the child as acquiring is the disposition to accept or reject a given sentence on the basis of having come to accept or reject one or more other sentences. It is because language-users in general have acquired that disposition that the sentence is part of our theory, and can inform us about the world, truly or falsely.

Quine holds that we can clarify the relation of theory to evidence by reconstructing the links between observation categoricals and theoretical sentences in terms of logic. Schematically, at least, the matter is straightforward enough:

> A theory is tested by deducing an observational categorical from it and testing the categorical. If it fails so does the theory. One or another of its component assertions is false and needs to be retracted. If the categorical passes the test, then so far so good. A favorable test does not, of course, prove the theory to be true; it does not even prove the categorical to be true.
>
> (*FSS*, p. 44)

For this tidy schematism to apply with full generality, however, the theory has to be stated with full explicitness. Assumptions which working scientists regard as too obvious to mention—or which they may simply be unaware of making—would need to be spelled out and used as premises. Also, the language in which the theory was stated would have to be reformulated and regularized, so as to make it conform to the demands of logic. (As we have indicated, this is the Quinean project which will occupy us in Chapters 9–13, below.)

Quine does suggest that this sort of explicitness and reformulation might have advantages for the science concerned: it would "perhaps contribute to the advancement of science by uncovering logical interconnections and suggesting a fruitful new hypothesis for testing." (*FSS*, p. 47.) Perhaps there might be something particular to the given subject-matter to be learnt from reformulating our theory of it in this fully explicit fashion. For the most

184

part, however, it seems more plausible to think that what is to be learnt from the idea of a fully explicit theory is something general about the nature and structure of science, and thus also about the world (something philosophical, one might say, in virtue of its generality and abstractness). From this point of view, what is of interest is not the actual reformulation of a particular theory, but rather the general claim that such a reformulation should in principle be possible, and the general methods by which it might proceed.

Speaking of observation categoricals as logically implied by a theory thus presupposes a degree of logical rigour and precision in the theory which will not be found in practice. It also idealizes in other ways. One is that an observation categorical is in principle compounded of observation sentences—sentences understood by all fully functioning speakers of the language. In any given circumstances, the verdict that would be given by any speaker on that sentence is the same as would be given by any other speaker (some qualification is needed here, to allow for the issue of the corrigibility in principle of observation sentences). This social agreement "renders science objective, or anyway intersubjective" (*FSS*, pp. 44–45). A working scientist, however, will rarely or never take matters to that extreme. He or she will rest content with what commands agreement from all those working within the same speciality or subspeciality. Such sentences will usually be more theoretical, and less widely used, than observation sentences. We might perhaps assimilate this situation to Quine's idealized picture by thinking of the scientist's practice as a matter of the employment of sentences which are observation sentences relative to a particular and rather narrow community of speakers—we think of those working in the given subspeciality as forming a small linguistic community. In any case, if agreement on those sentences fails within this small community, our scientist could, at least in principle, resort to categoricals compounded from what are observation sentences by anyone's standards. It is in this sense, rather than in any very practical sense, that observation sentences, and the observation categoricals compounded from them, form the ultimate evidence for science. As long as there is a common language, there must be such sentences; cases in which we actually appeal to them, however, are likely to be extremely rare.

Two other doubts about Quine's use of observation categoricals are potentially more threatening to his general picture of evidence and its relation to theory. First, we often presuppose background conditions which are not answerable to what is concurrently observed. To use an example of Quine's: litholite, a substance with distinctive appearance, emits a gas with a distinctive smell when its temperature is 180 degrees Celsius. (See *PT*, pp.

9f.) But the observation categorical will not mention the temperature, for that is not directly observable. Perhaps it will say: whenever you have litholite and a thermometer connected to it reads 180 degrees, you have the smell of hydrogen sulphite. But this assumes that the thermometer is in good working order and connected in the right way with the sample of litholite. In such cases we may imagine that there are notes on earlier tests of the thermometer, and that the observation categorical mentions the concurrent observation of notes. But sometimes there will be no notes or they may not be in view. Even where notes are in view, the connection between them and the situation they record is not merely a matter of observation. A second doubt along the same general lines is that most or all observation categoricals may hold only subject to *ceteris paribus* clauses which cannot be fully spelled out, or which mention conditions not subject to current observation. Quine's view, however, is that all evidence reduces, ultimately and in principle, to the observed concomitance of the truth of observation sentences, or the failure of such concomitance.

II Observation categoricals and empirical content

A theoretical sentence, or a set of them, counts as cognitive, we said, because of its relations to observation categoricals. In the idealized case, these are relations of logical implication. On this basis Quine defines the *empirical content* of a sentence or a set of sentences as the set of observation categoricals that it implies.[1] A sentence or set of sentences that implies observation categoricals, one or more, is said to have *critical mass*, and to be *testable*. Seeing how Quine deploys these ideas shows some of his doctrines from a new angle, and also reveals something of his attitude towards our theorizing.

There are very many sentences of science which are essential constituents of empirical theories but which, taken individually and in isolation from others, imply no observation categoricals. (This is one way of stating holism, as Quine understands it.) In the ordinary sense of "theoretical", indeed, it seems that theoretical sentences generally will be in this situation; they are unlikely to imply any observation categoricals without at least some statement of initial conditions.

In particular, no sentence of logic or mathematics, taken by itself, has empirical content. This is not a distinctive trait of mathematics, however; the same holds for many theoretical sentences. Even the set of all true sentences of mathematics lacks empirical content; it will imply no observation categoricals. But again Quine sees no distinctive trait. The infinite set of all mathematical truths lacks empirical content, but "[t]here is no end of other equally infinite classes of truths ... of which we can say that the whole infinite class, like mathematics, lacks empirical content" (*FSS*, p. 53). Where Quine does sense something distinctive about mathematics is that in that case the infinite truths in the empirically contentless set "are somehow all of a kind" (ibid.). As for *how* they are all of a kind, he is undogmatic; nothing turns on this point for him, certainly not an account of the basis of mathematical truth. He suggests that a significant feature is "paucity of primitive predicates, with consequent emphasis on logical construction" (*FSS*, p. 55). Thus understood, as he points out, the relevant characteristic becomes a matter of degree.

Two paragraphs ago we said that many sentences of science have no empirical content, but are nevertheless essential constituents of empirical theories. Quine considers the idea of a criterion of significance constructed on this basis. Such a criterion might say that a sentence is empirically significant if it has empirical content or if it plays an essential role in a set of sentences which has empirical content. Two points are important here. First, as Quine recognizes, the criterion does not work. Second, even if such a criterion were possible, he would not welcome it; it is no part of his concern to distinguish the empirically significant from the empirically empty in the sort of way suggested. We shall elaborate on both points.

The proposed criterion is that a sentence is empirically significant just in case it plays an essential role in some set of sentences with empirical content, i.e. removing the given sentence would deprive the set of some or all of its empirical content. But this will not work.[2] Consider an arbitrary sentence, *s*, and some observation categorical, *c*. Now form the set consisting simply of *s*, and the sentence "If *s* then *c*". This set implies the observation categorical *c*, and *s* plays an essential role in the implication. So by our criterion *s* is empirically significant; but *s* here could be any sentence at all, so the argument shows that *every* sentence is empirically significant by this criterion, which is thus useless. (See *FSS*, p. 48; Quine's example of a sentence to play the role of *s* is "Quadruplicity drinks procrastination", which he attributes to Russell.) What we need, as Quine points out, is the idea of sentences which are essential members of "*interesting* sets" (*FSS*, p. 48; emphasis in the original) which are testable. But it is hard to see how this idea could be turned into a clear or rigorous criterion—especially as our view of what sets are interesting is liable to change as our theory progresses.

Quine thus holds that no criterion of empirical significance is to be had. More significantly, he also says that if such a criterion were available, he would not endorse it. The Logical Positivists hoped for a criterion of meaningfulness—in particular, one which would separate meaningful science from meaningless metaphysics. Quine has no such ambitions. He says of the idea of such a criterion: "I would not want to impose it in positivistic spirit as a condition of meaningfulness" (*FSS*, pp. 48–49). Let us see in more detail what he says on the point:

> Much that is accepted as true or plausible even in the hard sciences, I expect, is accepted without thought of its joining forces with other plausible hypotheses to form a testable set. Such acceptations may be prompted by symmetries and analogies, or as welcome unifying links in the structure of the theory. Surely it often happens that a hypothesis remote from all checkpoints suggests further hypotheses that are testable. This must be a major source of hypotheses worth testing. Positivistic insistence on empirical content could, if heeded, impede the progress of science.
>
> (*FSS*, p. 49)

It is notable that the main argument here concerns the progress of science. Quine's view of science is very abstract, and mostly does not take much account of its dynamic or diachronic aspect—that science is, now and for the foreseeable future, incomplete, and is thus changing and growing. But here the dynamic aspect comes to the fore: the role of (some) untestable hypotheses in promoting new theoretical development, and thus eventually new testable hypotheses, is the clearest argument for not banishing the untestable (were we able to do so). So it is still the relation to observation categoricals, and thus to stimulation, which is the crucial thing; here, though, the relation may be yet more indirect, since the untestable hypothesis simply plays the role of suggesting new testable hypotheses.

There are somewhat different considerations which also point towards the same conclusion. Quine emphasizes that while prediction is the *test* of science, it is by no means its only aim; understanding also looms large as a goal. (See *PT*, pp. 2, 20.) Presumably "symmetries and analogies" and "unifying links" play a major role in our having a theory which is comprehensible to us. This idea is encouraged by Quine's brief discussion of "softer sciences", where the emphasis is more clearly on the understanding that a theory may bring, in spite of the untestability of some of its components:

> In softer sciences, from psychology and economics through sociology to history (I use 'science' broadly), checkpoints are sparser and sparser, to the point where their absence becomes rather the rule than the exception. Having reasonable grounds is one thing, and implying observation categoricals is another. Observation categoricals are

implicit still in the predicting of archaeological finds and the deciphering of inscriptions, but the glories of history would be lost if we stopped and stayed at the checkpoints.

(*FSS*, p. 49)

These passages are quite revealing of Quine's general views; we should be struck by his willingness to accept as scientific sentences which violate our imagined criterion. Holism shows that no criterion is in fact possible here; still, it's one thing to acquiesce in this result grudgingly, and another to welcome it, as Quine clearly does.

Quine's rejection of the idea of a criterion of meaningfulness is of a piece with the views he puts forward in "Meaning in Linguistics", discussed in Chapter 3, section II above. There we saw that the meaningfulness of a sentence, for Quine, is simply a matter of its being actually or potentially used by speakers of the given language. There is no test which could show that a sentence accepted as meaningful by speakers is in fact meaningless. In the passages we have discussed in the last few pages Quine makes it clear that even if a criterion could be devised, he would not want to impose it to show that sentences which speakers of the language accept as meaningful are in fact not so. The idea of meaningfulness, and of its opposite, nonsense, plays an important role in much of the history of twentieth-century analytic philosophy. The idea is implicit in Russell's work early in the century; it is increasingly explicit in his slightly later work and in Wittgenstein's *Tractatus*; it plays a significant role in Carnap's work. Not so for Quine. This marks a very large break, often unnoticed, between his work and that of his predecessors.

III Underdetermination

Our theory of the world, when stated with full explicitness, *implies* observation categoricals. But the relation does not hold in the other direction: no (consistent) set of observation categoricals will imply our theory of the world. Apart from other considerations, our theory contains terms which do not occur in observation categoricals—"electron", for example. No set of sentences which do not contain a given word can imply a sentence which does contain that word, unless the containment is vacuous.[3] The terms that occur in observation categoricals, however, also occur in other parts of our theory, so the implication of evidence by theory is not similarly blocked. So: theory, in principle, implies the observation categoricals which are its evidence, but the observation categoricals do not imply the theory. The asymmetry here echoes that of the relation between observation sentences and the observation categoricals which are constructed from them. Observation sentences, as we saw, can conclusively falsify observation categoricals but cannot conclusively verify them. Likewise, observation categoricals, being implied by theory, refute it if they do not turn out as theory predicts; they cannot, however, conclusively verify it, at least not in the sense of implying it.

The fact that our theory of the world is not implied by any (consistent) set of observation categoricals suggests that more than one theory of the world might be compatible with the evidence and might imply the same observation categoricals, and thus have the same empirical content in the sense discussed in the previous section. This idea is the underdetermination of theory by evidence, the view that our choice of theory is not determined by the evidence; this idea will require some clarification.

Note first that it is global theories that we are considering here. A theory of limited scope must mesh with our other theories so as to form a global theory which, taken as a whole, is empirically successful. Given two limited theories which implied the same observation categoricals, one might still be preferable on straightforward empirical grounds, if it did much better than the other in facilitating a successful global theory. Hence Quine suggests that we consider the issue of underdetermination only for "global systems of the world, so there is no question of fitting the rival theories into a broader context" (*PT*, p. 98).

We have been talking, without further specification, of "the evidence". Is it all possible evidence, the set of all true observation categoricals, that is at stake? Or rather the observation categoricals implied by some given theory? This is a point on which Quine has vacillated to some extent.[4] There is, I think, reason to focus on theories which imply *all* true observation categoricals. (We would, of course, not know that we had a theory which met this criterion.) A theory which implies only some of the true observation categoricals will be modified and extended as new ones become known. Even though two theories imply exactly the same observation categoricals, one of them may lend itself to that sort of extension and modification much better than the other; that would clearly be a reason to prefer it. Like the question of how a theory meshes with other theories, this reason raises considerations which are not relevant to the thesis of underdetermination. In most of his later discussions, however, Quine speaks simply of "our theory". Perhaps he is imagining that theory to be extended and perfected; or perhaps the point simply is not important for his purposes. (He is certainly not considering such limiting cases as a "theory" consisting of a single observation categorical.)

There is also another source of unclarity in the formulation of underdetermination. The thesis asserts that our theory has rivals which imply the same observation categoricals. Does it also assert that at least one of those rivals is also as good in other ways as our theory? Does it assert that more than one theory can be tied for first place when we take into account not only prediction of observations but also other theoretical virtues, such as clarity and simplicity? Some of Quine's formulations suggest this latter, stronger, version of the thesis, while others do not.[5] We shall make the distinction when it matters and otherwise ignore it, as Quine often does.

While we are refining and clarifying the thesis of underdetermination, there is one further issue to go into. In "Empirically Equivalent Systems of the World", Quine phrases it as the question whether there are empirically equivalent but *logically incompatible* theories of the world. The idea of logical incompatibility, however, turns out to be a red herring, and for interesting reasons. Suppose we had two empirically equivalent theories which were logically incompatible. The source of the incompatibility might be, say, that one of them contains the sentence "Molecules have greater mass than electrons" while the other contains the sentence "Molecules do not have greater mass than electrons". These theories of course *are* logically incompatible. But suppose we alter the second one by replacing the word "molecule" at every occurrence by the word "schmolecule". We thus obtain a third theory, which is a trivial variant of the second—it differs from it only in the spelling of a single word—and yet is *not* logically incompatible with the first. (We could, of course, ring the changes on the first theory rather than the second.) This kind of manoeuvre can always be applied where we have empirically equivalent but logically incompatible theories. The change does not affect the implication of observation categoricals, since they do not contain the word "molecule". So the third theory is empirically equivalent to the second, and thus also to the first. The first and the second are logically incompatible, but the third is not logically incompatible with either. But since the third is simply a trivial variant of the second, any significance that there is to the difference between the first and the second should also be found in the difference between the first and the third. So nothing of any interest turns on the logical incompatibility here.[6]

The broader moral here concerns the individuation of theories. Quine refuses to put any theoretical weight on the notion of synonymy. For him, therefore, a theory is simply a finite set of sentences, or their conjunction. (The finite set may of course imply infinitely many others.) The sentences are individuated simply as a sequence of letters, spaces, punctuation marks, and other symbols that compose them: change the spelling of one word in a sentence and you have a different sentence, hence a different theory. This is why we count the second theory and the third, of the previous paragraph, as distinct theories, even though they are trivial variants, each of the other. The mere fact that we have *different* theories, by Quine's literal-minded criterion, does not yet show that anything of any general significance can turn on the difference. We shall return to this general point in a couple of pages.

The thesis of underdetermination, as it emerges from this process of clarification, is this: we suppose there is a global theory, ours or an improved version. (In the limit, a theory which implies all true observation categoricals and no false ones.) Such a theory, the thesis claims, is bound to have empirically equivalent alternatives. At first sight one might think that the thesis follows directly from the fact that theory is not implied by evidence, or from holism. In neither case, however, does the implication hold in any straightforward fashion.

To begin with: underdetermination does not follow simply from the fact that theory is not implied by evidence. Suppose we had an improved version of our theory which implies all the evidence but is not implied by that evidence. It might be, conceivably, that this theory is the only one which implies all the true observation categoricals and none of the false ones; still that would not show that it was implied by the true observation categoricals. Indeed the argument given in the first paragraph of this section shows that this implication would *not* hold. (This assumes that our theory, or its successor, contains sentences which essentially—i.e. non-vacuously— contain terms which do not occur in any observation categoricals.) Under those circumstances, the theory we had would not be underdetermined. It would be the only possible theory, in the sense that none other would be available which implied all the true observation categoricals and none of the false ones. But still the theory would not be implied by the observation categoricals. It would outrun them and their implications. Creativity beyond the logical would be required to think up the theory.

Although underdetermination does not follow from the fact that evidence does not imply theory, it is still a very plausible idea. If our evidence does not imply our theory, then why should there not be another theory, also compatible with all the evidence? Underdetermination also gains plausibility from holism. That doctrine, we should recall, can be stated as saying that there are sentences of our theory which do not imply any observation categoricals when they are taken in isolation, but do have such implications when they are taken together with other sentences of our theory. It follows from this that there are sets of sentences such that the set as a whole implies some observation categoricals but removing any member will leave us with a set which implies fewer or none. Presumably there are many such sets.

Suppose that T_1 is one such set; suppose further that one of the implied observation categoricals turns out to be false. Since more than one sentence of our theory was required to imply the falsehood, there is in principle some choice as to how that theory should be revised. All members of the set are required for the implication, so it can be blocked by removing any one of them. Since there is more than one way of revising T_1, there is more than one successor theory: T_2 and T_3, let us say, are both possible replacements for T_1. (The theories here may be global theories, but the argument does not require that they are.)

It might thus seem that underdetermination is simply a consequence of holism. But this is not so, at least not if we understand holism as Quine does. T_2 and T_3 are both possible replacements for T_1, and both are acceptable in as much as neither implies the falsehood that T_1 implies. But it does not follow that either T_2 or T_3 implies the *negation* of the false observation categorical. If one of them does while the other does not then the two are not empirically equivalent; they may also fail to be empirically equivalent for other reasons. It may be that in modifying T_1 so as to block the implication of the falsehood we also block the implication of some true observation categoricals, perhaps different ones in each case. It is no part of Quine's understanding of holism that we can always find a modification of a refuted theory that continues to imply all of the truths that that theory implies.[7] (Still less to say that we can always find more than one such modification.)

Underdetermination of theory by evidence thus does not follow either from holism or from the fact that evidence does not imply theory. Each of those facts, however, indicates a looseness of fit between evidence and theory that seems to lend plausibility to underdetermination. Quine, however, argues that the thesis is less easy to make sense of than might at first appear. It is, he says, "plausible insofar as it is intelligible, but it is less readily intelligible than it may seem" (EESW, p. 313). In the rest of this section we shall explore Quine's reasons for thinking that its intelligibility is dubious, and his response to this situation.

The thesis of underdetermination is that if there is a global theory, ours or a superior version, then there is an empirically equivalent alternative. The difficulty in making sense of the thesis lies in the word "alternative". Clearly we do not want to count one theory as in any interesting sense an *alternative* to another if they are logically equivalent. (In what follows it will simplify matters to leave this point unstated; it is assumed throughout.) But there is also a more troubling point, which is connected with the one made in our discussion of logical incompatibility. If "alternative" means simply that we have two different sets of sentences then underdetermination is trivially true, for reasons that leave it without interest. As Quine remarks, if we interchange the word "electron" and the word "molecule" at all their occurrences, then we obtain a different theory, in the sense of a different set of sentences. (Quine attributes this idea to B. M. Humphries, "Indeterminacy of Translation and Theory".) The two sets imply the same observation categoricals; the word "molecule" does not occur in observation categoricals, so the replacement will make no difference to them. The natural response to such a case is that if we were to make this switch then we simply would mean by the word "electron" what we formerly meant by the word "molecule", and vice versa, so the two sets of sentences are not really different theories at all. (Similarly if we merely change the spelling of one theoretical term, as in the "molecule"/"schmolecule" example a few pages back.)

Similar remarks apply to the difference between, say, our theory as formulated in English, and our theory as formulated in German or Japanese or any other language. Here, however, the change of language will affect the observation categoricals too. It will not be *the same* observation categoricals which are implied—not, that is to say, the same sentences; but presumably the observation sentences implied by one version can be straightforwardly translated into those implied by another.

So now our question is: do we have a clear way of making sense of what should count as an *alternative* theory that eliminates the cases that strike us as trivial? Is there a way of formulating the thesis of underdetermination that leaves it with some interest? If we helped ourselves to the idea of a proposition, or the meaning of a sentence, then we could say: two sets of sentences express genuine alternative theories if the sentences of the one, beyond the observational level, do not mean the same as the sentences of the other. (Perhaps the requirement should be: a sufficient number of significant sentences of the one do not mean the same as any sentences of the other. There are other sources of vagueness here as well, but I shall leave this point aside.) In the case of the theory in English and the theory in German, the natural response is that although the sentences are different they mean the same, and hence are just different ways of saying the same thing. Quine, of course, is not willing to accept an unexplained notion of sentence meaning, or of two sentences "saying the same thing"; yet without something to that effect, the thesis seems to be in danger of collapsing into triviality.

In the case of variants like the "molecule"/"electron" case, the difference between the two theories strikes us as trivial because we can see how to turn the one theory into the other. We have a one-to-one correlation between the sentences of the one theory and the sentences of the other, and this mapping will, evidently, preserve all interesting properties. (In particular, if a sentence of the one theory stands in some evidential relation to an observation categorical, then its correlate under the mapping will stand in that same relation to the same observation categorical.) We have, in short, a translation between the two theories. Something similar, of course, holds in the case of a theory phrased in English and what we would intuitively call "the same theory" phrased in German, say. Quine would not, strictly speaking, call these the same theory. What matters, however, is that we have a translation from one to the other—a correlation which will, again, preserve all interesting properties. (This case is a little different. Although translation from English to German can certainly be done, it is not a trivial matter. Also the observation categoricals will be different, but inter-translatable, as noted.)

So we can perhaps formulate the thesis of underdetermination by appeal to translation: our global theory has an alternative which is empirically equivalent but which cannot be translated, sentence by sentence, into ours or into a theory logically equivalent to ours. In "Empirically Equivalent Systems of the World", Quine assumes that we are dealing with two theories, each of which is phrased in his preferred notation of first-order logic. In that case, the only way in which the language of the one can differ from the language of the other is in the predicates of the theory. (See Chapter 10, below.) Translating one theory into the other is then a matter of finding a reconstrual of predicates—for each theoretical predicate of the first theory we need to find a predicate, or at least an open sentence with the right number of free variables, of the second theory. Carrying out the replacement will then translate the first theory into the second. The replacement, however, may be exceedingly complex. Quine describes the situation like this:

> We might study two incompatible theory formulations, trying in vain to imagine an observation that could decide between them, and we might conclude that they are empirically equivalent; we might conclude this without seeing a reconciling reconstrual of predicates. This we might; but there still could be a reconciling reconstrual of predicates, subtle and complex and forever undiscovered. The thesis of underdetermination ... asserts that our system of the world is bound to have empirically equivalent alternatives that are not reconcilable by reconstrual of predicates, however devious. This, for me, is an open question.
>
> (EESW, p. 327)

He is thus agnostic about this version of the thesis. He does, however, accept a weaker version, which refers not to *there being* no way of translating the one theory into the other, but rather to our not being able to find such a way: "our system of the world is bound to have empirically equivalent alternatives which, if we were to discover them, *we would see no* way of reconciling by reconstrual of predicates." (Ibid.; emphasis added.) His formulation in *Pursuit of Truth* is similar: "Imagine now two theories, ours and another, such that we are persuaded of their empirical equivalence but *we see no way* of systematically converting one into the other by reinterpretation sentence by sentence". (*PT*, p. 97; emphasis added.)

Quine's resort to the weaker version here may seem uncharacteristic of him, as may his agnosticism about the stronger version. I think the right moral to draw from this, and from other ways in which his discussion of the thesis of underdetermination is inconclusive, is that the thesis is not of great significance to him. No other aspects of his thought depend on it. Some commentators have claimed that underdetermination poses a challenge to realism. From Quine's point of view, however, there is no real challenge here. We shall take up this issue in Chapter 12, section IV below.

8

RADICAL TRANSLATION AND
ITS INDETERMINACY

The scenario of radical translation imagines a linguist attempting to construct a systematic method of translating the language of a group of people. It is *radical* translation because we suppose that our linguist has no prior contact with the language, nor with anyone who has any knowledge of it. The purpose of this chapter is to explore the idea and, in particular, to investigate Quine's famous—or notorious—conjecture of the *indeterminacy* of radical translation. This is the claim that two linguists, independently engaged in radical translation, might come up with different and incompatible translation manuals, each of which was fully successful. The first section of this chapter will enlarge upon this statement, in an attempt to get clear on exactly what the claim is.

For many purposes, though not all, indeterminacy is best considered as two quite distinct doctrines. (Quine at one point even speaks of them as "indeterminacies in different senses"; "Response to Orenstein", p. 573.) One concerns the translation of complete sentences. Here Quine conjectures that two translation manuals, each fully acceptable, may give translations of a given sentence which are not in any sense equivalent. The other doctrine concerns not the translation of sentences but rather of parts of sentences. It is that two fully acceptable translations may give different translations of sub-sentential parts of language, but in such a way that the differences cancel out, so that for whole sentences the two translations give roughly equivalent readings. Here it is translations of referring expressions which have received the greatest attention; for that reason, we will call it "indeterminacy of reference".[1] There is, unfortunately, no generally accepted name for the first, as distinct from the second. Quine usually just calls it indeterminacy, for it is explicit that he takes this idea, not the indeterminacy of reference, to be "the serious and controversial thesis on indeterminacy of translation" (*PT*, p. 50), as giving the "real ground of the doctrine" ("On the Reasons for the Indeterminacy of Translation", p. 178). Usually I shall

197

follow Quine in just using the term "indeterminacy" to mean the first; when clarity calls for a separate term I shall speak, as Quine occasionally does, of "holophrastic indeterminacy".

The distinction between these two doctrines is of great importance, but is not clearly made in *Word and Object*. Holophrastic indeterminacy always seems to have been Quine's chief concern, but much of the early discussion of indeterminacy picked up on the indeterminacy of reference. The distinction did not emerge with full clarity in Quine's work until the 1970 essay, "Reasons for the Indeterminacy of Translation"; as time went by it became increasingly important. In his late works he speaks of holophrastic indeterminacy as a "conjecture", whereas he says that indeterminacy of reference "admits of trivial proof" ("Reply to Woods", H&S, p. 728; cf. also response to Antony, O&K, p. 419).

The scenario of radical translation, and its indeterminacy, achieves prominence with chapter 2 of *Word and Object* but can be traced further back in Quine's work. The idea of radical translation, as a way of making claims about meaning tangible, goes back almost as far as Quine's earliest work in philosophy.[2] In "Carnap and Logical Truth" he invokes something like that idea in a discussion of the idea of "pre-logical peoples" (WP, pp. 109, 112). Radical translation plays a significant role in his 1951 essay "Meaning in Linguistics" where he uses it to contrast the task of the grammarian, who is concerned merely to specify which strings of phonemes are sentences of a foreign language, with that of the lexicographer, who attempts to specify which pairs of expressions of the language are synonymous. Quine discusses the sort of empirical evidence that is available, and the way in which that evidence bears on the task at hand. He emphasizes the extent to which the lexicographer must rely on her creativity, and on projecting her own worldview onto that of the people whom she is translating. His point here is not the difficulty of *finding out* what that natives mean. His point is, rather, that "we have nothing for the lexicographer to be right or wrong about." (*FLPV*, p. 63); although not labelled as such, this is indeterminacy.

Carnap took up the idea of translation in response to Quine's doubts about synonymy, and about other semantical ideas. He used it to argue that synonymy is a perfectly reputable concept because there are empirical criteria for its application. (See Carnap's reply to Quine in Schilpp, *The Philosophy of Rudolf Carnap*, and also Carnap, "Meaning and Synonymy in Natural Languages".) Quine's explicit advocacy of indeterminacy, in *Word and Object* and later, has been widely held to be a response to this attempt, though there is little direct evidence that this was Quine's motivation.[3] Much later, he says explicitly that the "thought experiment in radical translation ... was meant as a challenge to the reality of propositions as meanings of cognitive sentences" (response to Horwich, O&K, p. 419; cf. B&G, "Comment on Hintikka", p. 176). Doubts about the determinacy of translation are "doubts about how empirical criteria could in general determine what intension is determined by a sentence" (B&G, "Comment on Katz", p. 199).

The point of the general idea of radical translation is to give an approach to language which is evidently empirical, to see how much can be made of the idea of meaning, and also to show how language could be learnt (by the linguist) within those constraints. Quine's linguists are idealized in a number of ways, but they are not credited with any kind of non-empirical insight into the minds of those they seek to translate. They begin simply with what is observable, and what can be inferred from that by ordinary uses of scientific method. Questions about the empirical basis of language and meaning can then be phrased by asking: how, on that basis, could the linguists come up with translations? (As emphasized earlier, Quine comes to prefer an approach which asks how infants could come to acquire cognitive language; this approach predominates in his later work.) The exploration of the scenario of radical translation thus belongs to what I have called the epistemological side of Quine's work. As indicated in the previous paragraph, however, Quine also thinks of (holophrastic) indeterminacy as an argument against synonymy, and thus against propositions, and meanings more generally. (An argument against meanings is not an argument against the idea of *meaningfulness*; see Chapter 3, section I above.) It is in service of an ontological claim, that there are no entities of a certain sort. The subject of radical translation and its indeterminacy thus spans the two aspects of Quine's work which I have distinguished, the epistemological and the metaphysical. This is the reason for the position of the present chapter, between the primarily epistemological discussions of Chapters 4–7 and the primarily metaphysical discussions of Chapters 9–13.

The first section of this chapter will be concerned to give a more detailed statement of exactly what the indeterminacy of translation amounts to. The second section will take up the indeterminacy of reference and Quine's argument for that claim. The third section considers a challenge, that indeterminacy, of either sort, is incoherent or obviously absurd; it will also consider responses to this idea. The fourth and fifth sections will consider the arguments for and against indeterminacy; here holophrastic indeterminacy will be our primary subject, though the indeterminacy of reference will receive some attention. The sixth and final section of the chapter will consider the significance of holophrastic indeterminacy.

Almost all aspects of the indeterminacy of translation have been the subject of great controversy: what it comes to; whether it is incoherent, absurd, or in some other way quite radically defective; whether there is any reason to accept it; what would show it to be true or false; and what follows if it is true. Since the publication of *Word and Object*, indeterminacy has provoked an immense volume of secondary literature, much of it highly critical of Quine. The volume and strength of the reaction might lead one to think that indeterminacy is a central Quinean doctrine; some have even argued that his position as a whole depends upon it. I think this is a mistake. For reasons that I shall explain at length in section VI, I think that the truth of the idea is of less importance to Quine than is often supposed, and is not crucial for his thought in general. The coherence of the idea is another matter. An appreciation of how the possibility of indeterminacy arises, and why the idea is not incoherent or obviously absurd, might be said to be a criterion of having fully assimilated Quine's naturalistic view of language.

I Indeterminacy of translation

What exactly is indeterminacy of translation? At the start of the chapter we phrased it like this: two linguists, independently engaged in radical translation of a language hitherto completely unknown to them, might come up with different and incompatible translation manuals, each of which was fully successful. This requires clarification. We shall make two relatively brief points, and then turn to an issue requiring rather more discussion.

To begin with, what is it for a translation manual to be "fully successful"? One might think that a manual is successful if it translates any sentence of the one language by an equivalent or synonymous sentence of the other; that would rule out indeterminacy from the start. Quine would of course reject an understanding of translation which relies upon synonymy; given his doubts about this latter notion, he needs to show that our ordinary practices of translation do not presuppose it. He understands the success of a translation manual in practical terms; it is a matter of the manual's efficacy in facilitating "fluent dialogue and successful negotiation" with the speakers of the translated language (*FSS*, p. 80; the same phrase occurs in O&K, p. 410). "The practical purpose of such a manual would be inculcation in us of fluency and effectiveness in the native language. ... I picture the whole enterprise as directed to the holistic objective of communication". (*FSS*, p. 82.) Quine's claim is that the two linguists might produce incompatible translation manuals each of which is fully successful in this sense.

Given this understanding of what success in translation amounts to, it is clear Quine does not take indeterminacy to imply or suggest that translation is impossible, or paradoxical, or in some way more problematic than is generally thought. He is not out to undermine the practice, or to discredit it in any way. In a response to Hintikka, he says: "I am in favor also of translation, even radical translation. I am concerned only to show what goes into it" (D&H, p. 312). And again, in a reply to the same commentator some twenty years later, "I don't recognize a problem of indeterminacy of translation". ("Comment on Hintikka", B&G, p. 176.) If one assumes that the only way to understand translation is as preserving synonymy, then an attack on that notion will look like an attack on translation. As we have just seen, however, Quine gives a different account of translation. Given that understanding of the matter, indeterminacy does not threaten the practice of translation. Fully successful translation is perfectly possible, in Quine's view; his conjecture, indeed, is that it may be possible in more ways than one, not less.[4]

Our second minor point of clarification concerns the question: in what sense are the two manuals "different and incompatible"? In *Word and Object*, Quine spoke of their producing as translations of a single sentence two sentences which are not equivalent "in any plausible sense of equivalence, however loose".[5] He quickly came to dislike even this minimal appeal to the notion of equivalence. In 1969 he endorsed a suggestion of Harman's: "it is just that one translator would reject the other's translation" of the given sentence (D&H, reply to Harman, p. 297). Later he improves upon the point by saying: "the English sentences prescribed as translation of a given Jungle sentence by two rival manuals might not be interchangeable in English contexts" (*PT*, p. 48). We are supposing that we have two translation manuals, each of which makes for smooth communication. Quine suggests an operational test for their being "different and incompatible". We employ them alternately, translating one sentence by one manual, then the next sentence by the other manual, the next by the first, and so on. If the result is that we regularly translate discourse in the target language into something incoherent in our language, if the alternating use of the manuals destroys our fluent interaction with the speakers of the target language, then the two manuals count as different and incompatible. (See, again, *PT*, p. 48.)

The rest of this section will be devoted to a point on which Quine has often been misinterpreted. Indeterminacy is an ontological matter, not, as sometimes thought, an epistemological matter.[6] It is not a question of the difficulty or impossibility of our *discovering* which of the two acceptable translations is correct. Indeterminacy is, rather, the claim that there is nothing to discover, "nothing for the lexicographer [or linguist] to be right or wrong about", as Quine says ("Meaning in Linguistics", *FLPV*, p. 63, quoted in context early in this chapter). Facilitating "fluent dialogue and successful negotiation" is not merely how we find out that we have a good translation manual; it is all that correctness can amount to for such manuals. If two manuals each fulfil this criterion completely, then each is completely correct. This is a fundamental matter, and one which will recur in later sections.

Some commentators have interpreted indeterminacy epistemologically, as the claim that, although there *is* a uniquely correct translation, the evidence available to the linguist, and the procedures she can legitimately employ, do not suffice to determine it. If that was what Quine meant, then indeterminacy would simply be a special case of the more general idea of underdetermination of theory by evidence—the idea that our evidence does not uniquely determine a single theory of the world. (See Chapter 7, sections III and IV above.) Chomsky, for example, puts the point like this:

> serious hypotheses concerning a native speaker's knowledge of English ... will "go beyond the evidence". If they did not, they would be without interest. Since they go beyond mere summary of data, it will be the case that there are competing assumptions consistent with the data. But why should all of this occasion any surprise or concern?
>
> (Chomsky, "Quine's Empirical Assumptions", pp. 66–67)

Quine does not think that indeterminacy should occasion any concern; perhaps, for those who have pondered the matter enough, it should not occasion any surprise either. But certainly he does not think it is merely a special case of the underdetermination of theory by evidence. The indeterminacy conjecture is not that two manuals of translation may each be compatible with the available *evidence*; it is, rather, that each may be compatible with all of the facts about the world. (In spite of his partial endorsement of underdetermination, Quine is a realist; see Chapter 12, below.) Quine replies to Chomsky as follows:

> adopt for the moment my fully realistic attitude toward electrons and muons and curved space-time, thus falling in with the current theory of the world, despite knowing that it is methodologically under-determined. Consider, from this realistic point of view, the totality of truths of nature, known and unknown, observable and

unobservable, past and future. The point about indeterminacy of translation is that it withstands even all this truth, the whole truth about nature. ... This is what I meant by saying that, where indeterminacy applies ... there is no fact of the matter even to *within* the acknowledged under-determination of a theory of nature.

(D&H, p. 303; emphasis in the original)

He is equally emphatic in "Things and Their Place in Theories". He repeats the point that in cases of indeterminacy there is "no fact of the matter" as to which translation manual is correct. He goes on to say: "The intended notion of fact of the matter is not transcendental or yet epistemological ... it is ontological, a question of reality, and to be taken naturalistically within our system of the world." ("Things and Their Place in Theories", *TT*, p. 23.)

The misreading of indeterminacy as an epistemological matter is understandable. Quine very often talks about the linguist's evidence, or data, and methods. In *Word and Object*, for example, he speaks of "the objective data he [the linguist] has to go on" (p. 28), and of "possible data and methods" (p. 72). In *Pursuit of Truth* he says, similarly, that "our only data are native utterances and their outwardly observable circumstances" (p. 38). He goes on to speak of the linguist's methods. She begins by "tentatively identifying and translating observation sentences" (p. 44); then she will attempt to identify analogues of our logical constants by considering utterances made up of two or more observation sentences (pp. 44f.); then she will form what Quine calls "analytical hypotheses" about how utterances may be analysed into units which can be recombined to form new utterances, and about how those units may be translated. Quine emphasizes the difficulty of the task, and the "freedom for conjecture" (pp. 45f.) that it leaves; he considers "what constraints our radical translator can bring to bear" (p. 46). All of this sounds like a highly schematized account of the procedures of radical translation, of the evidence and methods which bear on the construction of a translation manual.

If indeterminacy is not an epistemological matter, why does Quine's discussion so often proceed in terms of the linguist's evidence or data? No doubt he does so in part for heuristic reasons: talk of the evidence the linguist has, and the methods she can use, illustrates and dramatizes the situation. But the point is not merely rhetorical; the way the argument is framed, in terms of evidence and method, is significant. Quine's claim is that there is "no fact of the matter" as to which of two translation manuals is correct, that the whole truth about the world would not suffice to settle the issue. This is an ontological question, not an epistemological one. But what counts as a "truth about the world" here? What are the facts? A preliminary answer is that the facts are those for which our idealized linguist might, in principle, gather evidence. In particular, these will be facts about the dispositions of the speakers of the language being studied, dispositions which correlate their observable behaviour with observable circumstances. (Verbal dispositions will, no doubt, be particularly relevant, but not exclusively so.)

There will, of course, be a gap between the evidence that the linguist has and the facts about what dispositions speakers of the given language have. This gap, however, is a matter of ordinary inductive uncertainty, and is of no particular concern to Quine. (As already remarked, he envisages his linguist as beginning with what is observable, and what can be inferred from that by ordinary uses of scientific method. He is not concerned to question the use of scientific method.) This gap is not what gives rise to indeterminacy. Indeterminacy, rather, concerns the gap between the facts and the translation—in particular, of course, it concerns the question whether the facts suffice to determine a unique translation manual.

Why are only the sorts of facts relevant to translation ones for which the linguist might have evidence? We have already seen the crux of the answer, in our discussion of Quine's (alleged) behaviourism (Chapter 4, section IV, above). We quoted Quine as saying: "in linguistics one has no choice" but to "be a behaviorist". This view is based on how language is learnt: "Each of us learns his language by observing other people's verbal behavior and having his own faltering verbal behavior observed and reinforced or corrected by others". (*PT*, pp. 38.) Hence, quite generally: "There is nothing in linguistic meaning beyond what is to be gleaned from overt behavior in observable circumstances". (ibid.) What underlies this is Quine's fundamental empiricism, the fact that "our information about the world comes only through impacts on our sensory receptors" (*PT*, p. 19). This applies to the linguist as much as to the rest of us. Only what is intersubjectively available can play a role in the learning of language; hence only what is, at least in principle, available to the linguist can be relevant to the mastery of language. (We shall return to this point in section V, below.)

Indeterminacy is thus the claim that mutually incompatible manuals of translation can conform to all the same distributions of behavioural dispositions. Quine also holds that such dispositions are "the only facts of nature that bear on the correctness of translation". Hence the conjecture is the claim that "mutually incompatible manuals of translation conform to all the same overall states of nature".[7]

II Indeterminacy of reference

We emphasized at the beginning of this chapter that Quine sees holo-phrastic indeterminacy, indeterminacy of the translation of whole sentences, as more important than indeterminacy of reference. In spite of this, we will begin with the latter. It is in some ways more tangible than holophrastic indeterminacy; there is a fairly clear-cut argument, and examples. For this reason, it will be helpful to have this form of indeterminacy before us in discussing issues which arise from both forms.

How does the indeterminacy of reference come about? We shall begin by talking, somewhat loosely, about meaning, as Quine does in this context. We ascribe meanings to sub-sentential parts of language. In Quine's view, however, "words ... owe their meaning to their role in sentences" (*PT*, p. 37), rather than having meaning independently. One consequence of this idea is that our ascriptions of meaning quite generally are answerable only to the use of sentences. (The notion of a sentence here, as elsewhere, is simply that of a piece of language capable of correct or incorrect use without linguistic context. See Chapter 4, section VI.) There is slack between ascriptions of meaning to sentences and ascriptions of meaning to sub-sentential units of language. More than one way of ascribing meanings to the latter is compatible with any given way of ascribing meanings to sentences. Since only the meanings of sentences impose any constraints at all on ascriptions of meaning, no one of these ways of ascribing meanings to sub-sentential parts of language can claim to be cor-rect to the exclusion of the others. Provided they really are all fully compa-tible with ascriptions of meaning to sentences, they are all equally correct— though incompatible with one another. In particular, Quine argues, more than one account of the objects presupposed by our theory is possible.[8]

How are we to make this talk of meaning less vague? The point is that the fundamental relation between language and the world is not a refer-ential relation, between parts of language and *objects*. It is, rather, a relation between sentences—complete utterances—and sensory stimulations. This is the essential point of the semantic primacy of sentences. The point is most vividly seen in the case of observation sentences. Taken as unstructured responses to stimulation, as first learnt, such sentences get their meaning simply from their relation to sensory stimulation. These proto-observation sentences make no ontological claims. Reference is more complex than anything going on that level; it requires, for example, pronouns, plural endings, copulas of identity and of predication, the contrast between sin-gular and general terms. As we emphasized in Chapter 6, reference emerges only when observation sentences become part of a more sophisticated theory, which includes identity, plurals, and so on.

Fully fledged observation sentences, of course, *are* part of a more sophisticated theory and they do make ontological claims. But what does their being part of a wider theory amount to? It consists in there being connections among *sentences* of the theory, including the observation sentences. Such links, as we saw, consist ultimately in "the conditioning of sentences as responses to sentences as stimuli" (*WO*, p. 11; quoted in context in Chapter 6, section II above). Given Quine's general approach to language, this point should not be controversial. (The notion of a sentence, again, is simply that of a complete utterance; only a complete utterance can be a stimulus, or a response to a stimulus, of the sort relevant to language-use.)

Quite generally, no longer confining ourselves to observation sentences, only two sorts of factors are relevant to the correct use of language—and thus to meaning, if we use the term—on a Quinean approach. First, links between sentences and sensory stimulation. (The links consist in the fact that the occurrence of the stimulation makes it more or less likely that the given person will utter the sentence, or will assent to it when another utters it.) Second, the sorts of links among sentences indicated in the previous paragraph. For the indeterminacy of reference, what matters is that both of these sorts of factors deal with sentences, complete utterances. Sub-sentential units thus impose no independent constraint upon an account of language; any account which gives the right story about sentences and their use is acceptable (again, all complete utterances count as sentences). The semantic account of sub-sentential units is not basic; it is derivative upon the semantic account of complete sentences.

This is not to say that we could manage without the idea that sentences are made up of significant parts. For one thing, as has been often remarked, our ability to understand and to produce sentences which we have never heard before depends upon our combining sub-sentential parts of language, each of which will in general be familiar to us from its use in other sentences. For another, it may be impossible for us to use theoretical sentences correctly without at least implicitly analysing those sentences into significant constituent parts. Take the most obvious case, that of the "so-called logical connections" between sentences. A logical connection may be thought of as summing up infinitely many facts of the form: whenever it is appropriate to assert *those* sentences it is also appropriate to assert *this* one. But we could not learn all of these facts one-by-one. What we learn—implicitly at first, explicitly from logic books—is that whenever it is appropriate to assert a sentence of this *form*, it is appropriate also to assert a corresponding sentence of *that* form. But this requires that we attribute forms to sentences, i.e. see them as made up of constituent parts and patterns which are significant and which recur in other sentences.[9]

Our conclusion, a paragraph back, was that the meaning of sub-sentential parts of language is derivative upon the meanings of sentences. Since it is the sub-sentential parts of language that refer, reference is derivative upon the meanings of sentences. The referential aspect of language is not basic, not given; it is constructed or derived. Hence, as Quine says:

> Reference and ontology recede thus to the status of mere auxiliaries. True sentences, observational and theoretical, are the alpha and the omega of the scientific enterprise. They are related by structure, and objects figure as mere nodes of the structure. What particular objects there may be is indifferent to the truth of observation sentences, indifferent to the support they lend to theoretical sentences, indifferent to the success of the theory in its predictions.
>
> (PT, p. 31)

Objects are central to our theory of the world, for we cannot get by without analysing our sentences so as to reveal structure: otherwise we could never master the sentence-to-sentence links which are essential to language beyond the observational level. For all that, however, the role of objects is secondary in epistemology and in semantics; the truth of sentences, and their links to one another, are primary.

Reference is derivative. The thesis of the indeterminacy of reference—to come around to that again—is that there is more than one way that it could be derived, more than one way in which we could attribute reference to our terms while still preserving the relations of sentences to sensory stimulation and to one another. So far this idea is no more than an abstract possibility. Quine, however, is in no doubt at all that there are such alternative ways of ascribing reference; the matter "admits of trivial proof", he says (H&S, 2nd edn only, p. 728). There are a number of ways in which Quine thinks the point can be demonstrated. Perhaps the simplest, and certainly the one to which he most often appeals in later writings, employs the idea of a *proxy function*. The idea here is that we take a one-to-one function, f, defined over the objects to which our beliefs apparently commit us. For spatio-temporal objects, an example is *spatio-temporal complement of*; this function maps any given object onto the rest of space-time, i.e. to all of space-time excluding the given object. Now we reinterpret each sentence which appears to be about an object, x, as being, instead, about $f(x)$. And we also reconstrue each predicate, so that it holds of $f(x)$ (the spatio-temporal complement of x, in our example) just in case the original predicate held of x.

The reconstruals of objects and of predicates cancel out, in trivial fashion, so that the net import of each sentence is unaffected. A reconstrued sentence will be true, under any circumstances, just in case the original version was also true under the same circumstances. The inferential relations among sentences, and all of the sentence-to-sentence connections, are also unchanged. So at the level of sentences and truth, it seems as if speaking of the proxy-function language instead of our own would simply make no difference at all; hence it might seem as if these are not two separate languages, but one language described in two ways. At the level of the constituent parts of sentences, however, there is a difference. Does "Rover" refer to the family pet, or to all of space-time other than the family pet? (It makes no difference here whether we leave the name unanalysed or subject it to Russell's theory of descriptions.) We thought we knew the answer, but Quine's proxy functions may seem to call it into question.

We can put the matter in terms of translation. Suppose Martians were to land (or merely to observe us with their super-fine instruments); suppose also that for them the two translations result in discourse which is about equally natural or unnatural. Then two different Martians might come up with wholly different accounts of our ontology, two accounts which attributed the same net import to each human sentence.[10] And, crucially, there would then be nothing to which either of the Martians could appeal to show that the one account was correct and the other incorrect. The way in which evidence relates to a given sentence would be equally accounted for by the two translations. A gesture such as pointing would on the one account indicate an object in the direction of the pointing finger; on the other account, however, pointing would simply indicate the complement of something in the direction of the pointing finger. *Asking* the person pointing which object he intended would do no good: he might say "Rover, of course", but the issue is precisely whether his word "Rover" refers to the one object or to its complement. He might even say: "I mean the family pet, of course, not its space-time complement" but, again, these words are subject to the same reconstrual. Nor would more subtle questions help, for there is no agreement about the construal of the language in which the questions themselves would be asked and answered. In short there will simply be no settling the question as to which of the translations is correct; the case has been set up in such a way that this unsettleability is an intrinsic feature. And for Quine this means that there is no uniquely correct answer here: what the case shows is not the Martians' ignorance, their inability to get at some fact. It is, rather, that there is no fact to be got at.[11]

Indeterminacy of reference may be compared with ontological reduction, briefly discussed in Chapter 2 in connection with the natural numbers. (We shall return to the issue of ontological reduction in section III of the next chapter.) Superficially there are similarities: each relies on a technique of mapping objects of one kind onto other objects of another kind which can serve the same function. But the differences are more significant. Indeterminacy of reference depends on a mapping which is internal to a given ontology; objects of one kind within that ontology are mapped onto objects of another kind, also within that ontology. Our ontology contains both physical objects and their complements, for example; the claim of ontological relativity is that we could construe someone as talking about either one. Ontological reduction, by contrast, concerns the relationship between two ontologies. The reduction of numbers to sets shows that instead of using an ontology which contains both sets and numbers we can use one which eliminates the numbers and contains only the sets. (Or we may say that the reduction identifies the numbers with sets. Quine sees no real difference here; the point is that the new ontology does not contain numbers *in addition* to sets.) Mapping entities of one kind onto entities of another in order to effect an ontological reduction may thus enable us to eliminate entities which are in some way problematic, or simply superfluous; it may thus constitute theoretical progress. The mappings which bring about indeterminacy of reference, by contrast, are wholly unmotivated. Nor does Quine claim otherwise. His point is that the availability of such mappings shows that there is no fact of the matter as to whether we are talking about objects or their space-time complements.

III The threat of incoherence

The talk of Martians towards the end of the previous section was, of course, introduced only to illustrate a point which could also be made by talking about our own linguistic community. If two of us each undertake to translate a third, we could, in principle, come up with translations which agreed about the net import of each sentence, but still differed in the ontology which they ascribed to the one being translated. I might translate you as speaking the complement-language, and my translation would have just as much claim to correctness as the translation of someone who translates you as speaking a language in which short expressions refer to objects, not to their space-time complements. There would be no fact of the matter as to which translation was correct, and thus about which language you were really speaking. (Note that while I shall speak in terms of indeterminacy of reference, analogous points apply also to holophrastic indeterminacy. The availability of examples makes it convenient to discuss the matter in the context of indeterminacy of reference; my remarks in this section, however, apply to both forms of indeterminacy.)

At this point one may think that bringing indeterminacy home in this way shows that the whole idea collapses into incoherence. Suppose I translate you as speaking the complement-language. My words, like yours, are subject to various translations, equally correct. So someone else can claim that *I* am in fact speaking the complement-language, and that when I translate you I am really attributing to you the object-ontology, not the complement-ontology (since the complement of the complement of an object is simply that object). We now seem to be in danger of a regress. I say that your use of the word "Rover" refers to the space-time complement of the family dog; but if my words themselves are subject to various translations, what claim do they actually make? And if someone were to answer this question, still *her* words would be susceptible of various translations, and so on. If my talk of rabbits can be translated as talk of complements of rabbits, and my talk of rabbit-complements can be translated as talk of rabbits, then what difference is there between the two? Yet surely talking of the one is not the same as talking of the other. As Quine says:

> We seem to be maneuvering ourselves into the absurd position that there is no difference ... between referring to rabbits and referring to rabbit parts or stages. ... Reference would seem now to become nonsense not just in radical translation but at home.
>
> (*OR*, pp. 47f.)

The idea of translation seems to be undermined here by the lack of a stable language into which to translate, a language which simply says what it says.

Some commentators have responded to this (alleged) threat of incoherence with the idea that the problem is resolved by a special relation which each of us has to the meanings of his or her own words. On this view, the language into which I translate others is itself stable in the relevant sense because it is *my* language, and I know what I mean by its words. Even if others can come up with various translations of what I say, compatible with all behavioural dispositions, still only one such translation (at most) will be correct. My words have a meaning which is guaranteed, presumably by something in my mind; this meaning determines that by "Rover" I really do mean the family pet, not his space-time complement, that by "rabbit" I mean *rabbits*, not space-time complements of rabbits or rabbit-stages. The basis of this view is the supposed primacy of the first-person case, the insistence that *I* know what I mean, even though this meaning may not be fully manifested in my dispositions. (How anyone else might know this about me is, on this view, unclear, at best.) On this view of the matter, indeterminacy threatens us with a kind of solipsism of meaning: I know what I mean but can never know what anyone else means, for the behaviour of another person (or even her dispositions to behave) do not suffice to determine her meaning.

Some advocates of the idea of the primacy of first-person meaning have put it forward as an interpretation of Quine, as what he is really advocating. Others have used it to argue that his view is absurd or quite obviously wrong, since it denies what they take to be the evident fact of first-person meaning.[12] Both positions seem to me quite mistaken; the idea of "first-person meaning" which they share is irredeemably confused.

In the light of the previous chapters, it is clear, I hope, that we cannot plausibly interpret Quine as holding any view which makes "first-person meaning" different in principle from meaning in general. It is fundamental for him that "[l]anguage is a social art" (WO, p. ix), that "[t]here is nothing in linguistic meaning beyond what is to be gleaned from overt behavior in observable circumstances." (PT, p. 38.) The only merit of the interpretation is the hope that an appeal to "first-person meaning" will avoid the threatened incoherence. But all of this is quite misconceived. First, the threat of incoherence is an empty one. Second, if it were not, no appeal to the first-person case would help. We shall briefly discuss this second point and then revert to the first, which will shed light on Quine's general views from a new angle.

The idea behind the invoking of the first-person case is, presumably, that my meaning is underpinned—and made proof against indeterminacy—by something that I know, perhaps by introspection. For this to be cogent, however, the "something" that is meant to guarantee my meaning is not in any way manifest in the way I behave, or in any ways I would behave under other circumstances. If it were, Quine's linguist could take account of that behaviour. (We should not think of Quine as restricting his imagined linguist to certain kinds of dispositions to behaviour, although some of his formulations may encourage that view. Anything which is in principle publicly observable is grist for the Quinean mill.) So the objection asks us to suppose that the crucial thing about meaning is something which is in no way manifest in behaviour. It follows at once that I can have no reason to think that anyone else has it. But what reason do I have to think that *I* have it? Would I miss it if one day I did not? To say that I would not miss it is to undercut the whole idea. But to say that I would miss it is equally problematic. For my missing it could not in any way show up in what I said or did, because this "something" is not manifested in behaviour. But then what does it mean to say that I would miss it? Again, if it changed from one day to the next would I notice the change? What reason could I have to think that it has not changed?—Questions along these lines seem to me wholly to undermine the idea of meaning being guaranteed by a mysterious something that is completely divorced from any behavioural manifestations.[13]

The idea that Quine's views require the idea of "first-person meaning" is encouraged by the view that he thinks that understanding other people always involves translating them. If to understand someone's utterances is, in general, a matter of translation, then what of the language into which the translation takes place? If we are to avoid an endless regress, which leaves us understanding no language at all, we must have some other kind of understanding of language which does *not* consist in translating; at some point I have to have a language which I understand in some more immediate fashion. And a private language is an obvious candidate. (The support goes the other way around too. If real meaning lies in *my* language, then the only way to understand the words of someone else is to translate those words into my language.)

The idea that understanding someone's utterance involves translating them may be tempting. The linguist, after all, is already in full possession of a language. So one might think that, in the scenario of radical translation, what makes the target language meaningful is the fact that it can be translated into a language—the linguist's—the meaningfulness of which is simply taken for granted. In this view, talk of radical translation is an *indirect* approach to meaning, "one in which the native speech is to be meaningful just insofar as it is interpreted back into some other medium (the one the interpreter brings with him) about whose meaning we do not ask".[14] This idea is perhaps encouraged by some remarks of Quine.[15] But the tempting picture cannot be a correct account of Quine's views. It requires a language "about whose meaning we do not ask", something like a private language. But the idea of a such language is wholly alien to his thought.

This issue connects with the question considered in the first section, whether indeterminacy should be understood in an epistemological sense, as showing us limits on the translator's knowledge, or in an ontological sense, as showing a limit on what there is to be known. In spite of Quine's frequent talk of the linguist's evidence, it is clear that he intends the latter, stronger, view. On the tempting (but incorrect) picture, the scenario of radical translation has nothing to tell us about what meaningfulness *is*; it tells us only how the linguist can come to know the meaning of another language—by translating it. Presumably the meaningfulness of the target language, like that of the linguist's, really rests on something that plays no role within the scenario of radical translation (something about which "we do not ask"). But if that were correct then indeterminacy of translation could, at most, show us something about the linguist's *knowledge* of meaning.

If linguistic understanding does not always involve translation, how are we to think of it? And how is the threatened incoherence to be resolved along Quinean lines? The two questions are closely connected; we shall take them in order.

I may occasionally do something like translating you. If you use a word which I do not immediately understand, or if you make a remark which strikes me as excessively odd, then I may cast around to find a plausible meaning to attribute to you. But normally I do nothing of this kind. Normally I simply respond to what you say. To understand someone's utterances is not, in the usual case, to translate them; it is simply to be disposed to respond to them in appropriate ways, linguistic and non-linguistic, immediately and over the course of time. When I say that your word "Rover" refers to the family dog, and not to its space-time complement, what gives my words meaning is simply that they are part of our familiar shared language which we use, responding to one another's uses. The point is not that in this language there is reference which is in some more or less mysterious fashion not susceptible to the indeterminacy argument. It is, rather, that we have a language which we simply *use*, without attempting to consider it from the vantage point of some other language. As Quine says: "in practice we end the regress of background languages by acquiescing in our mother tongue and taking its words at face value." (*OR*, p. 42.)

The crucial point here is that what gives our words their meaning is simply our use of them. Quine enlarges on this idea, by specifying what kinds of uses are relevant, and how they might come about. This has been the subject of Chapters 5 and 6, which set out an approach to language and its acquisition which does not rely on mentalistic terms such as "meaning". As indicated at the start of this chapter, the relevance of radical translation to meaning is essentially of the same kind. The aspects of use which are relevant to the linguist's task of constructing a translation manual are the aspects which are relevant to its being a meaningful language, and to its words and sentences meaning what they do. But it is the use of language which is crucial, not our translating it. To take the words of our language "at face value" is not to attribute special meanings to them, meanings which escape the indeterminacy argument in some special way. It is simply using them, and not asking for an explanation of their meaning in other terms.

While we are simply using our language, there is no issue of indeterminacy, for that arises only with translation:

> To say what objects someone is talking about is to say no more than to say how we propose to translate his terms into ours. ...
>
> The point is not that we ourselves are casting about in vain for a mooring. Staying aboard our own language and not rocking the boat, we are borne smoothly along on it and all is well; "rabbit" denotes rabbits, and there is no sense in asking, "Rabbits in what sense of 'rabbit'?" Reference goes inscrutable if, rocking the boat, we contemplate a permutational mapping of our language, or if we undertake translation.
>
> (TT, p. 20)

We can of course accept that "rabbit" denotes rabbits, and not rabbit-stages or space-time complements of rabbits. But when we say what a term denotes, what we are asserting is simply part of our ordinary language. In the sentence: "'Rabbit' denotes rabbits" the second use of the word "rabbit" is an ordinary use. Accepting the truth of the sentence does not mean accepting that it carries with it some sort of guarantee against indeterminacy of reference:

> Within the home language, reference is best seen (I now hold) as unproblematic but trivial, on a par with Tarski's truth paradigm. Thus "London" denotes London (whatever *that* is) and "rabbit" denotes rabbits (whatever *they* are). Inscrutability of reference emerges only in translation.
>
> (H&S, p. 460; emphases in the original)

My "knowing what I mean" thus generally amounts to no more than my being a fluent speaker of the language. In his reply to an essay by Peter Pagin, Quine puts it like this: "knowing what expressions mean *consists*, for me, in being disposed to use them on appropriate occasions." (O&K, p. 420; emphasis in the original.) This is not to deny that I sometimes know what I mean better than others do. If I say something ambiguous, I generally know in which sense I intended it. But this is not because my meaning is something wholly distinct from my dispositions. My "knowing what I meant" here may amount to no more than my knowing which paraphrases of my remark I would be willing to accept, and which not. And Quine certainly need not deny that I often know what I am about to do, or that I often know (though by no means infallibly) what I would do in certain as yet unrealized circumstances.

IV Arguing for indeterminacy

What reason is there to accept holophrastic indeterminacy? Let us recall some points which frame the issue. At least in his later work, Quine accords that idea a conjectural status. So we should be wary about attributing to him, as a settled opinion, anything that purports to be a clear-cut and decisive argument for it. On the other hand, he clearly thinks that it is a reasonable and plausible conjecture; most commentators have taken the opposite view. What can account for this difference? It is crucial here that for Quine the criterion of success for a translation manual is simply that it facilitates "fluent dialogue and successful negotiation" with the speakers of the translated language (*FSS*, p. 80). Given the purely practical nature of this criterion, why should there *not* be more than one way of satisfying it? Why should we accept it as *prima facie* plausible that there is exactly one way in which it can be satisfied? From a Quinean point of view, it is only if we surreptitiously rely on an unexamined notion of synonymy that unique-ness of translation is overwhelmingly the more reasonable and plausible view. Quine of course holds that we should not presuppose an undefined notion of synonymy; we should, rather, think of success in translation as a practical matter of facilitation of smooth interaction. His view is that, given that criterion, indeterminacy is not particularly implausible on the face of it, and so confronts no particularly onerous burden of proof. To the contrary: he seems to hold that it is plausible that if there is one way of translating so as to ensure smooth interaction then there is more than one.

What reasons, of a more positive kind, does Quine give us to accept holophrastic indeterminacy as at least plausible? In some works he approa-ches the matter very abstractly, but often he talks in more concrete terms about the situation of the linguist undertaking radical translation. We shall briefly consider this latter kind of discussion, and then turn to the more abstract considerations.

In chapter 2 of *Word and Object*, where Quine first systematically sets out the idea of indeterminacy, he gives a schematic account of the situation of the field linguist, in these terms:

> The recovery of a man's current language from his currently observed responses is the task of the linguist who, unaided by an interpreter, is out to penetrate and translate a language hitherto unknown. *All the objective data he has to go on are the forces that he sees impinging on the native's surfaces and the observable behavior, vocal and otherwise, of the native.* Such data evince native "meanings" only of the most objectively empirical or stimulus-linked variety. And yet

the linguist apparently ends up with native "meanings" in some quite unrestricted sense; purported translations, anyway, of all possible native sentences.

(*WO*, p. 28; emphasis added)

The chapter is a heavily idealized account, in Quinean terms, of the linguist's procedures. Quine has the linguist picking up a sentence here and there by passive observation, and then querying the native speakers and seeing whether they assent or dissent to the sentence in various circumstances. (This presupposes, of course, that the linguist has been able to translate signs or words for assent and dissent.[16])

Quine's linguist is then in a position to gauge the stimulus meaning of native utterances. (See Chapter 5, section II, above; as emphasized there, the issue of stimulus meaning is more complicated than Quine held at the time of *Word and Object*; I shall ignore this issue here.) Stimulus meaning, Quine says, "may be properly looked upon ... as the objective reality that the linguist has to probe when he undertakes radical translation" (*WO*, p. 39). Drawing on stimulus meaning, the linguist may more or less confidently undertake the translation of observation sentences, and of truth-functions. (Or, strictly speaking, "verdict functions"; see *Roots of Reference*, pp. 76ff., and Chapter 6, section II above.) For sentences quite generally, the linguist can judge whether two are "stimulus-synonymous", i.e. would command the same verdict under any given stimulatory conditions; this knowledge will be more or less useless for standing sentences, but may be revelatory for non-observation occasion sentences. She can also judge which sentences are "stimulus-analytic" and which "stimulus-contradictory", i.e. which would be assented to under all stimulatory conditions and which under none. (These names are perhaps misleading; Quine does not claim to have a criterion which separates assent or dissent "based on meaning alone" from that based on knowledge, as factual as you like, which is shared by all speakers of the language.)

The sorts of facts indicated above, Quine says, "cover all the available evidence" (*WO*, p. 70). To get beyond them, the linguist segments native utterances into units—words, in effect—and attributes independent significance to these units, which may then be recombined to form new sentences. Her methods of analysing utterances form a system of what Quine calls "analytical hypotheses". They are *analytical* because they require the linguist to analyse utterances and to attribute significance to their parts. But if indeterminacy is true they are not *hypotheses* in the ordinary sense, for they are not answerable to evidence: "they exceed anything implicit in any native's dispositions to speech-behavior" (*WO*, p. 70). It is here that indeterminacy

216

sets in: Quine's claim is that rival systems of analytical hypotheses are possible, each leading to a manual of translation which is equally successful. (It
sets in earlier, of course, if translation of assent and dissent is also indeterminate; see note 16, above.)

What reason have we to accept this? We have no examples, except perhaps of the most artificial kind. Nor should we expect to be able to come up
with realistic examples. An alternative scheme for translating some hitherto
unknown language into English, say, would be no easier to construct than
the initial radical translation of the language would be. And once a translation was in place, those who knew any part of it would, in fact, be almost
certain to duplicate it rather than come up with a genuine alternative—even
if such alternatives are in principle available. So no example is to be expec-
ted. (Thus the case is unlike that of indeterminacy of reference, where there
are small-scale examples.) But Quine holds that the sparsity of the constraints makes it very plausible that more than one system of analytical
hypotheses is possible. As he puts it, in a statement that proved greatly
over-optimistic about the reception of his work: "one has only to reflect on
the nature of possible data and methods to appreciate the indeterminacy"
(WO, p. 72). Similarly, in *Pursuit of Truth* Quine gives a briefer account of
the linguist's evidence and procedures, and says: "These reflections leave us
little reason to expect that two radical translators, working independently
on Jungle, would come out with interchangeable manuals." (P. 47.)

We turn now to attempts to set out more abstract and general reasons for
the indeterminacy of translation. None of these seem to me to provide reasons more compelling than the plausibility considerations just discussed;
the reasons that they do not are instructive.

Quine gives his most detailed attempt at a general argument for indeterminacy in "On the Reasons for the Indeterminacy of Translation". The
argument takes as its starting point the underdetermination of theory by
evidence. Quine insists that indeterminacy of translation is not simply a
straightforward instance of underdetermination; to suppose that it is is to
construe it as an epistemological matter, which is not how Quine intends it.
In this argument, underdetermination is a crucial premise in an argument
for indeterminacy, but the latter is not simply an instance of the former.

We begin, more or less as before, by supposing that we are able to
translate the observation sentences of the target language, for these are the
ones which are fixed, more or less, by dispositions to observable behaviour
in observable circumstances. To get beyond these, "we have to project analytical hypotheses, whose ultimate justification is substantially just that the

implied observation sentences match up" ("On the Reasons for the Indeterminacy of Translation", p. 179). Our task, in short, is to impute a whole theory to the speakers of the target language, on the basis of our translations of their observation sentences. What theory should we impute to them? The underdetermination of theory by evidence tells us that more than one theory is compatible with a given set of observation sentences. So, Quine claims, there is more than one theory that we can reasonably impute to the speakers of the target language. This would be so even if we and they alike had access to all observational truths. They would agree with us on all observation sentences but, given underdetermination, this would not guarantee agreement on theory. "Where physical theories A and B are both compatible with all possible data, we might adopt A for ourselves and still remain free to translate the foreigner either as believing A or as believing B". (Op. cit., p. 180.)

Quine accepts that the choice between translating the foreigners as believing A and translating them as believing B may be settled on the grounds of simplicity: one option may make for much smoother, easier, and more natural translations than the other. Or either one might lead to translations so cumbersome and unmanageable that we abandon both, and attribute to the foreigner some third theory. "But", he says,

> we can imagine also ... the possibility that A and B are both reasonably attributable. It might turn out that with just moderate circuitousness of translation at certain points—different points—A and B could be imputed about equally well. In this event no basis for a choice can be gained by exposing the foreigner to new physical data and noting his verbal response, since the theories A and B fit all possible observations equally well. ... In this event our choice would be determined simply by the accident of hitting upon one of the two systems of translation first.
>
> ("On the Reasons for the Indeterminacy of Translation", p. 180)

Perhaps we should not think of this argument as representing Quine's considered opinion. In a later essay he says he has "lost [his] liking" for the argument in the case where one of the theories (A, B) is ours, "for in devising a manual of translation I would favour agreement, where I could, between the natives and myself regarding the truth of a sentence and its translation" ("Comment on Newton-Smith", pp. 66–67). In a still later work, however, he seems to accept that underdetermination does imply indeterminacy but speaks, enigmatically, of "the inferiority" of this approach ("Reply to Roth", H&S, pp. 459f.).

It is, in any case, notable that Quine claims in "On the Reasons for the Indeterminacy of Translation" only that "we can imagine ... the possibility" that we will be free to translate the foreigners in either of two ways, as believing *A* or as believing *B*. He says almost nothing about the sorts of simplicity considerations which might rule this out. What might they look like? What sorts of things might make one translation much more cumbersome than the other? The answer to this question reminds us that there is much more to a theory than its observational implications, and that a translator is not wholly limited to observation sentences. We might, for example, only be able to distinguish a very small number of theoretical terms in a language that we were attempting to translate. This would suggest, at least, that it would be better translated by another language which contains a relatively small number of theoretical terms, rather than some language in which such terms were abundant. Clearly the sheer number of theoretical terms is something that a radical translator might be able to gauge.

There is a more general point here. A theory has a structure, made up of links between sentences. On Quine's account such links "must finally be due to the conditioning of sentences as responses to sentences as stimuli" (*WO*, p. 11; quoted in context, Chapter 6, section II, p. 160, above); such links are thus dispositions, and hence correspond to internal states of the language-user. They are thus genuine facts and are, in principle, available to the radical translator. The linguist can probe how the natives' willingness to accept one sentence changes when they are told another; also their willingness to accept sentences which she translates as being of the form "If p then q", or "p implies q". All this is grist for the translator's mill, and it certainly takes us beyond observation sentences. The two translations—the *A*-translation and the *B*-translation—give us, we are supposing, the same observational implications, so the mere ability to translate observation sentences does not enable us to attribute one rather than the other. But still it may very well be that one of the two translations better preserves the sentence-to-sentence links of the native speakers than does the other, and this would clearly be a reason to prefer it. Quine claims that we can imagine that no such considerations in fact enable us to choose between two translations; we can imagine that situation, but nothing he says shows that it could in fact occur.

For the last couple of pages we have been concerned with an argument from underdetermination to indeterminacy. There is also an apparently somewhat different argument for indeterminacy to be found in Quine's work, of the same very abstract kind. In this case the premises are the fact of Quine's equating the kind of cognitive meaning that is of concern to him with evidence and the holistic view that he takes of evidence. Attributing the premises (perhaps a little dubiously) to Pierce and Duhem, respectively, he sums up the point like this:

> If we recognize with Pierce that the meaning of a sentence turns purely on what would count as evidence for its truth, and if we recognize with Duhem that theoretical sentences have their evidence not as single sentences but only as larger blocks of theory, then the indeterminacy of translation is the natural conclusion.
>
> (*OR*, pp. 80f.)

His previous paragraph spells out the argument in more detail:

> If English sentences have their meaning only together as a body, then we can justify their translation into Arunta only together as a body. There will be no justification for pairing off the component English sentences with component Arunta sentences except as these correlations make the translations of the theory as a whole come out right. *Any translations ... will be as correct as any other, so long as the net empirical implications of the theory as a whole are preserved in translation.* But it is to be expected that many different ways of translating the component sentences, essentially different individually, would deliver the same empirical implications for the theory as a whole; deviations in the translation of one component sentence could be compensated for in the translation of another component sentence. Insofar, there can be no ground for saying which of two glaringly unlike translations of individual sentences is right.
>
> (*OR*, p. 80; emphasis added)

Seen abstractly, holophrastic indeterminacy arises in the same way as indeterminacy of reference: we have constraints on wholes which do not determine translations of the parts. (Indeterminacy is, as Quine says in *Word and Object*, "a conflict of parts seen without the wholes", pp. 78f.) In the case of indeterminacy of reference, the wholes were sentences, and the parts were sub-sentential. In the case of holophrastic indeterminacy, the whole is our total theory, or a large chunk of it, and the parts are individual sentences. The idea behind the latest argument is that holism shows that it is only our theory as a whole that is answerable to evidence; holism might thus be taken to show that it is our whole theory that is in that sense the true "unit of empirical meaning". On this line of thought, indeterminacy arises because there is, so to speak, more than one way that the meaning of the whole can be shared out among the parts. Like the argument from underdetermination,

220

however, this argument fails to be conclusive, and for just the same reason. The relation of the whole theory, or some sizeable chunk, to experience is not all that there is, even on a Quinean account. The structure of the theory, the links among its component sentences, must also be taken into account. Will taking account of these matters suffice in every case to determine translation? Quine conjectures that it may not; it is hard to see how there could be a fully convincing reason which would make the claim more than a conjecture.

The abstract arguments for indeterminacy that we have examined over the last few pages thus do not seem to add anything to the bare assertion that, given the constraints, there is no reason to think that translation must be determinate. Nor is this surprising; Quine, after all, comes to think of indeterminacy as a conjecture. Agnosticism about indeterminacy, however, may be enough for Quine's philosophical purposes—enough, that is, to show that synonymy and the related idea of a proposition cannot be taken for granted, as ideas available for philosophical use.

V Arguing against indeterminacy

Many arguments have been put forward claiming to refute indeterminacy. I shall not attempt to set these out, or categorize them, or make any pretense to completeness. I shall, rather, simply discuss two kinds of argument which seem to me particularly important, either because they represent very natural reactions to the idea or because a Quinean response to them brings out something significant about his thought. The first kind of objection claims that Quine ignores facts which are relevant, although not available to the radical translator, and that these facts may rule out all possible translations except one. The second does not turn on facts of this sort, but argues Quine's linguist is too limited in her methods, in what she takes to count as evidence for the correctness of a translation.

The first sort of objection, then, claims that the range of facts that Quine considers leaves out something essential. In one important version, the objection is that Quine does not take into account the idea that states of the brain might determine translation. Quine's view is that nothing which is not, at least in principle, available to the translator can be relevant to meaning: "[t]here is nothing in linguistic meaning beyond what is to be gleaned from overt behavior in observable circumstances" (PT, p. 38). Even granting that point, however, we may still hold that it makes all the difference who is doing the gleaning. At least as far as we know, only creatures with normal human genetic endowment are capable of learning (human) language when exposed to the relevant behaviour.[17] Clearly that endowment, and the kind of brain that results from it, play a crucial role in language. Quine himself, as we saw, argues that we must have complex higher-order dispositions; if these dispositions are not themselves innate then the propensity to form them, under favourable circumstances, must be.

It is thus indisputable that human beings share an innate genetic endowment which plays a crucial role in their acquisition of language. What is disputable is whether that endowment is the sort of thing that might determine translation. Quine's answer is negative; he insists that "even a full understanding of neurology would in no way resolve the indeterminacy of translation" ("Reply to Nozick", H&S, p. 365). Let us suppose that all the behaviour of any given person can, in principle, be explained in terms of that person's brain, and of the forces acting on him. What exactly is the "behaviour" that is thus explained? In what terms should it be described? One might think that we should describe the behaviour as "referring to rabbits" or as "referring to rabbit-complements", as appropriate; in the sentential case, as "saying something which means A" or as "saying something which means B". Given that kind of description of the behaviour, one will, no doubt, find states of the brain which go along with referring to particular objects, or with meaning something in particular. But that result is obtained only by begging the question: we have simply assumed the subject of our experiment is determinately meaning A rather than B. To avoid begging the question, the relevant behaviour should instead be described without such terms as "refers" or "means", perhaps in terms of nerve firings and muscle contractions, or in terms of emissions of noises. The issue here is about the data which are to be explained; if we accept a Quinean description of the data then a neurophysiological explanation will not determine translation.[18]

The point here is that if two translations are each compatible with all behaviour, each will also be compatible with any explanation of that behaviour—provided the description of what is to be explained is in acceptable terms. (As Quine says of his "linguistic behaviourism": "It disciplines data, not explanation". O&K, p. 417.) A response to this might be to claim that no account of language will be possible if we insist on the sorts of terms acceptable to Quine. (This is the sort of claim that Quine's genetic project is designed to rebut; here we are coming at the point from a slightly different angle.) One might, in particular, argue that any account of language requires a level of description between the behaviour, on the one hand, and the brain, on the other hand. Indeed there is a very strong reason to believe this: your nervous system and mine are different objects. We require a level of description at which we can talk about what is common to all users of the language, and it is unlikely that any very useful description of this sort is available at the level of neurons. So we need an intermediate level of description. Quine's talk of dispositions, however, is just such an intermediate level of description. (See Chapter 4, fifth section, above.) A given person's disposition, on Quine's account, *is* a state of that person's nervous system. We do not in general have any description of that state in terms of nerves and neurons, but on Quine's account we do not need anything of the sort to make talk of dispositions legitimate. Given appropriate evidence, it is legitimate to posit dispositions to behaviour, provided the behaviour is described in physicalistic terms. But dispositions, or other entities, posited with that constraint will play no role in determining translation.

The second kind of objection to indeterminacy that we shall consider is that Quine's linguist is too limited in her methods, in what she takes to count as evidence for the correctness of a translation. Hookway gives, as an example, the maxim: "A community is more likely to have terms for rabbits than for undetached rabbit parts or stages in their histories". (Hookway, *Quine*, p. 135.) If there is reason to believe this maxim, and others like it, then there are constraints on translation which Quine leaves out of account.

How is Quine to respond to this charge? Hookway attributes to Quine the view that a maxim such as the above "provides a pragmatic reason for preferring one manual [of translation] over another without giving any reason for thinking it [i.e. the preferred manual] *true.*" (*Quine*, p. 135; emphasis in the original.) According to Hookway, Quine's acceptance of indeterminacy is based on a gap between what is justified by the (physical) facts and what "serves our practical needs in looking for a translation manual" (*Quine*, p. 136). The latter considerations are merely "subjective or pragmatic" (ibid.). Such considerations, according to Hookway's *Quine*, thus cannot justify the idea that one of two translation manuals is correct and the other is not. A "manual 'fits the facts' so long as it conforms to stimulus meanings" (ibid.); two manuals may each satisfy this condition so that each must be counted as fully correct, even if one is vastly inferior on "pragmatic" grounds. This interpretation seems to fit some of Quine's remarks (see, for example, *OR*, p. 34). But I do not think it is the right way to read Quine.

If Quine's position is as Hookway describes it, however, then it might seem rather arbitrary. A physicist, on this account, is entitled to use "pragmatic" factors in coming up with the best theory, without our impugning the truth of that theory. Why is the linguist not entitled to the same latitude? Some commentators have claimed that Quine presupposes, at the outset, a list of which subjects count as "real science" and which do not. On this account, he holds that only real sciences are entitled to use "pragmatic" factors and to count them as part of the search for *truth*; physics makes the list (along, presumably, with chemistry, behaviouristic psychology, biology, and perhaps others), while semantics, for some reason, does not. This idea of a list of "real sciences" brings out the arbitrariness of Quine's view, as Hookway interprets it. There is also another reason for not being satisfied with that interpretation. As we have emphasized, Quine's account of what it is for a translation manual to be *correct* in fact makes correctness a practical matter through and through. A translation manual is correct if it enables us to engage in "fluent dialogue and successful negotiation" with speakers of the other language; there is no more to it than that. But then the distinction that Hookway attributes to Quine, between a translation manual's having "pragmatic" advantages and its being correct, seems very dubious, at best.

Hookway's interpretation was his account of Quine's response to the objection that he (Quine) ignores such maxims as "a community is more likely to have terms for rabbits than for undetached rabbit parts or stages in their histories". If we do not accept the interpretation, how are we to think of Quine as responding to the objection? There are, I think, two rather different sorts of response. One is to question the basis for accepting a maxim such as the one given. We may think we have an inductive basis for believing it: our linguistic community conforms to it, and so do all the others that we know of. But do we really know this? To say that a linguistic community conforms to the maxim is to suppose that all acceptable translations of the language of that community obey the maxim. If we do not beg the question then we have no reason to think that this is so. If indeterminacy is not ruled out from the start then we must accept that the translation manuals that we already have may have alternatives which violate the maxim. In that case no claim about what sorts of terms most communities have is justified.

A second sort of Quinean response will perhaps not apply to indeterminacy of reference, the kind of case that Hookway considers, but may apply in some cases in which holophrastic indeterminacy is at stake. Our linguist may use "pragmatic" considerations as freely as the physicist. But why should we think that these always suffice to yield a unique translation? Quine suggests that they will not. In some cases, reasonable procedures of translation, even if accepted without question, may not determine a unique answer. There will be trade-offs to be made, and there may be no uniquely best way of making them. Quine asks: "How much grotesqueness may we allow to the native's beliefs, for instance, in order to avoid how much grotesqueness in his grammar or semantics?" (*PT*, p. 47.) Clearly he is here envisaging two translation manuals, each of which allows us to communicate

well enough, but neither of which makes for completely trouble-free communication—in the one case we have to attribute some peculiar beliefs to
our interlocutor, in the other case some different strange beliefs, or some
implausibly complex grammar, or something of the sort. Since either allows
for communication, and there is no better, each must be accepted as successful, in spite of their differences.

Quine's response here is not merely meant to point out that any scheme
of translation is underdetermined relative to the evidence for it. That much,
after all, may hold equally for any other subject, including physics. As
before, the point is ontological, not merely methodological or epistemological. Quine is suggesting that the totality of truth about the world—not
just the totality of evidence—fails to determine translation. But now the
suspicion of arbitrariness may reassert itself. The best theory of physics that
we come up with counts as telling us the truth about the world, even
though it is underdetermined, so that an equally good alternative is in fact
available. So why not say: the best scheme of translation that we come up
with equally counts as telling us the truth about what the natives mean,
even though an equally good alternative is in fact available. Quine holds
that in the first case "equally good" has a methodological or epistemological
sense: it means equally conforming to all the *evidence* (as summed up, perhaps, in all the true observation sentences); whereas in the second case
"equally good" has an ontological sense: equally conforming to all the facts.
But why the distinction? In his reply to Chomsky, addressing this point,
Quine says: "theory in physics is an ultimate parameter. There is no legitimate first philosophy, higher or firmer than physics, to which we can
appeal over the physicists' heads". (D&H, p. 303.) Quine is a physicalist; he
takes the real facts to be the physical facts. When he says that there is no
fact of the matter about which of two translations is correct he is relying on
a physical conception of "fact of the matter". On his view, however, there is
nothing arbitrary here, and certainly no a priori assumption of physicalism.
To the contrary: Quine's physicalism is based on the view that a reconstruction of our theory of the world along physicalist lines greatly enhances
its simplicity and its clarity, and omits nothing deserving inclusion. His
defence of this view, in turn, consists in his sketch of such a reconstruction;
this will occupy us in the next five chapters.

VI The significance of indeterminacy

The concern of this section is with the significance of holophrastic indeterminacy. (The significance of indeterminacy of reference will be considered

in connection with realism; see Chapter 12, below.) Some commentators claim that (holophrastic) indeterminacy is a central doctrine of Quine's, with very general implications for his thought.[19] In his late work, however, Quine speaks of the doctrine as a "conjecture", which suggests that he thinks no general or important aspects of his view rest on which way this conjecture comes out. As I indicated at the start of this chapter, I agree with that position; I think that much less turns on the correctness of the doctrine than might appear.

At first sight, one might think that the truth or falsehood of indeterminacy is of the greatest importance. Quine himself says that the motivation of the idea is "to undermine Frege's notion of a proposition or *Gedanke*" (B&G, p. 176; cf. pp. 198–9, above). If we can make sense of the idea of the meaning of a sentence then we can, presumably, make sense of the idea of linguistic meaning quite generally. (The meaning of a sub-sentential expression would be identified with the systematic contribution that the expression makes to the meanings of sentences in which it occurs.) So what is at stake is whether there are meanings. How can that not be an issue of great importance to Quine?

To answer this question, we need to see *how* the determinacy of transla-tion would enable us to make sense of the notion of a proposition. If translation were determinate, we could define two sentences as synonymous just in case the one is translated into the other by a fully acceptable trans-lation between the language of the one and the language of the other. (This does not exclude the case where the two are sentences of the same language.) We could then identify the proposition expressed by a given sentence with the set of sentences which are, in this sense, synonymous with it. A propo-sition would thus be a set of synonymous sentences. We could presumably extend the definition and take meanings to be sets of synonymous expres-sions more generally. As Quine says: "I keep urging that we could happily hypostatize meanings if we could admit synonymy. We could simply iden-tify meanings with the class of synonyms". (H&S, "Reply to Alston", p. 73; cf. also *WO*, p. 201.)

The idea of a set of synonymous expressions, however, is an extremely thin notion, relative to the idea of meanings and propositions as they have mostly figured in analytic philosophy. (Consider, most obviously, Russell's use of the word "proposition" in the first decade of the twentieth century and Frege's use of the word "*Gedanke*" from the 1890s onwards. These writings of Frege and of Russell are foundational for twentieth-century analytic philosophy; many subsequent thinkers have more or less taken over the idea of a proposition seen there.) Most of the philosophical purposes for which the word "proposition" and its close relatives have been invoked are not served by sets of synonymous sentences. In particular, a notion of meaning understood in that way will not play the sort of explanatory role that Quine is concerned to reject.

Consider what is, I think, the central use to which the idea of meaning has been put: to explain our understanding of language. In this use, a meaning is thought of either as a mental entity or as an abstract entity. If meanings are mental, they are perhaps known by introspection. As we have emphasized, Quine finds this sort of idea to be unscientific, and to impede the explanation of the phenomena rather than helping.[20] If they are abstract entities, we must postulate some sort of epistemic contact between the language-user and the meaning: one understands an expression by "grasping" its meaning. (This idea more or less fits the work of Frege and of Russell, mentioned parenthetically in the previous paragraph.) In either case, there must be some epistemic relation between the speaker and the meaning, if the meaning is to explain the speaker's understanding of language. If the meaning is a set of synonymous linguistic expressions, however, the matter is quite different. It will be of no help to know that a particular expression is in the set. Nor would a list of all the expressions in the set give one an understanding of any one of them, unless one already understood at least one of the other expressions in the set. Meanings, construed as sets of synonymous expressions, do nothing at all to explain the understanding of language.

For an explanation of the understanding of language, then, it simply doesn't matter whether there is an empirically grounded notion of synonymy which allows us to define meanings. The crucial philosophical issue is, rather, whether we can presuppose a notion of meaning, and of our epistemic access to meanings, independently of the empirical grounding of such notions. Quine, of course, thinks that such a presupposition is not legitimate. This view of his, however, is not dependent on the indeterminacy of translation. Nor does that idea provide any sort of argument against those who have assumed a notion of a proposition which is not empirically based; the question of the determinacy of translation, as Quine thinks of it, assumes that if a notion of meaning is to be acceptable then it must be empirically based. This assumption is central for Quine; the answer to the question of indeterminacy is, by comparison, a matter of detail. No doubt there are philosophers who have assumed that the notion of a proposition is justified on empirical grounds but have then gone on to attribute to propositions characteristics—explanatory powers, in particular—that no empirically based notion could have and that Quine's sets of synonymous sentences certainly do not have. A virtue of reflecting on indeterminacy is that it discourages this sort of muddle; but it is clarity of thought that is crucial here, not the correctness of indeterminacy.

Quine speaks of the indeterminacy conjecture as directed against the idea that there are propositions. What he means is, of course, that it is directed against the idea that the concept of a proposition can be shown to be empirically well grounded. Many of the philosophers who have relied most on the idea of a proposition, however, have not had in mind anything empirically grounded. Nor would an empirically grounded notion serve their purposes. In the fundamental disagreement between Quine, on the one hand, and those who have relied upon a non-empirical notion of a proposition, on the other hand, indeterminacy is irrelevant. Quine's real argument against that notion of a proposition, against the idea of meaning more generally, is simply that he has no need for it. This is the crucial point. Quine's physicalistic account of language, the subject of Chapters 5 and 6, is meant precisely to show that we can account for the phenomena of language-use without relying on a non-empirical notion of meaning, or anything of the sort.

It should be noted that indeterminacy simply plays no role in Quine's account of language, nor could it. What the adult language-user possesses, and the infant acquires, is a highly complex set of dispositions; there is no sense in which these are or are not indeterminate. Only with translation does the question of indeterminacy arise.

The understanding of language is the central context in which philosophers have appealed to the idea of meaning, but it is not, of course, the only one. Another is the idea that some sentences are true in virtue of meaning, and that this puts them in a fundamentally different epistemological category from all other sentences. We have discussed this idea in some detail in Chapter 3, above; our recent discussion enables us to put the matter in a slightly different light. For Quine, the idea would require that our accepting those sentences as true should be explicable purely in terms of their meanings. But if the notion of meaning here is empirical then it is based on our linguistic dispositions. Those dispositions include, among many others, our dispositions to accept those sentences; it cannot *explain* those dispositions. Meaning, in other words, is not a sufficiently fundamental notion to provide an explanation of the required kind.

These two philosophical uses of the idea of meaning are perhaps the most important, but they are by no means the only ones. Others include the idea that meaning is what is preserved by translation, i.e. that translation is to be understood as an endeavour which aims to preserve meaning; that philosophical analysis similarly aims to preserve meaning; that it is propositions, meanings of indicative sentences, which are, in the first instance, the bearers of truth and falsehood; and, finally, that belief and doubt and hope, and so on, are to be understood as attitudes towards propositions. In each case Quine provides a way of understanding the given kind of phenomena without invoking meaning. We have already seen this in the case of translation. He spells out a way of understanding that activity, and the criteria for its success, which make no mention of meaning. (See the beginning of the first section of this chapter.) We shall see him take analogous steps with regard to philosophical analysis (in Chapter 9), to truth (in Chapter 10) and to the so-called propositional attitudes (in Chapter 13). As in the case of understanding, we simply do not need to assume that there are meanings in any of these cases.

Quine argues that we can account for all the phenomena without invoking propositions, or anything analogous. But his way of understanding matters has more to be said for it than this negative point might suggest. For one thing, there is no reason to believe that the various uses which are made of propositions can all be accommodated with a single all-purpose notion. In the case of belief, we presumably want the result that if a competent speaker of the language accepts one sentence while denying another then the two sentences express different propositions. That criterion imposes very fine-grained identity conditions upon propositions: sentences which one might unreflectingly think of as meaning the same will come out, by this criterion, as expressing different propositions.[21] This criterion also yields a notion of a proposition which may fit poorly with other philosophical uses that are made of that notion. On some ways of understanding truth in virtue of meaning, for example, any two sentences which are logically equivalent express the same proposition. This criterion is extremely coarse-grained: many sentences which one might think of as quite unlike in meaning come out as expressing the same proposition. Certainly we cannot expect our competent language-user's assertions and denials to conform to this criterion. The fine-grained criterion suggested by a focus on propositional attitudes also fits poorly with an understanding of philosophical analysis. On any reasonable account of that process, surely, we want to allow that it might lead us from one sentence to another even if there are some competent speakers who would accept the one and deny the other. All this may undermine the idea that there is a single intuitive notion of a proposition, such as many philosophers have assumed. It may also, therefore, undermine the idea that accepting propositions is the natural position, from which Quine's views are a dubious philosophical departure.

It is thus far from clear that there is a single notion of a proposition which will suit the various philosophical purposes to which that notion has been put. Even apart from that issue, however, there is the question whether positing propositions in fact advances or impedes our understanding of various phenomena. In the cases of propositional attitudes and of philosophical analysis, Quine argues that it tends in fact to impede understanding. It requires that there be clear-cut answers to matters which may be intrinsically vague or purpose-relative. Is someone who utters a certain sentence thereby also expressing *the same* belief as that expressed by another sentence? Some questions of this sort are not always happily thought of as having definite answers, if only we could get at them; in some cases complex contextual factors come into play, and the matter is distorted if we insist upon an answer, yes or no. (We shall return to this point in Chapter 13.) In the case of philosophical analysis, again, Quine claims that all that is required is that the purposes served by the unanalysed sentence are equally or better served by its counterpart; he even allows that those purposes may shift as analysis proceeds, perhaps as the process brings clarity. (See for example *WO*, pp. 159f.) This criterion may be laxer and more purpose-relative than a synonymy requirement. (It depends, of course, on what the supposed definition of synonymy looks like in detail.) If so, it may give us a better understanding of why philosophical analysis is worthwhile. Certainly this is Quine's view. Requiring that the end points of the process of analysis be synonymous, he says, "would be out of place ... even if the notion of synonymy were in the best of shape" (*WO*, p. 208).[22]

The burden of this section has been that the issue of the determinacy or indeterminacy of translation is of relatively little significance from Quine's point of view. If translation were determinate then we could use that fact to define a notion of synonymy, and hence of meaning. But *that* kind of notion of meaning would play neither of the roles which have chiefly led philosophers to invoke the term "meaning". It would not explain language-acquisition or language-mastery. It would not underpin a notion of truth by meaning which would play a fundamental epistemological role; hence it would not contradict Quine's views on that topic. In the case of other philosophical uses of propositions and meanings, Quine also argues that we can avoid postulating such notions; in some cases, indeed, he argues that even if there were a legitimate notion of meaning we would still achieve a better account of the phenomena if we do not employ it.

9

QUINEAN METAPHYSICS
Limning the structure of reality

In Chapter 1 we made a rough distinction between two general aspects of Quine's work, or two sorts of projects that he is engaged in. On the one hand there is an epistemological aspect, which has to do with our relation to the world. As Quine conceives it, this project includes not only questions of knowledge, how we can come to have theories which have been reliable guides to the world, but also questions as to how our language can be about the world. These issues occupied us in Chapters 4–7. The second of the two general aspects concerns not our relation to the world, but rather what the world is like, at least in its broad structural features; Quine speaks, in this connection, of "limning the true and ultimate structure of reality" (WO, p. 221). It is this latter aspect of his work that is our subject in this chapter and the next four. Here Quine's concern is with ontological issues, or with metaphysics more generally. (We should note that while Quine explicitly uses the word "ontology" as a description of part of his own work he does not do the same with the word "metaphysics". But a concern with the "structure of reality" goes beyond ontology, so I use the broader term as well.)

The phrase "limning the true and ultimate structure of reality" at once raises a number of questions. Most obviously, perhaps, there are general questions of principle. What does ontology or metaphysics come to, on Quine's conception? How can there be room for such a subject? And how can the philosopher hope to tell us anything about the world? One might suppose that a scientifically minded philosopher such as Quine would think of that as the task of the special sciences: how can he hold that there is a philosophical contribution to be made here? These very general questions of principle will be the subject of the first section of this chapter. In addressing them, it will be useful to revert to the contrast between Quine and Carnap. Carnap denies that there is such a subject as ontology. Quine, by contrast, holds that there is, and that there is a philosophical contribution to be made to that subject. As he sees the matter, the philosopher considers how our science, our theory of the world, might best be organized and systematized, simplified and clarified. (Quine takes this to be the sort of activity that scientists engage in, in their more theoretical moments, for their own disciplines; the philosopher's concern is broader, but not in principle different.) The objects that are presupposed by that system, when it is organized and systematized in the best available fashion, are those that we are committed to. The philosopher's systematizing activity thus tells us what there is, if our theory of the world is broadly correct. Quine's view of the world—his metaphysics, as I am calling it—is answerable to our best theory, as regimented or systematized. If we use the word "metaphysics", we must bear in mind that it is metaphysics embedded in science and constrained by the needs of science. (Metaphysics naturalized, one might say.)

The idea of organizing and systematizing our system of the world, as used above, is vague, or at best very abstract. In making it more concrete, the central idea is that of *regimentation*. Our knowledge is to be systematized by casting it in a clear and rigorous language. The idea of regimentation, and some of its ramifications, are the subject of the second section of the chapter. One of those ramifications is *ontological reduction*, which is the subject of the third section. This is an important point of method in ontology, as Quine conceives it: the use of definitions and paraphrases to show that our theory does not commit us to the existence of certain kinds of entities which it might appear to. (We briefly mentioned this issue in Chapter 2, and in Chapter 8 we discussed it in the context of the indeterminacy of reference.)

The point of regimentation, on Quine's view, is that it makes our overall theory of the world clearer, more precise, and more systematic. He sees the drive towards system as central to the improvement of our knowledge, central to the outgrowth of science from ordinary common sense knowledge. He raises the question "how science gets ahead of common sense" and says: "the answer, in a word, is 'system'. The scientist introduces system into his quest and scrutiny of evidence. System, moreover, dictates the scientist's hypotheses themselves" (SLS, WP, p. 233). The philosopher's concern with regimentation is thus, in his view, a continuation of the ordinary scientific procedure of imposing system upon theory. The scientist's efforts to clarify, simplify, and organize one or another area of theory enable us to command a better overview of that part of our knowledge and facilitate progress in various ways. The philosophical endeavour is broader in scope but essentially the same in motivation and payoff; philosophy, in Quine's view, is continuous with science.

How does the imposition of system upon our knowledge fit with Quine's overarching empiricism? He sees the two as separate matters; the success of our science is due to their combination. In an important passage from "What Price Bivalence?" he puts it like this:

> A good scientific theory is under tension from two opposing forces: the drive for evidence and the drive for system. Theoretical terms should be subject to observable criteria, the more the better, and the more directly the better, other things being equal; and they should lend themselves to systematic laws, the simpler the better, other things being equal. If either of these drives were unchecked by the other it would issue in something unworthy of the name of scientific theory: in the one case a mere record of observation, and in the other a myth without foundation.
>
> What we settle for ... is a trade-off. We gain simplicity of theory, within reason, by recourse to terms that relate only indirectly, intermittently, and rather tenuously to observation. The values that we thus trade off one against the other—evidential value and systematic value—are incommensurable. Scientists of different philosophical temper will differ in how much dilution of evidence they are prepared to accept for a given systematic benefit, and vice versa.
>
> ("What Price Bivalence?", *TT*, p. 31)

We need not deny Quine's empiricism in order to acknowledge his concern with system.

It is the concern with system that is prominent in this chapter and the next four; let us briefly look ahead at those chapters. This chapter, as indicated, is concerned with the general principles relevant to the idea of regimentation. That activity, on Quine's account, involves fitting our theory into the framework of first-order logic; this framework functions as a paradigm, and as an ideal of clarity. Here, as much as anywhere, we see that Quine is the heir of Frege and of Russell.[1] Like them, he exploits the resources of logic to metaphysical ends; in particular, many of the definitions which he uses for the purposes of ontological reduction exploit the resources of logic. Chapter 10 will take up various issues which are raised by the adoption of first-order logic as the framework. We need to see exactly what the language of first-order logic is, why Quine accords it a privileged status, and what the consequences of doing so are. The first point is more complicated than it might sound, because we need to see not only what is explicitly included in that language, but also how those elements can be manipulated so that we can achieve the effect of a much richer language.

233

Chapter 11 concerns extensionality, which is a consequence of Quine's use of first-order logic but deserves separate treatment. Chapter 12 deals with independent constraints on the ontology and the language of regimented theory: its ontology is to be physical objects and sets, its language is to be physicalistic, in Quine's somewhat complicated sense. In Chapter 13, the last of this group of four, we get down to cases. Much of what we take ourselves to know does not fit straightforwardly into Quine's favoured language, or is ruled out by his further constraints. So he has to show either that it can be reformulated so as to fit after all, or to argue that the loss is not a sufficient objection to the constraints he imposes.

I Theory, language, and reality

For Carnap, the words "metaphysics" and "ontology" are pejorative terms, applicable only to the misguided efforts of philosophers. He denies that our ordinary or scientific theories of the world carry with them commitments to any ontology. This view is sustained by two ideas. First, our claims to knowledge presuppose a language or conceptual scheme. We cannot settle ontological questions by some sort of direct confrontation with the objects concerned; our knowledge of objects is mediated. Here he is opposing the sort of view held by Russell, which relies upon our (alleged) direct knowledge of objects, unmediated by linguistic or conceptual structures. For Russell, this kind of (supposed) knowledge can serve as a foundation for our conceptual scheme precisely because it is direct, and so not itself conceptual. The second idea which Carnap relies upon is the Principle of Tolerance. Various languages, various conceptual schemes, are available, and the choice among them is not a matter of right or wrong. The objects we speak of when we employ one conceptual scheme may be different from those we speak of when we employ another. Claims about what there is are thus relative to the choice of language, and this is a free choice, with no right or wrong to it. My speaking of real numbers, say, does not imply that I hold that such things *exist*, in an absolute sense; it merely reflects my decision to use, for present purposes, a language which contains terms for real numbers.

In Carnap's view, then, there are no genuine ontological claims. A common sense or scientific assertion about what there is presupposes a particular conceptual scheme, or linguistic framework, though this will generally not have been explicitly formulated until the assertion is subjected to philosophical scrutiny. Any ordinary assertion is internal to a particular language, and is thus language-relative, i.e. true or false only relative to that language. There is no sense to the idea that one language is *correct*. The role of philosophy, on this account, is that of formulating languages explicitly, and drawing out the implications of a given formulation; this then enables us to consider which language to choose for a particular purpose. There is, however, no room for ontological assertions, i.e. assertions about what there is in an absolute sense. The metaphysician's attempts to make such assertions misfire. And we certainly should not construe the scientist or mathematician as attempting to make an absolute claim of this sort. Speaking about the acceptance of abstract objects, Carnap says: "the acceptance of a linguistic framework must not be regarded as implying a metaphysical doctrine concerning the entities in question." ("Empiricism, Semantics and Ontology", p. 214.)

It is important to be clear on how Carnap's views differ from Quine's here. The first idea above—that scientific knowledge presupposes a language or conceptual scheme—is common ground between them; neither of them accepts that any part of our knowledge is direct and unmediated. But on the second idea they disagree. We have already discussed issues relevant to each of these points; let us briefly review.

First, Quine does not accept any version of the idea that we have direct and unmediated knowledge of objects. Sense data are the only kind of thing that he considers even a possible candidate for some kind of direct and immediate knowledge.[2] As our earlier discussion makes clear, however, he rejects the idea that we have direct and presuppositionless knowledge even of sense data; he argues that our allegedly given knowledge of sense data in fact depends on what we take ourselves to know about the physical world. (See Chapter 4, section I, above.) The implication of this is that the determining of our ontology, for Quine, is dependent upon theory. We do not first settle what objects there are, in some presuppositionless or pre-theoretical fashion, and then construct a theory with that ontology. Rather, the theory comes first. Once it is in place we can consider what ontology it requires; in the process, of course, we may revise the theory, or modify the way in which it is phrased, so as to simplify and clarify our ontology, but still it is the theory which is prior. This point fits with Quine's account of how language is learned: we do not begin by naming objects which are immediately given to us. We begin, rather, with whole sentences, uttered or assented to in response to stimulations. (See Chapters 5 and 6, above.)

Second, Quine denies the Principle of Tolerance. He is dubious about our being able, in general, to make a clear distinction between choice of language and choice of theory within a language; he denies, in any case, that the two choices are sharply different in kind. In each case, we make the choice that leads to the best, simplest, and clearest theory. (See Chapter 3, section IV above, for a more detailed discussion.) For this reason,

Quine does not see our assertions as language-relative. Various languages are available, true, but they do not stand on a level; we choose the best. So if a scientist claims that there are neutrinos, say, there is no sense in which that claim is merely relative. Her words are to be taken seriously, as making a genuine claim about what there is in the world—an ontological claim. This does not, of course, go along with a view that ontological assertions are justified by a priori reflection on Being *qua* Being, or anything like that. Quine has no more sympathy with traditional metaphysics of that sort than does Carnap. Unlike Carnap, however, he never takes it seriously as a view to be combated; this is, no doubt, part of the reason that he is happy to use the word "ontology" to describe his own views.[3]

Carnap and Quine disagree as to whether we should attribute ontological implications to the ordinary assertions of scientists and non-philosophical persons in the street. Carnap denies it, on the grounds that such assertions are language-relative; Quine denies the relativity, and accepts the ontological implications. Given Quine's answer to this question, there is a subject that might reasonably be called ontology—there are genuine questions as to what there is. But our concern is not only with the possibility of ontology in general but also with the possibility of philosophical contributions to ontology. On Quine's conception, philosophy is part of science—it is that part concerned with the most general and abstract issues. Why is ontology a matter for philosophy in this sense?

On Quine's conception, the philosopher's most general concern is with our theory of the world as a whole. The epistemological aspect of the enterprise asks how we might acquire that theory and how it is related to sensory input. The metaphysical or ontological aspect considers that system of knowledge as a going concern, largely independent of genetic considerations. We want to clarify and systematize our theory, to see how it might best be reformulated: what are the simplest and clearest terms in which we can state it? We also want to command a clear overview of it, to see what it really says, to become self-conscious about what we are committed to in accepting that theory. The ontological question gives this issue one precise and important focus: what ontological claims does our theory of the world require us to accept? What sorts of objects must we acknowledge as real, given that we accept that theory?

One might think that there are two quite separable issues here, a descriptive project and a clarificatory project. The first would set out our theory of the world as we have it, to show what it really comes to, and what it commits us to; the second would be concerned with how that theory might best be reformulated so as to simplify and clarify it. If the two projects were indeed distinct, the first could be carried out in isolation from the second; the descriptive project would be independent of any idea of reformulating our knowledge. One might then hold the first project to be legitimate, while being agnostic, at best, about the legitimacy of the second. In something like this vein, Strawson, in the introduction to *Individuals*, describes his work as "descriptive metaphysics", which he contrasts with the more dubious enterprise of "revisionary metaphysics". The former aims "to lay bare the most general features of our conceptual structure", the latter "to produce a better structure" (p. 9).

Quine, however, denies the possibility of such a separation. In his view, "our [ordinary] conceptual structure" does not pick out anything definite; nothing sufficiently well defined is implicit in our ordinary knowledge and our ordinary language. This view shows up in his attitude towards ontology. He holds that the ontological question is artificial from the outset:

> a fenced ontology is just not implicit in ordinary language. The idea of a boundary between being and non-being is a philosophical idea, an idea of technical science in a broad sense. Scientists and philosophers seek a comprehensive system of the world, and one that is oriented to reference even more squarely and utterly than ordinary language. Ontological concern is not a correction of a lay thought and practice; it is foreign to the lay culture, though an outgrowth of it.
>
> (TPT, *TT*, p. 9; cf. also "Facts of the Matter", pp. 159f.)

When we are concerned with ontological questions, or metaphysical questions more generally, we cannot simply examine our beliefs in the terms in which we are at first prone to express them. Our beliefs must, rather, be cast into a linguistic form which will let their presuppositions shine forth. Ontology, as Quine interprets it, thus presupposes *regimentation*: it is only insofar as we conceive of our knowledge as cast in regimented notation that it makes sense to raise ontological questions. Since there is more than one method of regimenting, more than one notation that could be adopted as standard, we must choose. We choose the one that best systematizes our theory. Hence the project of describing our theory and its commitments is inseparable from the project of regimenting that theory.

Implicit here is the idea that the choice of a standard notation is not neutral; nor is the way that we settle the various choices that will face us about how to regiment our ordinary beliefs into this notation. The nature of the enterprise forces decisions on these issues. Here again Quine's rejection of Carnap's Principle of Tolerance is crucial. He does not take it that these choices are unconstrained, any more than he would take the choice of a physicist between Einstein's theory and Newton's to be unconstrained. The denial of the Principle of Tolerance undercuts not only the distinction between the analytic and the synthetic, but also the distinction between philosophy and science. The physicist, on Quine's account, chooses the best available theory, and counts that as correct until something better comes along. Similarly, the philosopher, on Quine's account, chooses the best available notation—*canonical notation*, Quine sometimes calls it—and the best method of regimenting theory into that notation. What does "best" come to here? Quine's answer again assimilates the philosopher's task to that of the scientist, who tries to formulate a theory which accommodates the various data in the simplest, clearest, and most fruitful way. For Quine, the virtues of the best canonical notation are precisely those of clarity, simplicity, and system. As we emphasized at the start of this chapter, Quine attributes great importance to these virtues of theory, and sees the philosopher's concern with them—and thus with regimentation—as continuous with the concerns of the working scientist.

II Regimentation

We begin with a revealing passage from *Word and Object,* which sums up many of the points we have made so far:

> Each reduction that we make in the variety of constituent constructions needed in building the sentences of the language of science is a simplification in the structure of the inclusive conceptual scheme of science. Each elimination of obscure constructions or notions that we manage to achieve, by paraphrase into more lucid elements, is a clarification of the conceptual scheme of science. The same motives that impel scientists to seek ever simpler and clearer theories adequate to the subject matter of their special sciences are motives for simplification and clarification of the broader framework shared by all the sciences. Here the objective is called philosophical, because of the breadth of the framework concerned; but the motivation is the same. *The quest of a simplest, clearest overall pattern of canonical notation is not to be distinguished from a quest of ultimate categories, a limning of the most general traits of reality.* Nor let it be retorted that such constructions are conventional affairs not dictated by reality; for may not the same be said of a physical theory? True, such is the nature of reality that one physical theory will get us around better than another; but similarly for canonical notations.
>
> (*WO*, p. 161; emphasis added)

The emphasis here is on paraphrase of the language of science as a means of simplifying and clarifying our overall conceptual scheme. We seek the "simplest, clearest pattern of canonical notation". Thus far, this looks like an idea that Carnap might endorse. Unlike Carnap, however, Quine identifies this endeavour with the search for "ultimate categories", or "the most general traits of reality". He also differs from Carnap in insisting that the claims implicit in the reformulation cannot be dismissed as conventional in a sense which implies that they are not also factual. He does not accept the opposition between the conventional and the factual. The choice of the framework for the reformulation is "conventional" only in a sense also shared by some supposedly empirical knowledge. If we find it convenient, all things considered, to adopt a framework according to which there are sets, say, then we have accepted the existence of sets as being among the "general traits of reality"; we are committed to there being sets. As compared with Carnap, this attitude may seem to reinstate metaphysics—for it is *reality* we are after. On the other hand, it makes no concessions at all to the traditional metaphysicians whom Carnap opposed. The philosopher has no special philosophical access to "the general traits of reality", by means distinct from the knowledge of the scientist or the person in the street. On the contrary: it is a matter of making our theory fully explicit, by seeing how it can best be organized. The philosopher is concerned to systematize and clarify the conceptual scheme of science; this systematization and clarification, however, is itself scientific both in its method and in its results.

Quine's regimented language is thus not an attempt to capture ordinary English, to systematize ordinary language or our supposed "intuitions".[4] It is not supposed to encapsulate ordinary language; at some points it diverges markedly from ordinary usage. On the other hand, it is not an attempt to replace ordinary usage; it is not a proposal for language-reform. Quine, indeed, explicitly acknowledges that various kinds of idiom may be suitable for various purposes. This idea may sound like a reversion to Carnap; the saving difference is that Quine holds that his canonical notation is the one to use when our concern is with the way the world really is. Various idioms may be suitable for various purposes, but not all purposes are equal. Over the next few pages we shall enlarge upon the points made in this paragraph.

First, then, Quine's regimented language does not aim to reflect ordinary English, or even to produce a more systematic version of it. Ordinary language is the starting point of Quine's endeavour, but not its end point. To think otherwise, he says, "is to exalt ordinary language to the exclusion of one of its own traits: its disposition to keep on evolving" (WO, p. 3). In our attempts at science, we do not simply accept ordinary common sense knowledge as adequate. Similarly, Quine holds, our attempts to find a suitable language for science should not rest content with ordinary language as we find it. "Scientific neologism is itself just linguistic evolution gone self-conscious, as science is self-conscious common sense" (ibid.). Quine is not attempting to capture in precise terms what we ordinarily think or say. As we have seen, indeed, he does not think that this describes a coherent enterprise, for the relevant sort of precision simply is not implicit in ordinary language. If we want to give a precise account of what our system of knowledge comes to, we must be in the business of reformulating it and imposing a systematic structure upon it.

This point is a source of common misunderstandings and criticisms of Quine. In an essay on the individuation of events we are told, for example, that Quine's account of this matter does not "accord with our intuitions", and thus that "the truth must lie somewhere else" (Unwin, "The Individuation of Events", pp. 316f.). Here the picture seems to be that there is such a thing as the truth about events and their individuation, and that somehow—through our intuitions—we have access to this truth; Quine's view does not conform to it, and so must be rejected. Such a picture, however, does not come close to meeting Quine on his own terms, because it underestimates what we might call the Carnapian strain in his thought. For Carnap, the choice of a language is to be justified on the grounds of its simplicity, its convenience, and so on. How well it conforms to pre-existing usage matters only to the extent that it affects those sorts of factors. More obviously: a language cannot be justified by saying that it conforms to the way things really are, independently of the language. For Carnap, there is no sense to the idea that there *really are* events, absolutely, independent of the choice of conceptual scheme, and they really do have such-and-such identity-criteria. It is absurd to suppose that we might first, by act of intuition, settle the real criteria of individuation for events, and then base our choice of language on the insight vouchsafed to us by that intuition. On this sort of point, Quine is in complete agreement with Carnap. There is no immediate knowledge—in that sense, no intuition. For Quine, unlike Carnap, the claim that there really are events does make sense, but not because he supposes that our "intuitions" give us some sort of direct access to the matter.

A second point is that Quine does not claim that we should, or even that we could, give up ordinary language and use only his reformed and regimented language. To the contrary, in a passage in which he is discussing idioms of ordinary language that have no place in that notation, he says:

> Not that the idioms thus renounced are supposed to be unneeded in the market place or in the laboratory. Not that indicator words and

240

subjunctive conditionals are supposed to be unneeded in teaching the very terms ... on which the canonical formulations may proceed.

(*WO*, p. 228)

Our "renouncing" idioms for the purpose of regimented notation does not imply that they are meaningless. (As we have seen, the idea of meaninglessness plays no real role in Quine's thought. See Chapter 7, section II above, and also Chapter 3, section II above.) Nor does it imply that they are unneeded in everyday life, or even in the ordinary conduct of science. Perhaps the regimented language could not be learnt as a first language; that would be no difficulty for Quine's project as he conceives it.

Even for the working scientist, Quine is no advocate of linguistic reform. He thinks that his project is continuous with that of the scientist, but he recognizes that he presses it further than would be feasible in the laboratory:

> Science, though it seeks traits of reality independent of language, can neither get on without language nor aspire to linguistic neutrality. To some degree, nevertheless, the scientist can enhance objectivity, and diminish the interference of language, by his very choice of language. And *we {i.e. we philosophers}, concerned to distill the essence of scientific discourse, can profitably purify the language of science beyond what might reasonably be urged upon the practicing scientist.*
>
> (SLS, *WP*, p. 235; emphasis added)

Philosophy is continuous with science, but the philosopher's concerns are typically more abstract and general than those of most scientists, who are usually concerned to formulate workable theories governing a limited domain of phenomena. The appropriate sorts of reformulation or regimentation are correspondingly different.

For Quine, as for Carnap, different regimentations, different languages, are suitable for different purposes. Unlike Carnap, however, Quine does not infer from this that (supposed) claims of ontology are language-relative. Both of these points are explicit in a passage where Quine is discussing statements of propositional attitude ("Mary believes that so-and-so", or hopes that, or fears that, and so on). He speaks of "a bifurcation in canonical notation", and says:

> If we are limning the true and ultimate structure of reality, the canonical scheme for us is the austere scheme that knows no quotation but direct quotation and no propositional attitudes but only the physical constitution and behavior of organisms. ... If we are

venturing to formulate the fundamental laws of a branch of science ... this austere idiom is again likely to be the one that suits. But if our use of canonical notation is meant only to dissolve verbal perplexities or facilitate logical deductions, we are often well advised to tolerate the idioms of propositional attitude.

(*WO*, p. 221)

Elsewhere he speaks, similarly, of propositional attitudes, among other things, as "Grade B idiom" ("Reply to Davidson", D&H, p. 335). We shall return to propositional attitudes in Chapter 13; here our focus is on the general issue. As before, the underlying point is Quine's rejection of the Principle of Tolerance. Various languages are suitable for various purposes; but one language, his fully regimented canonical notation, is appropriate when we are concerned with "the true and ultimate structure of reality". That notation is the one to use when our concern is to maximize objectivity, to get at the world as it really is. When our concerns are less fundamental we may be well advised to use other notations, but there is no equality among the various options here, no claim that the choice is a free one, and so no claim of language-relativity. On the contrary: if we have succeeded in choosing the best canonical notation, then our theory as phrased in that notation tells us what there really is in the world.

Talk of phrasing our theory in canonical notation presupposes some idea of the relation between the theory as it stands and the paraphrased version. What does Quine take to be the relation between the regimented and the unregimented versions of theory? The answer to this question distinguishes him from other philosophers who have employed similar techniques of analysis. Bertrand Russell, for example, says "the thought in the mind of a person using a proper name can only be expressed explicitly" by the fully analysed version of a sentence (*Problems of Philosophy*, p. 54). Other philosophers have claimed that a successfully analysed sentence is *synonymous* with the sentence subjected to analysis. Neither of these ideas is acceptable to Quine. He requires a way of making sense of his project of analysis and regimentation which does not rely on a notion of synonymy.

On the one hand we have an unreconstructed body of ordinary discourse; on the other we have some sentences in canonical notation. What makes the latter acceptable as a reformulation of the former? On Quine's account, all that matters is that the new version will perform the same function as the old, or at least as much of that function as we think it important to preserve: "We fix on the particular functions of the unclear expression that make it worth troubling about, and then devise a substitute, clear and couched in terms to our liking, that fills these functions". (*WO*, pp. 258–59.) Who is to make the decision as to what aspects of the use of an expression are worth preserving? In the paradigmatic case, the decision is made by the user of the expression, who is presumably best placed to judge which aspects are crucial to his or her purposes. Thus Quine considers a sentence S, reformulated as S', and says:

> there is no call to think of S' as synonymous with S. Its relation to S is just that the particular business that the speaker was on that occasion trying to get on with, with the help of S among other things, can be managed well enough to suit him by using S' instead of S. We can even let him modify his purposes under the shift, if he pleases.
>
> Hence the importance of taking as the paradigmatic situation that in which the original speaker does his own paraphrase, as laymen do in their routine dodging of ambiguities.
>
> (WO, p. 160)

This paradigm is a good fit for cases of "[p]ractical temporary departures from ordinary language" (WO, p. 157), but seems less good for the more enduring and thoroughgoing paraphrases required by Quine's ontological concerns. In that sort of case, presumably, we project ourselves into the position of one who might utter the words being paraphrased. So claims about the acceptability of a given paraphrase must be based on substantive judgments about the "scientific and philosophical purposes" which are served by certain idioms or certain kinds of discourse. For this reason, Quine's proposals for paraphrase are accompanied by arguments about the purposes to be achieved by use of a given idiom, and how those purposes might be achieved in a better way—how what we say might be modified so as to contribute to the simplification and clarification of theory.

The idea of the simplification and clarification of theory, invoked throughout this chapter, is rather vague and abstract. A more concrete understanding will emerge case-by-case, but it may be helpful to set out two general ways in which regimentation can contribute to the simplification and clarification of theory. The first is by enabling us to avoid philosophical problems, thereby, in effect, resolving them. There is an important assumption here. Our ordinary language contains constructions and idioms which give rise to puzzling questions. The assumption is that if we can see how to avoid those constructions and idioms then we have equally avoided the puzzling questions. Quine puts the point like this:

> Philosophy is in large part concerned ... with what science could get along with, could be reconstructed by means of, as distinct

from what science has historically made use of. If certain problems of ontology, say, or modality, or causality, or contrary-to-fact conditionals, which arise in ordinary language, turn out not to arise in science as reconstituted with the help of formal logic, then those problems have in an important sense been solved: they have been shown not to be implicated in any necessary foundation of science. Such solutions are good to just the extent that (a) philosophy of science is philosophy enough and (b) the refashioned logical underpinnings of science do not engender new philosophical problems of their own.

(MSLT, *WP*, p. 151)

Quine does not here directly assert that "philosophy of science is philosophy enough", but I think that the implication, both of this passage and of his work in general, is that the serious philosophical issues do indeed concern science, in his broad sense of the word—our general theory of the world. Part of the "simplification and clarification" of that system of beliefs is to show how we can reformulate it so as to avoid puzzling and irresoluble questions which have characterized much philosophy; scientific work can then go forward without the distraction or impediment of such questions. In a similar passage in *Word and Object*, Quine speaks of cases in which "problems are dissolved in the important sense of being shown to be purely verbal, and purely verbal in the important sense of arising from usages that can be avoided" (p. 261). Here we have an idea which, allowing for differences in idiom, is common to Carnap and Quine.[5]

A second way in which regimentation contributes to theory is by facilitating inference and our understanding of inferential links. In Chapter 6 we saw that the idea of links among sentences plays a crucial role in Quine's account of language learning. The child must acquire the dispositions to connect sentences to sentences. (A little more exactly: he must acquire dispositions to change his verdict on one sentence when he changes his verdicts on others.) The theory that the child is learning is holistic, made up of sentences which are linked not only to sensory stimulation but also to other sentences. For most sentences, indeed, the links to sensory stimulation are indirect, through other sentences. Quine's empiricism requires that theory be answerable to sensory stimulation; connections among sentences are essential here. Such connections stitch our theory together into a whole and relate sentences from even its most abstract parts to sentences which are directly answerable to the occurrence of sensory stimulations. As initially acquired, such connections among sentences are a brute behavioural matter: "any such interconnections of sentences must finally be due to the conditioning of sentences as responses to sentences as stimuli" (*WO*, p. 11, quoted in context in Chapter 6, p. 160, above). Regimentation brings order and system to the situation. It brings insight "concerning the general relation of premise to conclusion in actual science and common sense" (MSLT, *WP*, p. 149). It gives a clear and precise account of the logical links. It will also help to make it clear what is presupposed by those links which are not simply a matter of logic. Regimentation makes it clear that such connections require extra premises, which can then be formulated and explicitly considered.

Ordinary discourse requires considerable reworking before the techniques of logic can be applied to it. In Quine's view, the advantage of this reworking is not a merely practical matter; it has theoretical ramifications, for it brings insight into the theories concerned. Quine compares the use of logic here with the use of mathematics in science: "the motivation of the Procrustean treatment of ordinary language at the hands of logicians has been ... that of achieving theoretical insights comparable to those which Arabic numeration and algebra made possible." (MSLT, *WP*, p. 149.) In each case, significant reworking of the theories is required; in each case, Quine holds, it is more than justified by its theoretical rewards:

> The ancillary activity of analyzing and paraphrasing scientific sentences of ordinary language, so as to abstract out their logical form and explore the formal consequences, is comparable in principle to the activity of the physicist who reworks and rethinks his data and hypotheses in stereotyped mathematical form so as to bring to bear the techniques of tensor analysis or differential equations upon them.
>
> (MSLT, *WP*, p. 149)

III Ontological reduction: definition, explication, and elimination

Quine holds that the ontological claims of a given body of discourse are unclear, except relative to some scheme of regimentation, either envisaged or actually implemented. We can, nevertheless, think of our ordinary discourse as having certain *prima facie* ontological commitments. For example, where we have a singular term which is the subject in simple subject-predicate sentences which we accept as literally true, it may be said that we have a *prima facie* ontological commitment to a corresponding object. According to how we choose to regiment the given body of discourse, the *prima facie* commitment may be preserved as an all-things-considered commitment; or

it may disappear, as we show how to achieve the effects of the given sentences without reference to any such alleged object. In the latter kind of
case, we have achieved an *ontological reduction*: we have shown that an
apparent commitment to a certain object or kind of object need not be
taken as a real commitment. We have shown that our body of beliefs does
not in fact require us to accept the existence of a certain object or kind of
object which it might appear to require. In Chapter 2 we briefly mentioned
one important example: the reduction of number-theory to set-theory. The
idea is of quite general importance in Quine's thought; the purpose of this
section is to explain the idea in greater detail, and also to discuss Quine's
attitude towards it.

Let us begin with a trivial case. As ordinarily formulated, our knowledge
contains such expressions as "the average family" (of a given country or city,
perhaps). The words function as a singular term, as if they named an entity
of which various puzzling things are true (that it has 1.8 children, for
example). What we mean when we use the words "the average family",
however, can be explained in other terms, which do not suggest that there is
any such entity. Although trivial, this is a good example of ontological
reduction. There is a systematic method of translating (reducing) discourse
which might seem to presuppose a given sort of object into discourse which
serves the same purpose but does not make that presupposition. This will be
a particularly useful technique when we have some reason to find the alleged
sort of object in some way problematic or dubious. In the present case, we
can easily offer a paraphrase of any statement about the average family into
statements about actual families. This is why we can use the words, and use
them to make serious statements which we take to be true, even though we
do not accept that there is an entity which they name. In the present case,
also, we have every reason to accept the reduction, for no one thinks that, in
addition to the actual families living in a given country, there really is such
an entity as *the average family* of that country, which really does have 1.8
children. To suppose that there is gives rise to various unanswerable questions: where does this family live? how do we come by information about
it? how can it have 1.8 children? and so on. (As we saw towards the end of
the previous section, avoiding unanswerable questions, or philosophical
problems, is precisely the sort of thing that Quine sees as a reason for
paraphrase.)

Quine is, evidently, not urging language-reform. He is not proposing that
we should refrain from using such terms as "the average family". If what we
currently say by means of terms of that sort always had to be spelt out in
full detail our discourse would become inconveniently lengthy. A thoroughly

eliminative language, one in which all definitions of this kind have been carried out, would be too prolix for actual use. Quine's point is not that we ought to use such a language. As he says about a different example: "The purpose of the definition is to enable us to lapse back into the eliminated notation, or a convenient approximation, while maintaining a key to how the strict canonical transcription would run". (*WO*, p. 188; cf. also TDE, *FLPV*, p. 26.) Even though we do not use the eliminative language in practice, its availability may be of great interest; according to Quine, at least, it reveals the commitments of our knowledge.

Let us see what Quine says about a less trivial, though still uncontroversial, example, namely the definition of an ordered pair. Significantly, he refers to this definition as a "philosophical paradigm".[6] The fundamental notion of a set is indifferent to order: the set consisting of me and my shadow is the same set as that consisting of my shadow and me. For certain set-theoretic purposes we need ordered pairs—set-like entities, containing two objects, which are not order-indifferent.[7] (The ordered pair $<a, b>$, as it is written, is a different entity from $<b, a>$, unless, indeed, a and b are the same object.) Such entities must obey the fundamental postulate that the ordered pair consisting of a and b is identical to the ordered pair consisting of x and y if and only if $a = x$ and $b = y$. Do we need to assume the existence of ordered pairs, i.e. kinds of entity, distinct from sets, of which the fundamental postulate is true? The definability of ordered pairs establishes a negative answer. (It was shown by Wiener in 1914 and, by a slightly different method, by Kuratowski in 1921.) The resources of set-theory are already sufficient to provide for ordered pairs, with a little manipulation. We can, that is to say, systematically equate each ordered pair with a set. One way to do it is this: we identify the ordered pair $<x, y>$ "with the [set] $\{\{x\}, \{y, \emptyset\}\}$, whose members are just (a) the [set] $\{x\}$, whose sole member is x, and (b) the [set] $\{y, \emptyset\}$, whose sole members are y and the empty [set]" (*WO*, p. 258; note that this assumes that y is not itself the empty set).[8] When translated via the definition, the fundamental postulate becomes simply a theorem of ordinary set-theory. This is all we need; to justify identifying a given kind of entity with ordered pairs nothing more is necessary than that we be able to prove that this postulate holds of that kind of entity.

By adopting one of the definitions, we clarify the commitments of our set-theory, and avoid potentially difficult questions about the nature of ordered pairs. The definition does not claim to capture a "real structure" underlying our notation for ordered pairs, or to embody facts about ordered pairs beyond the fundamental postulate. What justifies it is simply its convenience: it enables us to do the set-theory that we want to do while avoiding unnecessary assumptions and entities. Quine claims a general significance for this case:

> This construction is paradigmatic of what we are most typically up to when in a philosophical spirit we offer an "analysis" or an "explication" of some hitherto inadequately formulated "idea" or expression. We do not claim synonymy. We do not claim to make clear and explicit what the users of the unclear expression had in mind all along. We do not expose hidden meanings. ... We fix on the particular functions of the unclear expression that make it worth troubling about, and then devise a substitute, clear and couched in terms to our liking, that fills these functions. Beyond those conditions of partial agreement, dictated by our interests and purposes, any traits of the explicans come under the head of "don't-cares".
>
> (WO, pp. 258–59)

Any definition of ordered pair will do violence to what one might think of as "ordinary set-theoretic language". On Wiener's definition, for example, the empty set is a member of a member of every ordered pair, which surely runs counter to "what we ordinarily say" about ordered pairs (insofar as one can give substance to such an idea). For Quine this does not matter at all. Our use of ordered pairs requires only that they fulfil the fundamental postulate, so any objects which do so can be identified with ordered pairs; their other properties are irrelevant. Nor does it matter that there are various ways in which an ordered pair can be defined; any definition which fulfils the fundamental postulate is acceptable. This again might seem paradoxical. One can imagine the complaint: does every ordered pair contain a set containing the empty set, or not? Surely both answers cannot be correct! Quine has no sympathy here: "Any air of paradox comes only of supposing that there is a unique right analysis—a mistake that is encouraged by the practice, otherwise convenient, of retaining the term 'ordered pair' for each version." (WO, p. 260.) The point here is that what the definition shows is that we can in fact get by without ordered pairs. It is convenient to talk as if there were ordered pairs, but if that seems to raise troubling questions we can always fall back on the fundamental language of set-theory, where there is no mention of ordered pairs, and such troubles do not arise. There is no such thing as "the notion of ordered pair" which our definitions are trying to capture; this, indeed, is what the definitions show.

Ordered pairs perhaps threaten to raise difficult philosophical questions, if taken absolutely at face value: what are these entities? Quine quotes Pierce's puzzling answer to this question, an answer which invokes a "mental Diagram" and relies on unexplained notions of "Firstness" and "Secondness". He comments: "We do better to face the fact that 'ordered pair' is (pending added conventions) a defective noun" (*WO*, p. 258). This may overstate the problem: we could have said that ordered pairs are entities of which the fundamental postulate holds true, and stop at that. (Those who have already accepted set-theory as a whole, way up into the transfinite, could surely find little reason to object at this point; having swallowed a camel, they have no reason to strain at a gnat.) Even so, there would be reason to accept a definition of ordered pairs for the sake of economy, both of entities and of assumptions. In the case of ordered pairs, our intuition or "what we might at first be inclined to say" has at most a weak grip on us, and there is every reason to override it.

It would be natural to think that the definition of ordered pair is clearly acceptable because we are dealing with a purely technical matter. But Quine, as we have noted, speaks of the definition of ordered pairs as a "philosophical paradigm" (*WO*, p. 257); clearly he thinks of the definition as having a moral which applies quite widely. How can he justify the idea that conclusions drawn from this technical kind of case apply more widely, to the non-technical as well as the technical? The hallmark of a "technical" question here is that it is answerable only to convenience, simplicity, economy, and considerations of that general sort. But given a broad enough view of those virtues, Quine holds that *all* ontological questions are technical in this sense—all are to be settled by criteria of that sort. As we emphasized in the first section, above, ontology, for Quine, is an artificial enterprise from the outset, so it should not be surprising if ontological questions are to be settled by considerations which may seem artificial.

Should we think of Wiener's definition as *explicating* the idea of an ordered pair, or as *eliminating* it? Should we take it as telling us what ordered pairs really are, or as telling us that in fact there are no such things as ordered pairs? More generally, do definitions of this kind, definitions which effect an ontological reduction, explain what the given kind of entity is? Or do they show that there are no entities of that kind? The two ideas might seem to contradict one another, but Quine does not think so. In some cases, he holds, both of them are applicable; in other cases we have elimination that is clearly not explication. It depends on the details of the case:

> Explication is elimination but not all elimination is explication. Showing how the useful purposes of some perplexing expression can be accomplished through new channels would seem to count

as explication just in case the new channels parallel the old ones sufficiently.

(*WO*, p. 261)

The kind of definition under consideration always enables us to eliminate a certain expression from our vocabulary, although often at the cost of considerable prolixity. Should we speak of it as also eliminating the things for which the given expression might be supposed to stand, or as explaining what things of that kind really are? It is more natural to speak of elimination if some significant number of the uses of the eliminated term are rejected, rather than subject to the definition. This is a matter of degree, of more and less rather than all or nothing. On Quine's account there simply is no sharp difference between elimination and explication; no point of principle is at stake in the choice. In any case, however, the definition does show that we do not need to include entities of the given kind in our ontology.

10

A FRAMEWORK FOR THEORY

The role of logic

Ontological questions, and metaphysical questions more generally, are to be settled by reference to our overall theory of the world. For these purposes, that theory must be thought of as regimented, that is, as set within a canonical form of notation. Regimentation may be thought of indifferently as the construction of a new theory or as the reformulation of our old unregimented one. The process is in principle answerable to all the usual virtues of theory construction but, in practice, the virtues of simplicity and clarity will predominate. In particular, theory cast in Quine's canonical notation has a definite ontology, whereas no definite ontology is implicit in unregimented theory. (See Chapter 9, section I above.) What we might think of as the more empirical end of the range of virtues will presumably play little role: we do not expect the regimented theory to differ from the unregimented in the correctness of its predictions; nor does regimentation aim primarily at gains in the familiarity, scope, or fecundity of the theory, although such benefits are conceivable.[1] (For this list of the virtues of a theory, see "Posits and Reality", *WP*, p. 247; see also Chapter 4, p. 84, above.) As with any change of theory, we begin with what we have—unregimented theory, in this case—and consider how we might improve it. Any improvement gives us a better understanding of the world; hence Quine equates "the quest of a simplest, clearest overall pattern of canonical notation" with "a limning of the most general traits of reality" (*WO*, p. 161; quoted in context p. 238, above).

None of this shows that we should or could abandon unregimented language. For the most part, we will continue to use it. In practice we will carry out the regimentation only in disputed cases, and even then only part way. The very general sorts of questions which regimentation answers are usually not at issue in the everyday practice of science. When they arise, we resort to regimentation to answer them; even here, it will usually be enough merely to indicate how regimentation could be carried out. It is a point that we have seen before: we philosophers "can profitably purify the language of science beyond what might reasonably be urged upon the practicing scientist" (SLS, *WP*, p. 235; quoted in context in Chapter 9, p. 241, above).

Quine claims that the best way to regiment our theory is to set it in the syntax of classical, two-valued, first-order logic with identity.[2] (When I speak of logic, unqualified, it is this system that I mean.) Logic is not exactly a language in the ordinary sense. It has no predicates of its own, except for the identity predicate; so it has no sentences of its own apart from the laws of identity. (In many contexts, as Quine points out, the identity predicate is definable. In those contexts logic has no predicates of its own at all, and hence no sentences of its own. See *PL*, pp. 61–64.) But the syntax of logic becomes a full-fledged language when we add a vocabulary consisting of predicates adequate for the particular matters we are discussing.[3] Regimented theory thus has logic as its structure. (Sometimes, as above, I shall follow Quine in speaking of logic as the "syntax" of theory. Logic, as Quine uses the term, perhaps goes beyond syntax, in the narrowest sense. For Quine, however, nothing turns on this except the choice of the word; in what follows I shall feel free to ignore the issue, and keep the word.)

Quine's taking first-order logic as the framework for theory is, on his account, a theoretical step like any other. The physicists adopt relativistic mechanics, rather than Newtonian mechanics, for the sake of the simplicity and clarity which this move brings to their theory. Similarly, Quine claims, setting theory within the syntax of first-order logic is the best way to simplify and clarify that theory; he thinks the step is justified on the same very general sort of basis as other developments of theory. Unlike some of his predecessors, Quine does not see the logical framework as a priori, as something that is imposed upon theory from without. This point perhaps needs particular emphasis because some parts of our theory do not, on the face of it, fit into the framework. If we are to retain the framework, we must show how parts of the theory could be reconfigured, more or less drastically, so as to fit after all; if we cannot do that, we must reject those apparent aspects of our knowledge as not reflecting "the true and ultimate structure of reality" (*WO*, p. 221). Focusing on a particular narrow area of putative knowledge may thus make the framework appear to be an external constraint on theory. It may even make the need to fit our knowledge into the framework seem to be merely an obstacle. Consideration of the theory as a whole, however, shows that local inconveniences are more than offset by global advantages. The details will emerge as we go, in this chapter and the next three, but I shall say a little about the advantages immediately.

As a framework for theory, logic earns its keep in virtue of the simplicity and clarity that it brings to that theory. The syntax of logic is itself wonderfully clear, simple, and transparent. Theory, when paraphrased so as to fit into that syntax, has a structure which is equally clear, simple, and transparent. When theory is thus paraphrased we can see exactly what it says, and what it does not say. We can thereby avoid puzzling questions which might otherwise divert the progress of science into fruitless channels; this is one of the advantages of regimentation noted in the previous chapter. Another advantage noted there concerned inference. On Quine's holistic view of knowledge, the links between sentences—the fact that we infer some sentences from others—are crucial. Logic allows for the systematization of these links; they are understood in terms of (logical) implication.[4] This is a large part of the gain of regimentation. The point here is not that all the inferences that we make should be logically valid. But holding our inferences up against that standard can make us aware of what premises we should need to add in order to make them logically valid. Those premises can then be subjected to critical scrutiny. Science, Quine says, is "self-conscious common sense" (WO, p. 3); regimenting our inferences, and making their premises explicit, will increase the self-consciousness. It will enable us to become more aware of our assumptions, and thus of points at which further work may be needed.

The notion of structure has a special role to play in logical truth and in implication. According to Quine's definition, a sentence is a logical truth if and only if it is true and every sentence with the same logical structure is also true. (See PL, p. 49; equivalently, the logical truths are those containing only the logical vocabulary essentially.) Implication is a matter of logical truth (see previous note), so implication is equally a matter of logical structure: "Logical implication rests wholly on ... the logical structures of the two sentences." (PL, p. 48.) Regimenting our theory reveals its logical structure; regimented sentences are grist for the logical mill. Logic, with its established methods of proof, can be applied to them directly and without further ado.

The first section of the chapter outlines the basic syntax of logic. For Quine, it is an advantage of this syntax that it provides a clear way of answering the ontological question; that issue is also discussed in the first section. The next two sections take up two aspects of Quine's logic that have been controversial: first, in section II, the fact that it is a bivalent (two-valued) logic—a logic of truth and falsehood; second, in section III, the fact that it is first-order logic rather than second-order logic (we shall explain the difference). Section IV takes up the question of the bearers of truth-values, what sorts of things are true or false. On Quine's account these are *eternal sentences*, sentences which do not change their truth-value with changes in the context in which they are uttered. Section V considers the concept of truth itself.

I The syntax of logic; ontological commitment

In order for logic to be applicable to sentences directly, those sentences must be paraphrased so as to employ a syntax which meshes smoothly with logic. From Quine's point of view this syntax also recommends itself on other grounds. It is transparent, economical, and powerful; by limiting our regimented language to a very small number of clearly understood grammatical constructions and categories, we obtain a language with far greater expressive power than its meagre basis might lead us to expect. Whether the language has *sufficient* expressive power is controversial; given the poverty of its constructions, however, its power is striking.

What is this syntax? The basic syntax consists of no more than the following:

1 truth-functional operators;[5]
2 quantifiers and variables (of which more below);
3 identity (which is, as noted, definable under some circumstances).

To apply the syntax to a particular subject we need to add predicates, of one or more places, drawn from that subject. (No particular predicate, except identity if not definable, is part of the basic syntax.) Further economies can be imposed on this already very economical syntax. A single truth-functional operator suffices, for they can all be defined in terms of one.[6] Similarly, as we shall see, we only need one of the two quantifiers.

An elementary sentence is constructed from this basic vocabulary by applying an *n*-place predicate to a sequence of *n* variables (not necessarily distinct). This yields expressions such as "*x* is red", or "*x* is the mother of *y*". Things of this sort are *open sentences*, meaning that they contain variables ("*x*", "*y*", and so on) which are not preceded by quantifiers; such variables are said to be *free*. (We shall make this more precise shortly.) Open sentences are not true or false as they stand, but only relative to an assignment of objects as values of the variables. (Equivalently, an open sentence is true or false *of* a sequence of objects.) The open sentence "*x* is red" is true if "*x*" is assigned a red object as its value, false otherwise. (Open sentences may thus be compared with English sentences which use pronouns, such as "It is red" or "She is his mother". Such sentences are true or false only relative to a context in which it is clear to what or to whom the pronoun refers.)

More complex sentences are formed from these elementary sentences by two operations: first, truth-functional compounding; second, affixing of quantifiers which bind their variables, an idea to be explained shortly. A crucial point is that these two operations are *iterative*: they can be applied in either order, and indefinitely often. For example, two open sentences may be conjoined, and quantifiers then prefixed to the conjunction; or one open sentence may have a quantifier prefixed to it and then be conjoined with another open sentence, and a quantifier affixed to the conjunction, and so on. The power of logic arises from the fact that these operations can be iterated without end, and in any order, thus generating an infinite number of non-elementary sentences from any given stock of one or more elementary sentences.

There are two quantifiers, the existential and the universal, written "∃" and "∀", respectively, and followed by a variable. When a sentence is preceded by a quantifier immediately followed by a given variable, occurrences of that variable in that sentence are said to be *bound*. (Variables which are not bound are *free*.) A sentence in which all variables are bound is a *closed* sentence. Thus "(∃x) x is red" is a closed sentence which is true just in case there is at least one way of assigning a value to "x" which makes the contained open sentence, "x is red". (Equivalently, it is true if the open sentence is true of at least one object.) It is thus a sentence that can be read as saying that *there is* a red object (at least one); that there exists at least one red object; or that something, at least one thing, is red. (I take all these formulations to be ways of saying more or less the same thing in English. The precise meaning of the existential quantifier, however, is given by the rule for evaluating the truth or falsehood of sentences containing it.) Similarly, "(∀x) x is red" is true just in case the open sentence "x is red" is true of everything, of all objects, i.e. the open sentence is true for every assignment of values to "x". Our universally quantified sentence thus says that everything is red. To say that nothing is red we do not need to introduce a further quantifier: we simply negate the sentence that says that something is red. Negation is a truth-functional operator which applies to a single sentence to produce a sentence which is true if the original sentence is false, false if it is true. Either quantifier can be defined in terms of the other. Using "~" for negation, and "F" to stand for any arbitrary predicate, we can define "(∀x) Fx" as "~(∃x) ~ Fx". (If it is not the case that there is an object of which "F" is not true, then "F" is true of every object.) Or we can define "(∃x) Fx" as "~(∀x) ~ Fx".

The interpretation of the quantifiers given here is objectual rather than substitutional. (See Chapter 6, section III, above.) On the substitutional interpretation, a sentence "$(\forall x)\ Fx$" (where "F" stands for any predicate) is true just in case every *name* which can replace "x" in "Fx" produces a true sentence when we make the replacement. On that account, the role of names, or of singular terms more generally, is crucial; the desired results are achieved only when every object has a name and every name names an object. If the first of these conditions fails, "$(\forall x)\ Fx$", substitutionally interpreted, may be true even though there is some (unnamed) object of which "Fx" is not true; or "$(\exists x)\ Fx$" may be false even though there is some (unnamed) object of which "Fx" *is* true. Can we assume that every object has a name? In artificially restricted cases perhaps we can, but in general we cannot. To claim that there are feral cats in the neighbourhood is not necessarily to be able to name any, or even to give a singular term which denotes any. That the objects outrun the names is, moreover, true as a matter of principle, not just of happenstance. Given the existence of the real numbers, or of sets which will play the analogous role, we can prove that there are more objects than names, so that not all can be named. This fact alone would, for Quine, be enough to justify the choice of an objectual rather than a substitutional interpretation of the quantifiers.

Quine attributes the greatest importance to the clarity and economy of the framework which we have been sketching:

> I hesitate to claim that this syntax, so trim and clear, can accommodate in translation all cognitive discourse. I can say, however, that no theory is fully clear to me unless I can see how this syntax would accommodate it.
>
> ("Promoting Extensionality", p. 144)

The point that Quine hesitates to assert here seems to function as something like a regulative principle for him: where we cannot yet see how to accommodate a body of discourse within our austere syntax, this fact indicates that we have not yet got to the bottom of the matter, and further work is called for. And when we come to see how to make the accommodation, that, for Quine, represents significant philosophical and scientific progress.

For Quine, an important purpose of regimenting theory is that we thereby clarify exactly what entities we have to accept if we accept the theory—we clarify the *ontological commitments* of the theory. (As we emphasized in the previous chapter, he thinks that unregimented theory has no definite ontological commitments.) On his account, the ontological commitments of a theory are conveyed by its bound variables. If we assert a sentence of the form "$(\exists x)\ Fx$", or a sentence implying such, we are thereby committed to there being objects, one or more, of which the predicate "F" is true. (Note that a sentence of the form "$(\forall x)\ Fx$" implies the corresponding sentence of the form "$(\exists x)\ Fx$".) If a theory implies some sentence of the form "$(\exists x)\ Fx$", then, the theory cannot be true unless there is an object of which the given predicate holds; the theory is committed to there being things of that kind. This, for Quine, is guaranteed by the nature of the quantifiers, given that they are objectual rather than substitutional. It is all that we need in order to be able to say what entities must be accepted by one who advocates a given theory: "a theory is committed to those and only those entities to which the bound variables of the theory must be capable of referring in order that the affirmations made in the theory be true." ("On What There Is", *FLPV*, pp. 13f.) This criterion does not settle the ontological question; it tells us only what things a given theory is committed to there being, not what things there actually are—unless, of course, we are assured that the theory is true (see op. cit., *FLPV*, p. 15).

For Quine, the sense that we give to the idea of existence, and to the ontological question, is thus bound up with logic, meaning first-order logic with identity.[7] Quantification here is inseparable from the rest of the logic; any change in logic shifts the ontological question:

> What I have been taking as the standard idiom for existential purposes, namely quantification, can serve as standard only when embedded in the standard form of regimented language that we have been picturing. ... If there is any deviation in this further apparatus, then there arises a question of foreign exchange: we cannot judge what existential content may be added by these foreign intrusions until we have settled on how to translate it all into our standard form.
>
> (*PT*, pp. 35f.)

This connection between logic and ontology does not imply that no change in the logic, and thus in the ontological question, is possible. To the contrary: Quine explicitly envisages that possibility. A change in the logic would mean a change in "the very notion of existence".[8] But that notion might then be replaced by a "kindred notion ... that seems sufficiently akin to warrant application of the same word; such is the way of terminology." (*PT*, p. 36.) But the ontological question as we understand it is bound up with our logic. Equally, the connection between logic and ontology does not imply that we cannot sensibly speak of the ontological commitments of bodies of unregimented theory—those of eighteenth-century chemistry, for example, or of current theories phrased in other terms. In such cases we have, again, "a question of foreign exchange". When we speak of ontology in such a case we are more or less explicitly envisaging the given theory as paraphrased into the terms of our logic; no doubt there will sometimes be room for dispute as to how such envisaged paraphrase would go, and thus about the ontological commitments of a given body of theory.

Quine's criterion of ontological commitment, and thus also of what it is to be an object, is thus inseparably bound up with his canonical notation. To accept that there are things of a certain kind is to commit oneself to using first-order logic with identity in reasoning about them. This, for Quine, functions as a crucial constraint on what objects we should accept. It is only if we are willing to apply the laws of identity that we should accept a putative object as indeed being an object; for such laws to be sensibly applicable, we must be able to make clear sense of the identity-criteria for objects of the given kind. As Quine asks: "what sense can be found in talking of entities which cannot meaningfully be said to be identical with themselves and distinct from one another?" ("On What There Is", *FLPV*, p. 4.) Or, more explicitly:

> We have an acceptable notion of class, of physical object, or attri-
> bute, or any other sort of object, only insofar as we have an accep-
> table principle of individuation for that sort of object. There is no
> entity without identity.
>
> (*TT*, p. 102)

This view plays an important role for Quine; in particular, it underpins his view that there are no such things as meanings or propositions.

Quine takes his criterion of ontological commitment to be *obvious*. Rightly understood, he thinks, it "is scarcely contestable, since the quanti-fiers are explained by the words 'each object x is such that' and 'there is an object x such that'." (*PL*, p. 89.) Similarly, he refers to this criterion of ontological commitment as a "triviality" (see *TT*, pp. 174–75). Not all philosophers, however, have found it obvious.

One point of possible disagreement is that Quine puts forward a single and univocal criterion of existence. The quantifiers, universal and existen-tial, are not ambiguous; nor is the idea of existence which they convey; there are not different kinds or modes of Being. "The variables of quantifi-cation in natural science range over physical objects and over numbers, functions, and other sets. All of these are equally assumed in the only sense that I understand". ("Immanence and Validity", p. 242.) This immediately distinguishes his view from those of many philosophers of a more obviously metaphysical stripe. Abstract objects, such as sets, *exist* in just the same sense as concrete objects, such as the desk in front of me. Likewise the entities of advanced science, such as electrons, quarks, and black holes, exist in just the same sense. This is not to deny that there are differences here. But we can think of these as differences between the sorts of things said to exist, and in our degree of certainty in making the claim, not between the senses of existence ascribed to each. There is no reason to say that the notion of existence is equivocal, and means one thing as applied to concrete objects and another as applied to abstract objects. (See *WO*, section 27.)

A second point is that a sentence such as "$(\exists x)$ (x is red)" commits us to the existence of a red object, but not, on Quine's criterion, to the existence of the property or attribute of redness. The sentence, after all, does not quantify over redness.[9] We are not required to posit an entity named by the predicate in order for the predicate to make sense; not every meaningful part of language functions as a name. More important, positing properties would not have any "real explanatory power" ("On What There Is", *FLPV*, p. 10); hence we have no reason to posit them. The notion of explanation here is, of course, naturalistic; Quine's rejection of properties rests on the idea of a purely naturalistic account of language-acquisition and language-use, sketched in Chapters 4–6, above, which does not invoke such entities. In Quine's view, the positing of properties is thus redundant. Moreover they lack clear identity-criteria, so we have every reason *not* to accept them.

A third controversial point about Quine's criterion is that ontological commitment is conveyed by the use of quantified variables, not by the presence in the language of names. Names, and singular terms more broadly, do not occur in Quine's canonical notation, strictly construed. Those who hold that names bear the burden of reference will, of course, take this point as a criticism of that notation. Quine, however, argues on independent grounds that it is bound variables, or their natural language analogues, that are, in the primary sense, referential. (See Chapter 6, section III, above; see also the first section of the next chapter.)

II Bivalence

In this section and the next we shall briefly consider two controversial features of Quine's canonical notation. For our purposes, the logic that Quine chooses matters less than the general principle underlying his choice. And the general principle is that we should choose our canonical notation in a way which maximizes the simplicity, clarity, and efficacy of our system of knowledge as a whole. For Quine this is all that matters—there are no other constraints.

In this section our concern is with the fact that the sentential logic that Quine advocates is classical truth-functional logic. In particular, it is two-valued, or bivalent: every closed sentence is either true or false; every open sentence is either true or false of a given object or sequence of objects. Quine accepts this logic because of the clarity, simplicity, and system that it brings to theory as a whole, but he explicitly accepts that there are countervailing considerations, chiefly that it increases the gap between our theory and its evidence. (For the important idea that our theory must result from a balancing of these two factors, see Chapter 9, p. 233, above, and especially the passage from "What Price Bivalence?" quoted there.) Let us enlarge upon the opposition between these factors in the case of bivalence.

If we adopt bivalent logic we have to accept that many sentences whose truth-value we do not know, and will never know, nevertheless *have* determinate truth-values. In *Philosophy of Logic* Quine speaks of a doubt about bivalence on this score as arising from "a confusion between knowledge and truth" (p. 85). In "What Price Bivalence?" written eleven years later, he treats the idea with more respect, and he is surely right to do so. For doubts about bivalence are equally doubts about the notion of truth that is presupposed in classical bivalent logic; merely to appeal to that notion of truth is not to answer the doubts. In "What Price Bivalence?" this issue appears as an absolutely fundamental one. Citing Michael Dummett, Quine says "Bivalence is ... the hallmark of realism." (WPB?, *TT*, p. 32.)[10] To be a realist about a certain kind of (alleged) entity is to accept that statements about entities of that kind are true or false, independent of our knowledge. Even while acknowledging this point, Quine says that he is inclined to maintain bivalence "for the simplicity of theory that it affords" (ibid.). An important point of Quine's method is illustrated here. Fundamental metaphysical issues are not settled by a priori insight or argument; they are settled by the choice of canonical notation, which is in turn governed by considerations of systematic simplicity of theory as a whole.

In treating every sentence, known or unknown, as having a determinate truth-value, classical logic idealizes our knowledge. Some idealization of this sort is no doubt required for anything worth calling a logic, but some forms of logic seek to minimize it. On some interpretations of intuitionistic logic, for example, a sentence is counted as neither true nor false unless we have some way of establishing its truth-value, at least in principle.[11] More exotic ideas have also been mooted. (Quine speaks of all departures from the classical as "deviant logics"; his most detailed discussion of them is in chapter 6 of *Philosophy of Logic*.) Classical two-valued logic, however, makes no compromises. Quine acknowledges that the "sweet simplicity" of two-valued logic is bought "at no small price" (WPB?, *TT*, p. 32). He has no doubt but that the price is worth paying. No logic is going to excise all undecidable sentences, and "the familiarity, the convenience, the simplicity, and the beauty" of classical logic makes it superior to any rival (*PL*, p. 87).

In *Pursuit of Truth* Quine invokes holism to reinforce the appeal to simplicity. Again alluding to Dummett, he considers the idea that we should "reckon a sentence of natural science neither true nor false if no procedure is known for making a strong empirical case for its truth or falsity" (*PT*, p. 94). His response is that this criterion does not mark a sharp distinction. Observation sentences, and the observation categoricals based on them, come out clearly true or false by this test, but after that matters get murky, for other sentences "share empirical content in varying degrees by implying observation categoricals jointly" (ibid.).

Bivalence is also threatened by vagueness, which is a widespread feature of language. Almost every sentence contains vague terms. In many cases, however, the vagueness makes no difference to the truth-value. "It's raining" may be vague, but still it is unproblematically true in a downpour, and unproblematically false on a cloudless day. Quine suggests a number of expedients to lessen vagueness in cases where we require precision. The use of some vague adjectives can be eliminated; we replace them with their comparatives. Whether a given cup of coffee is hot may be unclear, because of the vagueness of the term, but fewer problems afflict the question whether it is hotter than another, or than some paradigm. For more scientific purposes we use degrees Celsius or Kelvin. There is still some vagueness here (to how many decimal places can we measure temperature?), but we can generally achieve as much precision as we need and we usually understand, at least in principle, how more could be achieved if required.

Some vague nouns, such as "mountain" and "heap", can be made precise by stipulations, as and when needed.[12] In some cases, where it matters for scientific purposes, we will actually adopt and impose the relevant definitions. For other terms, playing less of a systematic role in our theory, we content ourselves with the idea that we could do this if necessary: "To reason *as if* our terms were precise seems pretty straightforward as long as we see that they could be made precise by arbitrary stipulations whenever occasion might arise". (WPB?, *TT*, p. 34; emphasis in the original.) In some cases, however, no stipulation of this sort is available, even in principle. Removing a single molecule from one of the surfaces of my desk would still leave my desk intact. Continuing the process would, at some point, leave me deskless.

Yet we cannot in fact specify any such point: we cannot specify, however arbitrarily, which molecules make up my desk. Quine suggests that we may be able to get by with no such stipulation:

> What I call my desk could be equated indifferently with countless almost coextensive aggregates of molecules, but I refer to it as a unique one of them, and I do not and cannot care which. Our standard logic takes this also in stride, imposing a tacit fiction of unique though unspecifiable reference.
>
> (FSS, p. 57)

No such tactic, however, will save the predicate " ... is a desk" from vagueness. Quine does at one point suggest that we can avoid even this source of vagueness by retreating to terms of "austere physical theory" (WPB?, TT, p. 37). On the whole, however, he seems content to live with a certain amount of vagueness: when it matters we will take steps to eliminate it, but we should not expect to attain a wholly precise language.

Ambiguity poses a threat to the idea that no sentence can be both true and false. An ambiguous sentence may be true in one sense and false in another; Quine, indeed, takes this as the clearest available way of understanding the idea of ambiguity (see WO, p. 131). Syntactic ambiguity will be removed by paraphrase into the syntax of logic. About other forms of ambiguity Quine has very little to say (section 27 of WO is the sole exception). Where they occur, and where it matters, we can presumably remove them quite easily by rephrasing the sentence.

Vagueness and ambiguity might be thought to cast in doubt the possibility of imposing classical logic upon our system of knowledge, or even of systematizing it at all. Other sorts of considerations have been held to cast doubt upon the desirability of choosing classical logic. In particular, it has been suggested that other forms of logic may be preferable for systematizing the reasoning that is involved in quantum mechanics. There are various proposals of this sort; Quine discusses one made in 1936 by Birkhoff and von Neumann. His comments on this proposal indicate his general attitude towards deviant logic.

Birkhoff and von Neumann suggest that some of the difficulties in understanding quantum mechanics arise from the use of standard truth-functional logic within a realm where such reasoning is not unrestrictedly valid. They accordingly propose a weakened version of logic, which they think appropriate to quantum mechanics.[13] The proposal has not been widely adopted by those working in the area; if it were, Quine would perhaps be more sympathetic towards it. What he says, however, very much emphasizes the drawbacks of such an idea, rather than its advantages:

> Whatever the technical merits of the case, I would cite again the maxim of minimum mutilation as a deterring consideration ... in any event let us not underestimate the price of a deviant logic. There is a serious loss of simplicity, especially when the new logic is not even a many-valued truth-functional logic. And there is a loss, still more serious, on the score of familiarity. ... The price is not quite prohibitive, but the returns had better be good.
>
> (*PL*, p. 86)

It might, of course, suit the purposes of the working physicist to use a non-standard logic solely for the purposes of quantum mechanics; or those working in some other branch of science might find the same tactic useful. As a temporary expedient, we might decide to use a non-standard logic in one branch of our knowledge. The use of such a logic would eventually require some explanation: why do the principles of inference which hold everywhere else fail *here*? How is the given branch of science to be integrated with others in such a way that the difference in logic makes sense? Such an explanation would, presumably, be couched in terms of the logic in general use. Quine seeks a single way of regimenting our knowledge. (See the remarks about his views on the unity of science in Chapter 1, above, towards the end of section IV.) Clearly he is not wholly ruling out the possibility that we might come to find some alternative logic preferable for this purpose. But equally clearly he thinks that to outweigh the simplicity and familiarity of first-order logic it would have to have great advantages of other kinds. He is not persuaded that any candidate has in fact met this criterion.

III First-order logic

The logic that Quine takes as canonical notation is first-order. Others have preferred second-order (or even higher-order) logic (we shall get to the difference shortly). It is not that Quine claims that first-order logic is necessary, or a priori, and that its rivals are not. (First-order logic is analytic, on Quine's late understanding of that term, while second-order logic presumably is not; Quine's understanding of analyticity, however, leaves this point without any general philosophical interest.) Nor is it a matter of what to count as *logic*: for Quine little or nothing turns on the use of that word. In a number of relatively early essays he uses the word much more broadly, counting set-theory, and hence mathematics, as logic—as Frege, Russell, and Carnap all more or less did. But even at that stage nothing is at stake for him in that usage. To adopt a narrower use of the word "logic", he says, "is merely to deprive '∈' [the symbol for set-membership] of the status of a logical word" (C&LT, *WP*, p. 111). His subsequently coming to do just that is more a change of usage than of doctrine. What *is* at stake for Quine is what we should take as the notation in which ontology is to be gauged, and in which arguments are to be formulated, when our concern is to state matters as clearly and explicitly as possible.

First-order logic is contrasted with second-order logic. In second-order logic quantifiers can bind predicate letters as well as variables ranging over objects. We say things like "Everything true of Plato is true of Socrates too"; the language of second-order logic allows us to capture the meaning of this sentence by paraphrasing it as "($\forall F$) [If F(Plato) then F(Socrates)]". The interpretation of second-order logic, however, is controversial. On one view, the second-order quantifiers range over properties or attributes: our second sentence would then mean that Socrates has every property that Plato has. On another view, which is now widely taken as standard, second-order quantifiers range over all the set of all subsets of the universe of discourse (where the latter is what the first-order quantifiers range over).—We shall return to this issue towards the end of the section.

Second-order logic brings with it a considerable increase both in inferential power and in expressive power. Some inferences which are not valid by the standards of first-order logic are valid by the standards of second-order logic; some concepts and sentences that cannot be expressed in a first-order logic can be expressed if we go second-order.[14] An important example of the expressive power of second-order logic concerns the infinite. In first-order logic we cannot say what it is for there to be infinitely many objects of a certain kind, at least not without quantifying over sets, or properties or the like (unless, of course, we simply help ourselves to the concept of infinity or that of finitude). In second-order logic, by contrast, we can analyse the concept. One way to do it is this: there are infinitely many Fs just in case there is at least one object which is F and there is a transitive asymmetrical relation (R in the schema below) which relates every object which is F to another object which is F. Schematically:

$$(\exists x) \ Fx \ \& \ (\exists R) \ [(\forall x)(\exists y) \ (\text{If } Fx \ \& \ xRy \text{ then } Fy) \ \&$$
$$(\forall x)(\forall y)(\forall z) \ (\text{If } xRy \ \& \ yRz \text{ then } xRz) \ \&$$
$$(\forall x)(\forall y) \ (\text{If } xRy \text{ then } \sim yRx]$$

Here it is essential that we quantify over relations between objects as well over objects; unless we resort to set-theory, nothing equivalent can be done without the second-order quantifier.[15]

Even more striking, perhaps, is the fact that certain quite ordinary looking sentences of English have no first-order symbolization, but can be symbolized in second-order logic. An example which has become famous is: "Some critics admire only one another". There is no first-order symbolization of this sentence unless, again, we quantify over sets, or other entities to the same effect;[16] yet the sentence certainly looks as if it is only about *critics*, not about sets or attributes. Using second-order logic, we can schematize it as follows:

$$(\exists F)[(\exists x)(Cx \ \& \ Fx) \ \& \ (\forall x)(\forall y) \ (\text{If } Cx \ \& \ Fx \ \& \ Cy \ \& \ Axy \text{ then } Fy)]$$

(Here "Cx" has as its intended interpretation "x is a critic"; "Axy" has "x admires y".)

Second-order logic thus has *prima facie* advantages over first-order logic. Yet Quine prefers the latter as canonical notation. In fact he argues quite generally against any sort of use of second-order logic, opting instead for set-theory when more than first-order logic is needed. We need to see why. I shall begin by discussing his reasons for preferring first-order logic as the framework for theory; his reasons for rejecting second-order logic more generally will emerge from this discussion.

Why, then, does Quine hold that first-order logic is peculiarly fitted to form the framework for theory—more fitted, in particular, than second-order logic? I shall distinguish two factors.[17] One is that there are formalisms for first-order logic which are complete. A *formalism* is a system of precise axioms and rules of inference for which it is a purely mechanical matter to check whether any given formula is an instance of an axiom, or follows from other formulas by application of a rule of inference. (Or we can give a so-called natural deduction system, consisting solely of rules of inference, and no axioms; this may seem to be little more than a technical trick, but it fits nicely with the emphasis on logic as facilitating inference.) To say that such a formalization is *complete* means that any logically valid schema can be obtained from the axioms by repeated (but finite) applications of the rules of inference; and that if a sentence is implied by one or more others (a finite number at most) then there is a proof which takes the implying sentences as premises and has the implied sentence as a conclusion. (It is, of course, also essential that the formalism be *sound*: that it does not enable us to prove any schemata which are not logically valid, or to infer a sentence from others which do not logically imply it. Soundness, however, is much easier to obtain, and to prove, than is completeness.) Completeness thus effects a link between first-order validity and provability, defined in purely syntactic terms. The two notions are quite distinct: to prove that they pick out exactly the same schemata and the same inference patterns—which is what soundness and completeness together show—was a remarkable result.[18]

The completeness of first-order logic shows that we can give a precise syntactic account of first-order logical implication, with no questionable presuppositions. We can define (first-order) logical truth and logically valid inference without presupposing the idea of truth or the notion of an interpretation. (An interpretation of a first-order schema consists of a specification of a universe of discourse, the set of objects which the quantifiers range over; a specification of a set of ordered n-tuples of such objects for each n-place predicate letter; and an assignment of values to free variables in the schema, if there are any. Validity can be defined as truth in all interpretations.) Completeness "shows that we *can* define logical truth by mere description of a proof procedure, without loss of any traits that made logical truth interesting to us in the first place" (*PL*, p. 57; emphasis in the original). It shows that we have, in our favoured proof procedure, a precise and surveyable compendium of the subject. Quine also connects it with the idea that all the truths of logic are actually or potentially *obvious*. If we choose a complete axiom system for logic in which each axiom is obviously true, and each rule of inference obviously truth-preserving, then we can obtain every logical truth by a series of obvious steps from obvious starting points. (See C&LT, *WP*, p. 111; also *PL*, pp. 82–83, 98.)

Second-order logic, at least on the standard interpretation, is not complete. The qualification is needed here because completeness is a matter of the relationship between the syntactic formulation of the logic (the formalism, whether axiom system or natural deduction system), on the one hand, and the semantics for the logic (what we count as an interpretation), on the other hand. A logic is sound and complete when there is a formalism, a syntax, which enables us to derive exactly those schemata which are true in all interpretations. Different understandings of the semantics for second-order logic give different definitions of an interpretation because they give different accounts of the range of the second-order quantifiers. According to the account that is now standard, in any interpretation the second-order quantifiers range over all subsets of the domain of that interpretation (where the domain is the range of the first-order quantifiers). This is perhaps the natural account, at least if we want to take the second-order quantifiers extensionally rather than as ranging over properties. Given that account of the semantics for second-order logic, it is incomplete: there is no formalism that enables us to prove all its valid schemata (and none that are not valid).[19] We can limit the range of the second-order quantifiers so that we obtain a formalism which is complete relative to that conception of an interpretation. If we do so, however, we lose much of the added inferential power which made second-order logic seem attractive.[20]

The completeness of first-order logic is thus one reason that Quine has for taking it, rather than second-order logic, as the framework for theory. Ontology provides another reason. First-order logic applies to all objects but it "has no objects it can call its own; its variables admit all values indiscriminately." (FSS, p. 52.) If our logic is first-order, there are no logical objects: to accept first-order logic is not to commit oneself to the existence of any particular kind of entity. It does commit one to accepting that at least one object exists, but it requires no assumptions at all about the nature of that object.[21] By contrast, it is quite unclear what ontological assumptions are implicit in second-order logic. (This unclarity alone might be taken as a reason to prefer first-order logic as the framework for theory.) Quine argues that considerable assumptions are implicit here. He holds that it is better to assert our existential assumptions explicitly, as and when needed, rather than building them into the framework for our theory.

The question of the ontological assumptions of second-order logic has given rise to much debate, but our account must be brief. In accordance with his criterion of ontological commitment, Quine has consistently argued that in treating predicate letters as quantifiable variables we are committing ourselves to a range of entities which those variables range over. On some accounts, it is attributes or properties to which we are committing ourselves. Quine, however, is not willing to accept that there are attributes and properties; in his view, they lack the clear identity-criteria that are required for an ontological assumption to be legitimate. Another account takes second-order variables as ranging over sets, in particular over all sub-sets of the domain of whatever interpretation is in question. (This is what I have been calling the standard account, and is more popular in recent work than the "properties" view.) In that case, Quine argues, we are committed to the existence of sets; in effect, we are simply doing set-theory with misleading notation. (See especially Set Theory and Its Logic, pp. 256–58.) It is misleading, above all, precisely because it tends to obscure the ontological assumptions involved: those assumptions are not conveyed by explicit claims, but merely by the form of the notation. The use of second-order logic with this interpretation also has results which Quine would object to. Given that use, even so innocent a sentence as "Socrates is mortal" implies the existence of sets: in second-order logic it implies "$(\exists F)$ F(Socrates)" and so implies that there are sets.

Some philosophers have attempted to argue, against Quine, that no particular ontological assumptions are implicit in second-order logic. One such attempt is by George Boolos, who directs our attention to sentences with plural subjects.[22] Some of these are straightforwardly schematizable in first-order logic: "Some critics admire Brahms" is an example; here the only ontological commitment is to there being critics (and Brahms). Other sentences, apparently very similar to the first kind, are not susceptible of first-order treatment: we have already seen an example, "Some critics admire only one another". Asserting this sentence commits us to there being critics but not, Boolos insists, to there being anything else. A plural subject of this sort carries no ontological commitment except to the ordinary entities within the range of the first-order quantifiers. Boolos takes it that the sentence is best symbolized in second-order logic, as in the third paragraph of this section. He then argues that the ontological innocence of the ordinary language sentence—which he takes to be evident—shows the ontological innocence of its second-order paraphrase. He argues, further, that all sentences in second-order logic can be understood in the same sort of way; they are symbolizations of ontologically innocent sentences with plural subjects, and hence are themselves ontologically innocent.

Quine would disagree. Perhaps it is on the face of it very plausible that the sentence about the critics, as ordinarily understood, has no ontological implications except to there being critics. Once we allow second-order quantification, however, we are committed to accepting second-order sentences of unlimited complexity. Appealing to sentences in ordinary English as giving us the ontological implications of complex second-order sentences has its drawbacks. Some of the English sentences would be quite unnatural and hard to understand; certainly their ontological implications would be very far from evident. The point here is one which we have already seen Quine make: when it comes to gauging the ontological commitment of our sentences we cannot, in general, rely upon what seems evident. Standard semantics for second-order logic gives us a way of understanding any second-order sentence, and its ontological implications, without any such reliance. But it does so at the cost of assuming the existence of sets. (In which case, Quine holds, we are better off simply doing set-theory explicitly.) Even in the case of the simple sentence about the critics, Quine would have no sympathy for the idea that its ontological commitments are to be judged by what strikes us as "evident". He thinks of ontology as an artificial matter, in which little weight is to be placed on pre-theoretic opinions. Any criterion, on his view, must be to some extent artificial. We should choose one which is clear, definite, and generally applicable. Quine's criterion satisfies these demands; he would not think that Boolos's arguments against that criterion suggest any alternative which comes close. The two philosophers also have rather different concerns. Boolos is interested in the question "whether the first-order predicate calculus with identity adequately represents quantification, generalization, and cross-reference in natural language" ("To Be Is to Be a Value of a Variable ... ", p. 62). Quine's concern is with the best framework for theory, not with whether the framework distorts ordinary language. On his view it is a great advantage of first-order logic that it carries with it a clear and straightforward criterion of ontological commitment. He has no qualms at all about representing the sentence about the critics as making an explicit claim that there is a *set* of critics each member of which admires only other members (see *Methods of Logic*, p. 293, where the point is explicit).[23]

IV The bearers of truth-values: eternal sentences

According to Quine's two-valued logic, every sentence of the regimented theory is true or false. This fact raises questions about the nature of truth and falsehood, which we shall consider in the next section. It also raises questions about what exactly it is to which truth and falsehood are ascribed; that question is our subject here.

Most of our utterances say what they say, and have the truth-values that they have, only because of the contexts in which they are uttered. By the "context" of an utterance I mean such factors as: who says it, to whom it is said, when it is said, where it is said, why it is said, what objects or events are salient on the occasion, and to whom, and so on. (For the written language it is the act of inscription, or the anticipated act of reading, that is presumably relevant.) In some cases, context-dependence is obvious. A sentence such as "I have a toothache" or "It's raining" will, quite evidently, be true in some contexts and false in others. (The same is true of any occasion sentence; such sentences, as we have seen, play a central role in Quine's account of the acquisition of language and knowledge.) So also, perhaps less obviously, a sentence such as "Russia is the largest country in the world". Countries come and go, changing their territorial extent, so that a claim about them which is not explicitly limited as to time may depend upon the context of utterance—in particular, upon when the utterance is made. Such instability in truth-value threatens the application of logic. If there are shifts of context, otherwise correct applications of logic may lead from true premises to a false conclusion. An example which Quine gives is: George married Mary; Mary is a widow; therefore George married a widow. (See *WO*, p. 170.) But Mary may not have been a widow at the time of her marriage to George; it may be precisely George's death which widowed her. In that case the conclusion is false, although the premises are true and the logic impeccable.

Context-dependence shows that for theoretical purposes we cannot take ordinary sentences as the bearers of truth-values. Most ordinary sentences have truth-values which vary with context; we need to eliminate the context-dependence. This is, no doubt, one of the impulses behind the idea of a *proposition*, thought of as an abstract entity more or less akin to the meaning of a declarative sentence. Even if the sentence varies in truth-value, *what the sentence says*—the proposition it expresses, on this view—may be timelessly true or timelessly false. The positing of propositions is, of course, not Quine's response to context-dependence. Instead, he thinks of truth as applying, in the first instance, to *utterances*, particular dateable events. "What are best seen as primarily true or false are not sentences but events of utterance". (*PL*, p. 13.) An inscription can be treated analogously: what is true or false is not the sentence but the event of writing it. On this view, it is particular events of uttering or inscribing that are, in the first instance, the bearers of truth and falsehood. The sentence "I have a headache" has no fixed truth-value, but any given act of uttering or inscribing it does. In *Word and Object* Quine speaks of truth as "a passing trait of a sentence for a man" (p. 191). This may seem to be a rather different view, but in fact it is not. A sentence counts as true or false for a person at a time: it is true in those cases where the utterance of that sentence at that time by that person would have been a truth. Again, truth is primarily, or in the first instance, a property of utterances, actual or counterfactual.

For the purposes of regimented theory, however, we need sentences as truth vehicles. Our logic is a logic of sentences, not of acts of utterance. So while truth may be *primarily* ascribed to events, or to sentences relative to a person and a time, we need to introduce a sense in which sentences themselves are true or false. Or, rather, we need to introduce sentences to which truth and falsehood may be ascribed without variability in truth-value—what Quine calls eternal sentences. (See Chapter 4, section VI, above.) Their truth-values are fixed once for all. (This does not, of course, imply that we cannot be uncertain or mistaken about the truth-value of an eternal sentence. It means only that its truth-value does not change, even if our opinion about it does.) The sentences of arithmetic are eternal sentences just as they stand; so too, perhaps, the fundamental laws of the natural sciences. For the most part, however, the sentences that we utter are not eternal sentences. So we need to show how we could replace the context-dependent sentences which are actually uttered with eternal sentences, true or false once for all. (One kind of context-dependence will remain. What is true or false is the eternal sentence *of a particular language*; since languages change, a sequence of words or marks is a true or false sentence *of early twenty-first-century English*, say. For the most part we can ignore this relativity and speak of eternal sentences as having truth-values, "tacitly understanding these as relativized to our present-day English language habits"; *PL*, p. 14.)

To begin with, we can eliminate what Quine, following Goodman, sometimes calls "indicator words": "here", "there", "now", "then", "tomorrow", "me", "you", "this", and so on. (Russell, in *Inquiry into Meaning and Truth*, calls such words "egocentric particulars"; they are now often referred to as "indexicals", a usage that I shall sometimes follow below.) In the place of indexicals we think of a fully regimented theory as containing specifications of objects or places or periods of time in terms of their locations in space and time. Such specifications make use of established systems for referring to space and time: longtitude and latitude for location in (terrestrial) space; years AD (or some other well established system), and hours and minutes GMT (or some other system with fixed relations to GMT). One point which has worried some philosophers here is whether the eternal sentence really says the same as the more mundane sentence that it replaces. If I am ignorant of the date, is my saying on 5 January 2006 "I will do it tomorrow" the same as my saying "I will do it on 6 January 2006"? Perhaps it is not, but this is the kind of issue that Quine is happy to ignore; quite generally he imposes no requirement that regimentation preserve synonymy.

Other instances of context-dependence are perhaps less obvious than indexicals, but will be dealt with along similar lines. The use of tensed verbs will be eliminated. Tense is a kind of implicit indexical; the use of the past tense, say, asserts that an event happened earlier than the time of utterance. Verbs will be timeless, with time indicated explicitly: rather than saying that the Greeks defeated the Persians, we can say the Greeks defeat the Persians on ... (or before ...), where what is added is a date. Similarly, the quantifiers of canonical notation are treated timelessly, even when they range over objects which exist in space and time. To say that there *is* an object which is identical to Socrates and is mortal does not commit us to Socrates's still being alive; what it implies is that there is, or was, or will be, such a person as Socrates and that he—whenever he may exist—is (or was or

271

will be) mortal. Specification of the time of that existence can be added explicitly if desired. Thus Quine says: "date is to be treated on a par with location, color, specific gravity, etc.—hence not as a qualification on '∃', but merely as one of sundry attributes of the thing-events which are the values of 'x'." (MSLT, WP, p. 147.) Again, most utterances of descriptions rely, as Quine puts it, on "supplementary information gleaned from the context and circumstances of utterance" (WO, p. 183). For the purposes of canonical notation, "we have to imagine that supplementary information made explicit as part of the ... sentence" (ibid.). And this gives us the general method: we are to think of a context-dependent sentence as replaced by one in which the relevant aspects of the context are stated explicitly. Worries about whether the two sentences really say the same thing are, again, beside the point—beside Quine's point, at least.

On the face of it, at least, the method of replacing a context-dependent sentence with a context-independent one seems unproblematic. But various philosophers have criticized it. One criticism is that a language wholly free of indexicals can only say things which are wholly general in nature. We specify an object by means of predicates which hold of it, but surely there might be other objects of which all the same predicates hold. How is an indexical-free language to guarantee uniqueness of reference? Our systems for referring to location in space and time might seem to answer this point, but they are themselves vulnerable to the same sort of question. Greenwich is at zero longitude: it is one of the places at which our system of longitude and latitude is, so to speak, nailed down to the surface of the Earth. But if our concern is with anchoring that system, we cannot specify Greenwich by saying that it is the place at zero longitude: to do so is blatantly circular. Of course we can specify other features of Greenwich, but not with a *guarantee* that our specification is unique. The situation is exacerbated by the idea that, even if that town *is* unique as far as this world goes, there might be another planet on which there is an exactly similar town, in exactly similar relations to coastlines and other towns and so on. As a scientific hypothesis this idea is exceedingly implausible. But if nothing rules it out absolutely, then nothing absolutely guarantees that our methods of locating things in space manage to single out places on this earth. (Similar remarks apply to time.) In the end, the objection goes, only reference to *here* and *now* can nail our theory down to the reality which we are trying to think about.[24]

The objection assumes that regimented language is independent and self-sufficient, that it could, at least in principle, function as our only language. But this is not Quine's claim:

It may indeed by protested that something tantamount to the use of indicator words is finally unavoidable, at least in the teaching of the terms which are to be made to supplant the indicator words. But this is no objection; all that matters is the *subsequent* avoidability of indicator words. All that matters is that it be possible in principle to couch science in a notation such that none of *its* sentences fluctuates between truth and falsity from utterance to utterance. Terms which are primitive or irreducible, from the point of view of that scientific notation, may still be intelligible to us only through explanations in an ordinary language rife with indicator words, tense, and ambiguity. Scientific language is in any event a splinter of ordinary language, not a substitute.

(SLS, *WP*, p. 236; emphases in the original)

In similar vein, he says in *Word and Object* that he is not supposing that indicator words are "unneeded in teaching the very terms ... on which the canonical formulations may proceed". His claim "is only that such a canonical idiom can be abstracted and then adhered to in the statement of one's scientific theory" (*WO*, p. 228). Quine does not dispute the idea that our language could not function as it does without indexicals. Regimented theory, indexical-free, may be parasitic upon ordinary language, which contains indexicals. But that is a result which Quine accepts without a qualm, for he does not envisage canonical notation as replacing ordinary language, only as enabling us to present our theory in clarified and simplified form.

Quine's eternal sentences play something of the role in his thought that propositions play in the thought of some other philosophers. If a sentence is not an eternal one, any relevant features of its context of utterance will be taken account of in the proposition that it is said to express; hence the proposition will, in effect, be the meaning of the corresponding eternal sentence. Quine, of course, rejects the appeal to propositions. He thinks their identity-conditions are unclear, as we have emphasized; he also thinks that they are simply an unnecessary shuffle. To specify a proposition we must use an eternal sentence, and speak of the proposition that it expresses. (Or we may say something like: the proposition expressed by "I have a headache" as uttered by Peter Hylton at noon on 6 January 2006; here we are a step away from the required eternal sentence, but it is a small step.) Since we must in any case accept eternal sentences, why should we burden ourselves with the further and quite unnecessary assumption of propositions? Doing so takes us further away from the actual facts of linguistic behaviour, from actual acts of utterance or inscription. It thereby obscures the question of the relation of the actual utterance to the proposition: the sentence, we are told, *expresses* the proposition, but this word is merely a label, affording us no help in understanding the situation. (See *WO*, p. 208.) Propositions are at best unnecessary; at worst they mislead us by seeming to explain without actually doing so. Quine's method, by contrast, allows for progress with the question of the relation of the eternal sentence to the actual utterance. At least as a first approximation, the relevant eternal sentence will be the one that the speaker accepts as performing the function he or she intended by the original utterance.

So Quine takes eternal sentences, not propositions, as the bearers of truth and falsehood. Our theory, as fully regimented, is made up of eternal sentences. This does not imply that Quine thinks that we will, or should, or could, forswear ordinary sentences in favour of their eternal cousins. Where ambiguity threatens we will paraphrase, taking steps in the direction of eternal sentences, but it will seldom be necessary to go all the way. The point is not that we should use eternal sentences in daily life, or even in our scientific endeavours. It is, rather, that eternal sentences are available, if needed, as unambiguous counterparts of our more wayward utterances. We can thus think of the context-dependence of those utterances as a feature that can in principle always be eliminated, and feel free to ignore it where it makes no difference. As Quine says, memorably if now perhaps anachronistically: "The relation of eternal sentences to our logic is like that of silver dollars to our economy: mostly we do not see them, but we reckon in terms of them". (*WO*, p. 227.) Less picturesquely, he says:

> In practice certainly one does not explicitly rid one's scientific work of indicator words, tense, and ambiguity, nor does one limit one's use of logic to sentences thus purified. In practice one merely *supposes* all such points of variation fixed for the space of one's logical argument; one does not need to resort to explicit paraphrase, except at points where local shifts of context *within* the logical argument itself threaten equivocations.
>
> (SLS, *WP*, p. 237)

V Truth

Quine's view of truth is close to what is sometimes called the "redundancy theory of truth", or the "disquotational" theory: to assert that a sentence is true adds nothing to a simple assertion of the sentence itself.[25] In ordinary discourse, no doubt, saying that a sentence is true emphasizes that one is fully serious in asserting it, that one means it literally, that one has ample evidence, and so on. Quine would not dispute that, but he is not concerned with those sorts of effects of the word; for one thing, all of the claims which he considers are fully serious and literal. So it might seem that the notion of truth is wholly redundant:

> In speaking of the truth of a given sentence there is only indirection; we do better simply to say the sentence and so speak not about language but about the world. So long as we are speaking only of the truth of singly given sentences, the perfect theory of truth is what Wilfred Sellars has called the disappearance theory of truth.
>
> (*PL*, p. 11)

What preserves an ineliminable role for truth is the qualification to each of these two sentences. When a particular sentence is in question, the ascription of truth *is* redundant (apart from indicating seriousness, and so on). Similarly for any (finite) number of given sentences. Matters are perhaps different if we consider a sentence such as "Everything Lincoln said was true". Even here, though, it might be argued that in a responsible theory no such assertion would be made apart from a listing of Lincoln's utterances, so we are back to the previous case: the sentences can then simply be asserted one-by-one. But there are other cases in which the truth predicate cannot be eliminated in this way; we shall draw on an example of Quine's to show how this happens.

We can generalize on "Socrates is mortal" in the obvious way, by saying about all relevant objects (people) what the given sentence says about Socrates: "All people are mortal". But no such straightforward method is available if we want to generalize on "If time flies then time flies". To do so we talk of the sentences themselves:

> We say "All sentences of the form 'If p then p' are true". We could not generalize as in "All men are mortal", because "time flies" is not, like "Socrates", a name of one of a range of objects (men) over which to generalize. We cleared this obstacle by *semantic ascent*: by ascending to a level where there were indeed objects over which to generalize, namely linguistic objects, sentences.
>
> (*PT*, p. 81; emphasis in the original)

In the case of Lincoln's utterances we could, ideally and in principle, simply assert each of his sentences on our own account, and drop the talk of truth. But no such recourse is available here since the number of sentences involved is infinite. So we talk about the sentences themselves. How do we get back, so to speak, from talking about the sentences to talking about their subject-matter? The answer is in the *disquotational* function of the truth predicate. Ascribing truth to the sentence "Socrates is mortal" has the same effect as asserting that Socrates is mortal. Quite generally, ascribing truth to a sentence results in an assertion which is about what the sentence is about. And this is precisely what is wanted. Ascribing truth to an infinite lot of sentences achieves the same effect which could have been achieved by asserting them one by one, had they been finite in number.

The disquotational function of the truth predicate is, in Quine's view, the reason for its usefulness. The passage quoted in the first paragraph of this section continues like this:

> Where the truth predicate has its utility is in just those places where, though still concerned with reality, we are impelled by certain technical complications to mention sentences. Here the truth predicate serves, as it were, to point through the sentences to the reality.
>
> (*PL*, p. 11)

Linking truth to disquotation as we have done is not a definition in the strictest sense: it does not enable us to eliminate the predicate from every context in which it has a use. Nevertheless, Quine clearly thinks that the link gives us as much of an explanation of truth as we can ask for:

> in a looser sense the disquotational account does define truth. It tells us what it is for any sentence to be true, and it tells us this in terms just as clear to us as the sentence in question itself. We understand what it is for the sentence "Snow is white" to be true as clearly as we understand what it is for snow to be white. Evidently one who puzzles over the adjective "true" should puzzle rather over the sentences to which he ascribes it. "True" is transparent.
>
> (*PT*, p. 82)

The disquotational view of truth, along with naturalism, give the basis for Quine's claim that truth is *immanent*. "To call a sentence true is just to include it in our own theory of the world"; and there is no "higher tribunal than our best scientific theory of the time" (L&S, p. 353; Quine also cites, in the same connection, the fact that truth is relative to a language: "[a] string of marks is true only as a sentence of some specific language", ibid.). In the same passage, however, Quine also acknowledges a sense in which truth is transcendent: "[t]o *call* a sentence true is just to include it in our science, but this is not to say that science fixes truth. It can prove wrong". He blithely sums up the situation by saying: "[v]ery well then: immanent in those other respects, transcendent in this" (ibid.).

Quine's position here may seem confusing, even contradictory, even apart from the contrast between the immanent and the transcendent ("the treacherous old dichotomy", he calls it; L&S, p. 353). If calling a sentence true is simply saying that it is included in our science, how can we conclude that a sentence which we once called true is in fact false? The worry here is, I think, superficial. A passage in *From Stimulus to Science* is helpful:

> We should and do currently accept the firmest scientific conclusions as true, but when one of these is dislodged by further research we do not say that it had been true but became false. We say that to our surprise it was not true after all. Science is seen as pursuing and discovering truth rather than as decreeing it. Such is the idiom of realism, and it is integral to the semantics of the predicate "true".
>
> (*FSS*, p. 67)

Our science changes, but truth does not. What lies behind this, however, is not a metaphysical mystery, not a conception of Truth as a grand and possibly quite unattainable ideal standing wholly above the enterprise of science. Our science is, of course, fallible, and further scientific work often leads us to correct our earlier views. When that happens, we do not say that those views used to be true but now are not; we say we used to think that they were true, but now know better. This is simply a fact of usage. It does not undermine the view that truth is immanent, and that its essential features are given by the disquotational account. To say that science changes but truth does not is just to say that whereas we didn't always assert, say, "mass is relative to inertial frames", it was always true—which is only to say: mass always was relative to inertial frames, whether or not we knew it.

In many contexts a distinction can be drawn between the attempt to find the truth and the attempt merely to find something that will work—will serve to convince others, or will enable us to get by for a time. In Quinean terms we can, I think, understand this as the distinction between, on the one hand, looking for an account which will solve a localized problem; and, on the other hand, looking for an account of a given subject which is best all things considered, and which, in particular, best fits with the rest of our knowledge into a coherent and successful whole. Where such a distinction can sensibly be drawn, Quine is on the side of truth. But that does not mean that he has any sympathy at all for a notion of truth which is transcendental in a stronger sense than that indicated in the last paragraph. We construct the best theory that we can, and count it as true until we find a better one—better by the standards internal to our knowledge, not by its measuring up to The Truth.

The view that there is little more to truth than disquotation may seem disappointing. The notion of truth has been the locus of major philosophical disputes, over the coherence theory of truth, for example. As Quine sees the matter, the disputes are mislocated. There are interesting questions in this general area, but they concern the question of the warrant of beliefs, not the notion of truth. To call a sentence true is equivalent to affirming it; this much is trivial. But there is certainly room for non-trivial discussion as to whether we are warranted in affirming a given sentence, and what provides that warrant. If we ask what in general warrants us in affirming sentences, then we are asking a question whose answer calls for nothing less than "a general analysis of . . . scientific method" (*PT*, p. 93).

Disquotation, we said, does not provide a definition of truth in the strictest sense. In that sense, indeed, no definition of truth is possible, on pain of paradox. The point here is given in the ancient story of the Cretan who says that all Cretans are liars, a story which nowadays is often boiled down to the sentence: "This sentence is not true". Quine's own tidy version is: " 'yields a falsehood when appended to its own quotation' yields a falsehood when appended to its own quotation." (*PT*, p. 82.) Is this sentence true or false? Clearly it should be true if and only if the phrase "yields a falsehood when appended to its own quotation" does indeed yield a falsehood when appended to its own quotation. So we append it to its quotation, and get back to the original sentence. So that sentence is true if and only if it is false: hence the paradox. The moral that Quine draws is that a language which contains "the innocent notations for treating of quoting and appending, and also the notations of elementary logic" (*PL*, p. 83) cannot—on pain of contradiction—contain a truth predicate which applies, truly or falsely, to *all* the sentences of the language, including those which themselves contain the truth predicate. If a language contains the resources to define its own truth-predicate it would also contain the resources to prove a contradiction. So if we introduce a truth-predicate for a regimented language there must be restrictions. Perhaps we apply the truth predicate only to sentences which do not themselves contain that predicate. Or, more artfully, we can introduce a hierarchy: we use the predicate "$true_0$" so as to apply, truly or falsely, to sentences which contain no use of the word "true"; "$true_1$" to apply, truly or falsely, to sentences which may contain "$true_0$" but not "$true_1$"; and so on up as far as we have reason to go.

On pain of contradiction, then, no definition of truth for a given language is possible within that language. Tarski, however, has shown how we can define truth for a suitably regimented language, using the resources of a more powerful meta-language. (The measure of "power" here is essentially how strong a set-theory is taken as part of the language.) Tarski's approach fits with the disquotational account. He puts forward, as a criterion of adequacy for any definition of truth, that it enable us to prove " 'Snow is white' is true if and only if snow is white", " 'Grass is white' is true if and only if grass is white", and so on. Avoiding the "and so on": if p is a given sentence and s is a name of that sentence (formed, for example, by putting it between quotation marks), then we should be able to prove each sentence of the form:

(1) s is true if and only if p.

A definition which can prove this, Tarski argues, is a satisfactory definition of truth.[26] He shows that his definition does indeed satisfy this criterion. Quine alludes to Tarski's work with some frequency, but it is unclear how much lasting significance it has for his thought. The adequacy condition encourages the disquotational idea and, with it, the idea that truth is immanent. (See *WO*, p. 24, note 3.) If all that we can ask of a definition of truth is that it enables us to prove each instance of (1), then it is plausible to think that truth simply amounts to disquotation—that calling a given sentence true simply amounts to asserting it. The claim that fulfilment of Tarski's adequacy condition is all that we need to be able to prove from a definition of truth is not itself susceptible of proof. But it is provable that any two predicates both of which satisfy the adequacy condition are co-extensive (apply to exactly the same sentences); this perhaps argues that fulfilment of the adequacy condition is all we need—that it deserves its name. Tarski's definition itself may well have led Quine to think of truth as an acceptable concept. That view, however, seems to me defensible without resort to the definition.

11

EXTENSIONALITY, REFERENCE, AND SINGULAR TERMS

In the previous chapter we examined Quine's version of the syntax of first-order logic. (When I speak of logic in what follows, it is this version that I mean.) Any language which uses this syntax is a long way from the language in which most of our knowledge is in fact formulated. One obvious gap concerns singular terms and reference. This is an issue that much occupies Quine; it is the focus of our concern in this chapter.

Quine holds that "[o]rdinary language is only loosely referential" ("Facts of the Matter", p. 168). Still, the referential aspect of regimented theory is, presumably, a precise and clarified version of this loosely referential structure. In ordinary language it is perhaps natural to think of reference as conveyed primarily by names, or by singular terms more generally.[1] A theory formulated in the syntax of logic, by contrast, does not even contain singular terms. In such a theory, reference is conveyed by quantified variables. How, then, is the referential structure of our ordinary knowledge, loose though it may be, to be fitted into the syntax of logic? Answering this question, Quine says, will "bring the referential business of our language more clearly into view" (*WO*, p. 125). Understanding reference in our own language is the chief concern of chapters 3–5 of *Word and Object*; in Quine's view we accomplish this task precisely by seeing how that language could be regimented into canonical notation, where reference is clear.

Our task, therefore, is to understand the referential structure of our language or, equivalently, to understand how our language is to be fitted into the clear and precise referential scheme given by regimented notation. Either way, the task raises two general issues. One concerns singular terms. The lack of such terms in regimented theory might be thought to constitute an immense difference between that theory and its unregimented version; it might be thought to be an important deficiency in the regimented language. But in fact the logic set out in the previous chapter can achieve the effect of singular terms. Any sentence containing a definite

280

description (a phrase of the form "the F") can be replaced with a sentence containing no singular term. This is Russell's well known theory of descriptions; the theory is controversial but Quine endorses it and puts it to his own uses. He extends it to include all singular terms, including names and functional expressions. It gives him a method of accommodating singular terms within regimented language. It remains true, of course, that singular terms are not primitive notation for Quine; he uses the theory of descriptions to argue that any unregimented sentence containing a singular term has an analogue in regimented language which will perform nearly enough the same function. Quine argues, indeed, that the replacement has advantages, even beyond its enabling us to make do with his austere version of logic. This issue is partly technical, and will occupy us in the first section.

The second general issue is more complex. The paraphrase of a sentence such as "Socrates is mortal" is, as we shall see in the first section, an existentially quantified sentence. The referential role which one might attribute to the name in the ordinary sentence will be played by the existentially quantified variable. Quine argues, however, that not all occurrences of singular terms in ordinary language should be counted as referential and treated in this way. The point is crucial for the regimentation of ordinary sentences. Occurrences of names which are not referential should not be replaced by variables which bear the burden of reference; those which are referential should be. But what is the distinction here? An answer to this question requires discussion of the idea of *extensionality*, which is the subject of the second section. (One issue which arises here requires treatment which is technically more demanding than our other discussions, and will be discussed in an appendix to the chapter.) In the third section we shall consider the referential structure of ordinary language and, in particular, failures of extensionality which occur there. These ideas raise complexities and technicalities which are not essential for Quine's overall position. I will not go into those complexities in this chapter; some of them will emerge when we see the application of these ideas, in Chapter 13, especially section VI.

I Singular terms

Theory regimented along Quinean lines contains no singular terms. There are no names, no functional expressions, and no definite descriptions. One advantage of this is simplification of the syntax. Another is that we do not have to face the question of singular terms that lack reference, an issue we shall come back to later in this section. On the face of it, however, these gains seem to be bought at a high price, namely a loss of expressive power as compared with ordinary language. But in fact, Quine argues, there is no real loss. Use of the restricted syntax enables us to achieve the effect of a language which does contain singular terms. The general idea here has some similarity to ontological reduction, which we discussed in section III of Chapter 9, above. Artful use of a restricted language allows us to achieve effects which would be more directly achieved by a richer language; we can use the expressions of the latter—singular terms, in this case—but explain our use of them in terms of the restricted language which lacks them. The difference is that here the strategy does not reduce our ontology. What it does is to show that the syntax of first-order logic enables us to achieve the expressive power of a richer syntax, in which there are singular terms. What Quine needs to show is that definitions enable us to eliminate singular terms from the richer language without loss or, equivalently, to introduce them into the sparer language.

Our ordinary language contains definite descriptions: phrases of the form "the *F*". An example is "the author of *Word and Object*". If the predicate "wrote *Word and Object*" (or: "authored *Word and Object*", to preserve the form) is true of exactly one object then we can use the definite description to say something about that object. (For example: "The author of *Word and Object* was a great philosopher".) But what if there is no object of which the predicate is true, or if it is true of more than one object? In such cases, it has been argued, the question of the truth of a statement in which the phrase occurs as a singular term *does not arise*, and the sentence is neither true nor false. (See, for example, Strawson, "On Referring".) One of Quine's concerns is precisely to avoid such truth-value gaps. Accordingly, he adopts Russell's technique of defining sentences containing definite description.[2] This definition has the further advantage of enabling us to exploit the structure of the defining phrase in logical inference, using only the ordinary rules of logic. According to Russell's definition, sentences of the form "the *F* is *G*"—i.e. that *G* holds of the unique thing of which *F* is true—are taken to say that there is one and only one thing which is *F*, and that it (that thing) is *G*. To phrase this in our logical notation we need the identity relation, to enable us to say that there is only one thing of which *F* is true. Then we understand "The *F* is *G*" as claiming that there is a thing satisfying three conditions: first, it is *F*; second, it is the only thing that is *F*; third it—the one and only thing that is *F*—is *G*. Saying of something that it is the only thing that is *F* is in turn understood as saying that anything which is *F* is identical to that thing. So the paraphrase of the whole, in the syntax of logic, is:[3]

$(\exists x)[Fx \;\&\; (\forall y)(Fy \rightarrow x = y) \;\&\; Gx]$

Equivalently, but a little more tidily:

$(\exists x)[(\forall y)(Fy \leftrightarrow x = y) \;\&\; Gx]$

Here there is no singular term; reference is conveyed by the bound variables.

Ordinary language contains functional expressions such as "the teacher of Plato" or "5 + 7"or "17^2". These are like definite descriptions in that they are complex expressions which play the role of singular terms. Such expressions are vital to mathematics, pure and applied; yet the syntax set out in the previous chapter has no explicit place for functional expressions. In response, Quine, again following Russell, shows how such expressions can be defined. (See Whitehead and Russell, *Principia Mathematica*, vol. 1, *30.) They are assimilated to definite descriptions, so that the analysis given above then applies. We define them from the relevant predicates. The plus function, for example, takes two numbers as argument and yields their sum as value. Sentences containing "plus" (or "+") can be defined in terms of the relevant three-place predicate. In ordinary English the predicate and the function are not sharply distinguished; to mark the distinction let us introduce the predicate "ADD (x, y, z)" to mean that x is the sum of y and z. (So then "ADD(5, 2, 3)" counts as a true sentence, "ADD(3, 4, 5)" as a false one, and so on.) We can now use the predicate to mimic the function. Suppose "F" represents some predicate that we want to attribute to (5 + 7). Instead of using the function sign "+" and saying "$F(5 + 7)$" we use the predicate "ADD" and say: "there is one and only one number, x, such that ADD(x, 5, 7) and $F(x)$". In the notation of logic:

$(\exists x)\{(\forall y)[\text{ADD}(x, 5, 7) \leftrightarrow x = y] \;\&\; Fx\}$

To say something about 5 + 7 is to say that same thing about *the* number x such that ADD(x, 5, 7); via the theory of descriptions, this is understood as an assertion that there is one and only one number that is the sum of five and seven, and .... Again, the singular term is eliminated. (A similar, somewhat more complicated, manoeuvre enables us to define contexts in which a functional expression is embedded in a more complex singular term, as in "(5 + 7) × 13".)

A notation which lacks functional expressions and definite descriptions can thus achieve the expressive power of one which has them. Using the more restricted notation in practice would greatly complicate the work of mathematicians and others. But Quine is not advocating that we abandon the richer notation. To give it up, to give up "the nesting of singular terms within singular terms without limit" and "the facile substitution of complexes for variables and equals" would, as he says, "diminish the power of mathematics catastrophically" (*WO*, p. 188). But no such sacrifice is in question. Rather, Quine claims, we remain free to use the richer notation in practice, while retreating to the more austere version when awkward theoretical questions arise:

> we can vacillate between two [notations], opportunistically enjoying their incompatible advantages. What modern logicians call *definitions* are largely instructions for doing just that. Thus we can cleave theoretically to a canonical notation in which there are no singular terms but variables, but at the same time we can define, relative to that notation, a shorthand use of the other singular terms after all.
>
> (*WO*, p. 188)

The general idea here is essential to Quine's conception of the whole enterprise of paraphrase, and of canonical notation. To repeat a phrase already quoted, the point is to show "what science could get along with, could be reconstructed by means of" (MSLT, *WP*, p. 151; quoted in context, Chapter 9, second section, above).

To this point we have been discussing complex singular terms. What of semantically simple singular terms or proper names? The relevant difference, from the present point of view, is that a complex singular term contains a predicate which can easily be extracted and taken as the basis for a definition in Russellian fashion. Names, by contrast, differ precisely because they are semantically simple: on the face if it, they contain no predicate which can be used in that way. Quine solves this problem by brute force, as it were. Given a name, say "Pegasus" or "Homer", we can, he argues, simply introduce a predicate which will play the required role. Thus "is-identical-to-Pegasus" or "is-identical-to-Homer"; for the purposes of canonical notation the predicate is looked upon as without significant structure (as indicated by the use of hyphens instead of spaces). In particular, it is not thought of as containing a singular term, for the point of the manoeuvre is precisely to eliminate singular terms. Or we can introduce a single word for the predicate, along the lines of "pegasizes", to avoid the appearance of the name's occurring. In either case, the name is in effect absorbed into a predicate, or a general term, rather than remaining as a singular term. This manoeuvre may seem quite artificial and unnatural, but from Quine's point of view that is no obstacle (see especially "On What There Is", *FLPV*, pp.

7f.). As we have emphasized, his business is not that of capturing ordinary language but rather that of finding a workable substitute which is clearer and more perspicuous.

The technique of defining sentences containing definite descriptions and proper names does not effect an ontological reduction of the sort discussed in Chapter 9.[4] If "Homer wrote the *Iliad*" is true, then there must be, in the timeless sense, such a person as Homer. As paraphrased, the sentence becomes:

$(\exists x)[(\forall y)(y$ is-identical-to-Homer $\leftrightarrow x = y)$ & x wrote the *Iliad*]

This sentence can only be true if there is, in the range of the variables, an object (and exactly one object) of which the predicate "is-identical-to-Homer" is true. Sentences which ought to carry a commitment to the existence of Homer thus evidently do. Equally important, sentences which, one might think, ought not to carry such a commitment evidently do not, when subjected to paraphrase. Consider "Homer did not exist" or, more idiomatically, "There was no such person as Homer". Quine's Russellian paraphrase renders the sentence like this:

$\sim(\exists x)(\forall y)(y$ is-identical-to-Homer $\leftrightarrow x = y)$

(Here I use "$\sim$" for truth-functional negation, as in the first section of the previous chapter.) The paraphrase is an unproblematic sentence which asserts that there is no object, x, such that x is-identical-to-Homer (more precisely, that there is no *unique* such object).

A virtue of this analysis emerges if we consider a sentence containing a proper name which names nothing, for example "Pegasus flies". The presence of the empty name here may lead us to say that the sentence is neither true nor false, thereby upending our tidy two-valued logic by allowing truth-value gaps; worse, we may get into philosophical tangles about how there can be names which name nothing; worse yet we may start thinking that Pegasus must *be* or subsist, in some shadowy sense short of existence, in order for the sentence denying his existence to make sense. When we subject the sentence to paraphrase, however, it is clear that none of these difficulties arise. As paraphrased, the sentence says:

$(\exists x)[(\forall y)(y$ is-identical-to-Pegasus $\leftrightarrow x = y)$ & x flies]

Given that there was no such thing as Pegasus—nothing of which " ... is-identical-to-Pegasus" is true—this sentence is straightforwardly false.[5]

285

Truth-value gaps, shadowy entities, and other threatening philosophical problems are all avoided.

The elimination of singular terms has been subjected to various criticisms—more, indeed, than we can go into here. One, already mentioned, is that treating names along Russellian lines distorts ordinary language. Quine is not concerned to render ordinary language undistorted. But he also disputes the assumption that ordinary language clearly treats names as singular terms rather than general terms. Ordinary language, as he sees the matter, is simply not clear-cut on this sort of issue. "In thus construing names as general terms, what we deviate from is only in part usage, and largely attitude towards usage" (*WO*, p. 181). And again:

> it would be pointless to defend either the singular term or the general term as *the* regular counterpart of the name "Socrates" of ordinary language. In paraphrasing some sentences for some purposes the singular term will come in handy; on other occasions the general term works better.
>
> (*WO*, p. 189; emphasis in the original)

The point here is of a piece with Quine's view that ontology is an intrinsically artificial enterprise, noted in Chapter 9, section I but it is more general. Ordinary language is simply too wayward and varying to be an exact fit for any precise scheme. To be a logician of any kind is to systematize our inferences and the language in which they are conducted, imposing upon ordinary discourse a regularity which is not inherent in it; we may choose whatever scheme of regularization best suits our purposes.

Quine does not deny that his methods distort ordinary language. An important example here is the distinction which some have found, within ordinary usage, between the use of an expression to pick out a certain object, and its use to say something about an object otherwise picked out. According to Strawson, the first performs "the referring (or identifying) task", the second performs "the attributive (or descriptive or classificatory or ascriptive) task" ("On Referring", p. 17). The first sort of use is liable to give rise to truth-value gaps. If someone uttered (with serious, non-fictional intent) a sentence containing an expression which does not, in fact, succeed in picking out a unique object then, Strawson holds, he did not say something false. Rather, it is said, "the question of whether his statement was true or false simply *did not arise*" (Strawson, "On Referring", p. 12, emphasis in the original). Quine's way with singular terms eliminates truth-value gaps—that, as we saw, was part of its motivation—and in doing so rides rough-shod over the distinction between the referential and the attributive uses. Quine does not, however, deny that such a distinction can be made for ordinary language. What he says is: "it would be a mistake to infer that modern logic errs in not keeping the idiosyncracy of ordinary language which that distinction brings out" (MSLT, *WP*, pp. 144f.). The point is a general one. It applies also, for example, to the replacement of the ordinary "if ... then ... " with the material conditional. Again, it is arguable that the ordinary use gives rise to truth-value gaps, and, again, Quine thinks that we do better to paraphrase into a notation which does not. As emphasized in Chapter 9, Quine does not think that our paraphrase of theory should aim at synonymy, even if the goal were intelligible. The point is, rather, that "[a] paraphrase into a canonical notation is good insofar as it tends to meet needs for which the original might be wanted" (*WO*, p. 182), while eliminating terms which tend to cause difficulties.

Another kind of objection frequently made to Quine's method of eliminating singular terms is exemplified by the claim that understanding the general term "is-identical-to-Pegasus" will depend upon a prior understanding of the singular term "Pegasus". (See for example Hans-Johann Glock, *Quine and Davidson on Language, Thought and Reality*, pp. 53f.) Quine's response is clear from points we have already emphasized: he does not claim that canonical notation could or should replace ordinary language in daily life, or in the practice of the working scientist ("in the market place or in the laboratory", *WO*, p. 228). A more general point is that canonical notation is not intended to reflect the structure of our understanding of language.[6] Hence, in particular, Quine does not claim that we could in fact learn such a reformed language, a language without singular terms, say, as a first language. The availability of such notation is, rather, important for abstract theoretical purposes, when we reflect upon our system of the world and its commitments—for philosophical purposes, we may say, if we are not misled by that phrase.

A third kind of objection to Quine's Russellian treatment of proper names is that names and descriptions behave differently in modal and counterfactual contexts.[7] We may use the description "the inventor of bifocals" to eliminate the name "Benjamin Franklin" from regimented language. But then we face the difficulty that "Benjamin Franklin might not have invented bifocals" seems to be true (someone else might surely have come up with the idea), whereas "The inventor of bifocals might not have invented bifocals" might be thought to be false. Here the Quinean response is that his concern is with regimented theory, from which modal contexts and counterfactual contexts are eliminated. (See Chapter 13, section VII, below.)

II Extensionality

According to the discussion of the previous section, we regiment a sentence such as "Socrates is mortal" by replacing it with a different sentence, existentially quantified rather than subject-predicate in form. The quantifier makes evident the ontological implications of the sentence: its truth evidently requires that there be (timelessly) such a person as Socrates. Similarly, the regimentation of the sentence "Homer never existed" is a negated existential quantification, which equally evidently denies that there is (timelessly) such a person as Homer. But now consider the sentence "Mary thinks that Homer never existed". We can regiment it along the same lines but, even as regimented, it has no clear ontological implications. Its truth does not settle the issue of the existence of Homer one way or the other. The issue which rises to the surface here is *extensionality*, a matter which is of considerable importance to Quine, and has received sustained attention in his work.

The idea of extensionality originates in the contrast, medieval or older, between the extension of a predicate and its intension. The extension of a predicate is made up of the objects of which it is true. The intension is presumably something like the meaning of the expression. Two predicates may have the same extension while having different intensions. On this account the distinction is, first and foremost, a distinction between kinds of entities. An "intensional entity" is the meaning of an expression, or is in some ways similar or analogous to a meaning. We might expect, however, that Quine's general suspicion of the notion of meanings would make him unsympathetic, at best, to the entities which are in this sense intensional; it also leads him to think that this way of making the distinction is obscure.

There is another, and clearer, way of distinguishing the extensional from the intensional; it is this sense that Quine uses. In this sense, it is *contexts* that are said, in the first instance, to be extensional or not. Let us define the term "co-extensive" for various parts of speech. Two *n*-place predicates (or open sentences) are co-extensive just in case they are true of exactly the same ordered *n*-tuples of objects; two singular terms are co-extensive just in case they denote the same object; and two (closed) sentences are co-extensive just in case they have the same truth-values. Now we can define a context as *extensional* if and only if replacing an expression in that context with a co-extensive expression results in a new expression which is co-extensive with the original. (In the true sentence "George Washington was a Virginian", for example, we can replace the name with any co-extensive expression—any other singular term denoting Washington—and we will obtain another sentence with the same truth-value, i.e. a sentence co-extensive with the original. Similarly if we replace the predicate " ... was a Virginian" with any other predicate true of exactly the same objects.) It is sentential contexts that chiefly concern us so we may say that a context is *extensional* if and only if replacing any expression within that context by another of the same extension leaves the truth-value of the whole unchanged. As the point is often put: in an extensional context an expression may be replaced by any co-extensive expression *salva veritate* (preserving truth-value). A language is said to be extensional if it contains no expressions which give rise to non-extensional contexts. Quine is a strong and consistent advocate of extensional languages; he calls himself "a confirmed extensionalist" and says: "Extensionalism is a policy I have clung to through thick, thin, and nearly seventy years of logicizing and philosophizing" ("Confessions of a Confirmed Extensionalist", p. 215).

Two main questions arise about extensionality, thus understood. One is simply why it is of such importance to Quine. The other is more complex both to state and to answer. Why do we have a single important concept here? We have defined the term "extension" separately for sentences, for predicates, and for singular terms. One might think that there would, correspondingly, be three separate conditions that a language might meet or fail to meet: co-extensive singular terms can be substituted for one another, *salva veritate*; co-extensive predicates can be substituted for one another, *salva veritate*; co-extensive sentences can be substituted for one another, *salva veritate*. So the question is: what is the reason to treat these three together, as defining a single criterion of extensionality? The answer is that we can, given weak and plausible assumptions, prove that a language which fulfils one of these conditions fulfils the others. The matter is technical, and will be discussed in an appendix to this chapter.

Our first question was why extensionality is so important to Quine. As a preliminary to that, we should note that any language which uses the syntax of logic, as set out in the previous chapter, is automatically extensional. Such a language, recall, is simply the syntax of logic with the addition of a stock of extra-logical predicates. It will, therefore, contain no singular terms, so only sentences and predicates are relevant. The only sentential connectives of the language are the truth-functional connectives (as opposed to, say, " ... because ... ", which is not truth-functional). So the only way in which sentences occur as parts of other sentences is truth-functionally, that is, in contexts in which the truth-value of the containing sentence is determined by the truth-value of the contained sentence or sentences. The point can be proved: from "$p \leftrightarrow q$" we can prove "$S \leftrightarrow S*$", where "S" differs from "$S*$" only in that the latter contains "q" in some or all of the places where the former contains "p". Hence all contexts for sentences are extensional. As for predicates, it is only through its extension that a predicate affects the truth-value of any sentence couched in the syntax of logic. Again the point is provable: from "$(\forall x)(Fx \leftrightarrow Gx)$" we can prove "$S \leftrightarrow S^*$", where, this time, "$S$" differs from "$S^*$" only in that the latter contains "G" in some or all of the places where the former contains "F". So, again, the requirement of extensionality, this time on predicates, is satisfied.

It is important to emphasize, however, that Quine does not merely accept extensionality as the price of a logical framework which he finds desirable for other reasons. To the contrary: extensionality is itself, in his view, a very highly desirable characteristic of a language, one that he would be extremely reluctant to abandon. He thus takes it to be an advantage of his canonical syntax that it yields an extensional language:

> Extensionality is much of the glory of predicate logic, and it is much of the glory of any science that can be grammatically embedded in predicate logic. *I find extensionality necessary, indeed, though not sufficient, for my full understanding of a theory.*
>
> (*FSS*, pp. 90–91; emphasis added)

Why does Quine hold this? Why does he put such a high value on extensionality? The short answer, for this point as for many others, is that he holds that the use of an extensional language brings great advantages to a theory phrased in that language: "The clarity and convenience conferred by extensionality are evident: free interchangeability of coextensive components *salva veritate*". ("Confessions of a Confirmed Extensionalist", p. 215.) There is more to the point than this, however. The sentence just quoted is immediately followed by this one: "When in particular those components are singular terms, indeed, their interchangeability would seem mandatory from any point of view; for this is simply the substitutivity of identity". Elsewhere Quine says: "it is an affront to common sense to see a true sentence go false when a singular term in it is supplanted by another that names the same thing. What is true of a thing is true of it, surely, under any name". (*FSS*, p. 91.) He takes as paradigmatically clear the situation in which a singular term functions simply by picking out an object. In that case, the truth or falsehood of the sentence as a whole depends only on what object is picked out, not on *how* it is picked out. It is unsurprising that Quine should wish to avoid reference to *how* an object is picked out. By his standards, whether two ways of picking out an object count as the same is vague, unclear, and context-relative—just the sort of issue that canonical notation should enable us to avoid. (Quine's attitude here goes all the way back to his early reaction to *Principia Mathematica*; see the last couple of pages of Chapter 2, section I above.) If our theory is set in an extensional language then we can evaluate the truth of its sentences without having to attend to such dubious issues.

The focus of the previous paragraph was on the requirement that co-extensive singular terms be substitutable *salva veritate*. The appeal of that requirement is more immediately evident than is the appeal of the analogous requirements for predicates and sentences, as Quine accepts. All forms of extensionality appeal to him, but still he acknowledges that one might wish to accept the one requirement while rejecting the other two. That course, however, is ruled out. As Quine says, "the three requirements interlock inseparably" (*FSS*, p. 91); this is the point to be proved in the appendix to this chapter. What it shows is that extensionality is not a group of three separate requirements lumped together under a single name, but is rather a single condition on a language.

Even apart from the argument given in the appendix, there is reason to think that the three apparently separate requirements of extensionality hang together. The kinds of contexts which violate one requirement also tend, without manipulation, to violate it in the others as well. A clear example is given by statements of propositional attitude, such as ascriptions of belief. It is evident that statements of belief violate the requirement of extensionality stated for sentences: the fact that someone believes one true sentence does not imply that she believes all true sentences. Equally, as we shall see in the next section, statements of belief violate the other two requirements of extensionality.

III Extensionality and reference

How is our knowledge, expressed in ordinary language, to be fitted into the syntax of logic? This question occupies a considerable amount of Quine's time, especially in *Word and Object*, and the aspect of it that most concerns him has to do with reference. In regimented notation, reference is conveyed with great clarity and simplicity by quantified variables. This, for Quine, functions as the very paradigm of reference. How are we best to map ordinary language onto the more limited notation? An answer to that question would give us an understanding of the referential structure of our language; we understand that structure by seeing how it relates to the paradigmatic cases of reference. The discussion here overlaps to some extent with that of Chapter 6, section III above, where we were concerned with the child's acquisition of referential language. Here, however, our focus is on the finished product, not on its acquisition. In this discussion, as we shall see, extensionality has a large role to play.

Much of what Quine has to say about the referential structure of our language is relatively uncontroversial, and we shall discuss it briefly or not at all. Much, indeed, is more or less familiar to anyone who has learnt to paraphrase English sentences using logical notation. (Quine himself played a large part both in clarifying such matters and in spreading the word; as a pedagogue of modern logic, and of the relation of logic to ordinary language, his influence is unrivalled.) Thus Quine emphasizes the relative clause, which creates general terms from open sentences: "it creates from a sentence ' ... *x* ... ' a complex adjective summing up what that sentence says about *x*" (*WO*, p. 110). Thus too he discusses the way in which indefinite terms ("some lion", "any mathematician", "all competent logicians", and so on) go over into the quantificational notation of regimented theory. (See especially *WO*, sections 23 and 34.) And, again, he discusses ambiguities, of terms, of syntax, and of scope, and ways in which they are to be eliminated when we paraphrase in order to regiment. (Here see especially *WO*, sections 27 and 28.)

Issues having to do with extensionality, and its failure, are more controversial, and perhaps less familiar, than the points just indicated. Quine introduces the issues by distinguishing two kinds of positions in which a singular term may occur: "in sentences there are positions where the term is used as a means simply of specifying its object, or purporting to, for the rest of the sentence to say something about" (*WO*, pp. 141f.). What is the criterion for the occurrence of a term fulfilling this condition? When is such an occurrence "purely referential", as Quine also says? It will be no surprise that it is the same as the criterion for the context's being extensional: "the position must be subject to the *substitutivity of identity*" (*WO*, p. 142).

There is a class of cases where a term violates this condition, if taken in the most literal fashion, but where the sentence is easily reconstrued so that there is no violation. These cases are generated by quotation; they might seem to be trivial, but they are important for Quine's work. Consider the sentence:

"Quine" rhymes with "twine".

If we take the word inside the first pair of quotation marks as a singular term referring to a man then clearly it is not a purely referential occurrence of that singular term. If it were purely referential, then it could be replaced by a co-extensive term, *salva veritate*. But it cannot be, for the sentence:

"The author of *Word and Object*" rhymes with "twine"

is false. So a singular term which occurs within quotation marks (at least when these are used in the way that has become standard among philosophers and logicians) may be in a non-referential position.[8] When we regiment a sentence such as the first of the pair above, therefore, we will not treat the occurrence of the name it contains in the way we would the occurrence of that name in "Quine was a great philosopher". In the latter case we would construe the sentence as claiming that there is one and only one object which fulfils a certain condition (that of having written *Word and Object*, perhaps), and that it is a great philosopher. In the former case, we would use a description uniquely true of the *word*. We might do this by spelling; it is the one and only word which is spelt: upper-case queue_lower-case yu_lower-case eye_lower-case enn_lower-case ee. (See *Word and Object*, p. 143. Here I use "_" as a symbol for concatenation, meaning that the symbol to its left is followed by the symbol to its right.) Or we might speak of the word made up of the seventeenth letter of the alphabet followed by the twenty-first letter followed by . . .

In practice, of course, we will do neither of these things, for either one leads to intolerable prolixity. In practice, even when we are concerned with precision, we will use quotation marks and assume that they and the word that they enclose are to be treated as a term referring to the *word* which is spelt: upper-case queue, lower-case yu, lower-case eye . . . and so on.

Quine speaks of non-extensional contexts for singular terms as "referentially opaque"; others he calls "referentially transparent" or "purely referential".[9] The case just discussed clarifies the reason for thinking that failure of extensionality is also failure of referentiality. As indicated in the previous section, if what we are saying is simply true or false *of the object* then it should hold true however that object is referred to. If we were really saying that *Quine*, the man, rhymes with "twine" then we would equally be saying that the well known author of *Word and Object* rhymes with "twine", for they are one and the same. But clearly that is not what is being said. What is being said is not about the man; it is about the name. The sentence, however, contains a singular term naming the man and is to that extent misleading; its wording suggests that it is about one thing, the man Quine, but is in fact about something else, the name "Quine". (Not that anyone is likely to be misled by this particular case.) Canonical notation, designed to maximize clarity and to facilitate inference, will not regiment a singular term in such a position as referring to the object which we take to be designated by that term in ordinary cases.[10]

Most cases of intensionality are not so easily dealt with as the one about "Quine" and "twine". Consider the sentence:

(1) Tom believes that Cicero denounced Catiline.

The "believes that" here creates a non-extensional context. On any account it is extensional for the embedded sentence, for clearly Tom may believe one truth without believing all truths, and may believe one falsehood without believing all falsehoods. In one sense of belief, at least, the sentence also forms a non-extensional context for the occurrence of the singular term "Cicero", for it may be that (1) is true while this one:

(2) Tom believes that Tully denounced Catiline

is false, even though in fact Cicero and Tully are the same person. (It may be argued that there is also another sense of belief, in which this fact and (1) together imply (2); in that case we do not have a non-extensional context for "Cicero" after all. See Chapter 13, below, where we return to these issues in a different context.) Hence "Tom believes that ... denounced Catiline" forms a non-extensional context.

In regimenting these sentences we will use definite descriptions, but this makes no difference to the failure of extensionality. We will, presumably, use two different predicates, each of which is true of Marcus Tullius Cicero and of no one else. Where the two predicates are "A" and "B", this partial regimentation gives us the following replacements for (1) and (2):

(1*) Tom believes that $(\exists x)[(\forall y)(Ay \leftrightarrow x = y)$ & x denounced Catiline]

(2*) Tom believes that $(\exists x)[(\forall y)(By \leftrightarrow x = y)$ & x denounced Catiline].

Here the failure of extensionality shows up in the fact that the replacement of a predicate by a *co-extensive* predicate may not preserve truth-value: (1*) may be true and (2*) false even though they differ only in that one has "A" where the other has "B", and these predicates are co-extensive because each, we are supposing, applies to Cicero and to no one else. (The failure of extensionality might also be thought to show up in the fact that the truth of either of these sentences is compatible with there being no person who denounced Catiline, since Tom might be wrong on that point. This use of the existential quantifier carries no ontological implications.)

Where singular terms occur in non-extensional positions, eliminating those terms in favour of definite descriptions thus does not eliminate the non-extensionality. We simply have a non-extensionality context for general terms instead. Hence some more drastic reconstrual is called for. This result could be reached also in more direct fashion. It is said that the creatures with a heart are exactly the creatures with kidneys. Even if this is true, still

Tom may believe that all mammals have hearts while not believing that all mammals have kidneys. A sentence such as "Tom believes that all mammals have hearts" as it stands, unregimented, can thus be changed from a truth to a falsehood by replacing one predicate with another co-extensive predicate. So reconstrual is called for if we are to embed theory within an extensional language. In Chapter 13, we shall take up the details of Quine's reconstrual of such sentences; quotation, discussed above, will have a significant role to play.

In our sentences (1*) and (2*), "believes that" forms a non-extensional context. On Quine's account the sentences require reconstrual, but still they make clear enough sense. Keeping to the same sense of belief, the same point applies to a sentence such as:

(3) Tom believes that someone denounced Catiline

or, in partially regimented notation:

(4) Tom believes that $(\exists x)(x$ denounced Catiline).

In these sentences, the embedded sentence (and indeed the name and the predicate) are in non-extensional position. So Quine holds that the sentences require reconstrual, but he does not doubt that they make clear enough sense. He argues, however, that the same does not hold for:

(5) $(\exists x)(x$ Tom believes that x denounced Catiline).

If we stick to the same non-extensional sense of belief, he claims, this sentence is ruled out. Given the standard (objectual) understanding of the quantifier, we cannot coherently combine it with a non-extensional operator in this way. Why not? Since we are dealing with a non-extensional sense of belief, we cannot think of "Tom believes that ... denounced Catiline" as an open sentence, true or false of objects in the usual way. If we do, we get no answer, or an incoherent answer, to the question whether it is true of Marcus Tullius Cicero: the truth of (1) would seem to show that it is, while the falsehood of (2) would seem to show that it is not. Hence we cannot think of "Tom believes that ... denounced Catiline" as being true or false *of objects* at all. Yet (5) attempts to say precisely that this open sentence is true of at least one object.

The moral of our discussion in this section as a whole is that when we paraphrase sentences in which terms occur in non-extensional contexts we will not treat those occurrences as referential. The moral of the last couple of paragraphs is that this point will show up in our use of quantified variables, since it is such variables which convey reference in regimented notation. Where both the variable and the quantifier are within the non-extensional context, the quantified variable does not make its usual ontological claim: (4), above, could be true even if no one had denounced Catiline. And we have ruled out the kind of case exemplified in (5), above. As Quine puts it: *"no variable inside an opaque construction is bound by an operator outside* [that construction]" (*WO*, p. 166; emphasis in the original). The significance of this restriction, as of some other aspects of this section, will become clearer in Chapter 13.

Appendix

We stated extensionality as three apparently separable requirements: that co-extensive singular terms are substitutable, one for another, *salva veritate*; that the same holds for co-extensive predicates; and that the same holds for co-extensive sentences (i.e. sentences alike in truth-value). Given weak and plausible assumptions, we can show that these requirements are not in fact separable. Since it is the requirement for singular terms that has the most evident independent motivation, what we really need to show is that a language which meets this requirement meets the others.

First, then, we show that a language in which all contexts for singular terms are extensional is also a language in which all contexts for predicates are extensional. The primary assumption that we need is that a predication, "Fa", always has the same truth-value as the statement that a is a member of the set of Fs, i.e. $a \in \{x/Fx\}$. (Note that we need only the assumption of likeness in truth-value, not a stronger assumption such as synonymy.) We also need to able to assume enough about the existence of sets to ensure that, at least in standard cases, $\{x/Fx\}$ will indeed exist.[11] Given this much, we can show if there is a non-extensional context for a predicate, "F" then there is also a non-extensional context for the singular term "$\{x/Fx\}$". Suppose we have a context which is non-extensional for predicates. So then there is some predicate "G", co-extensive with "F", and a sentence the truth-value of which can be changed by replacing some or all occurrences of "F" by occurrences of "G". (That is simply what it means to suppose that extensionality fails for predicates.) Let us suppose that the context gives us a true sentence when it contains "F" and a false one when it contains "G". Now in the first sentence replace everything of the form "Fa" with something of the form "$a \in \{x/Fx\}$"; and in the second sentence we replace everything of the form "Ga" with something of the form "$a \in \{x/Gx\}$". By the assumption made above this replacement will not alter the truth-values of the sentences. So now we have two sentences, one true and one false, which differ only in that one of them has the singular term "$\{x/Fx\}$" in exactly those places where the other has the singular term "$\{x/Gx\}$". But given the criterion for set-identity, these two singular terms refer to the same object—indifferently described as the set of Fs or the set of Gs. Thus the failure of substitutivity for predicates is turned into a failure of substitutivity for singular terms. Hence a language in which co-designative singular terms are intersubstitutable *salva veritate* must also be a language in which co-extensive predicates are intersubstitutable *salva veritate*. (One who denies extensionality might deny our first assumption, that "Fa" has the same truth-value as saying that a is a member of the set of Fs; this, however, will presumably lead to a rejection of set-theory as a whole as incoherent. From Quine's point of view, at least, this is too high a price for any right-minded person to be willing to pay.)

Second, we show that a language that meets the requirement of extensionality for singular terms also meets the requirement for sentences. The argument is very similar. Suppose, again, that we have enough set-theory to give us a set for every open sentence of straightforward structure. So, in particular, for each sentence, p, we have the following set: $\{x/\ p\ .\ x=x\}$. If our original sentence is true, this is the universal set, containing all objects.[12] If our original sentence is false, then this set is the null-set, containing no objects. In either case, if p and q have the same truth-value then $\{x/\ p\ .\ x=x\}$ = $\{x/\ q\ .\ x=x\}$. Any sentence containing a sentence, p, can be reconfigured into an equivalent sentence containing the name of the corresponding set, $\{x/\ p\ .\ x=x\}$. The result must have the same truth-value as the original. We then replace "$\{x/\ p\ .\ x=x\}$" with "$\{x/\ q\ .\ x=x\}$", where q is any sentence at all with the same truth-value as p. Given that p and q have the same truth-value, "$\{x/\ p\ .\ x=x\}$" refers to the same set as "$\{x/\ q\ .\ x=x\}$". By the assumption that co-extensive singular terms are intersubstitutable *salve veritate*, the result still has the same truth-value as the original sentence containing p. Then we undo the reconfiguring, to get back to the sentence with which we started, but now containing q rather than p. Again, it is hard to deny that every step here preserves truth-value; yet p and q need have nothing in common other than their truth-values. Given the very weak assumptions required for this argument, then, extensionality for singular terms implies extensionality for sentences.

12

ONTOLOGY, PHYSICALISM, REALISM

An important philosophical task, according to Quine, is to show how our theory of the world can best be clarified, simplified, and systematized. As we emphasized in Chapter 10, this is the motive that leads him to the idea of regimenting theory in canonical notation and, in particular, to the idea that first-order logic should be the syntax of regimented theory. First-order logic is not imposed on theory from a wholly distinct vantage point; Quine claims to be advocating it in the same spirit as that in which he might advocate any other scientific advance although it is, to be sure, far more general than most. With this same motive, and in this same spirit, Quine also considers the ontology of regimented theory, and the predicates that would be accepted within it. These are the subjects which occupy the first three sections of this chapter. The final section will discuss realism. This is an issue which we briefly addressed in Chapter 1. Since then we have examined both the indeterminacy of reference and the underdetermination of theory by evidence, each of which might be thought to make a difference to the issue of realism. So we need to return to the issue.

I Ontology: general principles; bodies and objects

How are we to settle what there is? The fundamental principle here is that ontology is to be settled by reference to our overall theory of the world. Our ontological claims are an integral part of our theory, and must be formed in the light of theory as a whole. Contrast this with the idea that (some) objects are *given*, wholly independent of wider theory, and that our theory must be tailored to fit the objects which are in this way given. As we have emphasized more than once, Quine has no sympathy at all with this idea. He denies that there are entities which are given prior to theory, and which have an ontological status higher or firmer than the entities posited by our best theory. (See Chapter 4, section I, and Chapter 9, section I, above.) On

Quine's account, everything, every object we accept as real, can be described as a posit; nothing is *given*, prior to and independent of our theory. Our ontology is drawn from our theory.

Accepting that ontology is in this sense a theoretical matter, how are we to settle what there is? It may be thought that we have already answered this question: given regimented theory, the objects that exist are those which must be in the range of the variables for the sentences of that theory to be true. But this is not a sufficient answer, because in regimenting theory we have considerable latitude. For the most part, decisions as to how theory should be regimented are to be guided by the usual theoretical *desiderata* of clarity, economy, and simplicity. (I omit efficacy in prediction of experience, because any two regimentations of a given body of unregimented theory will, presumably, be more or less equivalent in this respect.) These familiar ideas, however, can be given new expression when we consider the ontology of our theory. A minor point concerns the idea of economy: one theory can presumably be rated as more economical than another if it requires fewer entities or, perhaps, fewer kinds of entities. More importantly, Quine claims that to clarify and simplify our theory we should accept only objects for which we have clear identity-criteria.

For Quine, there is a fundamental connection between identity and objecthood: "the positing of first objects makes no sense except as keyed to identity" ("Speaking of Objects", *OR*, p. 23). We elaborated on the reasons for this connection in our discussion of reference in the last two sections of Chapter 6, above. As Quine acknowledges, however, the development of language has weakened this connection: "patterns of thing talk, once firmly inculcated, have in fact enabled us to talk of attributes and propositions in partial grammatical analogy, without an accompanying standard of identity for them" (ibid.). So then the question is: why should we reject this development, rather than welcoming it? Why should we not accept propositions as entities to which the concept of identity does not apply—accept them, as he says, "as twilight half-entities to which the concept of identity is not applicable" (ibid.)?

Quine's answer to this question is that accepting entities without identity would involve "a certain disruption to logic" ("Speaking of Objects", *OR*, p. 23). If we use first-order logic with identity to regiment theory, questions of identity become inescapable. If we accept that there are meanings, say, we cannot avoid the question whether the meaning of one expression is the same as that of another expression. So the use of first-order logic with identity is, *prima facie*, in conflict with the acceptance of "half-entities" without clear-cut identity-criteria. If we are to accept such half-entities "without abdication of philosophical responsibility", Quine says, "we must adjust the logic of our conceptual scheme to receive them, and then weigh any resulting complexity against the benefits of the half-entities" (ibid.). This assumes, however, that we are to have a single system of regimented theory. Quine suggests that we might respond to the situation by allowing for a more and a less narrow version of regimented theory. The narrower version would stick to the requirement that objects have clear identity-criteria, thus excluding the half-entities; this would be the one to use "for official scientific business" ("Speaking of Objects", *OR*, p. 24). The less austere would be counted as "a second-grade system" (ibid.; for more on this idea of more and less austere systems, see Chapter 13, section IV, below).

We should not be surprised that Quine accepts the demands of logic as a reason to ban entities without clear identity-criteria from the most austere, first-grade, version of regimented theory. As we have emphasized, he holds that objects are posited, not given; he holds that the advantages of positing them are the clarity and system that doing so brings to our theory. In particular, we clarify its structure by revealing and systematizing the inferential relations among the sentences which make it up; this, to his mind, is what makes it worth thinking in terms of objects at all. (See the final section of Chapter 6, above.) And logic, of course, is the systematization of these inferential relations.

The conclusion of our discussion to this point is twofold. On the one hand, our ontology is to be read off from our theory by regimenting that theory; the objects which we must acknowledge to exist are those which must be in the range of the variables for the theory to be true. On the other hand, the way in which we regiment theory is constrained by the need to have clear identity-criteria for those objects which we accept.

What objects, then, should we accept into our ontology? A natural first thought is that our ontology must include the ordinary objects that are most familiar, and most important in our lives: other people, tables and chairs, loaves of bread, cars and keys, trees and mountains, and in general the sorts of medium-sized objects that we constantly interact with. Quine refers to what I have here loosely called "ordinary objects" as *bodies*. A body is "roughly continuous spatially and rather chunky"; it "contrasts abruptly with most of its surroundings and is individuated over time by continuity of displacement, distortion, and discoloration" (TPT, *TT*, p. 13). Such things have an obvious connection with our survival and our flourishing.

Our concern with bodies is early, abiding, and inescapable. Our earliest utterances—"Mama", "Cookie", "Fido"—give rise to terms referring to

300

bodies. To learn to make such an utterance appropriately is to acquire a highly complex disposition. This sort of learning, however, comes naturally to us, as its non-linguistic analogue does to other animals. As Quine says: "Man is a body-minded animal, among body-minded animals". (*RR*, p. 54; for discussion of related points, see again the last two sections of Chapter 6, above.) For Quine's purposes it is also important that our earliest learning of such expressions is not yet the learning of referring terms; learning even the simplest referring terms requires learning other parts of the language, i.e. it requires the acquisition of other highly complex dispositions. Almost all humans, however, readily acquire such dispositions, provided they grow up in the company of those who already have them. An ontology of bodies comes naturally to us.

Bodies are thus included in any primitive ontology; they are assumed by any ontology that one might attribute to primitive humans or to a modern-day child. So they are the most obvious candidates for inclusion in our ontology. "Bodies are the charter members of our ontology, let the sub-sequent elections and expulsions proceed as they may". (*RR*, p. 85.) They are, Quine says, "the prime reality, the objects *par excellence*. Ontology, when it comes, is a generalization of somatology". (*RR*, p. 88.)

In Quine's view, however, this initial acceptance of bodies, ordinary objects, gives way before the demands of theory. The notion of a body is not a precise one. Being "roughly continuous" and contrasting with "most of its surroundings" are vague characterizations; there is little hope of replacing them with more precise versions. So there will be cases where it is unclear whether an alleged body really counts as such or not, and hence whether it should be counted among the things that there are. Regimented theory cannot tolerate this sort of unclarity. Accepting bodies in our ontology, moreover, commits us to precise demarcations, saying exactly what constitutes a given body. This Quine calls "a pointless task" (WPO?, p. 497), yet if an object is to be included in the ontology of our regimented theory we need precise identity-criteria for it. Even if we accept these difficulties, we do not gain full inclusiveness. No plausible attempt to make the idea of a body precise will include all of the (apparent) things that we talk about. Warm fronts, cold spells, bad moods, dire insults, and countless others, are unlikely to count as bodies.

So Quine argues that an ontology suitable for scientific and philosophical purposes—the ontology of our regimented theory—will not have a special category for bodies. The relevant category will, rather, be what he calls *physical object*, where the idea of a physical object is more inclusive than that of a body. The idea of a physical object is construed "simply as the aggregate material content of any portion of space-time, however ragged and discontinuous". (WPO?, p. 497. Some philosophers, we should note, use the term "physical objects" to mean more or less what Quine calls "bodies"; we shall stick to Quinean usage.) My left big toe and the Eiffel Tower taken together constitute a single physical object, but there is no single body made up of these things.

The notion of a physical object is more inclusive than that of a body. As long as precise identity-criteria are settled, any body will count also as a physical object, but not the other way around. We do not need to settle identity-criteria for bodies where nothing turns on it; bodies enter our ontology only insofar as we identify them with physical objects. Similarly, there is no problem in thinking of a warm front or a cold spell as a physical object, once we have settled upon definite criteria for individuation. We simply take the content of that portion of space-time which we have settled on as being occupied by the given state or condition. Bad moods might be thought of as mental, and thus in a different category, but Quine argues that things of that sort can also be identified with physical objects: in this case, with the body of the person concerned for as long as the mood lasts. (Quine's treatment of the mind, and mental entities, will occupy us further in the last section of this chapter and in the next chapter.) Another advantage of Quine's notion of a physical object is that its inclusiveness allows us to give a straightforward account of mass terms, such as "sugar". We can construe it as referring to "a single large and spatio-temporally scattered physical object, consisting of all the sugar anywhere, ever" (WPO?, p. 497). No body corresponds to such an entity, but it fits Quine's broader notion of a physical object.

The use of physical objects rather than bodies is a relatively minor modification of primitive ontology. A little reflection upon our theory suggests the need for what may appear to be a far more drastic change: including abstract objects among the things we take to exist. If the needs of theory are to govern ontology then there is certainly every reason to accept abstract objects. Much of our theorizing makes evident use of mathematics, and quantifies over numbers, of various kinds, and functions. (To a significant extent, indeed, the systematic character of our theory is due precisely to the role that mathematics plays in it.) This is most obvious in the case of physics, and the other natural sciences, but is by no means confined to those disciplines. There is no prospect of accommodating mathematics, or its applications, without accepting abstract objects of some kind.[1] But it is not only our systematic theory which requires the abstract. Almost any part of our knowledge will do the same. Even so casual a statement as that I own two copies of *Word and Object* is hard to make sense of without the idea of a book as a *type*, which many physical objects instantiate, and the most obvious way of making sense of a type, in this sense, is as an abstract entity. Or, again, the statement that there are sentences which no one has ever uttered requires that we think of a sentence not as a physical object but as a *sequence* of words, and a sequence is an abstract object.

In his mature philosophy, Quine sees every reason to accept abstract entities, and no compelling reason not to.[2] From Quine's point of view, there is thus ample theoretical reason to accept abstract objects. He suggests, indeed, that adding abstract objects to our ontology is not really a significant change at all because the distinction between the abstract and the concrete is less important, and perhaps also less clear-cut, than one might suppose: "General definition of the term 'abstract', or 'universal', and its opposite 'concrete' or 'particular' need not detain us. ... *no capital will be made of the distinction as such.*" (WO, p. 233; emphasis added.) And, perhaps more strikingly: "We ... seem to see a profound difference between abstract objects and concrete objects. ... But I am persuaded that this contrast is illusory". (TPT, *TT*, p. 16.)

The acceptance of abstract objects has met considerable resistance, at least as far back as the medieval disputes between nominalists and realists. Quine is, of course, well aware that many philosophers have looked sceptically upon the idea of such objects. He perhaps rather understates the point by saying "more confidence [has been] felt in there being physical objects than in there being classes, attributes, and the like" (WO, p. 233). He offers a number of explanations for this attitude.[3] Of these, only one seems to him to be a "defensible reason", namely, that "our terms for physical objects are commonly learned through fairly direct conditioning to stimulatory effects of the denoted objects" (WO, p. 234).

The objection suggests a criterion for existence—proximity to sensory experience, roughly—which would count even more strongly in favour of sense data than of physical objects. As we have seen, however, Quine thinks we have overwhelming theoretical reasons to reject sense data. It might seem that we have here "the collision of two standards", one being "directness of association with sensory stimulation", the other being "utility for theory" (WO, p. 236). But Quine rejects that diagnosis. In his view, directness of association with sensory stimulation cannot stand alone, as a standard independent of utility for theory; on the contrary, the former standard must be subordinate to the latter.

What is more or less directly associated with sensory stimulation is, on his account, an utterance. Such an utterance, or part of it, may be construed as a referring term. Whether it should be construed in that way, however, is a question which is to be decided by the needs of theory, not by the mere fact that the utterance is associated with sensory stimulation. As Quine puts it in *Word and Object*: "the stimulus meaning of an observation sentence in no way settles whether any part of the sentence should be distinguished as a term for sense data, or as a term for physical objects, or as a term at all" (WO, p. 236). Our use of a sentence, whether or not directly conditioned to sensory stimulation, "does not settle whether to posit objects of one sort or another for words of the sentence to denote in the capacity of terms" (ibid.). When have we posited objects? "[O]nly when we have brought the contemplated terms into suitable interplay with the whole distinctively objectificatory apparatus of our language: articles and pronouns and the idioms of identity, plurality, and predication, or, in canonical notation, quantification". (Ibid.; see again Chapter 6, above, especially section III.) What parts of a sentence to count as referential, if any, is thus a theoretical matter through and through. The criterion of directness of association with stimulation is not independent of theory. It is only in the light of theory—and in the light of a scheme for regimenting theory—that a part of a sentence emerges as a term at all. Objecthood, and termhood, are theoretical matters. Utility for theory, understood sufficiently broadly, is thus the only criterion by which we can decide what objects to accept.

This does not imply that closeness of association with sensory stimulation plays no role at all. As Quine points out, "sentences fairly directly associated with sensory stimulation exhibit terms for physical objects in all sorts of term positions, not just in rather special ones" (WO, pp. 237f.). We might take this as a reason for thinking that physical objects have a particularly clear and well established ontological status. But if we do so we are making a decision on the grounds of the role that terms for such objects play in theory, not on grounds independent of theory.

Reverting to the issue of abstract objects, we find little need for further discussion. The *prima facie* case for the theoretical utility of abstract objects is overwhelming, as noted a couple of pages back. More recently, we have been following Quine's argument that utility for theory is the only criterion by which we should decide whether to accept alleged entities of a given kind into our ontology. If we accept that criterion, then we can have no further doubts about accepting that there are abstract objects.

II Sets, hyper-Pythagoreanism, and the role of ontology

Much of the previous section was concerned with Quine's reasons for accepting abstract objects, where they are useful for theory. Relative to this important point of principle, the question of exactly which abstract objects we should accept is unimportant, a matter of detail. What Quine advocates here is that we should adopt sets as the only abstract objects. (As noted in Chapter 9, I consistently use the word "set", whereas Quine sometimes uses the word "class".) Sets are acceptable to Quine because their identity conditions are as clear as can be: a set is defined by its members; two sets with the same members are in fact a single set.

Sets are the only abstract objects that Quine accepts because they function as a more or less all-purpose kind of abstract object; they enable us to define all the others for which a good case can be made:

> the abstract objects that it is useful to admit to the universe of discourse at all seem to be adequately explicable in terms of a universe comprising just physical objects and all classes of the objects in the universe (hence classes of physical objects, classes of such classes, etc.). At any rate I can think of no persuasive exceptions.
>
> (WO, p. 267)

Mathematical entities, most obviously, are definable in terms of sets, as Frege and Russell showed. (See the very brief discussion of this point in Chapter 2, above.) Natural numbers can be identified with sets of equinumerous sets; rational numbers follow as ratios—ordered pairs—of natural numbers; real numbers can be treated, along the lines suggested by Dedekind, as sets of rational numbers. One-place functions, on this line, are sets of ordered pairs satisfying certain conditions. (Quite generally, n-place functions are sets of ordered $n+1$-tuples.) The power of sets, Quine holds, is such that if we admit them then no other kinds of abstract object are required.

Of the reasons against accepting sets, the one which weighs most heavily with Quine is that unrestricted positing of sets leads to paradox—most notably, and most simply, to Russell's paradox.[4] These paradoxes show that any theory of sets must impose restrictions on what sets there are. Quine has himself suggested various ways of doing this but is, for the most part, agnostic as to which should be adopted.

In *Word and Object*, Quine envisages a theory of sets with physical objects as the so-called "ground elements"—i.e. as the only entities which are members of sets but are not themselves sets. In "Whither Physical Objects?" he favours what is called "pure set theory": set-theory without ground elements. How is such a thing possible?

> There is the empty set [the set containing no members], there is the unit set of the empty set [the set containing the empty set and

nothing else], there is the set of these two sets, and so on. We get infinitely many finite sets in this way. Then we take all the finite and infinite sets having these as members. Continuing thus, we suffer no shortages.

(WPO?, pp. 501f.)

The difference between the two positions would not concern us if it were not for the fact that in "Whither Physical Objects?" Quine takes advantage of the possibility of pure set theory to suggest what may appear to be a very drastic ontological move: the elimination from our ontology of physical objects themselves.

A physical object, as Quine uses that term, is simply "the aggregate material content of any portion of space-time" (WPO?, p. 497). Quine raises the question of the status of these "portion[s] of space-time". Can we understand a physical object just as the material content of such a "portion", and eliminate the reference here to space-time? Quine takes it that this move is blocked by developments in physics, which suggest that it may not make clear sense to identify electrons over time, or even to distinguish between two electrons existing at the same time. More generally, physics seems to be not so much a theory of matter as of fields—"a theory of the distribution of states over space-time." (WPO?, p. 499.) Bodies, to begin with, and then physical objects, seemed clear enough to take as the basic elements in our ontology. But Quine thinks that physics has cast the objects themselves in doubt: "our physical objects have themselves gone so tenuous that we find ourselves turning to the space-time regions for something to cling to." (Ibid.) So we cannot eliminate the space-time regions in favour of their material content; we can, however, do the reverse, and eliminate physical objects in terms of space-time regions. But now, given some coordinate system, the space-time regions can themselves be understood as sets of ordered quadruples of real numbers.[5] Thus we end up in a position that Quine calls "hyper-Pythagoreanism": our ontology contains *only* the abstract objects of mathematics—in particular, it contains only sets.

Hyper-Pythagoreanism, as Quine considers it, does not imply that physics is wholly replaced by mathematics. The predicates which we ascribe to the ordered quadruples which stand in for regions of space-time will not all be drawn from mathematics. The displacement of the physical by the mathematical concerns ontology, what objects we accept; what we say about those objects will have non-mathematical content. (There is nothing abstruse about the idea of saying non-mathematical things about mathematical objects. I have four sisters; this statement can be understood as saying something about the number four, namely that it is the number of my sisters.)

Thus: "our system of the world does not reduce to set theory; for our lexicon of predicates and functors still stands stubbornly apart." (WPO?, p. 503.)

Quine sees the displacement of the physical from our ontology not as an abandonment of physics but, to the contrary, as suggested by the needs of that subject itself:

> Bodies ... needed to be generalized to physical objects for reasons that rested on physical concerns. ... Physical objects, next, evaporated into space-time regions; but this was the outcome of physics itself. Finally the regions went over into pure sets; still the set theory itself was there for no other reasons than the need for mathematics as an adjunct to physical theory. The bias is physical first and last, despite the airiness of the ontology.
>
> (WPO?, pp. 502–03)

He also holds that "the scheme has also a certain intrinsic appeal" (WPO?, p. 502) on the grounds of economy: "Numbers and other mathematical objects are wanted in physics anyhow, so we might as well enjoy their convenience as coordinates for physical objects; and then, having come thus far, one can economize a little by dispensing with the physical objects." (Ibid.)

One might think that hyper-Pythagoreanism is an extraordinary metaphysical doctrine, which would be the subject of much discussion in Quine's subsequent work. But in fact there is little mention of it. He raises the idea as a possibility in "Things and Their Place in Theories", but does not assert it. (See *TT*, p. 17.) In *From Stimulus to Science* he does not mention it at all, and seems to have tacitly given up on it, for he reverts to the idea of a system of sets with physical objects as ground elements, the position he advocated in *Word and Object*. (See *FSS*, pp. 40f.) But there is no real inconsistency here, and no change of mind on any issue that Quine sees as significant. The real moral of "Whither Physical Objects?" is not that only sets belong in our ontology but, rather, that it scarcely matters whether our ontology includes only sets or also includes physical objects.

How can it not matter whether we accept that there are physical objects? On almost any conception of ontology other than Quine's, any view which accepts that there is a subject deserving the name "ontology", the idea that it does not matter would be outrageous. But Quine is simply following out the implications of the idea of ontological reduction (and, indeed, of indeterminacy of reference). Consider sets and numbers. Denying that there are numbers as well as sets has advantages of economy; the view that accepts both numbers and sets perhaps has advantages of naturalness and convenience. Here Quine favours economy, but it could be argued that the advantages and disadvantages of these two views are more or less in balance, so that it is close to a matter of indifference which one we should adopt. Something like that is Quine's attitude towards the existence of physical objects, over and above sets. Once we have adopted one view, we are committed to that ontology; but we may nevertheless be able to see that little or nothing turns on our adopting one rather than the other.

The general moral here is that there is less to ontology than meets the eye. Quine concludes "Whither Physical Objects?" by saying:

> We might most naturally react to [the reducibility of all ontology to that of pure sets] by attaching less importance to mere ontological considerations than we used to do. We might come to look on pure mathematics as the locus of ontology as a matter of course, and consider rather that the lexicon of natural science, not the ontology, is where the metaphysical action is.
>
> (WPO?, pp. 503f.)

Similarly, in "Facts of the Matter", Quine draws the moral that "ontology is not what mainly matters. ... Sentences, in their truth or falsity, are what run deep; ontology is by the way" (pp. 164f.). In the second edition of *Pursuit of Truth* a similar point is made in terms of proxy functions and the indeterminacy of reference:

> A lesson of proxy functions is that our ontology, like our grammar, is part of our own conceptual contribution to our theory of the world. Man proposes; the world disposes, but only by holophrastic yes-or-no verdicts on the observation sentences that embody man's predictions.
>
> (PT, p. 36)

These words conclude a section which (again, only in the second edition) is appropriately entitled "Ontology defused".

At this point one might wonder why ontology is of any interest or significance at all. If a question so fundamental—or seemingly so fundamental—as the existence of physical objects is more or less a matter of indifference, why are we concerned with ontology at all? If I might as well be talking about cosmic complements of physical objects, or time-slices of objects, or sets of ordered quadruples of real numbers—then why think that the idea of "what I'm talking about" is interesting at all? Why should we be concerned with it? The question is a good one; the significance of ontology cannot simply be taken for granted, as self-evident.

Why does ontology matter? Quine says: "What is empirically significant in an ontology is just its contribution of neutral nodes to the structure of the theory". (*PT*, p. 33.) Again, speaking of the idea that we could interpret terms for bodies as referring to the cosmic complements of those bodies, he says:

> Bodies continue, under each interpretation, to be distinct from their cosmic complements ... they are distinguished in a relativistic way, by their roles relative to one another and to the rest on ontology.
>
> (*PT*, pp. 33f.)

The suggestion of these passages, and of others, is that all that matters about an object, abstractly considered, is the role that it plays in our theory. All that matters is that we have something suitable for playing the given role; no other demands are in place.

Consider the natural numbers. We need objects to play the theoretical role which we think of as played by those objects. We may be able to identify the objects playing that role with the objects playing another role, unless there is some theoretical reason to distinguish the objects. Thus we can identify each natural number with a set of a certain kind. The hard work of the reduction is to show that certain sets are, just in virtue of their theoretical role as sets, capable of playing the role of the numbers—that the one theoretical role already encompasses the other, so to speak. It is for that reason that the reduction seems like a real intellectual achievement; for that reason too, it effects a genuine ontological economy. Contrast the case of physical objects and their cosmic complements. Here we do not assimilate objects to complements or vice versa. Nor do we show that it is in fact already implicit in the way that we think about the complements that they can play the role of the objects, or vice versa. Instead, we simply interchange them, and in doing so we interchange the roles they have to play by altering the predicates to compensate. (Thus petting the family dog is not construed as petting the animal's cosmic complement but rather as *complement-petting* the dog's complement which is, of course, the same as petting the dog.) So no economy is effected; the interchange is pointless and seems like a mere trick. But then Quine is not recommending that we carry out the interchange of objects and their complements. He does not put forward the idea of the interchange as a desirable reform of theory; he argues for the feasibility of the interchange purely to illustrate the present point, that there is no more to an object than the role that it plays in our total theory.

Our question was: why does ontology matter at all, if an issue as drastic as the existence of physical objects turns out to be more or less a matter of indifference? In the last couple of paragraphs we have emphasized the idea that what matters about an object is the theoretical role that it plays; and here lies the answer to our question. What particular objects fill the theoretical roles in our theory may be a matter of indifference; the indeterminacy of reference might be taken to show that it is not even a question that we can make full sense of. But this is compatible with it being a crucial matter what sorts of roles our theory has which need to be filled by some object-or-other. In particular, as we have emphasized in several places, Quine aims to clarify theory by formulating it in a way that does not require objects whose identity-criteria are vague or unclear. "The main thing to settle, in the way of fixing the objects", he says, "is their individuation: we have to fix standards of sameness and difference." (FM, p. 158.)

III Physicalism

Some authors use the word "physicalism" to name the doctrine that only physical things exist.[6] Not Quine; he uses the term "materialism" for that view, which he rejects. Physicalism, as he uses the term, allows for the existence of abstract objects. In *Word and Object*, indeed, Quine seems to equate physicalism with the doctrine that there are only abstract objects and physical objects. Later, as we shall see, a rather more complicated view emerges under the same name.

In *Word and Object*, then, physicalism appears as an ontological doctrine. Its most controversial aspect is the denial that we need to accept the independent existence of minds and of mental states, in addition to physical and abstract objects. (Among mental states sense data, or our perceivings of sense data, have a special role to play because of views which make them epistemologically fundamental. We have discussed sense data elsewhere, however, and will not give them prominence here.) As we saw in the previous section, however, Quine comes to think that ontology is not "where the metaphysical action is" (WPO?, pp. 503f.). A further consideration, supporting this one, seems to be that he comes to think that the seemingly controversial claim of physicalism, ontologically construed, is trivial.

For Quine, the question whether we need to accept minds as well as physical objects is analogous to the question whether we need to accept ordered pairs, or numbers, as well as sets. The crucial claim is that there is nothing more to an object than the systematic role that it plays in our theory. For ordered pairs and numbers it is easy to show that another kind of entity, which is needed for independent reasons, can play the desired role. The application of these ideas to the mind is far more controversial, perhaps because many philosophers think that people have direct and immediate knowledge of their minds and the contents of their minds, knowledge which goes beyond any "theoretical role" which such things play. Except for the case of sense data, Quine says almost nothing about such views. But it is clear that he has no more sympathy with them than with the idea of sense data as directly and immediately given: "If there is a case for mental events and mental states, it must be just that the positing of them ... has some indirect systematic efficacy in the development of theory." (*WO*, p. 264.) On his view, minds and mental states and mental entities can be eliminated in just the same kind of way as ordered pairs, if we see reason to do so and a means of doing it.

Quine does not accept minds and mental things as independent, non-physical entities. In *Word and Object*, considerations of economy seem to be motive enough for this view (see *WO* pp. 264–65). Later he found more compelling reasons:

> I need hardly say that the dualism [of mind and body] is unat-tractive. If mind and body are to interact, we are at a loss for a plausible mechanism to the purpose. Also we are faced with the melancholy office of talking physicists out of their cherished con-servation laws. On the other hand, an aseptic dualistic parallelism is monumentally redundant.
>
> (*TT*, pp. 18f.)

A method of eliminating minds, or explicating them in terms of physical objects, is easily found. The paragraph just quoted ends like this:

> it is easily seen that dualism with or without interaction is reducible to physicalistic monism, unless disembodied spirits are assumed. For the dualist who rejects disembodied spirits is bound to agree that for every state of mind there is an exactly concurrent and readily spe-cifiable state of the accompanying body. Readily specifiable certainly; the bodily state is specifiable simply as the state accompanying a mind that is in that mental state. But then we can settle for the bodily states outright, bypassing the mental states in which I speci-fied them. We can just reinterpret the mentalistic terms as denoting those correlated bodily states, and who is to know the difference?
>
> (*TT*, pp. 18f.)

The idea that minds can be eliminated or explicated in this almost trivial way persists through Quine's mature work. (Cf. *FSS*, p. 85, where Quine speaks of "[e]ffortless monism ... form without substance".)

Should we take this treatment of minds as arguing for the apparently quite drastic conclusion that there are no minds? Or merely as telling us what minds really are? Is Quine, in short, *eliminating* minds or merely *explicating* them? Early and late Quine claims that "[t]he option ... is unreal" (*WO*, p. 265), "[t]here is no difference" (*FSS*, p. 86). (See also the end of the third section of Chapter 9, above.) The important thing is that we do not need to accept the existence of minds, and states of minds, in addition to bodies and states of bodies. Quine takes the availability of the reinterpretation to establish the truth of physicalism, understood as an ontological doctrine.

Quine does not claim that this extremely brief disposal of the mind–body problem is an important innovation. In *Word and Object* he says that it "adds ... nothing to what others have said".[7] Later he comes to speak of it as based on a "triviality" (*FSS*, p. 85). This later view fits well with the general downplaying of ontology which we saw in the previous section. It also suggests that if physicalism is to be an interesting doctrine we cannot think of it purely in ontological terms. The only alternative, given Quine's canonical notation, is to think of physicalism as constraining the vocabulary we employ to talk about the objects we quantify over. This is, indeed, the conclusion that Quine comes to. In "Facts of the Matter", after discussing the idea of dispensing with physical objects in favour of an ontology of abstract objects only, he comments: "The principle of physicalism must thereupon be formulated by reference not to physical objects but to physical vocabulary". (P. 165.)

How, then, are we to understand physicalism? Quine's favoured formulation is that there is no difference without a physical difference or that "nothing happens in the world ... without some redistribution of microphysical states" (review of Goodman, *TT*, p. 98). We can phrase this as a restriction on the vocabulary of our theory: a predicate is only acceptable if the difference between the situation in which it holds of a given object at a given time and the situation in which it does not is a *physical* difference.

What are the implications of this view? Quine maintains that it does not commit him to any strong form of reductionism:

> It is not a reductionist doctrine of the sort sometimes imagined. It is not a utopian dream of our being able to specify all mental events in physiological or microbiological terms. It is not a claim that such correlations even exist, in general, to be discovered; the groupings of events in mentalistic terms need not stand in any systematic relation to biological groupings.
>
> (FM, p. 163)

312

The reductionist doctrine which Quine does not embrace would imply that there is a particular kind of physical event that occurs in each person (presumably in his or her brain) every time he or she begins thinking about Vienna, say. We could then translate our mentalistic utterances by speaking about the physical event instead of the mental event. But that view is not what Quine is asserting. His is a "nonreductive, nontranslational" form of physicalism; his claim "is not that everything worth saying can be translated into the technical vocabulary of physics; not even that all good science can be translated into that vocabulary." (Review of Goodman, *TT*, p. 98.)

Quine does not even assert that for a particular person who thinks about Vienna on a number of different occasions the same kind of event occurs in his or her brain each time. His claim is merely that the particular mental event—Hylton's thinking about Vienna at 9:06 a.m., 7 February 2006, say—can be identified with some particular physical event, presumably taking place in Hylton's brain at the same time. It is the doctrine sometimes known as token-token identity of the mental and the physical, because it implies merely that each token—each particular mental event, say—can be identified with a physical event; this is opposed to what is called type-type identity, which would require that a given *type* of mental event (thinking about Vienna, say) should be identifiable with a given type of physical event (some particular pattern of firing of neurons, say). The doctrine is also widely known as anomalous monism.[8] (As we shall see in the next chapter, Quine thinks that the stronger reductionist programme may be plausible for some sorts of mental states—sensations, for example; but nothing crucial for him turns on this point. What is crucial is that he does not think that it is plausible for all mental events.)

Quine clearly holds that his nonreductive physicalism is an important and underestimated doctrine: "Most of us nowadays are so ready to agree to this principle that we fail to sense its magnitude". (FM, p. 163.) Why does Quine hold the principle to be so important? He thinks that the principle "accords physics its rightful place as the basic natural science" (ibid.):

> Why ... this special deference to physics? ... The answer is ... this: nothing happens in the world, not the flutter of an eyelid, not the flicker of a thought, without some redistribution of microphysical states. ... If the physicist suspected that there was any event that did not consist in the redistribution of the elementary states allowed for in his physical theory, he would seek a way of supplementing his theory. Full coverage in this sense is the very business of physics, and only of physics.
>
> (review of Goodman, *TT*, p. 98)

313

Psychology investigates a very limited range of phenomena, biology a wider but still limited range. It is, on Quine's account, physics and physics alone that seeks to bring every event under universal and exceptionless laws: "Physics investigates the essential nature of the world, and biology describes a local bump. Psychology, human psychology, describes a bump on the bump". (Review of Smart, *TT*, p. 93.) For this reason, physics promises the fundamental explanation for all phenomena: "Casual explanations of psychology are to be sought in physiology, of physiology in biology, of biology in chemistry, and of chemistry in physics—in the elementary physical states". (FM, p. 169.)

Quine thus draws strong conclusions from physicalism. This may seem surprising, for the most obvious difficulty that the doctrine faces is that it seems to be in danger of collapsing into triviality. The principle is that there is no difference without a physical difference, but what counts as a *physical* difference? We can hardly say that a difference counts as physical if it is stated in terms that *current* physics takes as fundamental; that would seem, quite unrealistically, to rule out fundamental changes in physics. Quine accepts that developments within physics itself may change our views as to what counts as a fundamental physical predicate: "The physical-state predicates are the predicates of some specific lexicon, which I have only just begun to imagine and which the physicists themselves are not ready to enumerate with complete conviction". (FM, p. 166.) Indeed he sees finding that lexicon—coming up with a complete list of the fundamental predicates of physics—as a large part of the task of physics, not as something which can be assumed to be complete, at least not until fundamental physics itself is complete. But then what answer can we make to the mentalist who insists that what Quine would think of as a mentalistic predicate, such as "understands", should be included among the physical predicates? If we accept the mentalist's claim, physicalism becomes completely vacuous; without a conception of the physical, however, how are we to block the mentalist's move?

Quine says at one point that the incompleteness of the fundamental lexicon of physics gives him "no choice but to leave my formulation of physicalism incomplete" (FM, p. 162). An incomplete formulation of physicalism, however, need not be trivial or empty. While we have no final theory of fundamental physics we have every reason to think that the theory which we do have is a good start in that direction, and that a final theory would be continuous with what we have. In particular, we have reason to think that it will not accept as fundamental anything that looks like a mentalistic term. This claim is not the result of an a priori view about what constitutes physics. It is, rather, the result of reflection on our current physics, the extent to which it is successful, what sorts of developments might contribute to its further success, and so on.

What if wholly unexpected phenomena should occur, and for that reason our physics were not to develop along lines that currently seem plausible? Quine imagines such an occurrence, and comments as follows:

> If telepathic effects were established beyond peradventure and they were clearly inexplicable on the basis of the present catalogue of microphysical states, it would still not devolve upon the psychologist to supplement physics with an irreducibly psychological annex. It would devolve upon the physicist to go back to the drawing board and have another try at full coverage, which is his business.
>
> (H&S, pp. 430f.)

In rejecting the idea of "an irreducibly psychological annex" Quine is insisting that physics must have a certain degree of unity and coherence. In a slightly different context he says that mentalistic predicates do not "interlock productively with the self-sufficient concepts and causal laws of natural science." (PT, 72); this gives some idea of what he is insisting upon. We cannot rule out the possibility that the physics which we currently have will require additions which are quite different from anything which we can, at the moment, envisage. On the other hand, we do have a theory which is to some extent coherent and unified. The unity and coherence are easy to overstate, but clearly they surpass anything that would result if we simply added some mentalistic terms to current physics, along with some supposed truths phrased using those terms. What counts as a "physical difference" should thus be understood, somewhat vaguely, in terms of the predicates of a theory which is recognizably continuous with current physics and which has (at least) the sort of coherence and unity displayed by that subject.

There is an assumption here, namely that there is an adequate theory, of the kind just indicated, to be had. If this should turn out not to be so then Quine's physicalism would be false—or perhaps it could not even be stated, for lack of a clear sense of the term "physical". Those who think that philosophy must be a priori will insist that Quine is here making an empirical assumption, and that this is a decisive objection to his physicalism. Quine would be untroubled; indeed the point provides a good illustration of his general view of the relation of philosophy to empirical science. From his point of view it is no objection to a philosophical doctrine that it makes an empirical assumption. And in this case he certainly thinks that the assumption is overwhelmingly plausible, given the physics that we do in fact have. He holds, that is to say, that we have every reason to think that a

fully adequate physics can be found, a theory which is a natural development of our current theory and recognizably continuous with it. His physicalism is predicated on that substantive, if very plausible, claim.

Quine's physicalism is: no difference without a physical difference. To see
how this principle could be non-trivial, imagine someone who rejects the
indeterminacy of reference. Such a view might, of course, be based on the
idea that there must be some physical state—the speaker's dispositions, or
brain-state, or what have you—which, if we knew it, would settle whether
the native is referring to rabbits or to rabbithood, say. (Recall that dispositions, on Quine's account, are indeed physical states.) But let us imagine a
different sort of opponent of Quine, who accepts that there is no physical
fact which, if known, would settle what the speaker is referring to but who
insists that there is, nonetheless, a fact of the matter about the speaker's
reference. Quine's opponent insists, perhaps, that there are *semantic* facts,
which are wholly independent of physical facts. This is just the sort of
position that Quine's physicalism rules out. If there is a difference between
referring to rabbits and referring to rabbithood, then there must be a physical difference between the two events. If there is no physical difference
then there is no difference at all—and so no fact of the matter as to whether
the speaker is referring to rabbits or referring to rabbithood.

Quine's opponent can, of course, claim that this example refutes physicalism—that the (alleged) difference between the two imagined situations *is*
a difference without a physical difference. Does the example refute physicalism, or does physicalism show that the difference alleged in the example is
not really a difference at all? It perhaps speaks for physicalism that the
alleged event of the speaker's determinately meaning rabbits rather than
determinately meaning rabbithood is not one for which we have, or could
have, any kind of evidence. Anything which could count as evidence must
be a physical event. (Only if an observer's sensory nerves are stimulated does
he or she have evidence; only physical events will result in the stimulation
of nerves.) So if there is no physical difference between the two allegedly
different situations then there can be no evidence as to which one obtains.
The insistence that there are nevertheless two genuinely different situations,
one of which obtains to the exclusion of the other, is sustained only by the
dogmatic view that our words refer determinately, even in cases where there
can be no evidence which shows what they refer to. Is Quine's position
equally dogmatic? He would insist that the complete lack of evidence is all
that we need to insist that we should not postulate a category of facts—
otherwise epistemological anarchy reigns. And we should note that his
position is not as drastic as one might suppose. It does not exclude "the

flicker of a thought". That is an event for which we might have evidence; so, Quine would claim, even though the event is not described in physical terms it must consist in underlying physical events.

The example of the imagined dispute shows how Quine's physicalism clarifies his behaviourism. (If, indeed, "behaviourism" is the correct word for his position; see Chapter 4, section IV, above.) Where we have a behavioural difference, even a difference in behavioural dispositions, then we can be sure of an underlying physical difference, and so we can be sure that there is a substantive question. Suppose, to take another case, we have no decisive evidence as to whether A believes that p in a particular case. Can we nevertheless insist that there is a fact of the matter, could we but know it? Clearly we can do so if we can say in behavioural terms what A's having that belief consists in—if we can specify a behavioural disposition which would count as evidence on one side or the other. (Regardless of whether we have or can obtain evidence for the claim that A has any of those dispositions.) But what if it is certain that A has no dispositions which would settle the question? In that case, Quine would say that there simply is no fact of the matter about A's believing p. The point will hold for mental states quite generally. Where we can specify some physical occurrence which would be evidence for the alleged event, we can be sure that there is a genuine event under discussion; where alleged mental events are in question, the relevant physical occurrence will presumably be a matter of dispositions to behaviour. It is not that the mental event can be reduced to such dispositions. Rather, the mental event's being connected to dispositions, or other physical facts, shows that there is a genuine difference between its occurring and its not occurring, and hence that our talk of such an event is not wholly empty:

> Mental states and events do not reduce to behaviour, nor are they explained by behaviour. They are explained by neurology, when they are explained. *But their behavioural adjuncts serve to specify them objectively. When we talk of mental states or events subject to behavioural criteria, we can rest assured that we are not just bandying words; there is a physical fact of the matter, a fact ultimately of elementary physical states.*
> (FM, p. 167; emphasis added)

IV Realism

As we saw in section III of Chapter 1, Quine's realism is underpinned by his naturalism. This latter doctrine is "that it is within science itself, and not in some prior philosophy, that reality is to be identified and described" (*TT*, p. 21); Quine abandons any idea of "a foundation for scientific certainty firmer than scientific method itself" (*PT*, p. 19). One implication of this is that if an entity is assumed by our science, then there is no standard of reality to which we can appeal to justify the idea that it is not, after all, *real*. What counts as "our science" here are the well established all-things-considered claims of science in the broad sense; it may be difficult to say exactly which claims qualify, but this is a difficulty internal to science, to be solved by further application of scientific method, not by extra-scientific means. Given this understanding of "science", there is simply no standpoint from which we can judge that the entities accepted by our science are unreal. This, I take it, is why Quine insists that his view is "robust realism" (*TT*, p. 21).

Quine's reflections on epistemology do not in any way threaten his realism, or its underlying rationale. Those reflections give a privileged position to stimulations of our sensory nerves, as being the only source of "our information about the world" (*PT*, p. 19). But this privileged epistemological position does not translate into a privileged ontological position; sensory stimulations have no greater claim to reality than any entities accepted by well confirmed parts of our science. The reason is that Quine's epistemological claims are claims *within* our ongoing science, our overall theory of the world. They do not stand outside that theory and attempt to judge it from an independent perspective. (The point of Quine's naturalism, it might be said, is that there is no such perspective.) There is no distinctively philosophical standpoint; the philosopher's reflections on our science are part of that science.

Quine's epistemology thus takes our science for granted; it does not occupy a distinct position from which the claims of science might be called into question. This point requires emphasis, because if we do not take it into account we might interpret some of Quine's remarks as undermining realism. Thus he often speaks of the objects that we accept as "posits". And at the opening of "Things and Their Place in Theories" he says: "Our talk of external things, our very notion of things, is *just a conceptual apparatus* that helps us to foresee and control the triggering of our sensory receptors" (TPT, *TT*, p. 1; emphasis added). But these epistemological remarks are made from within our ongoing theory of the world. They presuppose the reality of the world that our science tells us about, and cannot threaten it. The only way in which epistemology might undermine science, for Quine, is if it showed that our claims to scientific knowledge are dubious by the standards of our science itself—that our science conflicts with our claims to know it.

This is the form of scepticism which Quine takes seriously and addresses; see section II of Chapter 4, above.

Even if one accepts the argument of the previous three paragraphs, one may still think that Quine's realism is threatened either by the indeterminacy of reference, discussed in Chapter 8, above, or by the underdetermination of theory by evidence, discussed in Chapter 7, above. Quine, however, does not think so; his reasons are the subject of the rest of this section.

We begin with the indeterminacy of reference; the idea that this doctrine poses a threat to realism can be fairly easily disposed of. Indeterminacy of reference asserts that there is no fact of the matter as to what our words refer to. How can Quine insist that he is a realist about electrons and quarks, say, when the theory which deals with such matters can be interpreted as dealing with quite different things, entities undreamt of by our science?

The distinction between indeterminacy of reference and ontological reduction is important here. (See the end of the second section of Chapter 8, above.) The latter is a change in theory, undertaken for the usual theoretical reasons, which involves a change of ontology. We can, for example, use an ontology which contains just sets instead of sets and numbers. If we accept the reduction, that means that we are not realists *about numbers* (except insofar as we identify numbers with sets), but it does not threaten realism more generally. It changes which objects we are committed to but it does not change the nature of the commitment: we are committed to the reality of those objects which must be in the range of our quantifiers for our theory to be true. Hyper-Pythagoreanism, discussed in a previous section of this chapter, is a proposal for ontological reduction, and thus for a change in theory. Quine does not in the end accept that this is a worthwhile change. If he had accepted it he would have rejected realism *about physical objects* (except insofar as they are identified with sets) but, again, this is not a rejection of realism more generally, not a rejection of realism *tout court*.

The proxy functions used to show the indeterminacy of reference, by contrast, are functions *within* our present ontology. They do not take us from familiar objects to objects wholly alien to our ontology. They take us, rather, from familiar objects to objects which are less familiar but still part of our ontology. Given set-theory, the space-time complement of the family dog is, presumably, already in our ontology; it is something which we are already committed to accepting as real. Similarly, even if I, perversely, translate you as referring to space-time complements, I will still attribute to you an ontology which includes the ordinary objects as well as their space-time complements. It may, on my account, be the space-time complements which you explicitly talk about, but still the ordinary objects must be in your ontology. You accept set-theory, presumably, and you accept that there are space-time points, so you accept the space-time complements of the things you talk about. But then on my perverse translation you must accept ordinary things, for these are simply the space-time complements of the space-time complements which I translate you as talking about. (The complement of the complement is the thing itself.)

Quine's proxy functions map ordinary entities within our ontology onto (usually) more exotic counterparts—space-time complements, or sets of time-slices, or what have you—which are also within our ontology. Following the functions thus does not add entities to our ontology or subtract entities from it. Systematically reconstruing theory using such functions would alter our account of what is referred to by each sentence, but it would not alter our overall ontology—our account of what there is to be referred to. Nor would it give us any reason to take a less realistic attitude towards the entities, ordinary and otherwise, in our ontology.

The idea that underdetermination of theory by evidence might threaten realism is far more plausible. Here it is truth that is at stake, not just reference. (The indeterminacy of reference, by contrast, does not question the truth of any sentence of our theory; it merely says that alternative accounts of what the terms in each sentence refer to are available.) If there are alternative theories, just as good as ours, why should we accept that ours is the true one? If the truth of our theory is thus cast in doubt, so too is the reality of the objects in our ontology. But does Quine in fact hold that the truth of our theory is cast in doubt by underdetermination? I shall argue that he does not. The opposite idea, however, may be encouraged by the fact that Quine vacillates in the conclusion that he draws from underdetermination; we shall spend a couple of paragraphs setting out the alternatives, and his final position.

If we have two global theories which are empirically equivalent, and equally good on other grounds, should we count both of them as true? This Quine comes to call the *ecumenical* attitude. Or should we insist that in spite of their empirical equivalence we should count only one as true? The view that we should he comes to call, in similar spirit, the *sectarian* attitude. His vacillation is nicely illustrated by two versions of a single essay. In the first version of "Empirical Content", published in the first printing of *Theories and Things*, he invites us to suppose that we have two theories which cannot be reconciled by reconstruing the terms of one—i.e. that there is no translation between them which justifies us to treat them as two different ways of saying the same thing. We are also to suppose that they are empirically equivalent (although we might not know it) and that the observation categoricals implied by each theory are true (though, again, we would not know

320

it). He comments: "Nothing more, surely, can be required for the truth of either theory formulation. Are they both true? I say yes." (*TT*, p. 29.)

In a later version of the same essay, prompted by comments by Roger Gibson, he adopts a sectarian attitude. (See Gibson, "Translation, Physics, and Facts of the Matter".) In a later printing of *Theories and Things*, the remark just quoted is replaced by this one:[9]

> we should indeed recognize the two as equally well *warranted*. We might even oscillate between them, for the sake of a richer perspective on nature. But we should still limit the ascription of truth to whichever theory formulation we are entertaining at the time, for there is no wider frame of reference.

The theory which rivals our own contains some terms not translatable into the terms of our theory, otherwise the difference between them can be treated as trivial. (They are no more genuine rivals than physics formulated in English is a genuine rival of physics formulated in Japanese; see Chapter 7, section III, above.) But then if we accept both theories as true we are accepting redundancies:

> The sentences [of the rival theory] containing them [i.e. the untranslatable terms] constitute a gratuitous annex to the original theory, since the whole combination is still equivalent to the original theory. It is as if some scientifically undigested terms of metaphysics or religion, say "essence" or "grace" or "Nirvana", were admitted into science along with all their pertinent doctrine, and tolerated on the grounds merely that they contravene no observations. It would be an abandonment of the scientist's quest for economy and of the empiricist's standard of meaningfulness.
>
> (reply to Gibson, H&S, p. 157)

Given this attitude, it is unsurprising that in this work he comes out unequivocally in favour of the sectarian position. Sectarianism certainly seems to fit better than does ecumenism with his maintaining that his view is "robust realism" (TPT, *TT*, p. 21).

In *Pursuit of Truth*, written some years later than any of the works quoted in the previous paragraph, Quine is less sharply opposed to the ecumenical position, and ends up suggesting that there is no genuine difference between the two positions:

> What is to be gained [from the ecumenical position] is not evident, apart from the satisfaction of conferring the cachet of truth

evenhandedly. The sectarian is no less capable than the ecumenist of appreciating the equal evidential claims of the two rival theories of the world. He can still be evenhanded with the cachet of warrantedness, if not of truth. Moreover he is as free as the ecumenist to oscillate between the two theories for the sake of added perspective from which to triangulate on problems.

(p. 100)

The only real difference seems to be whether we choose to apply the word "true" to the rival theory or withhold it; no consequences seem to follow from our making one choice rather than the other. And as for which choice is correct, Quine suggests that the idea of correctness may simply not apply here. The next paragraph of the book starts like this:

The fantasy of irresolubly rival systems of the world is a thought experiment out beyond where linguistic usage has been crystallized by use. No wonder the cosmic question whether to call two such world systems true should simmer down, bathetically, to a question of words.

(pp. 100f.)

He may, however, have reverted to the idea that there is a sharp difference, and that sectarianism is clearly to be preferred. In a yet later work, he speaks of himself as "settled into the sectarian [attitude]".[10]

The last two paragraphs are a very brief discussion of Quine's shifting views on the implications of underdetermination. (For a more discursive account, see Bergström, "Underdetermination of Physical Theory" and works cited there.) The reason for our brevity is that our primary concern in this section is realism, and at no point do Quine's views about underdetermination cast his realism in doubt; at no point does he suggest that our theory might be other than flat-out true. Of course we might find an empirically equivalent rival to our theory which was clearly superior in is simplicity and clarity. In that case we would simply adopt the new theory. Our theory is not an object which is fixed over time; at any given time, "our theory" is simply the best that we have at that time, but it will evolve as times change. If we find a superior one, we adopt it. This is scientific progress, whether the superiority of the new theory is a matter of better predictions or of other virtues. At any given time we accept the best theory that we have as true, and we are realists about the entities posited by that theory.

To revert to our theme: Quine's responses to underdetermination do not, by his lights, do anything to cast the truth of our theory in doubt; the question for him is only whether an empirically equivalent rival should also be counted as true. Given his general views, this is exactly what we should expect. Our epistemology is part of our science; it does not pronounce on it from an independent standpoint. We define empirical equivalence in terms of the implication of observation categoricals because these latter are made up of observation sentences, which are in turn more or less directly answerable to stimulations of our sensory nerves, and all of our information about the world comes from such stimulations. But these epistemological claims, and the definition of empirical equivalence which is based on them, presuppose a theory of physical and abstract objects, including sensory nerves. It is the same naturalistic point as in the first two paragraphs of this section. Our epistemology is based on our theory of the world, and cannot cast it in doubt. (Except, as we saw, by arguing that our science is self-refuting—the kind of scepticism we discussed in section II of Chapter 4, above.)

Quine's realism, as we have said, is based on his naturalism. Our epistemology does not undermine our science, since epistemology is based on science—is part of it, indeed—and presupposes it at every turn. This point applies, in particular, to underdetermination. Taking our own theory for granted as true, we discover that there is or may be another, just as good, which has the same empirical consequences. Then there are decisions to be made—we have to say whether both would count as true, or only ours, or whether the question is too ill defined to answer. But one thing we are not going to say is that our own theory is, after all, not true, for to say that would be to undermine the considerations that led us to under-determination in the first place. For Quine, underdetermination thus does not threaten the idea that our theory should be counted as fully true. It does raise the question whether we are going to count some other theory as *also* being true, but neither answer to that question threatens the truth of our theory. Since the truth of our theory is not cast in doubt neither, in Quine's view, is the reality of the objects posited by that theory.

13

MINDS, BELIEFS, AND MODALITY

The last three chapters have explored conditions which Quine envisages fully regimented theory as meeting. That theory, as we saw, is to be made up of context-independent sentences set in the framework of first-order logic; it is thus to be extensional; it is to have an ontology of physical objects and sets; and its predicates are to meet the standards of physicalism. Why should we be concerned with the idea of regimenting our theory so that it fulfils these conditions? The short answer is that doing so, or seeing how we could do so, contributes to the clarity, the simplicity, and the explicitness of that theory. This, as we have emphasized, is the justification for the conditions. They are not imposed a priori. Neither does Quine aim to capture every aspect of ordinary language. (He does not even think that this task is a sensible one, since he does not think that there is sufficient definiteness implicit in our ordinary discourse.) Nor is he in the business of replacing ordinary language with a modified or cleaned-up version. He is not urging any changes on the language as it is spoken, either in ordinary life or in the laboratory. His concern is theoretical: how are we best to understand our theory, to make it explicit, to see what it commits us to? And how should our theory as a whole be understood so as to maximize its simplicity, clarity, and coherence?

Can what we take to be our serious and systematic knowledge be regimented so as to meet the conditions which Quine envisages? The area of knowledge which seems least likely to fit is that which concerns the human mind. Along with it will go large portions of our knowledge of human history, for that subject is full of claims about what such-and-such a person believed, or feared, or intended by an action, and so on. Sociology and the other social sciences include similar claims, as does the study of human culture and literature and all of what are generally called "the humanities". The natural sciences, by contrast, seem much more likely to fit within

Quinean constraints, and Quine more or less takes it for granted that they can, without significant difficulties of principle, be regimented so as to do so. This idea is controversial but Quine does not, for the most part, engage in these controversies, and we shall follow him in this. The only major exceptions are modality and causality, which we shall discuss in the last two sections.

The main subject of this chapter, then, is how Quine thinks our knowledge of the human mind can best be clarified and regimented so as to meet the conditions which we have examined. Most of Quine's efforts here deal with what he, following Russell, calls *propositional attitudes* (see Russell, *Inquiry into Meaning and Truth*, p. 18). We shall discuss the reason for this concentration in the first section. Propositional attitudes are mental states which can be attributed to someone using a "that"-clause, such as belief. One believes or thinks *that* it will not rain on the day of the picnic, or fears that it will, or hopes that it won't, or doubts that the sun will shine, and so on. As we shall see, Quine takes it that a very wide range of ascriptions of mental states can be fitted into this category.

An advocate of propositions can think of each of the propositional attitude ascriptions in the way the name suggests: as ascribing an attitude towards a proposition. Someone can be said to believe that a given proposition is true, or hope that it is true, or wonder whether it is true, and so on. This is perhaps a natural way to understand such expressions; it is, in any case, quite straightforward, as long as we accept that there are propositions. Quine, of course, does not accept that, so he needs to put forward another way of understanding statements of propositional attitude.

Further complicating the issue of propositional attitude ascriptions is the fact that they appear to be of two distinct kinds, *de re* and *de dicto*. Until 1968 Quine accorded the two kinds of ascription equal status. After that time, however, his views change, and he excludes ascriptions of *de re* attitudes from regimented theory. We shall briefly indicate the nature of the distinction in the first section, below; the fifth section will go into details, discussing Quine's early treatment of *de re* propositional attitudes and his later reasons for excluding them. Our main focus, however will be on the *de dicto* attitudes. Ascriptions of *de dicto* attitudes may seem to violate both the syntactic and the ontological constraints which Quine seeks to impose on regimented theory; the second section will deal with Quine's way of fitting those ascriptions within the constraints. This issue is relatively straightforward, at least compared with the question of the semantics of attitude ascriptions, and the question whether they should be thought of as genuine fact-stating discourse. Those matters occupy the third and fourth sections, respectively. The sixth section will deal with modality, i.e. with the idea that some truths are *necessarily* true, and that a sentence may be *possibly* true, even if it is in fact false. The seventh section, finally, will deal with the related issues of causality and natural necessity.

I The mind and the attitudes

Quine devotes far more time to the discussion of statements of propositional attitude than he does to statements about other aspects of our mental lives. We can distinguish four reasons for this concentration. One, which Quine does not state but which may be operating in the background, is that Quine is simply more concerned with our beliefs and our questions than he is with our emotions and our passions. Human knowledge is his primary concern, and on Quine's account knowledge is itself a propositional attitude, although of a peculiar kind, since one cannot know that so-and-so unless so-and-so is indeed the case.

Another reason for Quine's concern with propositional attitudes is that he holds that they are far more inclusive than might at first appear. Our saying that Tom wants some chocolate, for example, can be regimented in the form: Tom wants it to be the case that Tom has some chocolate. Similarly with trying: "Tom is trying to understand Quine" becomes "Tom is trying to make it the case [or: to bring it about] that Tom understands Quine". Looking for, hunting, intending, avoiding, wishing, fearing, dreading are all subject to the same sort of treatment. Whenever the ascription of a mental state can be phrased using a "that"-clause, Quine will treat it as the ascription of a propositional attitude. A very wide range of mental phenomena can thus be brought under the heading "propositional attitudes".

A third reason for Quine's concentration on propositional attitude ascriptions is that they are problematic because they appear, at least, to give rise to violations of extensionality: one may think that it will rain on Friday while also thinking that it will be sunny on the day of the picnic because one is under the mistaken impression that the picnic is on Saturday, whereas in fact it is scheduled for Friday. Propositional attitude ascriptions thus threaten to violate extensionality; some way of defusing the threat must be found before such attributions can be accepted as part of regimented theory. No such threat appears to arise from the attribution of sensations. Saying that a person is feeling pain or seeing red or tasting chocolate seems no less extensional than saying that he has dark hair or weighs 200 pounds.

An incidental matter can now be taken care of, before turning to the last of our four reasons. The mention of the *prima facie* failure of extensionality for the propositional attitudes enables us to give a preliminary explanation of the distinction between the *de dicto* attitudes and the (supposed) *de re* attitudes. To attribute a belief *de re* is to ascribe to someone a belief about an object however that object is described. If we attribute to Tom the *de re* belief that Cicero denounced Catiline then we must equally attribute to him the *de re* belief that Tully denounced Catiline, since Cicero and Tully are in fact one and the same person. We may phrase it by saying, as Quine does at one stage, that Tom believes *of* Cicero—that is, of Marcus Tullius Cicero, of the man however described—that he denounced Catiline. In the fifth section we shall enlarge on the issue of the *de re* attitudes, both their superficial plausibility and their more fundamental drawbacks.

Our fourth and final reason for Quine's focus on propositional attitudes, rather than sensations and other mental states, is that he thinks that the latter can be treated as physical phenomena, along more or less straightforward lines. Quine takes pain as an example, and argues that we can simply identify it with its neural mechanism (*FSS*, p. 86). It may turn out that there is more than one mechanism which gives rise to a given sensation but this, for Quine, is no obstacle: "we can take their alternation" (ibid.). We can simply regiment our talk of pain as talk of the neural mechanism or mechanisms:

> Whatever can be said about pain can be so rephrased as to be said about its mechanism. Where "*Fx*" means that *x* is a dull ache, we reinterpret *x* as the neural mechanism and then reinterpret "*Fx*" compensatorily as "the pain *that* x *produces* is a dull ache".
>
> (ibid.; emphasis in the original)

What if the neural mechanism for pain, say, varies from person to person? In that case, Quine says, the physicalist "might just say that pain is a state of an individual's nerves that tends to be manifested by writhing and wincing and to be caused by strains, bruises, lesions, and the like." (Ibid.)

There are ways in which talk of neural states does not fit our ordinary talk of pain, and other sensations. Each of us has introspective knowledge of his or her own pains; it sounds odd, at best, to say that one can have introspective knowledge of the states of one's own brain, especially as most of us have no idea what the relevant states are. But this is the kind of oddity that Quine readily tolerates. Again, our knowledge of our own pain is usually thought of as infallible, whereas even the neurophysiologist presumably does not have infallible knowledge of her own brain states. (Neurophysiology is, after all, no less fallible than the rest of science.) Again, however, Quine would be undeterred by the failure of his version of the attribution of

327

sensation to correspond to ordinary language. He thus holds that we can identify sensations with neural states and deal with them in regimented theory in that way. (This is not, of course, to say that he thinks that our ordinary talk of pain *means the same as* talk of neural states. To worry about that, however, is to misconstrue the point of regimentation.)

Quine makes some brief remarks about emotions which suggest that he more or less identifies them with sensations. (See *FSS*, p. 86.) This is surely too simple a view of emotions. But perhaps we can reasonably think of them as made up of propositional attitudes together with sensations and patterns of action. (See, for example, Kenny, *Action, Emotion and Will*.) In that case they will not require separate treatment; once treatments of sensations and of propositional attitudes are in place they can, presumably, be combined and extended so as to encompass emotions. It is propositional attitudes that are the difficult case, from Quine's point of view.

Quine has no hope that attributions of propositional attitudes can be understood as attributions of neural states. A given case of a person being in a propositional attitude is a case of her being in a particular neurophysiological state. To use an example of Quine's: if at a certain moment I think about Fermat's Last Theorem then that particular act of thought can be identified with my being in whatever physical state I am in at that moment. (This is a consequence of the ontological aspect of Quine's physicalism, which he takes to be a more or less trivial doctrine. See Chapter 12, section III, above.) Unlike the case of sensations, however, we have no reason to think that the same type of neurophysiological event takes place in me on two occasions on which I think about the theorem—still less that there is any significant cross-person similarity here. Nor is it plausible to think that we can identify the relevant neurophysiological event by saying that it is that state responsible for the characteristic behaviour that goes with thinking about Fermat's Last Theorem; it is not plausible to think that there is any such characteristic behaviour. This last point indicates a sense of the word "behaviourism" in which Quine is not a behaviourist: he does not think that we can give translations of all mentalistic predicates in behavioural terms, any more than he thinks we can do so in physiological terms.

Quine makes no attempt to reduce a predicate such as "thinking about Fermat's Last Theorem" either to neurophysiology or to behaviour. It is here, in the case of propositional attitudes, that we see the full force of the fact that his is a "non-reductive, non-translational" sort of physicalism (see his review of Goodman, *TT*, p. 98, discussed above, pp. 312–13) and of his anomalous monism:

The general predicate "thinking about Fermat's Last Theorem" . . . is irreducibly mentalistic. It still denotes physical objects in its intermittent way (usually mathematicians), and it has its place in our meaningful physicalistic language. The point of anomalous monism is just that our mentalistic predicate imposes on bodily states and events a grouping that cannot be defined in the special vocabulary of physiology. Each of the individual states and events is physiologically describable, we presume, given all pertinent information.

(FSS, pp. 87f.)

If we cannot analyse attributions of propositional attitudes as attributions of physiological states (or patterns of behaviour) then we have to give some other account of them; this account and some of its ramifications will occupy us in the next three sections.

II The *de dicto* attitudes: syntax and ontology

How are attributions of propositional attitude to be incorporated into regimented theory? We shall talk chiefly of belief, but the discussion is intended to apply quite generally. We cannot treat ascriptions of belief in what might seem to be the most straightforward possible manner. We take a sentence such as "The book is on the table" to assert a relation between the book and the table; we cannot treat "Tom believes that Cicero denounced Catiline" similarly, as asserting a relation between two objects, Tom and Cicero. The obstacle here, as already indicated, is the failure of extensionality. Tom may confidently assert that Cicero denounced Catiline; "Tully" is another name for Cicero; yet Tom, ignorant of this fact, may strenuously deny the sentence "Tully denounced Catiline". We might, of course, insist that he believes it anyway, since it can be obtained from a sentence he is willing to accept by replacing a term with a co-referential term. This step amounts to taking the belief ascription *de re*; Quine comes to think that such ascriptions have no place in regimented theory, as we shall see in the fifth section, below. In any case, we must surely accept that there is a place for *de dicto* ascriptions of belief, in which we are willing to accept that someone may believe that Cicero denounced Catiline while not believing that Tully denounced Catiline. (From this point on I shall ignore *de re* belief ascriptions until the fifth section.) So we must undertake some analysis of attributions of propositional attitudes if they are to fit into the extensional syntax of regimented theory.

If we construe propositional attitudes in the way the term suggests, as attitudes towards propositions, then extensionality is restored—but at a

329

price.[1] Our sentence about Tom is construed as a genuine relation between two objects; it is construed as a relation between Tom, on the one hand, and the proposition expressed by "Cicero denounced Catiline", on the other. Construed in this way, the assertion that Tom has that belief does not commit us to accepting that he also believes that Tully denounced Catiline: "Cicero" and "Tully" name the same man, but "Cicero denounced Catiline" and "Tully denounced Catiline" need not be taken as expressing the same proposition. If we take the two propositions to be distinct, we can represent Tom as believing the one but not the other. As in other cases, whether a given kind of idiom gives rise to a failure of extensionality depends on how we construe the idiom.

One idea which Quine is concerned to combat is that propositional attitudes are, indeed, attitudes towards propositions. He rejects this idea because, as we have already seen in some detail, he does not accept that there are propositions. (See Chapter 8, sixth section.) How then does he propose to construe statements of propositional attitude? The answer will be no surprise: an ascription of belief, say, is interpreted as stating a relation between a believer and a sentence.[2] Although unsurprising, this answer raises a number of questions and apparent difficulties; the rest of this section will be devoted to Quine's responses to these points.

To begin with: when Quine says that belief is a relation between a person and a sentence, what does he understand by a sentence? The answer is that he takes it as simply a linguistic object, a sequence of characters and spaces, or sounds, or gestures. Each particular mark or sound or gesture can be taken as a physical object or, better, as a set of the relevant physical objects. (These are simply tokens of inscriptions or utterances or movements, each made at a particular place and time. Thus we would identify the written letter "q", say, with the set of all actual inscriptions of that letter.) A sentence is then a sequence—an ordered set—of such sets. Quine recognizes that linguists often take a sentence not as a mere string of marks, but rather as the string together with a syntactic or semantic tree. He has no argument with linguists who wish to speak this way, but insists that for "philosophers or psychologists of language" that terminology would be misleading, since it "presupposes the very connections and distinctions that most concern them" (*FSS*, p. 94).

This answer immediately gives rise to another question. A sentence, as Quine construes it, is simply a linguistic object, a string of characters and spaces (or sounds, or gestures). How can such an object—the mere sequence of marks—be what is believed? How can a sentence, in this sense, be meaningful? The answer is that the sentence has a use, actual or potential, as part of a language. The idea of "potential use" is to be understood in terms of dispositions to use a sentence or to respond to uses of it: each of us has countless such dispositions, most of which will never be activated. The "mere marks" have their place in the fantastically complex network of interlocked dispositions which, taken together, make up the linguistic ability of speakers of the language. These dispositions relate sentences to occasions on which they would be used and also to other sentences, including observation sentences. Quine puts the point like this:

> There is a shortsighted but stubborn notion that a mere string of marks on paper cannot be true, false, doubted, or believed. Of course it can, because of conventions relating it to speech habits and because of neural mechanisms linking speech habits causally to mental activity.
>
> (FSS, p. 94)

The sentence, the marks or sounds, seem to be "mere"—seem to be, so to speak, dead—because we consider them apart from their use, and from the use of the language as a whole. (Cf. Wittgenstein, *Blue and Brown Books*, pp. 4f.)

Taking the object of a propositional attitude as a sentence, as simply the marks or sounds, is enough to block difficulties arising from the apparent non-extensionality of attributions of such attitudes. We make it explicit that when we say "Tom believes that Cicero denounced Catiline" we are ascribing to Tom an attitude towards the *sentence*, the string of letters and spaces, "Cicero denounced Catiline". We are saying of this sentence that Tom believes it (or, more idiomatically, believes it to be true). Propositional attitudes are thus assimilated to the well understood case of quotation; failure of extensionality is trivial, and can be removed by resorting to spelling. (See Chapter 11, section II above.)

According to Quine, then, the ascription of a propositional attitude asserts a relation between the person in the attitude and a sentence of a language. The relation here is complex and indirect. Take the case of belief. It is not that the believer has uttered the sentence, or even that he is inclined to utter the sentence under appropriate circumstances, or to assent to the sentence upon hearing it queried, or anything of that sort. To say that Aristotle believed that the Earth is round is not to attribute to Aristotle a disposition to utter or assent to the English sentence "The Earth is round". Presumably Aristotle had no dispositions with regard to any English sentences (except perhaps a disposition to look and act puzzled when hearing one uttered). Yet we certainly want to be able to attribute beliefs to Aristotle. What goes for Aristotle goes for the dog who—we say—thinks that I have a biscuit in my hand, or that I am about to throw a stick. The sentence is in the language of the one who ascribes the belief, not the language of the believer; if we accept the case of the dog, indeed, it is evident that the believer may not have a language at all.

Quine thus takes an attribution of a propositional attitude to assert a relation between a person and a sentence, i.e. a sequence of marks or sounds or gestures. That sequence must be taken as part of a language. So it might seem that the belief ascription must be relativized to language. Suppose that a given sequence of marks is a sentence of more than one language, with the two sentences clearly not equivalent by any reasonable criteria. (We can explain this last idea without invoking synonymy, or determinate translation, by saying: no plausible scheme of translation translates the one into the other.) If the ascription is not language-relative, it seems unclear what belief is then being attributed. But if we do relativize ascriptions to languages then we face another problem: the individuation of languages. And this problem is surely intractable. The obvious criterion—that two people speak the same language just in case they can speak fluently and otherwise interact successfully—fails for lack of transitivity. The inhabitants of each town along a coastline may be able to communicate with the inhabitants of the next town with complete success, but this does not imply that those in two distant towns on the coast will manage as well, or at all. Again, languages change over time; Chaucer's English is not ours. But readers in one decade can read the writing of the previous decade with no difficulty. So our "obvious criterion" cannot be taken as the criterion of identity between languages, because identity is transitive. No other plausible criterion of identity for languages readily suggests itself.

Quine evades this problem by relativizing ascriptions of propositional attitude not to the language but to the person. What is ascribed, strictly speaking, is belief (say) in a given sentence *in so-and-so's sense*. (See especially *WO*, p. 214.) In normal cases, no mention is made of this variable, and so-and-so is simply assumed to be the person who ascribes the attitude. I ascribe to Aristotle a belief in the sentence "The Earth is round", used as *I* would use it. It is *my* complex network of verbal dispositions which is relevant. What is ascribed to the believer is the belief that a certain sentence is true, where the sentence is taken as part of the language of the one who *ascribes* the propositional attitude, not the language of the one to whom it is ascribed. What is ascribed is an attitude towards a sentence, in the language of the ascriber.

Quine's analysis of the syntax of ascriptions of propositional attitudes is, evidently, motivated by ontological constraints as well as by syntactic ones.

(If we had propositions in our ontology then, as indicated, a rather different kind of analysis might seem natural.) The ontological constraints and the syntactic constraints work together. The resulting analysis conforms to Quine's ontology. The person to whom the attitude is ascribed is a physical object. What is ascribed is an attitude towards a sentence which, as we have emphasized, is a sequence of marks or sounds or gestures and thus an ordered set of sets of physical objects. To say that belief is belief in a proposition, by contrast, would require entities of a new type; Quine, as we have seen, thinks that we have every reason to reject such alleged entities.

Where does this ontological discussion leave our beliefs, our thoughts and fears, our hopes and dreams? The answer is not entirely straightforward. Each of my acts of thinking—my thinking about Fermat's Last Theorem at a particular time, say—is identified with my bodily state at that time; so it is accepted into our ontology. But my belief that the theorem is true cannot be treated in the same way, for it is, presumably, not something that exists or takes place at a particular time. (If I am convinced of the truth of the theorem then it is correct to count me among its adherents even when I am asleep.) We could identify my belief with my disposition to accept the sentences expressing the theorem. But this strategy would undermine much of the point of talking about beliefs at all. We want, for example, to be able to talk about shared beliefs. Clearly I may share beliefs with Aristotle even though there is no sentence that he and I are (timelessly) both disposed to assent to. The point here is that identifying beliefs with sentences, or with dispositions to assent to sentences, individuates beliefs exceedingly finely— too finely, perhaps, for them to be useful at all. An attempt to individuate beliefs less finely than sentences, but still finely enough to do what we want of them, would land us with propositions. Hence Quine does not accept that beliefs are objects at all.

On Quine's account, then, there are no beliefs. We can speak freely of a person as believing this or that, but we do not construe this as meaning that there is an object, a belief, which she has. This may seem to be a gross violation of our ordinary ways of talking, but in fact the matter is not so clear. In ordinary discourse we sometimes treat beliefs as objects and sometimes do not. In some contexts we speak of them as definite objects, which can be counted: I may say, for example, that while I accept much of a person's view there are two beliefs of his that I wish to challenge. In other contexts we do not: if I ask someone how many beliefs she holds about Quine, I shall most likely be taken as making a poor philosophical joke rather than asking a serious question. Reflection on this latter kind of case suggests that Quine's denial of propositions is not simply a constraint artificially imposed upon our account of belief, and the other attitudes. Accepting propositions, and thinking of belief as an attitude towards a proposition, would require us to accept that my silly question is a sensible one, which has in all cases a definite answer. That seems just as unnatural as Quine's view of belief; in many sorts of cases the question clearly is silly, and the idea that it has a definite answer is absurd.

Ordinary discourse is highly context-dependent and interest-relative. Sensitive as we are to the context and to the interests and assumptions of our audience, we have no trouble knowing when it is appropriate to talk of beliefs as if they were objects and when it is not. But this sort of variability and context-dependence is incompatible with the enterprise of regimentation, at least as Quine conceives it. Quine's method of regimenting has consequences which do not accord with ordinary usage. But so would any other scheme of regimentation. The enterprise, on his account, is inherently artificial; but so is the more general enterprise of science, of which it is a part.

III The *de dicto* attitudes: semantics

The upshot of the previous section is that Quine construes a statement of propositional attitude as an ascription of an attitude towards a *sentence*. In the usual case, the sentence is in the language of the ascriber. I ascribe to Aristotle a belief in the sentence—the string of marks—"The Earth is round". The worry about how a mere string of marks can be being the object of belief is deflected because this is not a *mere* string, it is a string of marks in my language, i.e. one which has a use, actual or potential—namely the use that I and other speakers of modern English give it, and the use that we would give it under any of countless circumstances. From a Quinean perspective, this view makes satisfactory sense of the syntax and the ontology of (*de dicto*) propositional attitudes. But this is by no means the end of what there is to say about them: "To have cleared away the ontology of the propositional attitudes is not to have made scientific sense of them". (*WO*, p. 216.) What remains to be done is to consider the sorts of bases on which ascriptions of propositional attitude are made, and the extent to which those ascriptions thus based make "scientific sense"; we may conveniently group these questions, and the issues to which they lead, under the vague heading "semantics".

Quine argues that the epistemological status of propositional attitude ascriptions is more problematic than that of our best cases of theorizing: "the underlying methodology of the idioms of propositional attitude contrasts markedly with the spirit of objective science at its most representative." (*WO*, p. 218.) To make out this claim, he contrasts direct quotation, where we simply repeat someone's words, with indirect quotation, where we seek rather to convey the gist of what he said, usually in other words. He finds direct quotation unproblematic: "When we quote a man's utterance directly we report it almost as we might a bird call. ... direct quotation merely reports the physical incident and leaves any implications to us." (WO, p. 219.) Indirect quotation, and ascriptions of propositional attitudes in general, are on Quine's account quite different:

> For the case of sentences generally ... surely there is nothing approaching a fixed standard of how far indirect quotation may deviate from the direct. Commonly the degree of allowable deviation depends on why we are quoting. It is a question of what traits of the quoted speaker's remarks we want to make something of; those are the traits that must be kept straight if our indirect quotation is to count as true. Similar remarks apply to sentences of belief and other propositional attitudes.
>
> (p. 218; footnote omitted)

In the face of difficulties of these sorts, how do we judge when to ascribe a propositional attitude?

> in indirect quotation we project ourselves into what, from his remarks and other indications, we imagine the speaker's state of mind to have been, and then we say what, in our language, is natural and relevant for us in the state of mind thus feigned. An indirect quotation we can usually expect to rate only as better or worse, more or less faithful, and we cannot even hope for a strict standard of more and less; what is involved is evaluation, relative to special purposes, of an essentially dramatic act. Correspondingly for the other propositional attitudes.
>
> (WO, p. 219)

He sums up the difficulty like this: "Casting our real selves ... in unreal roles, we do not generally know how much reality to hold constant" (WO, p. 219).

In some cases, doubt about the truth of an indirect quotation may arise simply because we do not know enough about the surrounding context and circumstances. But in others, Quine claims, even complete knowledge would not eliminate the uncertainty:

> Evidently we must recognize in indirect quotation and other idioms of propositional attitude a source of truth-value variation. ... It

will often happen also that there is just no saying whether to count an affirmation of propositional attitude as true or false, even given full knowledge of its circumstances and purposes.

(WO, p. 218)

The point here is not merely that we often lack evidence either way about the ascription of some propositional attitude; it is the stronger point that some such ascriptions are not answerable to evidence in any clear and decisive fashion.

In *Pursuit of Truth* Quine enlarges on the method by which we ascribe propositional attitudes, and connects this method with the earliest stages of language acquisition. Both require empathy. In the language-learning case the point was that for a child to learn, say, "It's raining" from an adult it is not enough that each of them perceives that it's raining; one of them, at least, must also perceive that the other perceives that it's raining. If the child is to learn this sentence as an observation sentence from the adult then one party or the other—and in practice, presumably, often both—must have the capacity to discriminate not only those occasions on which it is raining from those on which it is not but also those occasions on which the other party perceives that it is raining from those on which he or she does not. (See Chapter 5, above, especially section III.) This holds equally for the linguist engaged in radical translation. "Learning a language in the field and teaching it in the nursery are much the same at the level of observation sentences: a matter of perceiving that the subject is perceiving that *p*". (PT, pp. 62f.). As Quine puts it elsewhere: "We have an uncanny knack for empathizing another's perceptual situation, however ignorant of the physiological or optical mechanism of his perception". (B&G, p. 4.)

Invoking empathy here is not, by Quine's standards, explanatory; the explanation of our ability to perceive what others are perceiving is presumably an exceedingly complex neurophysiological matter. The point is not to explain the phenomenon but to get clear on just what it is. On Quine's account the sort of empathy required for learning language is the capacity to perceive that someone else is perceiving that *p*, for some cases in which *p* is an observation sentence. In his view, we could not learn language at all unless we had this sort of empathetic ability.

Cases of this sort are also the core cases of propositional attitude ascriptions, the cases in which the ascriptions are most definite and most soundly based, although we quickly get beyond them. The first step beyond, Quine suggests, is that we adapt the "perceives that *p*" idiom to non-observation sentences. How do we make such judgments? Quine considers the example "Tom perceives the train is late" and comments:

The evidence is not assembled deliberately. One empathizes, projecting oneself into Tom's situation and Tom's behavior pattern, and thereby finds that the sentence "The train is late" is what comes naturally. Such is the somewhat haphazard basis for saying that Tom perceives that the train is late. The basis becomes more conclusive if the observed behavior on Tom's part includes a statement of his own that the train is late.

(PT, p. 63)

Quine sees the ascription of other propositional attitudes as evolving from ascriptions of this kind. The ascription of belief, for example, differs from that of perception in various ways (see PT, p. 66) but the role of empathy, of projecting oneself into another's position, remains the same:

When we ascribe a belief in the idiom "x believes that p", our evidence is similar [to the case of ascribing perception] but usually more tenuous. We reflect on the believer's behaviour, verbal and otherwise, and what we know of his past, and conjecture that we in his place would feel prepared to assent, overtly or covertly, to the content clause.

(PT, p. 66)

The same holds when we consider other propositional attitudes, including indirect quotation:

Empathy figures in most ascriptions of these kinds, to subjects other than oneself. This is true even of "says that p": the allowable departures from direct quotation depend on what the ascriber deems the quoted subject to have had in mind. Whether to paraphrase "the commissioner" as "that scoundrel", in an indirect quotation, is a question not of the commissioner's character, but of the quoted speaker's view of it.

(PT, p. 68)

To give a name—"empathy"—to the way in which we judge how to ascribe propositional attitudes is not to have shown that such ascriptions are answerable to clear empirical criteria. Quine holds that in many cases they are, but in some cases they are not. Where p is an observation sentence, "A perceives that p" is "well under the control of empirical evidence" (PT, p. 67). Other attitudes too have transparently clear cases, sometimes even as ascribed to members of other species, as in Quine's example of "a tail-wagging dog's belief that his dinner is forthcoming" (ibid.). But the syntax

337

of belief ascription allows "p" to be replaced by any declarative sentence whatsoever; ascriptions of belief that p will vary greatly in the extent to which they are answerable to evidence. For some cases where we have no evidence we can still imagine evidence which would settle the matter one way or the other—the subject's willingness to take a bet, for example, or some other action which in imagined circumstances would be decisive. But other sorts of cases defy attempts to devise or imagine empirical tests. One example that Quine gives is belief in transubstantiation of the Eucharist; another is a belief about ancient history. In such cases we have nothing to go on except what the believer tells us, with no test of his sincerity. We are "loath to equate belief with lip service" (FM, p. 168), Quine says, but in some cases we have no other way of knowing whether someone believes or not—in some cases, indeed, we may have no reason to think that the subject has dispositions which would settle the matter, if we could bring about the appropriate circumstances. Quine thinks that there is no line to be drawn between cases which are answerable to clear evidence and those which are not. "Responsible [ascriptions of belief] grade off into the irresponsible, and one despairs of drawing a line." (PT, p. 67.)

IV Attitudes and facts

What should we conclude from our discussion of the semantics of ascriptions of propositional attitudes? Quine concludes that for the most rigorous scientific purposes we should avoid idioms of propositional attitude entirely: "In the strictest scientific spirit we can report all the behavior, verbal and otherwise, that may underlie our imputations of propositional attitudes ... but ... the essentially dramatic idiom of propositional attitudes will find no place." (WO, p. 219.) And, again:

> If we are limning the true and ultimate structure of reality, the canonical scheme for us is the austere scheme that knows no quotation but direct quotation and no propositional attitudes but only the physical constitution and behavior of organisms. ... If we are venturing to formulate the fundamental laws of a branch of science, however tentatively, this austere idiom is again likely to be the one that suits.
>
> (WO, p. 221)

In the same spirit, Quine speaks of "the idioms of propositional attitude" as "Grade B idiom" (D&H, p. 335).
One might interpret these passages as making merely a methodological point, a point about how best to construct our theories. Other passages, however,

show that Quine holds the ontological view that in some cases there is no fact of the matter about ascriptions of propositional attitude. In his reply to an essay of Putnam's, Quine says: "Some beliefs, perhaps belief in the essential nobility of man *quâ* man, are ... not readily distinguishable from mere lip service, and in such cases there is no fact of the matter by any reasonable standard." (H&S, p. 429; we shall return to this passage later.) In saying this he is, as he makes clear on the same page, drawing on physicalism, on his "identification of facts of the matter with distribution of microphysical states." (Ibid.)

Let us elaborate on Quine's example. Suppose there is someone who is known to have said that he believes in the essential nobility of man *quâ* man; the question arises whether this belief was sincere or mere lip service. There might, of course, be evidence which settles the question—there might be a secret diary, discovered after his death, in which he complains about having to utter such nonsense in order to be elected to office, say. Even without evidence, it might be argued that the man had a disposition which, if activated, would have provided clear evidence one way or the other. But must this be the case? Might it not be the case that in no circumstances would the man have done anything which made it clear whether his alleged belief was more than consistent lip service? In such a case it would be no use to devise bets that we might have offered him, or forced him to take, because the alleged belief is, after all, not answerable to evidence in any straightforward fashion—hence nothing counts as winning or as losing the bet. (Quine's example of belief in the transubstantiation of the Eucharist is even clearer on this count.)

If there is a fact of the matter as to whether someone has a given belief then that fact, for Quine, consists in that person's dispositions. There being a (physical) fact of the matter about someone's having a given propositional attitude depends on that person's having or lacking relevant dispositions. (A disposition, as we have emphasized, is a physical state of an object—of a person, in this case.) The man from the previous paragraph, let us suppose, has the disposition to utter the sentence or agree to it, but only in circumstances in which the action could be dismissed as lip service. He may lack any disposition which, if activated, would definitely settle whether he really held the belief. In such a case, Quine concludes, there is no fact of the matter.

The point is not simply one of lack of evidence. Often we do not know what someone really believes, and the person may die without leaving clear evidence one way or the other. But that does not directly threaten the idea that there is a fact of the matter, for his having held the belief or not held it may consist in his having had some disposition which was never activated. Still there is a connection between there being a fact of the matter and there being at least the potential for evidence. The activation of the disposition, had it occurred, would have provided evidence. But what if we have no reason to think that the person had a disposition which, if activated, would have provided evidence one way or the other? In that case, we have no reason to think that there is, by Quine's physicalistic standards, a fact of the matter.

So far in this section we have been concerned to explain Quine's consigning of mentalistic predicates, in particular ascriptions of propositional attitudes, to "Grade B idiom". In saying that mentalistic predicates are "Grade B idiom" Quine is not, of course, saying that they are meaningless. Nor is he proposing that we abandon them. But he is impugning their status as part of fully factual discourse. How is the use of idioms of propositional attitude to be explained and justified, in view of the deficiencies which Quine finds in those idioms? And how, in particular, can statements using such idioms form part of our science? Quine says that he uses the word "science" broadly, as including "psychology and economics through sociology to history" (*FSS*, p. 49). History and the social sciences surely make essential use of idioms of propositional attitude (cf. *PT*, pp. 72f.). But how can something that he wants to count as science be lacking in fully factual status?

We begin, then, with the fact that Quine does not propose that we abandon idioms of propositional attitude. In a discussion of indirect quotation he says that it is not "humanly dispensable" to manage without them, and supplies a reason why this is so: "We tend, even if we hear a remark directly and not by hearsay, to forget its exact words and remember only enough to report by indirect quotation". (*WO*, p. 218.) Mentalistic predicates quite generally are indispensable for reasons that go beyond this point: "for all their vagueness", such predicates "have long interacted with one another, engendering age-old strategies for predicting and explaining human action." (*PT*, pp. 72f.) By the standards of natural science the interactions may be limited, and the predictive strategies only partially successful, but still we understand each other, and understand ourselves, in terms which make indispensable use of such predicates. So we are not going to give up using them; nor does Quine think that we will or that we should. As we have emphasized elsewhere, language-reform is not part of his concern. The question, then, is to say how Quine thinks such idioms can be useful—indispensable, indeed—even though they are Grade B idiom; putting the matter the other way around, it is to say what their being Grade B idiom comes to, given that we will not and cannot do without them.

The key to answering these questions is that most uses of mentalistic idioms *are* factual. The idioms are excluded from the most austere version of canonical notation because some uses of them are not factual. That is to say: the idioms allow for the formation of sentences, such as the one discussed a couple of pages back, which we have no reason to count as making a factual claim. Such sentences will not be answerable to evidence, either actually available or available under counterfactual circumstances, since evidence is a matter of physical fact. But most uses of such idioms, and surely all of the indispensable ones, are not of this kind. Most uses are in sentences which are answerable to evidence, and for which there is a matter of fact; a true sentence of this kind asserts underlying physical facts which are, or would be, manifested in the sorts of things which count as evidence in favour of that sentence. (We cannot specify, in physical terms, which physical facts those are; if we could then Quine's monism would be translational and reductive, not anomalous.)

That this is indeed Quine's view may be seen from two passages. The first is from the reply to Putnam, which we have already quoted in part. The paragraph as a whole is as follows:

> Contemplating the application of my standard of fact of the matter to beliefs and desires, Putnam feels impelled to *modus tollens* [i.e. to reject the physicalistic standard]. Is it because he supposes that in beliefs and desires I recognize no fact of the matter? Then he misconstrues me. Some beliefs, perhaps belief in the essential nobility of man *qua* man, are indeed not readily distinguishable from mere lip service, and in such cases there is no fact of the matter by any reasonable standard. But most attributions or confessions of belief do make sense, within varying limits of vagueness. The states of belief, where real, are dispositions to behaviour, and so, again, states of nerves. Similar remarks apply to desires, except that desire has less tendency than belief to grade off into meaninglessness.
>
> (H&S, p. 429)

In most cases, then, Quine holds that there *is* a fact of the matter about ascriptions of belief. The general idiom "*A* believes that *p*", however, allows us to formulate sentences which outrun factuality.

A second relevant passage specifically addresses the issue of the learning of propositional attitude idioms. We do learn them, and the uses thus learnt are largely in accord with those of other people. Such learning would be impossible unless ascriptions of propositional attitude were physicalistically grounded, at least initially. The idioms, however, can outstrip their grounding, leaving them with no correspondence to any matter of fact:

> We learn mentalistic idioms ... in distinctive and intersubjectively observable circumstances. Those circumstances differ from others in respect of the distribution, however inscrutable, of elementary physical states. As long as we use such an idiom in a form and in circumstances closely similar to the original, we communicate information: there is a fact of the matter. But our mentalistic idioms, like other idioms, go on growing and stretching by analogy. Factual content becomes meanwhile more tenuous and elusive and can disappear altogether.
>
> (FM, p. 168)

Quine thus holds that in most cases our uses of propositional attitude idioms do "communicate information"; there is a fact of the matter. So he is not making the implausible claim that mentalistic sentences quite generally are non-factual, convey no information, and yet are nevertheless indispensable. The point is simply that the idioms which make those indispensable sentences possible also make it possible to formulate others which do not live up to his standards of factuality. Nor does he see any prospect of drawing a clear line between the factual uses of the mentalistic idioms and the other uses. So his response is that we should ban the idioms themselves from our vocabulary when our purposes are narrowly focused on stating facts—when we are concerned with "limning the true and ultimate structure of reality"—while not impugning the usefulness of those idioms in other contexts.

This mention of purpose may sound reminiscent of Carnap's Principle of Tolerance and the associated language-relativity, the idea that we make a free choice of a language for this or that purpose and that all our claims are then relative to that language. Is Quine surreptitiously embracing the Carnapian ideas which he ostensibly rejects? I think he is not. First, the relativity to language, and to purpose, is very limited. Our purposes, on Quine's picture, affect only which predicates we should accept in stating theory. Other matters are not depicted as in any way purpose-relative. These "other matters" include the logic of the theory and its syntax. More strikingly, they also include its ontology; accepting mentalistic idioms for certain purposes does not mean departing from the physicalistic ontology, even for those purposes. Second, and more important, Quine is quite clear that when our purpose is making judgments of ultimate reality the austere version of canonical notation is the one to use. That purpose, moreover, and hence that version of canonical notation, are the ones which go hand-in-hand with metaphysical ideas of reality and fact; those are exactly the ideas which Carnap had wanted to insist are language-relative, and hence without metaphysical significance. There is no real concession to Carnap here.

We have been discussing how mentalistic idioms can be practically indispensable even though they are factually deficient, and hence not part of what we might call "Grade A idiom". The same considerations also indicate how those idioms can be part of what Quine wants to include under the term "science". Quine wants to include human history, say, within science, so he presumably wants to count the statements of historians as making factual claims; yet history is full of ascriptions of propositional attitudes. This apparent tension is resolved by the fact that most ascriptions of propositional attitude *do* make factual claims. Statements accepted by a conscientious historian will be securely based on evidence. Those even considered by such an historian will be answerable to clear evidence, actual or potential—in other words, even if our historian lacks evidence she will at least have a clear conception of what would count as evidence, one way or the other. So for the historian's ascriptions there is a fact of the matter; hence the status of her subject as representing genuine knowledge is not impugned. History, like the rest of the humanities and social sciences, inevitably uses idioms of propositional attitude, and those idioms lend themselves to uses which lack factual content. But the non-factual uses are ones which an historian would repudiate in any case, as being too remote from any possible evidence; uses which have a place in the subject will be ones that Quine would take as making factual claims and, if all goes well, as genuinely true.

V The *de re* attitudes: a blind alley

The *de dicto* sense of belief which has concerned us in the previous three sections is non-extensional. In that sense of belief it may be true to say "Tom believes that Cicero denounced Catiline" and false to say "Tom believes that Tully denounced Catiline" even though Cicero and Tully are the same person. Our concern now is with the *de re* sense of belief, in which the two sentences must have the same truth-value.[3] For a time Quine embraced the idea that statements of belief in this sense have the same status as statements of *de dicto* belief, and attempted to clarify such statements. (See especially the 1956 essay "Quantifiers and Propositional Attitudes", WP, pp. 185–96; also sections 30, 31, 35, and 44 of *Word and Object*.) In the late 1960s he changed his mind, persuaded in large part by an argument first published by Robert Sleigh.[4] The purpose of this section is to explain the idea of *de re* belief, how Quine originally thought to fit it to his regimented notation, why he gave up the idea that this sense of belief can be accommodated within regimented notation, and how he subsequently sought to allow for the phenomena which had led him to think that it must be so accommodated. Our discussion will be of *de re* belief, but, as before, the remarks will apply, *mutatis mutandis*, to the other attitudes.

In *Word and Object* Quine motivates the idea of *de re* belief by talking about two senses in which a person might be said to believe that someone is a spy. Following Quine, let us suppose that it is Ralph to whom we attribute the belief. Suppose, further, that we want to say not merely that Ralph, like most of the rest of us, thinks that there are spies in the world. We want to say something much stronger—that there is some particular person whom he suspects, that he has "urgent information", which should presumably be conveyed to the relevant authorities as soon as possible (*WO*, p. 148). In 1956 Quine speaks of statements of this latter kind as "indispensable relational statements of belief" ("Quantifiers and Propositional Attitudes", *WP*, p. 191).

The first or weaker of the attributions above is unproblematic. In the light of our previous discussions, we can regiment it like this:

(1) Ralph believes-true "$(\exists x)(x$ is a spy)".

This is the (*de dicto*) belief which Ralph presumably shares with almost all of us, and which calls for no particular action on his part. But how are we to understand the stronger statement? A first attempt might be: "There is someone (some one particular person) whom Ralph believes to be a spy". Regimenting part way, this will give us:

(2) $(\exists x)(x$ Ralph believes-true that x is a spy).

From this we can see why Quine insists that in this kind of case we have a different sense of belief attribution. As we saw in section II of Chapter 11, Quine argues that it makes no sense to quantify into a non-extensional context from outside of that context. But in the *de dicto* sense of belief, "Ralph believes that ... is a spy" forms a non-extensional context. So this expression is not an open sentence, true or false of each object in the usual way. The failure of extensionality means that it cannot be thought of as true or false of *objects* at all. Hence there is no sense to affixing an existential quantifier in front of the expression in the attempt to say that it is true of at least one object.

Our conclusion so far is that the attempt to do justice to the idea that Ralph's belief is of interest to the counter-espionage agencies leads us to a new sense of belief ascription. The two sentences (1) and (2) use the word "believes" in different senses. For this new sense of belief ascription we then face the same two questions that we discussed above for the *de dicto* case. First, how are we to accommodate it within the syntax of regimented discourse? Second, can we find a coherent account of the semantics of assertions of belief, in this sense? We will take up these issues in order.

One might think that to say that Ralph believes, in the *de re* sense, that Ortcutt is a spy, is to assert a relation among Ralph, Ortcutt and the *property* of being a spy. The quantified sentence above, (2), is then taken to say that there is someone such that Ralph and that person have the relevant relation to the property. This idea is analogous to the idea that *de dicto* belief is a relation between a person and a proposition. Quine's objection to it is also analogous, as is his suggested alternative. The objection is that properties, like propositions, are entities with dubious or unclear identity-criteria and, since we have no need for them, we are better off not assuming them. As an alternative, he urges that we make do with open sentences, i.e. sentences containing a free variable. Thus our sentence about Ralph and Ortcutt becomes "Ralph believes-true 'y is a spy' of Ortcutt". The quantified sentence (2) becomes

(3) $(\exists x)$(Ralph believes-true "y is a spy" of x).

This method enables us to single out some but not all of the positions in an ascription of belief as referential. We can distinguish "Tom believes-true 'x denounced Catiline' of Cicero" from "Tom believes-true 'Cicero denounced y' of Catiline" and distinguish each of them from "Tom believes-true 'x denounced y' of Cicero and Catiline"; the first accords referential position (i.e. transparent occurrence) to the word "Cicero" but not the word "Catiline"; the second has it the other way around; the third accords both words referential occurrence.

In this way, the *de re* sense of belief can be fitted into the syntax of Quine's logic. That fact, however, does nothing to assure us that there is a coherent semantics which makes the right sort of sense of statements of *de re* belief. What we need is guidance as to when it is correct to attribute a *de re* belief to someone. In his writings before 1968 Quine endorses the idea that if we have reason to attribute to someone a *de dicto* belief of the form that a is F then we also have reason to attribute to him the corresponding *de re* belief, i.e. a belief of a (under any description) that it is F; we thus also have reason to say that there is something such that the given person believes that it is *F*. Thus we would take Tom's assertion that Cicero denounced Catiline as justifying us in making not only the *de dicto* belief attribution: "Tom believes-true 'Cicero denounced Catiline'" but also the *de re* attribution: "Tom believes-true '*y* denounced Catiline' of Cicero", and hence also: "($\exists x$)(Tom believes-true '*y* denounced Catiline' of *x*)". Quine refers to this inferential step from the *de dicto* belief attribution to the *de re* belief attribution as *exportation*, and says that it "should doubtless be viewed in general as implicative" ("Quantifiers and Propositional Attitudes", *WP*, p. 190; cf. also *WO*, p. 148). On Quine's pre-1968 account, this inference is central to the semantics of *de re* belief, for it tells us when we are justified in making a *de re* belief attribution. A difficulty with exportation leads Quine to abandon the whole idea of *de re* attitudes. Before discussing this, however, we shall take up one other matter.

Tom, we are supposing, denies that Tully denounced Catiline. So we are also justified in saying, in the *de dicto* sense, "Tom believes that Tully did not denounce Catiline". Hence, by exportation, we are justified in saying: "Tom believes-true '*x* did not denounce Catiline' of Tully". But since Tully is Cicero, and since those names occur in referential position in these sentences, we also have to accept: "Tom believes-true '*x* denounced Catiline' of Tully". We have to accept, that is, that Tom believes of Cicero (a.k.a. Tully) both that he did denounce Catiline and that he did not. But this, says Quine,

> is not yet a self-contradiction on our part or even on Tom's, for a distinction can be reserved between (a) Tom's believing that Tully did and that Tully did not denounce Catiline, and (b) Tom's believing that Tully did and did not denounce Catiline.
>
> (*WO*, p. 148)

He recognizes that there is an "oddity" here, but he is willing to accept it as the price of making sense of the relational sense of belief.

We now return to the difficulty with exportation. Putting the principle generally, it is the inference from the attribution of a *de dicto* belief of the form: "*A* believes-true '*Fa*'" to the attribution of the *de re* belief of the form: "*A* believes-true '*Fx*' of *a*". Quine, before 1968, thinks we must view this step as "in general ... implicative". Sleigh, Kaplan, and others argue that the inference is not generally correct. Suppose that Ralph in fact has no information of interest to the counter-espionage authorities; he knows no more about spies than I do. Still, he may well believe that one among spies is the shortest; let us suppose that he is right.[5] Being a logical fellow, Ralph also believes that the shortest spy is a spy. But then, by the principle of exportation, we must also accept "Ralph believes-true 'x is a spy' of the shortest spy". Hence we must accept (3), i.e. "($\exists x$)(Ralph believes-true 'y is a spy' of x)". This last belief was meant to be the kind that is of interest to the authorities; we now see, however, that Ralph may hold that belief even though he has nothing of interest to tell the authorities. What this shows is that the supposedly stronger belief is not stronger at all. So accepting exportation undermines the motivation for the *de re* attitudes.

One way to think of the problem is this: we attribute beliefs by considering what we would be inclined to say if we were in (what we take to be) the subject's place. (See the discussion of the role of empathy in *de dicto* attributions in the third section, above.) But this is, in the first place, evidence for *de dicto* belief attributions. The semantics of such attributions has its problems, as we saw, but the subject's sincere, earnest assertions generally give us a good guide here. For *de re* attributions they do not; Tom's denying (sincerely and earnestly) that he believes that Tully denounced Catiline does not count as evidence against the attribution to him of the *de re* belief of Tully (i.e. Cicero) that he denounced Catiline. So we need some idea of when it is correct to infer a *de re* attribution from *de dicto* attributions. Quine puts forward exportation as the principle of inference here, but it turns out to be irredeemably flawed. Hence he gives up on the idea of incorporating the *de re* attitudes into regimented notation.

There are, of course, other possible responses to the flaws of the principle of exportation. The argument against the principle given above turns on our counting "the shortest spy" as a singular term denoting a spy. So, one might think, the principle can be retrieved if we restrict the sorts of singular terms for which we allow it. If A believes-true "Fa" for some singular term, "a" *of the right sort*, then we may infer that A believes-true "Fx" of a; but "the shortest spy" and the like will be excluded as not being singular terms of the right sort. This idea is advanced by Kaplan, who introduces the idea of a *vivid name* of an object, for a person. (See the essay cited in note 4, above.) Kaplan's move reduces the idea of *de re* belief to that of *de dicto* belief: to have a *de re* belief is to have a *de dicto* belief that can be expressed using the right sort of singular term.

From Quine's point of view, however, the idea of a vivid name is too vague and, in particular, too context-bound, to be useable in regimented discourse. The ability to use a vivid name for something or someone presumably goes with knowing who or what that thing or person is. But this idea, Quine says, "is utterly dependent on context. Sometimes when we ask who someone is, we see the fact and want the name; sometimes the reverse.

Sometimes we want to know his role in the community. *Of itself the notion is empty*". ("Intensions Revisited", *TT*, p. 121; emphasis added.) Quine considers the possibility of a revision of logic which would enable us to make sense of the *de re* attitudes by taking context into account. (See *FSS*, p. 98; Quine cites Howard Burdick, "A Logical Form for Propositional Attitudes".) But his final position is that we should "omit propositional attitudes *de re* from our overall scientific language couched in the extensional grammar of predicate logic" (*FSS*, p. 97).

Excluding the *de re* attitudes from scientific language means excluding from that language any way of making sense of what Quine at one stage called the "vast" distinction represented by the difference between (1) and (2), above (see "Quantifiers and Propositional Attitudes", *WP*, p. 186). How great a loss is this? In "Intensions Revisited" Quine says that excluding the *de re*

> virtually annuls the seemingly vital contrast between [(1)] and [(2)]: between merely believing that there are spies and suspecting a specific person. At first this seems intolerable, but it grows on one. I now think the distinction is every bit as empty, apart from context as ... that of knowing or believing who someone is. In context it can still be important. In one case we can be of service by pointing out the suspect; in another, by naming him; in others, by giving his address or specifying his ostensible employment.
>
> (*TT*, p. 121)

The point here, I take it, is that in any case in which it seems reasonable to attribute a *de re* belief to someone (Ralph, say) he will have certain relevant *de dicto* beliefs. These may take the form of believing that his neighbour is a spy, or that the man he saw skulking down the alley a few minutes ago is a spy. In no readily imaginable context will the belief that the shortest spy is a spy count as relevant. What Quine despairs of, in giving up on the idea of the *de re* attitudes, is our being able to demarcate relevant from irrelevant beliefs in advance, without looking at the particular context in question.

Quine's view is a rejection of the *de re* idiom from scientific language, not a reduction of it to the *de dicto* idiom. It is not that we attribute a given *de re* belief to someone if and only if he or she has *de dicto* beliefs satisfying the right conditions, for it is impossible to specify such conditions in a sufficiently clear, general and context-free fashion. But someone to whom we are inclined to attribute a *de re* belief will have some *de dicto* beliefs which, so to speak, underlie the supposed *de re* belief. The value of a *de re* belief attribution is that it sums up a number of *de dicto* attributions without requiring us to specify them—which we may in a given case be unable to do. The situation here is analogous to that of *de dicto* beliefs and their relation to the physical facts—the real facts—which underlie them. *De re* beliefs are thus doubly removed from the real facts; in their case also we lack the sort of paradigm that we have for *de dicto* beliefs, that of sincere affirmation, as tested by, for example, willingness to take a bet. Hence Quine's more favourable attitude towards the *de dicto* than towards the *de re*.

VI Modality

There is a long philosophical tradition of taking some statements to be not merely true or false but *necessarily* true or false. The concept of possibility can be defined in terms of necessity: if a statement is not necessarily false then it is possibly true, whether or not it actually is true. (Alternatively, beginning with possibility, we can define necessity: a statement is necessarily true if it is not possible that it should be false.) Quine holds that the ideas of necessity and possibility have no place in regimented theory. The subject has been much disputed; we need to understand the issues involved and Quine's reasons for excluding modality.

In Quine's view, there are many resemblances between the issue of modality and the issue of propositional attitudes, which was discussed in the previous four sections. To summarize the relevant points: propositional attitudes give rise to non-extensional contexts; this in turn gives rise to syntactic problems, which are, however, fairly easily solved. Some have claimed that ascriptions of propositional attitudes have not only a *de dicto* sense but also a *de re* sense, in which they are extensional for some of the expressions in the scope of the attitude; this gives rise to further syntactic problems for which Quine, again, offers a solution. Quine has doubts about the interpretation of the terms which express propositional attitudes. He rejects the *de re* sense as unsuitable for regimented theory, but has a more welcoming attitude towards the *de dicto* sense.

Quine holds that all of these points apply also to modality, as we shall see, although the last only in very qualified form. In the case of modality, Quine does not think that either sense, *de dicto* or *de re*, has a place in regimented theory. He thinks that (*de dicto*) propositional attitudes are needed in our theory of the world (even if perhaps not in its most austere version), whereas modality, however construed, is not. Contrasting the two, he writes: "the propositional attitudes are less readily dispensable. . . . We cannot easily forswear daily reference to belief. . . . We can much more easily do without reference to necessity". (Reply to Føllesdal, D&H, p. 336; cf. also *PT*, p. 73, where the point is repeated.)

Quine dispenses with modality, in regimented theory, because he thinks that the idea is unclear and that little is lost when we do without it. Regimented theory is a systematization of the more serious aspects of ordinary knowledge, so it is relevant to see how we actually use such words as "possibly", "necessarily", "must", and so on. Quine is at some pains to distinguish our ordinary usage from the idea of modality put forward by other philosophers:

> In ordinary non-philosophical usage "possibly" usually serves merely as a modestly impersonal rewording of . . . "I am not sure but what" [*sic*]. Ordinarily the construction "necessarily" . . . connotes . . . a propositional attitude of purpose or resolve. Sometimes, also, "necessarily" and "possibly" provide a condensed way of saying that a sentence follows from or is compatible with some fixed premises understood as a background. And sometimes they provide little more than a variant style for "all" and "some".
>
> But what is called logical modality is none of these things. Used as a logical modality, "necessarily" imputes necessity unconditionally and impersonally, as an absolute mode of truth; and "possibly" denies necessity, in that sense, of the negation.
>
> (*WO*, p. 195)

Thirty-five years later he makes a similar point, saying that: "The adverb 'necessarily' is useful indeed, but only as an expository guide". (*FSS*, p. 99.) The implication here is that the sense of necessity which philosophers have emphasized, what Quine calls "an absolute mode of truth", has no real role to play in ordinary knowledge. The notion is a philosophers' invention; this already suggests that it has no place in our theory.

Philosophers and logicians have formalized necessity (in the sense which Quine calls "logical modality"). Their efforts have been both wide-ranging and technically successful.[6] Quine raises objections, especially to quantified modal logic (hereafter QML), i.e. systems in which modal operators can occur within the scope of quantifiers. (More accurately: systems in which variables may occur within the scope of a modal operator either unbound or bound by a quantifier which is not within the scope of the operator.) Quine's argument against QML sometimes appears as technical, but this appearance is misleading. The serious and enduring disputes concern questions of interpretation, and are not technical in any narrow sense. (It is chiefly the interpretation of the modal notions which is disputed, though

350

the nature of quantification is also sometimes in question.) Taken simply as uninterpreted formalisms, systems of modal logic—including QML—are unassailable, and have found uncontentious and technically significant use.[7]

Much of the debate over modality revolves around issues of non-extensionality. It is very plausible, on the face of it, to think that the modal operators give rise to non-extensional contexts. Consider the following pair of sentences:

(1) It is necessary that nine is greater than seven.
(2) It is necessary that the number of planets is greater than seven.

(2) can be obtained from (1) by replacing one expression, "nine", by another, "the number of planets", which designates the same thing.[8] Independent of any particular philosophical interpretation of modality, it is natural to think that (1) is true and that (2) is false. Elementary truths of arithmetic are widely taken to be among the strongest candidates for necessity. Surely the solar system might have formed with only six planets, or a succession of huge meteors might come along and knock three of the planets out of their orbits and off into deep space. So replacing one singular term by a co-designative term within a modal context can, it seems, turn a truth into a falsehood.

Quine takes it that there is indeed a failure of extensionality here, and that it shows that sentences such as (1) and (2) cannot be taken at face value, as simply being about the objects that they might seem to be about. On his view, some rephrasing is called for. His response is much the same as it is to the analogous situation in the case of (*de dicto*) propositional attitudes. He thinks that the best way to make sense of sentences such as (1) and (2) is by treating necessity as "a *semantical predicate* attributable to statements as notational forms—hence attachable to names of statements" ("Three Grades of Modal Involvement", *WP*, p. 158; emphasis in the original). Thus we should tacitly or overtly construe (1) as:

(1*) The sentence "Nine is greater than seven" is necessary,

and similarly for other ascriptions of necessity or possibility. Given this treatment, the failure of extensionality seen in the differing truth-values of (1) and (2) is attributable to the well understood failure of extensionality engendered by quotation, as in Quine's treatment of the propositional attitudes. Modal statements without quantifiers thus pose no syntactic problems as far as Quine is concerned; if he thought that the notion of necessity were clear enough and useful enough to be worthwhile, he could

treat such statements as he treats *de dicto* ascriptions of propositional attitude. (At the end of the section we shall consider the interpretation of *de
dicto* necessity.)

Other philosophers have argued that there is no failure of extensionality
illustrated by (1) and (2), and hence that such sentences can simply be taken
at face value.[9] Sentence (2) contains a definite description. Treating this in
Russellian fashion uncovers an ambiguity, for it can lead us to either of two
sentences. Using "Px" to mean that "x numbers the planets" and "N" as a
necessity operator, we have either:

(2a) $N(\exists x)[(\forall y)(Py \leftrightarrow x = y)$ & (x is greater than seven)$]$

or, alternatively:

(2b) $(\exists x)[(\forall y)(Py \leftrightarrow x = y)$ & $N(x$ is greater than seven)$]$.

The sentence (2a), it is admitted, is false, but (2b), it is argued, is true:
there is a number which numbers the planets and that number is necessarily
greater than seven.

The sentence (2b) is, at least from Quine's point of view, a drastic step
beyond the sort of necessity exhibited in (1), at least if we allow that (1) can
be paraphrased as (1*). In (2b) we have a quantifier which is *outside* the
scope of a necessity operator binding a variable which is *inside* the scope of
that operator. Quine, however, denies that this situation is legitimate.

Quine's objection here is to the interpretation of *de re* modality, not to the
syntax it requires. Syntactically, there is no difficulty in accommodating the
idea within regimented theory. As Quine sees, statements in which modal
operators are combined with quantifiers could be treated in the way in
which Quine himself, before 1968, proposed treating *de re* ascriptions of
propositional attitude. (See section V, above.) Along these lines, we could
say that the open sentence "x is greater than seven" is necessarily true of nine,
and hence also of the number of planets. Quite generally: what would be said
to be necessary is that a certain open sentence is true of an object, or of an
ordered pair of objects, or in general of an ordered n-tuple of objects. Along the
same lines, we can give a coherent syntax for quantification into modal contexts; there is something which is necessarily greater than seven becomes:

$(\exists y)[N("x$ is greater than seven" is true of $y)]$.

The availability of this manoeuvre removes any purely syntactic objections
to *de re* modality and to QML. (See "Intensions Revisited", *TT*, pp. 113–17.)

This does not make *de re* modality acceptable to Quine; what it shows is that his objections are not purely syntactic.

Quine's objection, then, is to the idea of *de re* modality which is involved when we quantify into modal contexts. That idea, he argues, presupposes what he pejoratively refers to as "Aristotelian essentialism" ("Three Grades of Modal Involvement", *WP*, p. 175; cf. also *WO*, p. 199); this idea is anathema to him. In asserting (2b) we are saying that there is an object such that *it*, in and of itself, regardless of how it is specified, is necessarily greater than seven; this is necessity *de re*. Presumably the advocates of such a view do not hold that *everything* true of an object is true of it necessarily, in this sense—if it were, modal distinctions would collapse. So quantifying into modal contexts requires "an invidious attitude toward certain ways of uniquely specifying *x* ... and favoring other ways ... as somehow better revealing the 'essence' of the object." ("Reference and Modality", *FLPV*, p. 155.)[10] He points out that it is "abruptly at variance with the idea, favored by Carnap, Lewis, and others, of explaining necessity by analyticity" (ibid.). It is, indeed, "abruptly at variance" with any view of necessity which sees it as due to *us*—to our language, our concepts, our categories, our forms of intuition—rather than grounded in the nature of things. Quine finds the latter idea of necessity almost incomprehensible—a view that was widely shared until the bravura articulation of the contrary point of view by Kripke (see Kripke, "Identity and Necessity" as well as his "Naming and Necessity").

In *Word and Object* Quine argues against essentialism, or at least puts forward an example which seeks to convey what he takes to be "the appropriate sense of bewilderment":

> Mathematicians may conceivably be said to be necessarily rational and not necessarily two-legged; and cyclists necessarily two-legged and not necessarily rational. But what of an individual who counts among his eccentricities both mathematics and cycling? Is this concrete individual necessarily rational and contingently two-legged or vice versa?
>
> (*WO*, p. 199)

He holds that these are not questions which we should answer, or sensibly can answer. If we are simply considering the object, not the object *qua* cyclist or *qua* mathematician, then he says:

> there is no semblance of sense in rating some of his attributes as necessary and others as contingent. Some of his attributes count as

important and others as unimportant, yes; some as enduring and others as fleeting; but none as necessary or contingent.

(ibid.)

He thus rejects the idea of *de re* necessity, and hence also the legitimacy of quantification into modal contexts, as QML requires.

Quine holds that questions about which traits are essential and which accidental are barely intelligible. From his point of view, such questions are wholly pointless. He simply takes it as evident that the idea of essence has no serious scientific use; modern science, unlike Aristotelian science, simply has no place for the notion. The closest we come is "picking out those minimum distinctive traits of a chemical, or of a species, or whatever, that link it most directly to the central laws of the science." ("Vagaries of Definition", *WP*, p. 52). There is, however, no comfort for the essentialist, or the modal logician, in this "vestige of essentialism" (ibid.). Many philosophers, unpersuaded by Quinean considerations, have come up with theories which distinguish the essential from the accidental properties of various objects. (Theories that purport to provide a basis for the claim that, say, the definition of human beings as rational animals gets at the essence of what it is to be human, while defining the species as featherless bipeds does not.) For Quine, however, such theories are neither clear nor useful; certainly they have no place in a theory which aims at "limning the true and ultimate structure of reality" (*WO*, p. 221).

Since the pioneering work of Kripke on the formal semantics of modal logic, it has become common to discuss modal notions in terms of possible worlds.[11] A statement is possible just in case it is true in at least one possible world; an object in one possible world is deemed to be identical to an object in another possible world just in case they share their essence. Quine insists, however, that while these ideas may dramatize modal logic they presuppose the modalities, and cannot explain them: "Talk of possible worlds is a graphic way of waging the essentialist philosophy, but it is only that; it is not an explication. Essence is needed to identify an object from one possible world to another". ("Intensions Revisited", *TT*, p. 118.)

Finally, in this section, we should return to Quine's view of the interpretation of *de dicto* necessity, as it occurs in sentential modal logic. Until the early 1960s, Quine takes it for granted that the necessary truths are to be identified with the analytic truths.[12] He takes it as undisputed, that is, that no *other* conception of necessity is acceptable. (During the 1950s this assumption was, for the most part, correct. Later, other views were put forward, especially by Kripke, as noted above.) We saw in Chapter 3, above, that Quine comes to accept that clear sense can be made of some sort of notion of analyticity but that on the crucial issues he makes no concession. Two points discussed there are of particular importance here. First, the truths of mathematics are not analytic in any sense acceptable to Quine. Second, within science there is no enduring significant difference between two kinds of truths. If some are introduced by explicit postulation or definition, this is a fact about how we first come to accept the truth which has no consequences for its subsequent status; it is "a trait of the passing event rather than of the truth which is thereby instituted" (C&LT, WP, p. 131). For these reasons, a notion of analyticity acceptable to Quine makes a very poor candidate for an explication of necessity in the philosophers' sense, necessity as "an absolute mode of truth".

There are other ideas, acceptable from a Quinean point of view, which could be identified with (de dicto) necessity. Most obvious, perhaps, is the idea of logical necessity. Quine comments as follows:

> Can I make sense of logical necessity? Extensionally, yes: I can make sense of logical truth. Given truth and an inventory of our logical vocabulary, I can demarcate the set of all logical truths. Similarly, given the chemical vocabulary, the chemical truths. They are the truths that remain under all substitutions on the component lexicon that leave the chemical vocabulary undisturbed; and correspondingly for the logical truths. *Calling them necessary adds nothing for me.*
> (B&G, comment on Marcus, p. 244; emphasis added)

Quine's "yes" here, however, is no concession to the advocates of modality. We can demarcate the logical truths from others, yes, but we can similarly demarcate any set consisting of all and only those truths which make essential use of some specified limited vocabulary. Perhaps in some contexts there is a real use for the demarcation, because it is useful to know which are the logical truths; but equally there might be contexts in which it was useful to know which are the chemical truths. If advocates of modality have nothing more in mind than that, then they would do well to give up the potentially misleading term "necessary" and speak instead of logical truth (or chemical truth, etc.).

VII Causality, counterfactuals, and natural necessity

Our subject in this section is a group of more or less closely related ideas: causality, natural law, physical necessity, subjunctive or counterfactual conditionals, and disposition terms. Let us begin with causality. The idiom "*p* because *q*" is, on the face of it, non-extensional: replacing one true sentence with another can lead us from a truth to a falsehood. It may be true to say: "Hylton got wet yesterday because it rained yesterday" but it is false to say: "Hylton got wet yesterday because snow is white". A natural response to this fact is to construe causality not as a statement operator but rather as relating *events*. Thus we would say: the event of yesterday's rain caused the event of Hylton's getting wet yesterday. Invoking events raises the question of their identity-criteria. In the example just given, events are referred to by "the event of" followed by a nominalized sentence. More awkwardly but equivalently and more perspicuously, one might take the sentence as it stands and precede it by: "the event that". (Thus: "The event that it rained yesterday caused the event that Hylton got wet yesterday".) But here "the event that" figures as a sentential context and, clearly, a non-extensional one.

Quine's solution to this problem is to identify an event with a physical object: an event which involves certain participants, each over a certain stretch of time (not necessarily the same stretch for each), is taken to be the physical object made up of the relevant objects at the relevant times. Thus he says: "A ball game ... might be identified with the scattered sum of the appropriate temporal segments of the players, taking each player for just the duration of his play." (WPO?, p. 497); one might perhaps add the relevant temporal segment of the ball, of other equipment used, and of the field where the play took place. With or without these additions, the various temporal segments make up a single physical object, in Quine's wide-ranging sense. On this account, events are physical objects, their identity-criteria are simply those for physical objects generally.

Quine's approach has a consequence which some have found objectionable. Where a single object or group of objects is involved over a single given stretch of time, we have a single event. Thus if we suppose that "a man whistled some song all the while he was walking to the bus stop, and not a moment longer", then both the whistling and the walking are identified with the relevant temporal segment of the whistler/walker, hence they are identified with one another (WPO?, p. 497; cf. also *TT*, pp. 11f.). Intuitively, we might think that the walking and the whistling are separate events, but Quine's account identifies them. Quine says of this consequence: "It is perhaps unnatural, but it is not clear to me that we lose anything". (WPO?, p. 497.) Let us consider why it may be acceptable, even though unnatural. To begin with, we identify only the particular act of walking and the particular act of whistling; walking and whistling are not identified in general, for there will be many walkings which are not whistlings, and vice versa. So the general distinction between walking and whistling does not collapse. We can also still do justice to the idea that some things are true of our event *qua* walking, while others are true of it *qua* whistling. From Quine's point of view this is just to say that some things will be true of it which are true also of other walkings and not of other whistlings, or not many; others the other way around. Thus in his reply to Føllesdal in the Hahn and Schilpp volume, Quine says:

> Føllesdal cites causality as a case where austere science itself has to exceed the bounds of extensionality. I am unconvinced. I am prepared to identify a particular event of walking with a particular event of gum-chewing if the agent is involved simultaneously in both, and then I am prepared to say that *that* gum-chewing, being a walking, did cause his displacement across town. We are still not committed to a general law that gum-chewings cause displacements.
>
> (H&S, p. 115; emphasis in the original)

Accepting the unnatural conclusion is the price to be paid for having events with clear extensional criteria of identity; for Quine it is the price to be paid for admitting events into our ontology at all.

To say that the causal relation holds among events, as Quine understands them, is not yet to say anything about the nature of that relation. Quine's most sustained discussion is in section 2 of *Roots of Reference*. He argues that the "root notion of causality" is to be found in "the flow of energy", as in that paradigm of causality, one billiard ball's hitting another and causing it to move. Elaborating the idea, he says: "Given an event *e*, then, imagine all its energy traced backward through time. Any earlier event that intercepts all of these energetic world-lines qualifies as a cause of *e*". (*RR*, p. 5.) As we shall see, he does not put this forward as a fully acceptable notion of cause; his claim rather seems to be that this is the best we can do in that direction.

This definition of cause is thoroughly physicalistic. For Quine, of course, this is no drawback; on his view, "all events, mental and social included, are a matter ultimately of the action of physical forces upon particles" (*RR*, p. 6). The definition does have one very peculiar consequence: causes of *e*, at least those that are at all distant from it in time, will usually be very widely dispersed in space. That is because each cause is the *total* cause of *e* at a given time. But we can consider contributory causes by defining them as events "intercepting merely some of the energetic lines that lead into the effect" (*RR*, p. 7). As Quine points out, our interest in a contributory cause is "conspicuously independent of the proportion of energy contributed" (ibid.). The potential energy in the wood and the oxygen vastly outweighs the energy of the lit match, yet it is to the match that we look when asked for the cause of the forest fire, not to the air and the wood. But which contributory cause we are interested in is bound to be a highly context-relative and (obviously) interest-relative matter. Perhaps the best we can hope for from an understanding of cause is that it explains what it is for one event to be a (contributory) cause of another, however uninteresting; the selection of the interesting causes will then be made by whatever criteria happen to strike us as appropriate in the particular case.

There is, however, another objection to the above definition of cause which Quine does accept. The definition relies on our being able to identify two events as "two manifestations of one and the same continuing bit of energy" (RR, p. 6). Quine holds that modern physics undermines such identification: "The very distinction between matter and energy wavers in modern physics, and even the notion of the identity of an elementary particle from moment to moment has fallen on evil days, what with quantum jumps". (Ibid.)

Quine's conclusion from this is not that we should seek another under-standing of cause. It is, rather, that the notion of cause, while useful in limited contexts, cannot be applied with the complete generality character-istic of advanced science. As a technical scientific notion, he claims, it is simply not needed: "a notion of cause is out of place in modern physics. ... Clearly the term plays no technical role at austere levels of the subject". (RR, p. 6.) Quine has held this view early and late. In "The Scope and Language of Science" he says:

> Now it is an ironical but familiar fact that though the business of science is describable in unscientific language as the discovery of causes, the notion of cause itself has no firm place in science. The disappearance of causal terminology from the jargon of one branch of science and another has seemed to mark the progress in the understanding of the branches concerned.
>
> (WP, p. 242)

The point here, perhaps, is that in the less advanced branches of science we may find ourselves saying that things of one kind tend to cause things of another, but the most advanced branches simply present us with excep-tionless generalizations embedded in an explanatory theory. In Pursuit of Truth he puts the point more bluntly and more briefly: "Science at its most austere bypasses the notion [of cause] and settles for concomitances". (P. 76.)

An idea which is often connected with causality is that of natural or physical necessity, or of a law of nature. The idea is that some true generalizations are accidental while others are laws of nature, and thus in some sense necessary, although not in the absolute sense of necessity discussed in the previous section. One way in which the difference is sometimes explained is that laws of nature support subjunctive conditionals, whereas accidental generalizations do not. All glasses of a certain kind dropped onto a stone floor from a certain height have broken. We have no hesitation in asserting that if I had dropped this glass, which is of the relevant kind, onto this stone floor then it would have broken. All the books on a given shelf in my study are by Quine. But no one thinks that if I had put a novel on that shelf then it would have been written by Quine. The difference, on many accounts, is that the generalization about the glasses is law-like, or causally necessary: a glass's being dropped *causes* it to break. Nothing similar holds for the books and the shelf. If we assume the notion of a law of nature, we can explain what it is for a subjunctive conditional to be correct: it must be underpinned by laws of nature which imply that things of that kind always act in the given way when the given circumstances occur. Similarly, given a clear understanding of counterfactuals we can distinguish laws of nature from accidental true generalizations: the laws of nature are the ones which support counterfactuals. Dispositions are often thought to belong to the same family of ideas: to say that an undropped glass would break if it were dropped is to say that it has a certain disposition—it is fragile. The novel has no disposition to change its authorship according to the shelf it is placed on.

Given Quine's general views, we should not be surprised that he takes a dim view of the idea of a law of nature. In "Necessary Truth" he endorses the view, which he attributes to Hume, "that necessity is no more than regularity" (*WP*, p. 71). Twenty years or so later he says: "along with the notion of logical or mathematical necessity I reject also the notion of physical or natural necessity, and thus also the distinction between law and accidental generalization." (H&S, pp. 397–98.) The most important points in favour of this view are that no persuasive understanding has been offered of natural necessity; also that we do not need such a notion to account for at least some of the phenomena which have led philosophers to invoke it.

Physical laws are sometimes thought of as *causal* laws, so one might suppose that Quine's denial of the former notion depends upon his view that the idea of causality is unnecessary in the most developed branches of science. But Quine's idea of causality, even if fully acceptable, would not support a notion of natural necessity or physical law. It might happen that

events of one kind always had events of another kind among their contributory causes, in Quine's sense; from his point of view, however, that fact
would be one more true generalization, with no intrinsic property of
"necessity" or "law-likeness" about it.

The denial of natural necessity does not rule out all differences among true
generalizations. Some generalizations are more theoretically embedded than
others. Let us revert to the glass and the book. Consider the following two
statements: (A) all glasses of a given micro-structure which have been dropped
from a given height onto a floor of a given hardness on or near the surface of
the earth have shattered; (B) all the books on a given shelf in my study are
by Quine. We are happy to infer from (A) that the next glass of similar micro-
structure that is similarly dropped will also break. We are much less inclined
to infer from (B) that the next book on the shelf will be by Quine; certainly
we will *not* infer that if an arbitrary book were placed on the shelf then it
would become a book by Quine. What justifies this difference? If the next
glass dropped does not shatter then rather significant and extensive modifications in our theory may be necessary to accommodate this fact. Perhaps
it will turn out that if the glass hits the floor at exactly the right angle then it
survives (or, indeed, it may turn out that its micro-structure is different from
that of the other glasses). But if no local explanation of that sort is available
then we may be forced to reconsider other generalizations, with far-reaching
effects on other aspects of our theory. Our confidence in our theory as a
whole, then, justifies us in making an inference from (A) to the fate of the
next dropped glass. Generalization (B) is in sharp contrast. If it were to turn
out that the next book placed on the shelf is not by Quine, no significant
theoretical changes threaten; it would, indeed, be entirely unsurprising.

The previous paragraph does no more than gesture at the sorts of differences that may be found among true generalizations. Even that brief discussion, however, may indicate why some generalizations strike us as more
accidental than others and, by the same token, why some true generalizations support subjunctive conditionals and others do not. To put the
point very generally: it is a matter of the way in which a supposed general
truth connects with the rest of our knowledge. This may be a matter of
degree, rather than of a clear bifurcation of generalizations into those which
are necessary or law-like and those which are not.

Let us consider the issue of subjunctive conditionals in somewhat more
detail. Quine does not think that the idiom in general has a place in canonical notation, for lack of clear and objective truth-conditions. He finds an
analogy here with idioms of propositional attitude:

The subjunctive conditional depends, like indirect quotation and more so, on a dramatic projection: we feign belief in the antecedent and see how convincing we then find the consequent. What traits of the real world to suppose preserved in the feigned world of the contrary-to-fact antecedent can only be guessed from a sympathetic sense of the fabulist's likely purpose in spinning his fable.

(WO, p. 222)

If we allow for the unconstrained formulation of subjunctive conditionals, sentences of the form: "If X were (timelessly) the case then Y would (timelessly) be the case", then we will have to accept many sentences whose truth-conditions are quite unclear. Quine gives a pair of examples, which he attributes to Goodman, to illustrate the point: "If Caesar were in command, he would use the atom bomb; If Caesar were in command, he would use catapults". (Ibid.)[13]

In Quine's view we thus have ample reason to ban the general idiom of subjunctive conditionals from canonical notation. But this is not to say that all such conditionals are unacceptable. Disposition terms are essential to Quine's account of language, as we have emphasized, and such terms embody subjunctive conditionals: "To say that an object a is (water-) soluble at time t is to say that if a were placed in water at t, a would dissolve at t". (WO, p. 222.) Quine takes dispositions to be "a better-behaved lot than the general run of subjunctive conditionals" because "they are conceived as built-in, enduring structural traits" (WO, p. 223). To ascribe a disposition to an object is thus to claim that it has a micro-structure of a given kind. Quine, as we saw, defends terms such as "soluble" by arguing that they refer to the known or unknown micro-structure of the object: other objects which we assume to have a micro-structure similar to this one have been observed to dissolve, and this gives us reason to suppose that this object too is soluble, whether or not it is ever in water. Adding a note from our recent discussion, the presumption is that the object has a micro-structure which is connected with dissolving-when-in-water by a generalization which is embedded in the rest of our knowledge in a way that encourages us to think that it will hold even novel cases—a generalization more like (A) above, rather than like (B).

Caesar too has his micro-structure, or any given time-slice of Caesar does. But to imagine an object with that micro-structure in charge of a twentieth-century army is absurd: it would be a person who spoke only Latin and (probably) Ancient Greek, and had no knowledge at all of modern weaponry, strategy, or political constraints. That is not what we imagine when we say that Caesar would have used the atom bomb; we imagine a person like Caesar in some ways and unlike in others, with no clarity in detail about which is which. So claims about what Caesar would do under such-and-such circumstances are unclear, in a way that is in sharp contrast with claims about the solubility of sugar-lumps or the fragility of glasses. The point here is not that human beings are far more complex than glasses and sugar-lumps, though they are. We may find that people who learn one foreign language easily also learn others easily if they make the attempt. This may give us reason to postulate a "built-in, enduring structural trait" that such persons have and others of us lack. The complexity of persons makes it impossible, currently at least, to specify that trait in micro-structural terms, but Quine argues that that does not matter. All we need is reason to believe that there is such a micro-structure, perhaps of highly disjunctive form, and that it is connected by a generalization which is embedded in the right sort of way with the exceedingly complex nexus of activities and responses that we call "learning a foreign language easily". But it is only if we have such reason that we can be confident that there is such a structural trait, or that we can give a reasonable basis for such subjunctive conditionals as: "If Mary had studied Spanish she would have learnt it easily".

It is thus Quine's view that some disposition terms, and some subjunctive conditionals, have relatively clear truth-conditions and a respectable physicalistic basis, while others do not. Since some do not, he does not admit "the subjunctive conditional or the dispositional operator '-ble' as a freely applicable ingredient of canonical notation" (WO, p. 225); admitting those would be admitting all subjunctive conditionals, and every disposition term that can be formed. This general ban, however, is compatible with Quine's position that we can accept, as part of regimented theory, sentences dealing with respectable cases of disposition terms and subjunctive conditionals. Those respectable cases include the dispositions which are emphasized in Quine's discussion of language; those dispositions, he claims, can be identified with structural traits of language-users.

CONCLUSION

We have distinguished two very general aspects of Quine's philosophy. What I have called the epistemological aspect chiefly takes the form of a genetic project: an account, in purely naturalistic terms, of how an infant might acquire knowledge, and the language in which that knowledge is expressed. What I have called the metaphysical aspect takes the form of a clarificatory project. This involves both setting out what Quine takes to be the clearest and simplest form of language in which our theory can be phrased and showing how our theory could be accommodated within that language. I speak of this aspect of Quine's work as *metaphysical* because of his claim that "all traits of reality worthy of the name can be set down in an idiom of this austere form if in any idiom." (*WO*, p. 228); its methods and its point, however, are quite unlike those of traditional metaphysics.

We have mentioned, in passing, one way in which the two aspects of Quine's work are related: the "naturalistic terms" in which the genetic project is to be carried out are those set out in the metaphysical project. But we have so far said little else about the relation between the two aspects. Nor have we said much about what it would be for either one—or Quine's philosophy as a whole—to be successful. These issues, the relation between the two aspects of his thought and the criteria for its success, are connected. A consideration of this matter will lead to a brief discussion of various ways in which one might disagree with Quine.

To begin with, it may seem as if the criteria for the success of Quine's genetic project are clear-cut. At least as Quine presents that project, it is a more or less straightforward scientific issue: can we give a purely naturalistic account of a child's acquisition of language and knowledge? (Of particular importance here is the fact that a purely naturalistic account would not presuppose terms or principles which Quine would dismiss as mentalistic.) Or better, perhaps: do we have a reason to think that such an account

363

is in principle available, even if we are not, and may never be, in a position to give it in detail? The project would, presumably, succeed if we had a clear affirmative answer to this question. Quine claims to have given a sketch of an account of the required kind, a sketch that makes it plausible that a full account is in principle available. A crucial presupposition which he makes here concerns the nature of the phenomena for which we are seeking to account. His project has no chance of success unless we assume that the phenomena are described in what he counts as a scientific, naturalistic, fashion. For example: if we think that what must be explained is *understanding*, construed, in a mentalistic fashion, as something more than simply the ability to use the language in ways that accord with other speakers, then we will presumably find any sort of naturalistic explanation to be lacking. So Quine must be understood as aiming to make it plausible that it is, in principle, possible to give a purely naturalistic account of the phenomena of the acquisition of knowledge and of cognitive language, when those phenomena are described in what he would take to be a naturalistic fashion. Opinions may differ as to whether he has in fact succeeded in this task; my concern here is with the criteria for the success of his philosophy as a whole.

The idea that the genetic project has relatively clear-cut criteria for success, that it is a relatively straightforward scientific issue, goes naturally with another kind of question about it. What is its philosophical interest? Why should we—we philosophers, that is—care about the answer to this question, any more than we care about the answers to myriads of other scientific questions? Why should we be particularly interested in an account of human cognition which avoids taking for granted terms which Quine would count as mentalistic, such as "meaning" or "proposition"? Regardless of the question of the *success* of the project, what is its *significance*?

The answer to these questions leads us to the metaphysical aspect of Quine's work, i.e. to the idea that "all traits of reality worthy of the name" can be described in a suitably clarified and simplified language—the sort of language that we examined in the previous five chapters. The philosophical significance of the genetic project is primarily that it functions as a defence of the metaphysical claim. The most obvious reason to doubt that claim is that our knowledge of the human mind may not seem to fit into Quine's framework; that sort of knowledge, it might be thought, must be phrased using just the sort of mentalistic terms which Quine excludes from his austere language. The genetic project is a sustained response to this issue, or at least to the narrower issue of fitting our knowledge of human cognition into the framework. How are we to understand human cognition in a scientific way, using only methods which have proved themselves in application to the natural world? Quine tackles this question with a seriousness which is almost without precedent among philosophers.[1] He attempts to sketch an account which takes for granted only principles and ideas which are justified by their role in our most successful sciences; in consequence, he expends great effort in attempting to explain even the most rudimentary kind of cognitive language. Quine's genetic project is thus primarily in service of his metaphysical claim: if our knowledge of human cognition, and perhaps of the human mind in general, can be fitted into Quine's austere idiom then, he holds, we have reason to think that that idiom can indeed encompass "all traits of reality worthy of the name".

We should note in passing that many philosophers who call themselves naturalists take for granted ideas of a very different sort from those used in successful empirical sciences—ideas such as belief, say, or reference, or meaning. The austerity of Quine's regimented theory, by contrast, is marked, and is crucial for naturalism as he understands it. Only by looking at the details of his genetic project, as we did in Chapters 5 and 6, can one see what naturalism comes to, in Quine's hands, and how seriously he takes it.

We might sum up the relation between the two aspects of Quine's work by saying that each depends upon the other, but in different ways. On the one hand: much of the philosophical *significance* of the epistemological aspect of Quine's work, at least of the genetic project, depends on the metaphysical aspect of that work; without the metaphysical claim, Quine's genetic project might succeed, but its philosophical interest would be unclear. On the other hand: the *feasibility* of the metaphysical project depends on the genetic project. If the latter project were to fail, the metaphysical claim would be quite implausible. For in that case there would be a range of phenomena—those concerning human cognition— which could not be fitted into Quine's austere idiom. So the success of the genetic project is a necessary condition for the success of the metaphysical aspect of Quine's work.

The success of the genetic project is not, however, a *sufficient* condition for the success of the metaphysical project. One might accept the former and still deny the latter, and for any one of various reasons; we shall discuss three. The first can be very briefly explained. One might think that even if we can in principle account for human cognition along what Quine would take to be naturalistic lines, still there may be other aspects of the mind that are less tractable. That is an issue which could, presumably, be transformed into a scientific task, along the general lines of Quine's genetic project. Perhaps its chances of success would be lower, but no new issues of principle seem to arise. Although the question here is relatively easy to explain, answering it might prove extremely difficult.

A second kind of reason for thinking Quine wrong will require a little more discussion, since it comes in two importantly different varieties. Stated quite generally, it is that one might think that Quine's austere language wrongly excludes some parts of our knowledge from our account of "the true and ultimate structure of reality" (WO, p. 221). One kind of example would be mental phenomena, where these are not described in Quine's extensionalist and physicalist language but rather in an ordinary unscientific way. Another example is modality; modal facts, it might be said, are real, and Quine's exclusion of them is arbitrary and baseless. Each of these issues has been, and continues to be, the subject of much recent philosophical discussion, most of which, from Quine's point of view, is not useful. My discussion will proceed in terms of modality, but is intended to apply more broadly.

The two varieties of the idea we are now considering can be distinguished by separating two claims which might be cited in justification of the view that Quine is wrong to exclude modality. (The distinction, we should note, is itself made from a Quinean point of view—as, indeed, is our whole discussion of how one might disagree with Quine.) One is the claim that modality is, contrary to Quine's view, indispensable to science—to what Quine himself would accept as science. Quine holds that modal notions are unclear, but it might conceivably be shown that trying to do science without them results in a degree of inconvenience and complication which outweighs the unclarity which results from accepting them as part of the austere language of regimented theory. (It might also be the case that their scientific use would enable us to clarify them so they came closer to meeting Quine's standards.) If some such claim were indeed convincingly made out, the Quinean response would be to expand the language of regimented theory so as to include modality. The idea of an austere scientific idiom which encompassed "all traits of reality worthy of the name" would presumably remain, although it would turn out to be in one respect significantly less austere than Quine himself thought. (Perhaps we cannot exclude the possibility that relaxing Quinean constraints in this way would, when thought through, somehow undermine the whole enterprise; hence "presumably".)

The claims of modality might also be advanced on the basis of a different sort of reason, however. It might be asserted that modality, although not indispensable to science, is an undeniable part of our ordinary way of conceiving the world and that it therefore deserves to be counted as a trait of reality. (More or less equivalently, for our purposes, it might be asserted that our "intuitions" give us knowledge of modal facts, which must be given a place in any account of reality.) Here the Quinean disagreement would be at a deeper level. Fundamental to Quine's view is the idea that our ordinary ways of thinking, just as we find them, should not be taken as telling us the way the world is; that those ways of thinking should only be taken in that way when they are revised and systematized in the light of the ideal of a systematic, overarching, and empirically based theory of the world. The point can be made by talking about metaphysics. As against Carnap, for example, Quine's philosophy allows for a revival of what may well look like metaphysics: it makes sense of the question whether there really are numbers, for example, or modal facts. But there is nothing transcendent, or even transcendental, in Quinean metaphysics. To the contrary: that subject is constrained by what Quine thinks of as the requirements of systematic empirical science. Although exceedingly remote from anything that one might count as empirical evidence, metaphysics as Quine understands it is supposed to be under some sort of empirical control; it thus counts as a respectable enterprise for the scientific philosopher to engage in. It is, we might say, metaphysics naturalized; in some contexts, indeed, it may seem odd to call it "metaphysics" at all.

This Quinean construal of metaphysics contrasts sharply with the anti-Quinean idea presently under consideration. By relying on unreconstructed common sense, or on "intuition", this latter idea reinstates metaphysics with no reliable constraints—or so Quine would see it. It is metaphysics in a stronger and more traditional sense, in what Quine would think of as a pejorative sense. It allows us to take ordinary ideas or alleged intuitions and on that basis to erect a complex structure of ideas, far beyond anything that is found in unreconstructed common sense. (The techniques of modern logic, and set-theory, are often used to erect an elaborate structure on what Quine would claim to be a very flimsy base.) In the process we generate questions, problems, and even paradoxes; as Quine would see the matter, we are thus reinstating an irresponsible kind of metaphysics which the scientific philosopher has every reason to reject. There is considerable historical irony here. Quine would certainly have less sympathy with this sort of non-scientific metaphysics than he has with the views of Carnap. His arguments against Carnap, and against Logical Positivism more generally, however, undermined the idea that there was a basis on which attempts at metaphysics could be definitely ruled out as meaningless. By doing that, Quine's work may well have had the effect of encouraging a revival of just the sort of metaphysics which he would most strongly oppose.

The anti-Quinean ideas discussed in the two previous paragraphs might be expressed by saying that by subordinating claims about reality to science, by naturalizing metaphysics, Quine leaves too little room for real metaphysics—that he unjustly denigrates the legitimate claims of non-scientific metaphysics. But his work might also be criticized on the grounds that it is too metaphysical; this is the third of our three ways in which one might reject Quine's metaphysics while not casting doubt on the possibility of a naturalistic and scientific account of the human mind. (Although perhaps leaving such an account without any very evident philosophical interest.)

One philosopher whose name is associated with this thoroughgoing kind of opposition to metaphysics is Rudolf Carnap. In the main body of the book we discussed Carnap as an influence on Quine, but made no attempt to give a balanced depiction of his ideas. Perhaps those ideas, more sympathetically interpreted or suitably modified, might be made the basis for a plausible scientific philosophy which rejects the whole idea of "all traits of reality worthy of the name", i.e. which rejects any form of metaphysics, including both Quine's constrained version and the unconstrained version recently discussed. One difficulty likely to face an attempt to interpret or modify Carnap's ideas in this sort of way is that any basis on which metaphysics can be rejected is liable to have its own philosophical presuppositions. The attempt to reject metaphysics may thus involve one in metaphysics after all. It is a dialectic that is familiar from other moments in the history of philosophy: an attempt to reject metaphysics may rest on what other philosophers argue are metaphysical assumptions after all; the anti-metaphysician stands accused of metaphysics. (Hume, on some interpretations, is a good example.)

A philosopher who is acutely conscious of this danger is Wittgenstein. By his own account, he does not, in his later writings, put forward a doctrine which shows that metaphysics is impossible or nonsensical—a doctrine which might be charged with making metaphysical assumptions of its own. He seeks, rather, to expose and to undermine the intellectual steps that first lead us towards metaphysics—that lead us, for example, to think that we should take seriously the idea of a language in which "all traits of reality worthy of the name" can be described. He does not so much attempt to show metaphysics to be nonsensical, or based on faulty reasoning, as to show us the nature of the intellectual temptations which lead us towards metaphysics, in the hope that when those temptations are exposed we will see that we can, and should, resist them.

Quine's work can be seen as a different kind of response to the dialectic of metaphysics and anti-metaphysics. He does not repudiate metaphysics, but neither does he embrace it in anything like its traditional form. Rather, he reinterprets it; he naturalizes it, making it responsible to the idea of the best language for accommodating our science. As always, however, there is a price to be paid. The price is that we have to accept that "the best language for accommodating our science" is an idiom in which "all traits of reality worthy of the name can be set down" (if, indeed, they can be set down in any idiom). This is a presupposition of Quine's naturalized metaphysics, not a result that can be drawn from it. What reasons can be offered in favour of the presupposition? In Quine's view, "our science" is just what we take ourselves to know about the world, when that knowledge has been refined and critically scrutinized in ways which enhance its objectivity, clarity, simplicity, and fruitfulness. He envisages this knowledge being expressed in a regimented language, extensional and physicalistic; this idea is, on his account, simply a further development along the same lines, a further way of refining and improving our knowledge. He holds that there is thus every reason to accept that our knowledge, as improved in this way, gives us the best available picture of reality.

NOTES

Introduction

1 But some have, of course; see for example Roger Gibson, *The Philosophy of W. V. Quine* (especially pp. xvii f.) and *Enlightened Empiricism* (especially pp. xv f.).

2 I have elaborated on this latter idea elsewhere; see especially the introductions to *Russell, Idealism, and the Emergence of Analytic Philosophy* and to *Propositions, Functions, and Analysis*.

3 In distinguishing two projects, or two aspects of Quine's work, I disagree to some extent with Roger Gibson, who at times seems to take the first aspect to be Quine's only concern. He says: "[Quine's] philosophy is best understood as a systematic attempt to answer ... what he takes to be the central question of epistemology, namely, 'How do we acquire our theory of the world?' " (*Enlightened Empiricism*, p. 1, *et passim*). There is, however, much in Quine's thought that does not fall happily into that category.

1   Overview: Quine's naturalism

1 "Philosophers in the professional sense have no peculiar fitness ... for helping to get society on an even keel, though we should all do what we can", "Has Philosophy Lost Contact with People?" *TT*, p. 193.

2 See "On the Nature of Moral Values", *TT*, pp. 55–66. The essay concludes by contrasting our claims about "ultimate values" unfavourably with science, which at least has "empirical checkpoints".

3 "Wie Schiffer sind wir, die ihr Schiff auf offener See umbauen müssen, ohne es jemals in einem Dock zerlegen und aus besten Bestandteilen neu errichten zu können". Neurath, "Protokollsätze"; the translation is mine.

4 In this usage "science" applies to any systematic and organized body of knowledge; Quine often uses that word instead of the term "knowledge", about which he has doubts. (This usage is perhaps closer to that of the German word *Wissenschaft* than to that of the English word as it is now commonly used.)

5 See Gilbert Harman, "Quine on Meaning and Existence, I"; the most explicit statement of this view is on the first page of the essay.

6 Not all such airwaves will be relevant, of course. And language can equally be a matter of writing or signing. Quine's view can take account of these facts.

7 The phrase "pure inquiry" here is intended to echo Bernard Williams's apt description of Descartes' epistemological project; see his: *Descartes: The Project of Pure Inquiry*.

8 *Almost* unimaginable: for an attempt to imagine such a thing, see again Paul M. Churchland, op. cit., pp. 20–21. That attempt, however, takes us well beyond what might be suggested by current neurological research and into the realm of science fiction. If it became plausible then perhaps the correct Quinean attitude would be to give up on the idea of knowledge as embodied in language.

9 The question, what is it for our language to be about the world?, could easily be thought of as metaphysical rather than epistemological. Given Quine's approach, however, it is easier to treat it along with more straightforwardly epistemological questions. No issue of principle is at stake here: Quinean epistemology is contained within metaphysics, as we saw in the discussion of reciprocal containment, a few pages back.

10 As indicated in the Introduction, my emphasis on the second aspect of Quine's work is a point of disagreement with Roger Gibson (see note 2 of the Introduction). Christopher Hookway's *Quine*, by contrast, does not mention the genetic project at all; this strikes me as a more significant distortion of Quine's thought.

2   Quine's philosophical background: beginnings; logic; Carnap

1 TDR, p. 266. I have discussed the early lectures mentioned here in "'the defensible province of philosophy': Quine's 1934 Lectures on Carnap".

2 Of these works Quine says: "I read them compulsively and believed and forgot all". (H&S, p. 6).

3 H&S, p. 7. Quine may have been more influenced by a course he took on psychology, where he read John B. Watson's *Psychology from the Standpoint of a Behaviourist*. He says of this course: "Nor do I recall that it shocked any preconceptions. It chimed in with my predilections". (TDR, pp. 265–66).

4 On Duhem, Quine says: "when I wrote and presented 'Two Dogmas' . . . I didn't know about Duhem. Both Hempel and Philip Frank subsequently brought Duhem to my attention, so I inserted a footnote" (TDR, p. 269). On pragmatism, Quine says of his use of that word near the end of "Two Dogmas": "This passage had unforeseen consequences. I suspect it is responsible for my being widely classified as a pragmatist. I don't object, except that I am not clear on what it takes to qualify as a pragmatist. I was merely taking Carnap's word and handing it back to him". (TDR, p. 272; see also B&G, p. 292). In fact, however, Carnap never, or almost never, uses the word "pragmatism" or its cognates in the relevant sense; Quine may here be influenced by C. I. Lewis, who certainly did use the word in that sense and was explicitly indebted to the pragmatists. (See, for example, section 1 of *An Analysis of Knowledge and Valuation*.) There may have been some indirect influence of the pragmatists on Quine, via Lewis's teaching.

5 Russell's *Our Knowledge of the External World* is subtitled "as a field for scientific method in philosophy"; "On Scientific Method in Philosophy" is also the title of an important essay that he published in 1914.

6 Quine's dissertation was submitted in 1932 under the title "The Logic of Sequences: A Generalization of *Principia Mathematica*"; it was published as a book in 1990.

7 They consistently use the word "class" rather than "set" but the latter is the modern usage, and I shall stick to it. In some technical contexts a distinction is made between sets and classes, but no such matter will concern us in this work.

8 Readers wanting more detail, and less compression, could hardly do better than Frege's *Foundations of Arithmetic* or Russell's *Introduction to Mathematical Philosophy*, both of them non-technical works.

9 On the back of the paperback edition of portions of the book (Cambridge: Cambridge University Press, 1962). The sentence was no doubt offered in response to a request from the publisher, but there is no reason to doubt its sincerity.

10 Joseph S. Ullian, "Quine and the Field of Mathematical Logic", p. 569. Ullian perhaps overstates the infancy of mathematical logic at the time of Quine's engagement with it.

11 H&S, p. 10. Quine goes on to emphasize the significance of clarity about use and mention, and the fact that the system put forward in his dissertation, unlike that of *Principia Mathematica*, is extensional. In a discussion of the same matter in "Two Dogmas in Retrospect" it is again extensionality that is chiefly emphasized; see p. 266.

12 Our concern, of course, is with explaining Carnap's influence on Quine, rather than with giving a balanced or comprehensive account of his work. I shall focus on those aspects of his work which are most important from this perspective; I shall interpret that work in the sort of way in which Quine seems to have done, without worrying whether this distorts Carnap's thought.

13 We should emphasize again that this is *Quine's* interpretation of the *Aufbau*. (See, for example, "Russell's Ontological Development", *TT*, p. 84.) Recent scholars have disputed it. See especially Michael Friedman, *Reconsidering Logical Positivism*, particularly the introduction and essays five and six; and Alan Richardson, *Carnap's Construction of the World*.

14 This statement requires rather complicated qualifications, which we cannot spell out fully here. Roughly: *my* construction of the world uses *my* experiences, but they can only be identified as mine when the construction is complete; the construction does not begin by assuming that they are mine, or that there is a me at all. It simply begins with unowned experiences: "the given has no subject" (*das Gegebene ist subjectlos*), as Carnap says (the phrase is the title of section 65; I have slightly modified the translation).

15 This paragraph is largely drawn from the present author's "Analyticity and the Indeterminacy of Translation"; see especially pp. 171–72.

16 This is, disregarding some subtleties, Carnap's mature view of analyticity. His earlier view is significantly different, and owes more to the notion of a tautology as it occurs in Wittgenstein's *Tractatus*.

3   The analytic–synthetic distinction

1 Lewis says, for example: "Mind makes classifications and determines meanings; in so doing it creates the *a priori* truth of analytic judgments". "A Pragmatic Conception of the *A Priori*", p. 233. For a short sentence, this contains, from Quine's point of view, a remarkable amount of error. See also, for example, Lewis's *Mind and the World Order*, Chapter VII.

2 It seems to have been this insight that led Quine, in the early 1950s, to go public with his long-held doubts about Carnap's distinction; in the late 1930s and the 1940s the doubts were purely negative, and he did not think them worth publishing. See TDR, p. 267.

3 We shall return to questions of existence and ontology, and of what it means to "accept" entities of a given kind; see Chapter 12, below.

4 See, for example, Grice and Strawson, "In Defense of a Dogma", pp. 146–47.

5 A third context, perhaps the fundamental one, is knowing the meaning, or understanding. Quine was slow to recognize this third context explicitly; see, however, "Mind and Verbal Dispositions", especially p. 86. As we have stressed, a crucial part of Quine's thought is the attempt to show that we can give a purely naturalistic account of language-use (hence of "understanding", or of the real facts behind that vague and mentalistic idea).— This is essentially the project that I discuss in Chapters 4–6, below.

6 "Meaning and Synonymy in Natural Languages", p. 234; he does not, however, accept that such criteria are necessary for the legitimacy of the concepts; see p. 235 of the same essay.

7 It is often thought that Quine takes the idea of approaching language via questions about translation from this work of Carnap's, and that the indeterminacy thesis is a response to "Meaning and Synonymy in Natural Languages". (E.g. Soames, *Philosophical Analysis in the Twentieth Century*, vol. II, p. 225.) But this cannot be entirely correct; see Chapter 8, especially pp. 198–9 for details.

8 See, for example, Gary Ebbs, *Rule-Following and Realism*, especially chapter 5.

9 Carnap makes just this point in his reply to "Two Dogmas", a reply unpublished in Carnap's lifetime, now printed in *Dear Carnap, Dear Van*, ed. Richard Creath. I shall cite this elsewhere in this section as "Reply to TDE".

10 That we share such intuitions—that we almost always agree in classifying sentences as analytic or as synthetic—is a point that Grice and Strawson insist upon. See "In Defense of a Dogma", pp. 142–43.

11 This focus on assertions does not imply that Quine thinks that assertion is the only form of behaviour that is in principle relevant to meaning; to the contrary, any form of behaviour may play this role. See the third section of Chapter 5, below.

12 It might be thought that we need no reason, but make a wholly arbitrary choice. This is more or less the position that Quine approvingly attributes to Carnap in his 1934 "Lectures on Carnap". It is implausible on the face of it that an arbitrary choice can generate an epistemologically significant distinction; we shall come to the general issue shortly.

13 I inject a note of qualification here because I think it is in fact unclear whether Carnap is trying to provide an epistemological distinction of exactly the sort that Quine requires. I shall ignore this worry in what follows: the focus of our interest is Quine, not Carnap.

14 It might be argued that a *meta-language* is presupposed and that we can appeal to its rules; but then the crucial question concerns choice of meta-language, and this question will raise exactly the same issues as those which were supposed to be settled by invoking a meta-language.

15 In the next two paragraphs, and elsewhere in this section, I draw on my essay "Analyticity and the Indeterminacy of Translation".

16 In practice, however, hardly any sentences will have interesting ramifications outside a fragment of theory significantly smaller than the whole. In TDR Quine says of holism which takes the whole theory as the relevant unit that it: "is true enough in a legalistic sort of way, but it diverts attention from what is more to the point: the varying degrees of proximity to observation" (p. 268).

17 Frege, indeed, takes the fact that arithmetic shares the universality of logic to be a reason for thinking the subjects identical; see "On Formal Theories of Arithmetic", p. 112.

18 But only *almost* certain: a modification to the law of the excluded middle was in fact proposed by Birkhoff and von Neumann in 1936, as a way of accommodating quantum mechanics. See Quine's *Philosophy of Logic*, pp. 85–86; also Hilary Putnam's "The Logic of Quantum Mechanics".

19 For one version of a worked out Quinean view of mathematics, see Michael D. Resnik, *Mathematics as a Science of Patterns*.

4 Reconceiving epistemology

1 An important source of this picture is Russell's *Problems of Philosophy*, an immensely influential work. In that book, both sources of knowledge are said to be based on an immediate and presuppositionless relation in which we stand to certain entities, the relation of acquaintance. In the one case, our acquaintance with abstract entities plays the crucial role; in the other case our acquaintance with entities given in sensation—sense data—and memories of such entities. See especially Chapter IV, V, and VII of *Problems*. In later twentieth-century philosophy the a priori element in knowledge was often more or less identified with logic, and often held to be purely tautological or conventional.

2 EN, *OR*, p. 72; on Quine's views about Hume, see his "1946 Lectures on Hume" and also Michael Pakaluk, "Quine's 1946 Lectures on Hume". Robert Fogelin argues for a considerable sympathy between Quine and Hume on the issue of the justification of knowledge. (See Fogelin, "Aspects of Quine's Naturalized Epistemology".) In a late work Quine goes so far as to say that we are not "entitled" to rely on induction; see "Response to Hookway". This may be an overstatement: insofar as induction is part of the ordinary

scientific method, a naturalist presumably *is* entitled to rely on it. What we cannot do, however, is to appeal to induction to justify scientific method itself.

3 It might be thought that Quine's position here illegitimately excludes the idea of innate knowledge. As we shall see, Quine fully accepts the idea of innate predispositions to form beliefs. (This is a point that we shall return to in the fifth section, below.) From his point of view it is not clear what could justify us in going beyond this, and speaking also of innate *knowledge*. It is also important to emphasize that our primary concern here is with how people know about their current physical environment; in that context the idea of innate knowledge seems quite unpromising.

4 In his late work Quine uses the expression "neural intake" rather than "stimulation". The change is terminological, made because some readers found the latter term misleading; no shift in doctrine is being signalled. See L&S, p. 349.

5 We should not, however, exaggerate Quine's claims to continuity here; on the same page he says: "I call the pursuit naturalized epistemology, but I have no quarrel with traditionalists who protest my retention of the latter word. I agree with them that repudiation of the Cartesian dream is no minor deviation".

6 The "more or less" is important here: "One may be perfectly intelligible in broken English and entirely unintelligible though one's sentences are constructed perfectly". H. O. Mounce, *Wittgenstein's Tractatus*, p. 121.

7 Yet stimulations of my sensory surfaces, while in principle observable, are certainly not shared. A large issue lurks here; we shall postpone consideration of it until the next chapter.

8 I gain some encouragement for this view from two passages. One is from a letter written by Quine to Roger Gibson in December of 1984:

> When I have stressed that language is learned through observation of overt behavior without telepathic aids, I have encapsulated the point by saying that linguistics has to be behavioristic; but if the term ["behaviourism"] does not fit my account, the term is what should be dropped.
>
> (Quoted in Gibson, *Enlightened Empiricism*, p. 129)

The other is from one of Quine's most vehement critics:

> I shall also make no objection to Quine's statement that "the behaviorist approach is mandatory". The behaviorism he has in mind here is not the dreaded reductive doctrine of days gone by, but merely a way of putting the study of language on a par with other sciences by requiring the linguist's theoretical constructions to be justified on the basis of objective evidence in the form of overt behavior of speakers. ... Quine's behaviorism is thus a behaviorism one can live with. ... Quine's behaviorism merely takes linguists out of their armchairs and puts them in the field facing the task of having to arrive at a theory of language on the basis of the overt behavior of its speakers in overt circumstances.
>
> (Jerrold Katz, "The Refutation of Indeterminacy", in B&G, pp. 179–80)

9 This does not guarantee that, in the relevant circumstances, each of us would in fact say "Yes". As we have already said, dispositions come with a *ceteris paribus* clause. The manifestation of a disposition may be inhibited, perhaps by another and more powerful disposition.

10 See "Philosophical Progress in Language Theory", where Quine speaks of the "behaviorizing of meaning" as "simply a proposal to approach semantical matters in the empirical spirit of natural science"; he then says: "An aid to taking this proposal seriously is the *Gedankenexperiment* [thought experiment] of radical translation". (P. 8.) Although Quine's radical translation is very much an idealization, there are actual cases which approximate it, most famously those involving Kenneth Pike; see Pike, "Into the Unknown".

374

11 Quine does not, of course, think of the infant as proceeding in anything like this way. This point might seem too obvious to state, but it has been claimed that on an empiricist account *all* learning involves the forming and testing of hypotheses, and hence that an empiricist is committed to the view that the learning of a first (public) language must take place in another language, which is not learned but wholly innate. See, most notably, J. A. Fodor, *The Language of Thought* and Fodor, *RePresentations*. Quine's account is an empiricist one on his understanding of empiricism, but not in Fodor's perhaps eccentric sense of that term.

12 Cf., among many others, Christopher Peacocke, "The Philosophy of Language". The most immediately relevant discussion is on pp. 74ff.

13 See *Word and Object*, pp. 35f. Quine speaks there of *verdicts* (assent or dissent) changing from occasion to occasion; elsewhere he speaks, as I have done, of *truth-values*; see for example *Word and Object*, p. 193.

5 The beginnings of cognitive language

1 As mentioned in the previous chapter, Quine comes to prefer the term "neural intake" to "sensory stimulation". I shall use them more or less interchangeably.

2 It is sometimes claimed that language is innate, at least in its essential aspects. No doubt there is much which is innate in animals which can acquire human language, and absent in those that cannot. Still, a German child grows up saying "Baum" under roughly the circumstances under which a French child says "arbre" and an English child says "tree". How a child comes to respond to tree-like sensory stimulations is clearly a matter of nurture, not of nature only, so there are aspects to language that are not innate. Because of Quine's focus on language as embodying knowledge, it is those aspects which are relevant here. See also Chapter 4, third section, above.

3 Assent and dissent need to be mentioned separately, as here, since one does not determine the other; sometimes speakers will neither assent nor dissent, because they are uncertain, or in a state of shock, or for some other reason. For the sake of brevity, however, I shall often simply speak of assent.

It might seem more natural to take the relevant form of behaviour to be *uttering* the observation sentence, rather than assenting or dissenting. Some children do seem to acquire a disposition to utter some observation sentences whenever they are undergoing the relevant stimulation; that disposition, however, is fairly rapidly inhibited by the response of adults to such ceaseless babbling.

4 In *Roots of Reference*, though not in *From Stimulus to Science*, Quine adapts the mathematical idea of a *neighbourhood* to clarify the idea of two episodes being "sufficiently receptually similar"; see *RR*, p. 17.

5 Strictly speaking, it is not necessary that all of these stimulation patterns should be perceptually similar to one another. Each might be perceptually similar to some paradigm, but not to all of the others, because transitivity may fail. More drastically, it may be that there are a number of distinct paradigms, and that what is required is perceptual similarity to any one of them; provided the number were reasonably small this would be no obstacle. I shall ignore these complications.

6 Here I ignore the fact that we have explained perceptual similarity as a three-place relation, not a two-place relation; the points could be translated to the more accurate idiom, but at the cost of some complexity.

7 Quine introduced the notion of stimulus meaning at a time when the privacy of stimulations was not clear to him (see especially *WO*, section 8). As the matter became clearer to him, he eventually advocated dropping the term "stimulus meaning" entirely. Citing Føllesdal, he says: "the word 'meaning' is misleading here, since a linguistic meaning should be the same for the whole linguistic community, whereas neural intakes

are clearly not comparable from person to person. So I drop the term". (L&S, p. 350.) The change, however, is more terminological than substantive, and I shall occasionally use the term.

8 Compare a nice comment of Quine's, on the role of innate endowments beyond mere quality spacing in the learning of language:

> Two generations ago, the supplementary innate endowment that got the main credit was an instinct for mimicry. One generation ago, a babbling instinct moved to first place; the infant babbles at random and the parent reinforces these utterances selectively. Currently, the babbling instinct is losing favor and the instinct for mimicry is back in the ascendancy. I expect that both of these innate aids are there, and also of course the innate spacing of qualities, as well as some further innate apparatus which has not yet been identified.
>
> ("Philosophical Progress in Language Theory",
> p. 6; note that this was written in 1970)

9 Stephen Pinker speaks of communities in which parents "do not speak to their children at all, except to make occasional demands and rebukes" (*The Language Instinct*, p. 40). He even goes so far as to claim in his introductory chapter that language "develops in the child spontaneously" (p. 18)—a claim that is, however, contradicted by his more careful discussion at pp. 276–83.

10 Merely witnessing talk, regardless of its content, will not do. Pinker cites the fact that hearing children born to deaf parents do not learn to speak by watching television. He comments: "Live human speakers tend to talk about the here and now in the presence of children" (op. cit., p. 278). Talk about "the here and now" will no doubt consist largely of what Quine calls observation sentences, or at least those which are observational relative to the child's immediate social circle. It is exposure to that kind of talk—to the assertion of observation sentences in appropriate circumstances—which is required if a child is to acquire language.

11 Strictly, the adult's response is keyed to her own global stimulations—those which are typically caused by events or objects in the environment which give rise, in the child, to global stimulations which are perceptually similar for the child.

12 I say "almost any" so as not to rule out, dogmatically, the possibility of sentences which escape this kind of argument. But it is hard to see how any could. Even a sentence such as "It *looks* red" may be corrigible; some device might be contrived to stimulate the utterer's retinal nerves directly, rather than by a red object or an object with red light shining on it; in that case the utterer may be mistaken. Note that "It looks red *to me*" is presumably not an observation sentence at all, for it fails the intersubjectivity requirement.

13 Quine's late appeal to immediate and unreflective assent thus does not fully accommodate deceptive situations. If situations of this kind are possible for a sentence then in appropriate conditions a person will assent immediately to such a sentence *unless* she has reason to think that the situation is a deceptive one. If she does have reason to think that, then she may dissent, or hesitate, pending further investigation.

14 In "I, You, and It", Quine defines the degree of observationality of a sentence along the lines that I am suggesting here, and for much the same reasons; see O&K, pp. 4–5. In *Word and Object*, however, he gives a rather different definition of the term.

15 Louise Antony claims that "there appear to be physical features of the speech stream that are universally indicative of phrasal boundaries", and, more generally, that language-learning "relies on a body of evidence that is ... composed of stuff of which mature speakers are generally unaware (prosodic patterns, syllabic contingencies)" (Antony, "Naturalizing Radical Translation", pp. 148–49). She makes these claims as if they told against Quine, but it is hard to see anything here that Quine would not readily accept, or that his view could not readily accommodate.

16 See, for example, Elizabeth S. Spelke and Gretchen A. Van de Walle, "Perceiving and Reasoning about Objects: Insights from Infants", and references given there.

17 Quine uses "body" here where others might use "physical object". He uses this latter term in a more general way, for what occupies any collection of spatiotemporal points, contiguous or not, no matter how miscellaneous the occupants. See Chapter 12, second section, below.

6 Beyond the observation sentences

1 Some qualification is needed here because of the corrigibility of observation sentences, discussed in the fourth section of the previous chapter. We might say that when you have acquired those dispositions you have learnt the sentence to a high degree, but not completely. This point complicates the picture but does not fundamentally alter it. I shall often ignore it in what follows.

2 An important example here is P. F. Strawson, who published a series of essays on related topics from the early 1950s to the mid-1980s. See especially "Reference and its Roots", and *Subject and Predicate in Logic and Grammar*.

3 There is a brief explanation of the symbolism and terminology used here in Chapter 10, first section, below.

4 This is a consistent theme in Quine's work. The words quoted occur both in the 1957 essay "Speaking of Objects" (*OR*, p. 23) and in the posthumously published essay "Confessions of a Confirmed Extensionalist" (p. 217).

5 The obvious example of such a view is that of Russell, who postulated a notion of acquaintance which brings us into direct contact with abstract objects as well as others.

7 Theory and evidence

1 See *PT*, p. 17, and *FSS*, p. 48. Strictly speaking it is the set of *synthetic* observation categoricals. (See *FSS*, p. 45; here Quine seems to get "first" and "second" the wrong way round; this was pointed out to me by Paul Gregory.) Also the notion of analytic observation categorical is relativized to speakers, so the notion of empirical content is too.—In what follows I shall feel free to ignore the points in this endnote.

2 Neither the criterion, nor its failure, are original with Quine. See Hempel, "The Empiricist Criterion of Meaning", section (2.3). Hempel in turn cites the first edition of Ayer, *Language, Truth and Logic* as putting forward the idea, and the second edition as making the criticism which shows that it fails.

3 A sentence contains a term *vacuously* if replacing it, at all its occurrences in the sentence, with any other term of the same grammatical category would result in a sentence with the same truth-value as the original. Quine speaks of a term which does not occur vacuously in a sentence as occurring *essentially*.

4 In EESW it is explicitly the former that is at stake. Quine speaks of "the doctrine that natural science is empirically under-determined; under-determined not just by past observation but by all observable events." (P. 313.) In his 1990 comment on an essay of Bergström's, however, he says: "In treating of the underdetermination of theories it is a poor idea to assume compatibility with all possible data. ... it is both unrealistic and irrelevant. What matters is that the theories ... imply ... all the same observation categoricals." (B&G, p. 53.) But later still, in the 1992 essay "Structure and Nature", Quine again speaks of "all possible observations" (p. 9; the phrase occurs also in both editions of *PT*, the first published in 1990, the second in 1992).

5 The distinction is emphasized by Bergström, who introduces the expression "weak underdetermination" to mean merely that there is a rival theory which implies the same observation categoricals as the one we are considering. The stronger version is, he thinks, "very unlikely". See Bergström, "Underdetermination of Physical Theory", especially pp.

100f. The fact that Quine does not rule out the stronger thesis is clear in *PT* where he says "now suppose rather that the rival theory is as neat and as natural as our own" (p. 99).

6 Quine sometimes attributes the manoeuvre that yields this conclusion to Donald Davidson; see, for example, *PT*, p. 97.

7 That Quine intends his holism in this sense, rather than the stronger sense, is explicit in his comment on Grünbaum in S. G. Harding, *Can Theories Be Refuted? Essays on the Duhem-Quine Thesis.* Quine accepts here that holism is "probably trivial" (p. 132). See also *PT*, p. 16.

8   Radical translation and its indeterminacy

1 Quine comes to favour this name for it, but sometimes also speaks of this second doctrine as "inscrutability of reference", or "ontological relativity". Some commentators have supposed that these names refer to different doctrines, but Quine explicitly denies this. See his "Reply to Roth", H&S, p. 459.

2 See Quine's 1937 essay "Is Logic a Matter of Words?" He suggests that the idea that the truth of logic is due to language can be approached by means of "the abstract consideration of an anthropological problem: the problem of determining whether a certain tribe of unknown tongue shares our logic" (ts. p. 5). He goes on to discuss ways in which a linguist might gather evidence for proposed translations.

3 Those who hold this view of the matter tend to ignore both Quine's early use of radical translation, noted above, and the way in which he introduces the subject in chapter 2 of *Word and Object.* He says the chapter will "consider how much of language can be made sense of in terms of its stimulus conditions, and what scope this leaves for empirically unconditioned variation in one's conceptual scheme" (p. 26). This closely follows his description in chapter 1 of his more general epistemological project:

> we can investigate the world, and man as a part of it, and thus find out what cues he could have of what goes on around him. Subtracting his cues from his world view, we get man's net contribution as the difference. This difference marks the extent of man's conceptual sovereignty
>
> (p. 5)

4 Part of the challenge issued by Grice and Strawson to Quine's views on meaning was to ask: "Is all talk of correct or incorrect *translation* of sentences of one language into sentences of another meaningless?" ("In Defense of a Dogma", p. 146.) Soames speaks of Quine's advocacy of indeterminacy as his "giving up on meaning and translation entirely" (*Philosophical Analysis in the Twentieth Century*, vol. I, p. 377); I hope it is clear that I completely disagree with this view of the matter.

5 *WO*, p. 27; this phrase occurs in a slightly different context, that in which Quine is imagining a given language mapped onto, or translated into, itself, rather than another language. But the point is the same.

6 This point is usefully stressed by Michael Friedman in "Physicalism and the Indeterminacy of Translation" and by Roger Gibson in chapter 5 of *Enlightened Empiricism* and in the overlapping essay "Translation, Physics, and Facts of the Matter".

7 Quine, "Reply to Putnam", H&S, p. 429. Both quoted passages are from this page. So also is the first sentence of the paragraph, except that I speak of "behavioural dispositions" instead of "speech dispositions" as Quine does there.

8 The doctrine is akin to one advanced by Ramsey about theoretical entities: that there is, so to speak, no more to such an object than the role that it plays in the structure of the relevant theory. All that matters is the truth-values of the theoretical sentences in which the object figures. For Quine, the point holds for all objects, since he "see[s] all objects as theoretical. ... Even our most primordial objects, bodies, are already theoretical—most

conspicuously so when we look to their individuation over time". (TPT, *TT*, p. 20.) See F. P. Ramsey, "Theories".

9 This paragraph overlaps one in my essay "Quine on Reference and Ontology"; I have also drawn on sections IV and V of that essay elsewhere in this section and in the next.

10 The idea that two Martians might come up with equally correct translations which did *not* attribute the same net import to each human sentence is the indeterminacy of holophrastic translation.

11 Once a general scheme of translation is in place, however, there is room for factual dispute. Two Martians who have both adopted the complement-translation may argue about whether "Rover" refers to the complement of the family dog or to the complement of the family cat. In this case one of them is right and one wrong, and the matter is settled in exactly the same way as the analogous dispute between two adherents of the other general scheme of translation.

12 The first of these positions has been expressed, somewhat tentatively, by Simon Blackburn in *Spreading the Word*, chapter 2, especially section 4. The second has been put forward, with characteristic vigour, by John Searle in "Indeterminacy, Empiricism, and the First Person". Dagfinn Føllesdal's "Indeterminacy and Mental States" is a powerful Quinean response to Searle. The latter explicitly denies that he intends his "meanings" to be private introspectible entities "or any of the Cartesian paraphernalia" (p. 146). But in that case it is hard to know what he takes them to be, or how he thinks they are known. This point is well expressed by Føllesdal, who says of Searle's denial of privacy: "[a]ll he offers us is a piece of negative theology" (op. cit., p. 100). So I shall speak of the more general idea which Searle exemplifies as if it were arguing for a private language. I have discussed Blackburn's views in "Translation, Meaning, and Self-Knowledge"; this section as a whole draws on that essay.

13 The considerations which rise to the surface here are closely connected with those often attributed to Wittgenstein, under the heading "the private language argument". See Wittgenstein, *Philosophical Investigations*, especially sections 243–315. For further discussion of these ideas in the Quinean context, see the essay by the present author cited in the previous note.

14 Simon Blackburn, *Spreading the Word*, p. 58. Blackburn asks this as a question, rather than asserting it; his discussion as a whole, however, makes it clear that he is strongly inclined to accept this interpretation, perhaps because he thinks no other is available.

15 See, for example, *OR*, p. 46. I do not think, however, that Quine's remarks there must be read as equating understanding with translating. Note also that in the opening pages of the same essay he explicitly rejects the idea of a private language—and does so in a way that makes it seem as if he simply never takes the idea seriously at all; see *OR*, pp. 26–27.

16 In a few places Quine seems to accept that there is indeterminacy even in the "linguist's decision as to what to treat as native signs of assent and dissent" ("Reply to Hintikka", D&H, p. 312). This goes along with the idea that indeterminacy comes in degrees: there will be some degree of indeterminacy even given the translation of assent and dissent. For the most part, however, the idea of indeterminacy in assent and dissent plays no role in Quine's thought, and I shall largely ignore it in what follows.

17 It does not matter here if in fact other creatures also prove to be capable of that feat. What matters is that the genetic endowment is crucial, and this is demonstrated by the fact that not *all* creatures have the relevant capability.

18 Nozick usefully discusses the idea that neurology might determine translation. He imagines two groups, one speaking ordinary English and one speaking English in which terms refer to temporal stages of the relevant objects. By a process of abbreviation of the latter language, the languages of the two groups come to be phonetically identical. He further imagines a child, brought up in a "mixed marriage". Which language does the child speak? If there were genuinely different languages here, there would be a determinate

answer. But clearly, Nozick says, there is not; hence we do not have two genuinely different languages. See Robert Nozick, "Experience, Theory and Language" in H&S, especially pp. 346f. Quine applauds what he calls "Nozick's parable"; see p. 365 of the same volume.

19 See for example Ebbs, cited in Chapter 3, note 8, and Soames, cited in note 4 of this chapter.

20 It might be said that we should consider mental meanings not as more or less mysterious introspectible items but rather as postulates of an empirically based theory of the mind. Quine would be sceptical, but open to argument. A theory of this sort which was acceptable to him would be part of an empirical account of what it is to understand a language, an account very different from that proposed by advocates of a more traditional notion of a proposition. A notion of meaning which was part of such a theory would not itself be explanatory; the work of explanation would be done by the imagined theory.

21 Philosophers have generated puzzles and paradoxes from the disparity; see, for example, Saul Kripke, "A Puzzle about Belief". From Quine's point of view, of course, the paradoxes simply serve to reinforce the idea that there is no conception of a proposition which will play the role in which many philosophers have attempted to cast it.

22 A view which *does* require the end points of analysis to be synonymous is vulnerable to what is sometimes called "Moore's paradox": how can the transition from one sentence to another which is synonymous with it represent philosophical progress? Quine's view is clearly not vulnerable to this question, since it does not require that analysis should preserve synonymy.

9 Quinean metaphysics: limning the structure of reality

1 The logic of Frege and of Russell, however, is not first-order logic. (See the third section of Chapter 10 for an explanation of this idea, and for alternatives.) Also, Quine's account of the philosophical significance of logic is quite different from that of his predecessors.

2 Such a view of sense data is found, for example, in Russell's *Problems of Philosophy*. Russell speaks of the direct and immediate knowledge that he thinks we have of sense data as "acquaintance", and argues that we must also be acquainted with abstract entities. There is no sign that Quine considers this latter idea at all; certainly it is not one that he would take seriously.

3 For some remarks on this choice of terminology, see Quine, "On Carnap's Views on Ontology", *WP*, pp. 201f. Quine explicitly dissociates himself from "traditional metaphysics", but adds: "I suspect that the sense in which I use this crusty old word ['ontology'] has been nuclear to its usage all along".

4 Sometimes the appeal to "intuition" in philosophy seems to mean no more than an appeal to usage, to what we ordinarily say about some matter; sometimes it seems to rely on the idea that there are structures or facts quite independent of us and our linguistic usages, and that something called "intuition" can somehow give us access to them. One of the attractions of the word may be precisely that it hovers between these two ideas, without forcing one to commit oneself to either.

5 In "Carnap and Logical Truth", discussing an imaginary logical positivist, Quine says:

> Ixmann's answer [to the metaphysician] consists in showing in detail how people (on Mars, say) might speak a language quite adequate to all of our science but, unlike our language, incapable of expressing the alleged metaphysical issues. (I applaud this answer, and think it embodies the most telling component of Carnap's own anti-metaphysical representations. ...)
>
> (*WP*, pp. 126f.)

6 See the title to section 53 of *Word and Object*. The phrase "that paradigm of philosophy" was used by Ramsey to describe Russell's theory of descriptions, and endorsed by Moore.

See Moore's essay "Russell's Theory of Descriptions", pp. 177, 225. Quine is surely consciously echoing Ramsey and Moore.

7 Quine sometimes speaks of classes rather than sets. We shall stick to the latter word; in quotations we shall replace Quine's uses of "class" with "[set]". As noted in Chapter 2, above, some theories make a technical distinction between sets and classes but that will not concern us.

8 This is Wiener's definition. Kuratowski's method is to identify the ordered pair of a and b, in that order, with the set $\{\{a\}, \{a, b\}\}$. The two methods work equally well. In particular, either definition enables us to prove the fundamental postulate, so it now becomes a theorem of ordinary set-theory, not an additional axiom; ordered pairs become special kinds of sets, rather than objects of a new kind. Other methods are also possible. Note that once we have a definition in place for ordered pairs, we can extend it to ordered triples, ordered quadruples and, in general, ordered n-tuples.

10 A framework for theory: the role of logic

1 Regimenting our theory may also lead to our developing what is, by any standards, a different theory, with different observational consequences. There is no sharp line to be drawn here, nor does Quine need one.

2 A rather different technique, predicate functor logic, can simulate the effect of standard first-order logic. Quine discusses this technique in "Variables Explained Away" and reverts to the point in an appendix to *From Stimulus to Science*. This form of logic is a relatively minor variant of standard first-order logic, and I shall ignore it in what follows.

3 Compare Russell:

The language of *Principia Mathematica* is ... a language which has only syntax and no vocabulary whatsoever. Barring the omission of a vocabulary I maintain that it is quite a nice language. It aims at being that sort of language which, if you add a vocabulary, would be a logically perfect language.
(Russell, "Lectures on the Philosophy of Logical Atomism", p. 176)

Quine's idea of logic as the framework of theory can be seen as a descendant of Russell's idea of a logically perfect language. There are sharp differences, however. In particular, regimentation into Quine's canonical notation is not an external constraint on theory; see the next paragraph of the main text.

4 As I am using the word here, a conclusion is *implied* by one or more premises just in case it follows from them as a matter of logic. (Equivalently, if the conditional, in which the conjunction of the premises form the antecedent and the conclusion is the consequent, is a logical truth. A conditional, in turn, is a sentence of the form "If ... then ... ", construed truth-functionally.) The converse of an implication is a logically valid *inference*, from the premises to the conclusion.

5 Truth-functional operators are ways of compounding sentences to form more complex sentences, where the truth-value of the compound—whether it is true or false—depends only on the truth-values of its constituent sentences. I am assuming that it is *sentences* to which truth and falsehood are ascribed; this assumption will come under scrutiny in the fourth section.

6 There are, in fact, two, either of which suffices to define all the others. One is "neither ... nor", that truth-function of two sentences which is true if both of the contained sentences are false; the other is "not both", that truth-function of two sentences which is true provided at least one of the contained sentences is false. They are both known as Sheffer strokes, after Harry M. Sheffer, who first devised them and proved them adequate for all the rest.

7 A system of logic which is readily translatable into first-order logic, such as predicate functor logic, will have the same effect. See note 2, above.

8 Here, it might be said, Quine is relying on the idea of meaning. Is this illegitimate, in view of his doubts about philosophical uses of that word? His use of the idea here does not seem to bear any explanatory burden, or to be of systematic importance in his thought. It is certainly not invoked to say that such a change is impossible, or must be made in a different way from any other change of doctrine.

9 We can formulate sentences which do quantify over redness: "(∃x) (x is the property which an object has if and only if it is red)", for example. Quine's criterion of ontological commitment is a formalistic matter: it does not, by itself, answer the substantive question, whether properties exist. If we accept the existence of properties, however, it is perhaps more natural to work in second-order logic. Then we could assert the existence of redness by saying, for example, that there is a property that applies to all and only the red objects: "(∃F) (∀x) (Fx if and only if x is a red object)". We shall return to this point in the third section, below.

10 The omitted portion of this sentence is a reference to Dummett's essay "Realism". This strong connection between realism and bivalence is not one that Quine explicitly endorses anywhere else.

11 "Intuitionism" as used here refers primarily to an approach to the philosophy of mathematics; its rejection of classical logic arises from the fact that there are mathematical claims which we have, even in principle, no way of establishing or refuting. Such claims, according to the intuitionists, should not be counted as either true or false until we have adopted methods of proof which can, at least in principle, determine which truth-value they have. See, for example, Michael Dummett, *Elements of Intuitionism*, and references given there.

12 Quine, who is fond of matters geographical, suggests a precise definition for "mountain"; see WPB?, *TT*, p. 33. W. D. Hart has argued that a precise definition is in fact implicit in the ordinary use of the word "heap", so that no stipulation is needed; see Hart, "Hat-tricks and Heaps".

13 Garrett Birkhoff and John von Neumann, "The Logic of Quantum Mechanics". Note that if their proposal were for a *strengthening* of classical logic it could be accommodated by our using a special axiom when reasoning about quantum mechanics. This would not suggest a change to logic; there would be no reason for counting such an axiom part of logic, rather than a fundamental law of quantum mechanics. But their idea is that classical truth-functional logic is too strong to employ without restriction when quantum mechanics is our subject, and that does require a change of logic.

14 I focus on expressive power rather than inferential power because cases of the latter tend to be technically rather complicated. An important example of the inferential power of second-order logic is that it enables us to derive (second-order) Peano Arithmetic from the apparently rather weak principle that the number of Fs is identical to the number of Gs just in case there is a one-to-one correlation between the F things and the G things. (This principle, now widely known as "Hume's Principle", must itself be phrased in second-order logic.) This fact has been taken by some to vindicate the idea that mathematics is reducible to logic. See Crispin Wright, *Frege's Conception of Numbers as Objects*.

15 We can give a first-order schema which is only true in infinite domains; removing the second-order quantifier from the sentence in the text results in such a first-order schema. But this does not amount to a general definition of infinity.

16 The example is due to Geach and to Kaplan; see *Roots of Reference*, p. 111, and *Methods of Logic*, p. 293 (where it is modified to use "people" rather than "critics"). The proof that it cannot be expressed in first-order logic is due to Kaplan; see George Boolos, "To Be Is to Be a Value of a Variable (or to Be Some Values of Some Variables)".

17 There is a third which might be mentioned: first-order logic might be thought to be especially suitable as a framework for theory because in a clear sense it has no subject-matter of its own. There are no *sentences*, true or false, which use only the vocabulary of first-order logic; that vocabulary enables us to form schemata, which are true or false only

relative to an interpretation of their predicate letters. (As noted early in the chapter, the identity predicate creates exception in contexts in which it is not definable.) First-order logic is in this way unlike second-order logic, and set-theory. This reason, however, seems to me less important than the two I discuss in the text.

18 The result is due to Gödel; see "The Completeness of the Axioms of the Functional Calculus of Logic". Presentations of the proof may be found in many places, including Quine's own *Methods of Logic*.

19 The underlying result here is the incompleteness of any formalism for elementary arithmetic. This is incompleteness relative to truth rather than to validity (a different sense from that in which first-order logic is complete). The point is that no formalism will enable us to prove all (and only) the truths of elementary arithmetic. This result, again, is due to Gödel; see "On Formally Undecidable Propositions of *Principia Mathematica* and Related Systems".

20 In particular, we no longer obtain the important result mentioned in note 14, above.

21 On some approaches, the requirement that at least one object exist is a drawback or a difficulty, perhaps because it is held that logic is a priori, and that we cannot know a priori that anything at all exists. For Quine, however, there is no problem, because he does not require that logic be a priori. Clearly it is *true* that at least one thing exists; since building this assumption into our logic simplifies matters, we have every reason to do so. There are variants of first-order logic which avoid the requirement, but Quine is not persuaded to adopt one. See "Meaning and Existential Inference", *FLPV*, pp. 160–67.

22 In addition to the essay cited in note 16 above, see also Boolos, "Nominalist Platonism". I should emphasize that I cannot do justice to Boolos's views here.

23 For further discussion of these issues, see also Philippe de Rouilhan, "On What There Are". De Rouilhan suggests that we should interpret second-order quantifiers as ranging over what he calls *multiplicities*, which "do not enjoy the same type of being as units do, but have their own type of being" (p. 197). Whatever its advantages in reflecting the structure of ordinary language, Quine would see this as an unnecessary complication. Set-theory is available, and clearly understood; and enables us to avoid such metaphysical excesses as distinguishing various "types of being".

24 This form of the objection goes back at least as far as F. H. Bradley; see his *Principles of Logic*, p. 64; for some discussion, see the present author's *Russell, Idealism, and the Emergence of Analytic Philosophy*, pp. 63f. In more general form, the objection goes back at least as far as Kant's criticism of Leibniz; see "The Amphiboly of Concepts of Reflection", in Kant, *Critique of Pure Reason*, A260/B310ff. More recent versions may be found in the work of P. F. Strawson; see, for example, his essay "Particular and General".

25 Quine may have learned of this idea from Tarski; see "Notes on the Theory of Reference", *FLPV*, pp. 134–36.

26 See A. Tarski, "The Concept of Truth in Formalized Languages"; for a simplified account of Tarski's definition, see *PL*, pp. 40ff.

11 Extensionality, reference, and singular terms

1 The distinction is that a name is without semantically significant structure whereas other singular terms, such as "The thirteenth prime number", may be made up of parts which are independently meaningful. The distinction is not of great importance to Quine, as we shall see.

2 See Russell, "On Denoting" and Whitehead and Russell, *Principia Mathematica*, *14. For discussion, see the present author's essay "The Theory of Descriptions". Quine's *technique* is the same as Russell's, but its application, and the philosophical motivation behind its application, are not. For one thing, Quine uses this technique to eliminate *all* singular

terms; for Russell, by contrast, it was important that there is a category of singular terms—genuine names, or logically proper names—which are not to be eliminated in this way.

3 Here I use "→" to symbolize the truth-functional "if ... then"; it forms a compound sentence which is false if the first sentence is true and the second is false, but true under the three other combinations. I use "↔" for the truth-functional "if and only if" or "just in case"; it forms a compound which is true if the two sentences are both true or both false, but false if one is true and the other false.

4 This is also largely true of Russell's use of that technique, in spite of his statements suggesting the contrary. (As compared with his earlier view, the technique does eliminate what he calls "denoting concepts"; but Russell often seems to make larger claims than that.) See again the present author's "The Theory of Descriptions".

5 Some might argue that the original English sentence *is* true—mythologically, because in all the stories Pegasus is indeed able to fly. Quine's concern is with science, not with myth, so he would disagree. But the analysis does not settle the issue: presumably the same claim can be made about the analysed sentence as about the unanalysed one (its use of the quantifier, with its unequivocal sense of existence, may make the claim less plausible; from Quine's point of view that is all to the good).

6 Here there is sharp distinction between Quine and Russell. Russell's logically perfect language, as I interpret the idea, *was* precisely intended to reflect the structure of our linguistic understanding, and to answer the question how such understanding is possible.

7 The classic source for objections of this kind is Kripke, *Naming and Necessity.*

8 I say "may be" rather than "is" because not all such positions are non-referential. Consider the sentence: "The singular term 'Quine' refers to a philosopher". In this sentence the proper name, although it occurs in quotation marks, is in referential position. The verb "refers" takes us from the name to its referent; even though it is a name of the name that occurs in the sentence, the sentence is thus about the referent of the name, not about the name. The expression "is true" functions similarly with regard to sentences. Hence the idea, discussed in the fifth section of the previous chapter, that the truth predicate has a disquotational function.

9 The use of the word "transparent" in this sort of context is Russell's, from Appendix C of the second edition of Whitehead and Russell's *Principia Mathematica*. See p. 665. (The appendices added to the second edition are due entirely to Russell.) The use of the word "opaque" here is Quine's.

10 This leaves open the possibility of taking the singular term, in such a position, to designate something *else*—as the name "Quine", when enclosed between quotation marks, is taken to designate the name, not the bearer of the name. Some philosophers hold that when terms occur in non-extensional contexts they sometimes designate the meanings or *intensions* which they have when they occur in other contexts. (Such views are clearly expressed by Frege; see, for example, "Sense and Meaning".) For this reason some philosophers speak of some, but not all, non-extensional contexts as intensional contexts for a given term or terms—meaning that they are contexts in which the truth-value of the whole is determined by the intension of that term or terms, together, perhaps, with the extensions of other terms in the context. (See for example Neale, *Facing Facts*, p. 149.) Since Quine rejects intensions he has no use for such an idea, and uses "intensional" simply to mean "non-extensional".

11 The qualification about standard cases here is simply to avoid predicates which are prone to give rise to paradoxical sets, such as Russell's case of "x is not a member of x". Some way must be found of blocking paradox in any case, but the argument in the text goes through on any plausible account.

12 If our set-theory does not have a universal set then we can impose appropriate restrictions by adding an extra condition. We choose some suitably large set, say $\{x/\ Hx\}$, and confine ourselves to objects which are members of that set by considering $\{x/\ p\ .\ Hx\}$. If p is true then

this is identical to {x/ Hx}; if p is false then it is the null set. If we are using set-theory with type restrictions we can confine ourselves to a set which contains all or none of the entities of a given type.—Like the first argument, this one is adaptable to any plausible restrictions on set existence.

12 Ontology, physicalism, realism

1 Arguments to the contrary invariably depend on assumptions that Quine rejects, perhaps most often on the idea that second-order logic is available, and involves us in no ontological commitments. As we saw in Chapter 9, Quine advocates the use of first-order rather than second-order logic. Even apart from that, he insists that second-order logic cannot coherently be thought of as ontologically innocent; the second-order quantifiers must range over some entities; hence its use requires abstract entities after all.

2 I say "in his mature philosophy" because there is evidence that in the early and mid-1940s Quine was attracted to nominalism, and hoped to find a way of dispensing with abstract objects entirely, while still maintaining enough mathematics for physical science. See especially the 1947 essay "Steps Toward a Constructive Nominalism", which Quine co-authored with Nelson Goodman. Even apart from an attraction to nominalism, Quine was always concerned with ontological economy, and with the question of how far such economy can be pressed. See *Word and Object*, section 55, which decidedly does not advocate nominalism.

3 There is a reason which Quine does not consider. Physical objects occupy space, endure over time, and interact causally. But why should these facts give us more confidence in the physical than in the abstract? From a Quinean point of view, the importance of space, time, and causality here is that they enable us to locate and re-identify physical objects. Many alleged abstract objects lack such clear criteria for re-identification. But the abstract objects which Quine accepts—sets—have identity-criteria as clear as those of physical objects.

4 Sets can be members of other sets. We can ask of a set whether it is a member of itself. Russell pointed out that if we can form the sets of those sets which are *not* members of themselves then we have the contradiction: that set is a member of itself if and only if it is not a member of itself. See, for example, Russell's *Introduction to Mathematical Philosophy*, chapter 13.

5 Does the need for a coordinate system matter? According to Quine it does not:

> it would simply not obtrude where it is unwelcome, namely in the most theoretical levels of physics. Laws at that level would quantify generally over quadruples of real numbers, picking out none specifically. The specificity of the coordinates would make itself known only when one descends to coarser matters of astronomy, geography, geology, and history, and here it is perhaps appropriate.
>
> (WPO?, p. 501)

6 The entry under "Physicalism" in *The Oxford Companion to Philosophy*, ed. Ted Honderich (Oxford: Oxford University Press, 1995), begins: "The doctrine that everything is physical. Also called materialism, the doctrine is associated with Democritus, Epicurus, Lucretius, Hobbes, Holbach, T. H. Huxley, J. B. Watson, Carnap, Quine, and Smart". (The entry is by Wayne A. Davis, and on p. 679.) Simon Blackburn's *Oxford Dictionary of Philosophy*, similarly, begins its entry under "Physicalism" like this:

> The view that the real world is nothing more than the physical world. ... Physicalism is opposed to ontologies including abstract objects ... and to mental

events and states in so far as any of these are thought of as independent of physical things, events, and states.

(p. 287)

7 *WO*, p. 265; Quine adds a footnote referring to Carnap's *Unity of Science* and to Herbert Feigl's essay "The 'mental' and the 'physical'".

8 The point of the term "anomalous monism" is that token-token identity, unlike type-type identity, will not give us laws relating the mental to the physical. The term seems to have been introduced by Donald Davidson in his essay "Mental Events", and the doctrine is widely attributed to him. The passage quoted in the previous paragraph from p. 163 of Quine's "Facts of the Matter" ends with a footnote to that essay of Davidson's. The doctrine of anomalous monism, however, although not the term, is clearly implied by Quine in section 54 of *Word and Object*. That section contains a footnote thanking Davidson but not, it seems, for that point.

9 No date is given for the printing of the book in which this altered passage occurs, nor is it billed as a new edition; the change is, however, signalled on the page where it occurs.

10 The later work is his reply to Roger Gibson's "Quine's Philosophy: A Brief Sketch", which appears only in the second edition of H&S (pp. 684f.) Gibson's essay is dated July 1997; Quine's reply is presumably somewhat later.

13   Minds, beliefs, and modality

1 Some philosophers might think of this as a case of intensionality, on the grounds that propositions are intensional entities. We shall not be concerned with this idea, since the distinction between intensional and extensional *entities* is not, by Quine's standards, a clear one. See Chapter 11, above, section II.

2 In *Word and Object* he adopts a different approach, although one which has very much the same net effect. He takes it that an ascription of a belief to Tom, say, does not relate Tom to a sentence or a proposition or anything else, but simply ascribes to him a complex one-place predicate. The predicate, however, is understood in terms of the relevant sentence: "The verb 'believes' here ceases to be a term and becomes part of an operator 'believes that', or 'believes [ ]' which, applied to a sentence, produces a composite absolute general term" (p. 216). The difference is thus very small, and in most later works Quine ignores the variant idea; I shall do the same from this point on.

3 The origins of the term *de dicto* and the contrasting term *de re* are medieval. Clearly the first has to do with what is said, while the second has to do with some thing; nothing that I say is intended as a claim about the claims or motives of those who introduced the terms.

4 Robert C. Sleigh, "On a Proposed System of Epistemic Logic". A very similar version of the argument was put forward independently by David Kaplan, "Quantifying In", which was published the following year.

5 Of course a number of spies might be tied for shortest. To avoid that we can ensure we have a unique description by referring to places and dates of birth as well as to heights; in what follows I shall ignore these complications, and continue to use "the shortest spy" as my example.

6 The earliest such attempts were those of C. I. Lewis. He objected to the use of the term "implication", in *Principia Mathematica*, to indicate a purely truth-functional relation. Beginning with his 1912 paper "Implication and the Algebra of Logic", he put forward the idea of "strict implication". (Roughly: a sentence p strictly implies a sentence q if the truth-functional "If p then q" is not merely true but *necessary*. For Lewis, however, strict implication was the fundamental modal notion.) In the 1940s systems of quantified modal logic were developed; see especially Rudolf Carnap, "Modalities and Quantification", and Ruth Barcan (Marcus), "A Functional Calculus of First Order Based on Strict

Implication", both published in 1946. For a modern treatment at a more introductory level, see Brian Chellas, *Modal Logic: An Introduction*; or Hughes and Cresswell, *A New Introduction to Modal Logic* (London: Routledge, 1996).

7 In particular, some forms of modal logic can be reinterpreted as provability logic, i.e. with the symbol that otherwise plays the role of necessity ("□") being taken to encode "It is provable that … ", via Gödel numbering. See Solovay, "Provability Interpretation of Modal Logic"; see also Boolos, *The Logic of Provability*, and further references given there. After explaining the provability interpretation of quantified modal logic, Boolos comments: "There is nothing in this explanation of the truth-conditions of □A to which even the strictest of Quineans could take exception." (P. 226.)

8 According to a decision by the International Astronomical Union taken in August 2006, there are eight planets, not nine. I stick to the traditional nine; the text can be made consistent with the new definition of "planet" if we simply replace "nine" by "eight" throughout.

9 See Church's "Review of Quine's 'Notes on Existence and Necessity'", and Smullyan, "Modality and Description". Note that the idea of dispelling non-extensionality by means of the theory of descriptions is compatible with the idea that some singular terms— proper names, or perhaps a subclass of proper names—do not threaten to give rise to non-extensionality in modal contexts. When names of this sort name the same objects, it is argued, they *can* be substituted within modal contexts *salva veritate*. See Føllesdal, *Referential Opacity and Modal Logic*, and Kripke, "Naming and Necessity". Following Kripke, such (alleged) terms are generally referred to as "rigid designators".

10 Føllesdal distinguishes weaker and stronger forms of essentialism; Quine, however, rejects both. See Føllesdal, "Essentialism and Reference", and Quine's reply (H&S, pp. 114f.).

11 See Kripke, "A Completeness Theorem in Modal Logic"; and "Semantical Considerations on Modal Logic".

12 In this he follows both Carnap and C. I. Lewis; see the former's *Meaning and Necessity*, section 39, and the latter's *Survey of Symbolic Logic*, chapter V.

13 The allusion, presumably, is to the Korean war of 1950–53. See James T. Patterson, *Grand Expectations: The United States, 1945–1974*, and references given there.

Conclusion

1 This is certainly not to deny that there are earlier attempts to answer the question, or something like it. Hume, for example, speaks of "a science of man" which would "explain the principles of human nature" and be based on "experience and observation". (See *Treatise of Human Nature*, Introduction. Note also that the book is subtitled: *Being an attempt to introduce the experimental method of reasoning into moral subjects*. "Moral subjects" for Hume meant primarily *mental* subjects.) What Hume envisages is a science constructed on its own principles but analogous to natural science—with Newton's physics, in particular; it would not be an attempt to use the principles of natural science to explain the human mind.

BIBLIOGRAPHY

Works by Quine

The Logic of Sequences: A Generalization of Principia Mathematica (dissertation, Harvard University, 1932; reprinted by Garland Press, 1990).

Methods of Logic (New York: Holt, 1950; 2nd edn, 1959; 3rd edn, 1972; 4th edn, Cambridge MA: Harvard University Press, 1982).

From a Logical Point of View (Cambridge MA: Harvard University Press, 1953; revised edn, 1980).

Word and Object (Cambridge MA: MIT Press, 1960).

Mathematical Logic, revised edn (New York: Harper & Row, 1962).

Set Theory and Its Logic (Cambridge MA: Harvard University Press, 1963; revised edn, 1969).

Selected Logic Papers (New York: Random House, 1966; 2nd edn, enlarged, Cambridge MA: Harvard University Press, 1995).

Ways of Paradox (New York: Random House, 1966; 2nd edn, enlarged, Cambridge MA: Harvard University Press, 1976).

Ontological Relativity and Other Essays (New York: Columbia University Press, 1969).

Philosophy of Logic (Englewood Cliffs NJ: Prentice-Hall, 1970).

Roots of Reference (La Salle IL: Open Court, 1974).

Theories and Things (Cambridge MA: Harvard University Press, 1981).

Pursuit of Truth (Cambridge MA: Harvard University Press, 1990; revised edn, 1992).

From Stimulus to Science (Cambridge MA: Harvard University Press, 1995).

Quine, W. V. and J. S. Ullian *The Web of Belief* (New York: Random House, 1970; 2nd edn, 1978).

"Is Logic a Matter of Words?" read to the American Philosophical Association meeting in Princeton, December 1937 (the typescript is in the University of Pittsburgh archives).

"New Foundations for Mathematical Logic", *American Mathematical Monthly* 44 (1937), pp. 70–80.

"Steps Toward a Constructive Nominalism" (with Nelson Goodman), *Journal of Symbolic Logic* 12 (1947), pp. 97–122.

"On Carnap's Views on Ontology", *Philosophical Studies* 2 (1951); reprinted in *Ways of Paradox and other Essays* (New York: Random House, 1966; second edition, enlarged, Cambridge MA: Harvard University Press, 1976), pp. 203–211.

"Two Dogmas of Empiricism", *Philosophical Review* 60 (1952), pp. 20–43; reprinted in *From a Logical Point of View* (Cambridge MA: Harvard University Press, 1953; revised edn, 1980), pp. 20–46.

"Identity, Ostension, and Hypostasis", in *From a Logical Point of View* (Cambridge MA: Harvard University Press, 1953; revised edn, 1980), pp. 65–79.

"Quantifiers and Propositional Attitudes", *Journal of Philosophy* 53 (1956); reprinted in *Ways of Paradox* (New York: Random House, 1966; 2nd edn, enlarged, Cambridge MA: Harvard University Press, 1976), pp. 185–96.

"Variables Explained Away", *Proceedings of the American Philosophial Society* 104 (1960), pp. 343–47; reprinted in *Selected Logic Papers* (New York: Random House, 1966; 2nd edn, enlarged, Cambridge MA: Harvard University Press, 1995), pp. 227–35.

"Posits and Reality", in S. Uyeda, ed., *Basis of the Contemporary Philosophy* (Tokyo: Waseda University Press, 1960); reprinted in *Ways of Paradox* (2nd edn, enlarged, Cambridge MA: Harvard University Press, 1976), pp. 246–54.

"Carnap and Logical Truth", in *Ways of Paradox* (New York: Random House, 1966; 2nd edn, enlarged, Cambridge MA: Harvard University Press, 1976), pp. 107–32.

"Immanence and Validity", in *Selected Logic Papers* (New York: Random House, 1966), pp. 242–50.

"Mr. Strawson on Logical Truth", in *Ways of Paradox* (New York: Random House, 1966; 2nd edn, enlarged, Cambridge MA: Harvard University Press, 1976), pp. 137–57.

Introduction to Russell's "Mathematical Logic as Based on the Theory of Types", in *From Frege to Gödel*, ed. Jean van Heijenoort (Cambridge MA: Harvard University Press, 1967), pp. 150–52.

"Epistemology Naturalized", in *Ontological Relativity and Other Essays* (New York: Columbia University Press, 1969), pp. 69–90.

"On the Reasons for the Indeterminacy of Translation", *The Journal of Philosophy* 67 (1970), pp. 178–83.

"Philosophical Progress in Language Theory", *Language, Belief and Metaphysics*, vol. 1 of *Contemporary Philosophic Thought* (Albany NY: State University of New York Press, 1970), pp. 2–19.

"Empirically Equivalent Systems of the World", *Erkenntnis* 9 (1975), pp. 313–28.

"Mind and Verbal Dispositions", in *Mind and Language*, ed. S. Guttenplan (Oxford: Oxford University Press, 1975), pp. 83–95.

"The Nature of Natural Knowledge", in *Mind and Language*, ed. S. Guttenplan (Oxford: Oxford University Press, 1975), pp. 67–81.

Comment on Grünbaum, in *Can Theories Be Refuted? Essays on the Duhem-Quine Thesis*, ed. S. G. Harding, Synthese Library, vol. 81 (Dordrecht: Reidel, 1976).

"Whither Physical Objects?" in *Essays in Memory of Imre Lakatos*, eds R. Cohen, P. Feyerabend and M. Wartofsky (Dordrecht: Reidel, 1976), pp. 497–504.

"Comment on Newton-Smith", *Analysis* 39 (1979), pp. 66–67.

"Facts of the Matter", in *Essays on the Philosophy of W. V. Quine*, eds R. W. Shahan and C. Swoyer (Norman OK: University of Oklahoma Press, 1979), pp. 155–69.

"The Variable and Its Place in Reference", in *Philosophical Subjects: Essays on the Work of P. F. Strawson*, ed. Z. van Straaten (Oxford: Oxford University Press, 1980), pp. 164–73.

"Empirical Content", in *Theories and Things* (Cambridge MA: Harvard University Press, 1981), pp. 24–30.

"What Price Bivalence?" *Journal of Philosophy* 78, no. 2 (February 1981), pp. 90–95. Reprinted, with additions, in *Theories and Things* (Cambridge MA: Harvard University Press, 1981), pp. 31–7.

"Relativism and Absolutism", *Monist* 67 (1984), pp. 293–96.

"1934 Lectures on Carnap", in *Dear Carnap, Dear Van*, ed. Richard Creath (Berkeley CA: University of California Press, 1990), pp. 47–103.

"Two Dogmas in Retrospect", *Canadian Journal of Philosophy* 21 (1991), pp. 265–74.

"Structure and Nature", *Journal of Philosophy* 89 (1992), pp. 6–9.

"In Praise of Observation Sentences", *Journal of Philosophy* 90, no. 3 (March 1993), pp.107–16.

"Promoting Extensionality", *Synthese* 98, no. 1 (1994), pp. 143–51.

"Response to Hookway", *Inquiry* 37 (1994), pp. 502–4.

"Naturalism, or Living within One's Means", *Dialectica* 49 (1995), pp. 251–61.

"Reactions", in *On Quine: New Essays*, eds P. Leonardi and M. Santambrogio (Cambridge: Cambridge University Press, 1995), pp. 349–61.

"Progress on Two Fronts", *Journal of Philosophy* 93 (1996), pp. 159–63.

"Response to Orenstein", *Revue Internationale de Philosophie* 4 (1997), pp. 573–74.

"I, You, and It", in *Knowledge, Language and Logic*, eds Alex Orenstein and Petr Kotatko (Dordrecht: Kluwer Academic, 2000), pp. 1–6.

"Quine's Responses", in *Knowledge, Language and Logic*, eds Alex Orenstein and Petr Kotatko (Dordrecht: Kluwer Academic, 2000), pp. 407–30.

"Confessions of a Confirmed Extensionalist", in *Future Pasts*, eds J. Floyd and S. Shieh (Oxford: Oxford University Press, 2001), pp. 215–21.

"Quine's 1946 Lectures on David Hume's Philosophy", ed. James G. Buickerood, *Eighteenth-Century Thought* 1 (2003), pp. 171–254.

Works by others

Alston, William P. "Quine on Meaning", in *The Philosophy of W. V. Quine*, eds E. Hahn and P. A. Schilpp (Peru IL: Open Court, 1986; 2nd, expanded edn, 1998), pp. 49–72.

Antony, Louise "Naturalizing Radical Translation", *Knowledge, Language and Logic* (Dordrecht: Kluwer, 2000), pp. 141–50.

Ayer, A. J. *Language, Truth and Logic* (London: Gollancz, 1936, 1946).

—— *Logical Positivism* (New York: Free Press, 1959).

Barrett, Robert and Roger Gibson *Perspectives on Quine* (Oxford: Blackwell, 1990).

Bergström, Lars "Underdetermination of Physical Theory", in *The Cambridge Companion to Quine*, ed. Roger F. Gibson Jr (Cambridge: Cambridge University Press, 2004), pp. 91–114.

Biletzki, Anat and Anat Matar, eds, *The Story of Analytic Philosophy* (London: Routledge, 1998).

Birkhoff, Garrett and John von Neumann "The Logic of Quantum Mechanics", *Annals of Mathematics* 37 (1936), pp. 823–43.

Blackburn, Simon *Spreading the Word* (Oxford: Oxford University Press, 1984).

—— *Oxford Dictionary of Philosophy* (Oxford: Oxford University Press, 1994).

Boolos, George *The Logic of Provability* (Cambridge: Cambridge University Press, 1993).

—— *Logic, Logic, and Logic*, ed. Richard Jeffrey (Cambridge MA: Harvard University Press, 1998).

—— "To Be Is to Be a Value of a Variable (or to Be Some Values of Some Variables)", *The Journal of Philosophy* 81 (1984), pp. 430–49; reprinted in *Logic, Logic, and Logic*, ed. Richard Jeffrey (Cambridge MA: Harvard University Press, 1998).

—— "Nominalist Plantonism", *Philosophical Review* 94 (1985), pp. 327–4; reprinted in *Logic, Logic, and Logic*, ed. Richard Jeffrey (Cambridge MA: Harvard University Press, 1998), pp. 73–87.

Bradley, F. H. *Principles of Logic*, 2nd edn (London: Oxford University Press, 1999; first published London: Kegan Paul and Trench, 1883).

Burdick, Howard "A Logical Form for Propositional Attitudes", *Synthese* 52 (1982), pp. 185–230.

Carnap, Rudolf *Der logische Aufbau der Welt* (Berlin: Weltkreis-Verlag, 1928); trans. by Rolf A. George as *The Logical Structure of the World* (London: Routledge and Kegan Paul, 1967).

—— *Logische Syntax der Sprache* (Vienna: Julius Springer Verlag, 1934); trans. by Amethe Smeaton as *Logical Syntax of Language* (London: Kegan Paul Trench, Trubner & Co., 1937).

—— *Unity of Science* (London: Kegan Paul, 1934).

—— "Testability and Meaning", *Philosophy of Science* 3 (1936), pp. 419–71; and 4 (1937), pp. 1–40.

—— *Introduction to Semantics* (Cambridge MA: Harvard University Press, 1942).

—— "Modalities and Quantification", *The Journal of Symbolic Logic* 11 (1946), pp. 33–64.

—— *Meaning and Necessity* (Chicago: University of Chicago Press, 1947; enlarged edn, 1956).

—— "Empiricism, Semantics and Ontology", *Revue Internationale de Philosophie* 4 (1950), pp. 20–40; reprinted in *Meaning and Necessity*, 2nd edn, pp. 205–21.

—— "Meaning and Synonymy in Natural Languages", *Philosophical Studies* 7 (1955), pp. 33–47; reprinted in *Meaning and Necessity*, 2nd edn, pp. 233–47.

—— "Intellectual Autobiography", in *The Philosophy of Rudolf Carnap*, ed. P. A. Schilpp (LaSalle IL: Open Court, 1963), pp. 1–84.

—— Reply to "Two Dogmas", a reply unpublished in Carnap's lifetime, now printed in *Dear Carnap, Dear Van*, ed. Richard Creath (Berkeley CA: University of California Press, 1990), pp. 427–32.

Chellas, Brian *Modal Logic: An Introduction* (Cambridge: Cambridge University Press, 1980).

Chomsky, Noam "Quine's Empirical Assumptions", in *Words and Objections*, eds Donald Davidson and Jaakko Hintikka (Dordrecht: Reidel, 1969), pp. 53–68.

Church, Alonzo "Review of Quine's 'Notes on Existence and Necessity'" *Journal of Symbolic Logic* 8 (1943), p. 31.

—— "Quine's Paradox about Modality", in *Propositions and Attitudes*, eds Nathan Salmon and S. Soames (Oxford: Oxford University Press, 1988), pp. 59–65.

Churchland, Paul M. *A Neurocomputational Perspective* (Cambridge MA: MIT Press, 1989), pp. 1–22.

—— "Eliminative Materialism and the Propositional Attitudes", reprinted in Churchland, *A Neurocomputational Perspective* (Cambridge MA: MIT Press, 1989), pp. 1–22.

Creath, Richard *Dear Carnap, Dear Van: The Carnap–Quine Correspondence and Related Work* (Berkeley CA: University of California Press, 1990).

Davidson, Donald *Essays on Actions and Events* (Oxford: Oxford University Press, 1980).

—— "Mental Events", in Davidson, *Essays on Actions and Events* (Oxford: Oxford University Press, 1980)

—— "Meaning, Truth and Evidence", in R. Barrett and R. Gibson, *Perspectives on Quine* (Oxford: Blackwell, 1990), pp. 68–79.

Davidson, Donald and Jaakko Hintikka, eds, *Words and Objections* (Dordrecht: Reidel, 1969).

Davis, Wayne A. "Physicalism", in *The Oxford Companion to Philosophy*, ed. Ted Honderich (Oxford: Oxford University Press, 1995), p. 679.

Dummett, Michael *Frege, Philosophy of Language* (London: Duckworth, 1973).

—— *Elements of Intuitionism* (Oxford: Oxford University Press, 1977).

—— *Truth and Other Enigmas* (Cambridge MA: Harvard University Press, 1978).

—— *Frege and Other Philosophers* (Oxford: Oxford University Press, 1991).

—— *Origins of Analytical Philosophy* (Cambridge MA: Harvard University Press, 1993).

—— "Realism", in Dummett, *Truth and Other Enigmas* (Cambridge MA: Harvard University Press, 1978), pp. 145–65.

Ebbs, Gary *Rule-Following and Realism* (Cambridge MA: Harvard University Press, 1997).

Eilan, Naomi, Rosaleen McCarthy and Bill Brewer, eds, *Spatial Representation* (Oxford: Oxford University Press, 1993).

Feigl, Herbert "The 'mental' and the 'physical'", *Minnesota Studies in Philosophy of Science*, vol. 2, eds Herbert Feigl and Michael Scriven (Minneapolis: University of Minnesota Press, 1958), pp. 370–497.

Floyd, Juliet and Sanford Shieh *Future Pasts: The Analytic Tradition in Twentieth-Century Philosophy* (Oxford: Oxford University Press, 2001).

391

Fodor, J. A. *The Language of Thought* (New York: Crowell, 1975).
—— *RePresentations* (Cambridge MA: MIT Press, 1981).
Fogelin, Robert "Aspects of Quine's Naturalized Epistemology", in *The Cambridge Companion to Quine*, ed. Roger Gibson, 2004, pp. 19–46.
Føllesdal, Dagfinn *Referential Opacity and Modal Logic*, Ph.D. dissertation (Harvard University, 1961), reprinted, with an introduction and addendum (London: Routledge, 2004).
——"Essentialism and Reference", in *The Philosophy of W. V. Quine*, eds E. Hahn and P. A. Schilpp (Peru IL: Open Court Press, 1986, 2nd, expanded edn, 1998), pp. 97–113.
—— "Indeterminacy and Mental States", in Robert Barrett and Roger Gibson, *Perspectives on Quine* (Oxford: Blackwell, 1990), pp. 98–109.
Frege, Gottlob *Die Grundlagen der Arithmetik* (Breslau: Verlag von Wilhelm Koebner, 1884); trans. by J. L. Austin as *The Foundations of Arithmetic* (Oxford: Blackwell, 1950, 2nd edn, 1953).
—— "Über formale Theorien der Arithmetik", *Sitzungsberichte der jenaischen Gesellschaft für Medizin und Naturwissenschaft* 19 (1885), suppl. 2, pp. 94–104; trans. by E.-H. W. Kluge as "On Formal Theories of Arithmetic", in Gottlob Frege, *Collected Papers on Mathematics, Logic, and Philosophy*, trans. Max Black *et al.*, ed. Brian McGuinness (Oxford: Blackwell, 1984), pp. 112–21.
—— *Collected Papers on Mathematics, Logic, and Philosophy*, trans. Max Black *et al.*, ed. Brian McGuinness (Oxford: Blackwell, 1984), pp. 157–77.
—— "On Sense and Meaning", in *Collected Papers on Mathematics, Logic, and Philosophy*, trans. Max Black *et al.*, ed. Brian McGuinness (Oxford: Blackwell, 1984), pp. 157–77.
Friedman, Michael *Reconsidering Logical Positivism* (Cambridge: Cambridge University Press, 1999).
—— "Physicalism and the Indeterminacy of Translation", *Nous* 9 (1975), pp. 353–74.
Geach, Peter Thomas *Reference and Generality* (Ithaca NY and London: Cornell University Press, 1962, amended edn, 1968).
Gibson Jr, Roger F. *The Philosophy of W. V. Quine* (Tampa FL: University of South Florida Press, 1982).
—— "Translation, Physics, and Facts of the Matter", in *The Philosophy of W. V. Quine*, eds E. Hahn and P. A. Schilpp (Peru IL: Open Court, 1986; 2nd, expanded edn, 1998), pp. 139–54.
—— "Quine's Philosophy: A Brief Sketch", in *The Philosophy of W. V. Quine*, eds E. Hahn and P. A. Schilpp (in the 2nd edn only) (Peru IL: Open Court, 1986; 2nd, expanded edn, 1998), pp. 667–83.
—— *Enlightened Empiricism* (Tampa FL: University of South Florida Press, 1988).
—— ed. *The Cambridge Companion to Quine* (Cambridge: Cambridge University Press, 2004).
Glock, Hans-Johann *Quine and Davidson on Language, Thought and Reality* (Cambridge: Cambridge University Press, 2003).
Gödel, Kurt *Collected Works, vol. I*, ed. Solomon Feferman (Oxford: Oxford University Press, 1986).
—— "Die Vollständigkeit der Axiome der logischen Funktionenkalküls", *Monatshefte für Mathematik und Physik* 37 (1930), pp. 349–60; reprinted, with a translation by Stefan Bauer-Mengelberg and Jean van Heijenoort under the title "The Completeness of the Axioms of the Functional Calculus of Logic", in Gödel, *Collected Works*, ed. Solomon Feferman (Oxford: Oxford University Press, 1986), vol. I, pp. 102–23.
—— "Über formal unentscheidbare Sätze der Principia Mathematica und verwandter Systeme", *Monatshefte für Mathematik und Physik* 38 (1931), pp. 173–98; reprinted, with a translation by Jean van Heijenoort under the title "On Formally Undecidable Propositions of *Principia Mathematica* and Related Systems", in Gödel, *Collected Works*, ed. Solomon Feferman (Oxford: Oxford University Press, 1986), vol. I, pp. 144–95.

Grayling, A. C., ed. *Philosophy 2: Further through the Subject* (Oxford: Oxford University Press, 1995).

Grice, H. Paul and P. Strawson "In Defense of a Dogma", *The Philosophical Review* LXV, no. 2 (1956), pp. 141–58; widely reprinted.

Hahn, Edwin and Paul Arthur Schilpp *The Philosophy of W. V. Quine* (Peru IL: Open Court, 1986; 2nd, expanded edn, 1998).

Harding, S. G., ed. *Can Theories be Refuted? Essays on the Duhem-Quine Thesis*, Synthese Library, vol. 81 (Dordrecht: Reidel, 1976).

Harman, Gilbert "Quine on Meaning and Existence, I", *Review of Metaphysics* 31 (1967), pp. 124–51.

Hart, W. D. "Hat-tricks and Heaps", *Philosophical Studies* 33 (1992), pp. 1–24.

Hempel, Carl "The Empiricist Criterion of Meaning", first published in *Revue Internationale de Philosophie* 4 (1950); reprinted in A. J. Ayer, *Logical Positivism* (New York: Free Press, 1959), pp. 108–29.

Hookway, Christopher *Quine* (Cambridge: Polity Press, 1998).

Hughes, G. E. and M. J. Cresswell *A New Introduction to Modal Logic* (London: Routledge, 1996).

Hume, David *Treatise of Human Nature*, eds T. M. Grose and T. H. Green, 4 vols (London: Longmans, 1874–75).

Humphries, Barbara M. "Indeterminacy of Translation and Theory", *The Journal of Philosophy* 67 (1970), pp. 167–78.

Hylton, Peter W. *Russell, Idealism, and the Emergence of Analytic Philosophy* (Oxford: Oxford University Press, 1990).

—— "Analyticity and the Indeterminacy of Translation", *Synthese* 52 (1982), pp. 167–84.

——"Translation, Meaning, and Self-Knowledge", *Proceedings of the Aristotelian Society* XCI, part 3 (1990/91), pp. 269–90.

—— "Analysis and Analytic Philosophy", in *The Story of Analytic Philosophy*, eds Anat Biletzki and Anat Matar (London: Routledge, 1998), pp. 37–55.

—— "'the defensible province of philosophy': Quine's 1934 Lectures on Carnap", in *Future Pasts: Reflections on the History and Nature of Analytic Philosophy*, eds J. Floyd and S. Shieh (Oxford: Oxford University Press, 2001), pp. 257–75.

—— "Quine on Reference and Ontology", in *The Cambridge Companion to Quine*, ed. Roger Gibson (Cambridge: Cambridge University Press, 2004), pp. 115–30.

—— *Propositions, Functions, and Analysis* (Oxford: Oxford University Press, 2005).

—— "The Theory of Descriptions", in *The Cambridge Companion to Russell*, ed. Nicholas Griffin (Cambridge: Cambridge University Press, 2003), pp. 202–40; reprinted in P. W. Hylton, *Propositions, Functions, and Analysis* (Oxford: Oxford University Press, 2005), pp. 185–215.

Kant, Immanuel *Critique of Pure Reason*, trans. Norman Kemp Smith (London: Macmillan, 1968; 1st edn, 1929).

Kaplan, David "Quantifying In", in *Words and Objections*, eds D. Davidson and J. Hintikka (Dordrecht: Reidel, 1969), pp. 206–42.

Katz, Jerrold "The Refutation of Indeterminacy", in R. Barrett and R. Gibson, *Perspectives on Quine* (Oxford: Blackwell, 1990), pp. 179–80.

Kenny, Anthony *Action, Emotion and Will* (London; New York: Routledge and Kegan Paul; Humanities Press, 1963).

Kripke, Saul A. *Naming and Necessity* (Cambridge MA: Harvard University Press, 1980). The text is based on lectures given in 1970; a slightly different version was published under the same title in *Semantics of Natural Language*, eds D. Davidson and G. Harman (Dordrecht: Reidel, 1972).

—— "A Completeness Theorem in Modal Logic", *Journal of Symbolic Logic* 24 (1959), pp. 1–11.

—— "Semantical Considerations on Modal Logic", proceedings of a colloquium in modal and many valued logic, *Acta Philosophical Fennica* (1963).

—— "Identity and Necessity", in *Identity and Individuation*, ed. Milton K. Munitz (New York: New York University Press, 1971).

—— "A Puzzle about Belief", in *Meaning and Use*, ed. A. Margalit (Dordrecht: Reidel, 1979), pp. 239–83.

Leonardi, Paolo and Marco Santambrogio, eds *On Quine: New Essays* (Cambridge: Cambridge University Press, 1995).

Lewis, C. I. *Survey of Symbolic Logic* (Berkeley: University of California Press, 1918).

—— *Mind and the World Order* (New York: Charles Scribner's and Sons, 1929).

—— *An Analysis of Knowledge and Valuation* (Paul Carus Lectures) (La Salle IL: Open Court, 1946).

—— *Collected Papers*, eds John D. Goheen and John L. Mothershead Jr (Stanford CA: Stanford University Press, 1970).

—— "Implication and the Algebra of Logic", *Mind*, n.s. 21 (1912), pp. 522–31, reprinted in C. I. Lewis, *Collected Papers*, eds John D. Goheen and John L. Mothershead Jr (Stanford CA: Stanford University Press, 1970).

—— "A Pragmatic Conception of the *A Priori*", *Journal of Philosophy* 20 (1923), pp. 169–77; reprinted in C. I. Lewis, *Collected Papers*, eds John D. Goheen and John L. Mothershead Jr (Stanford CA: Stanford University Press, 1970).

Marcus, Ruth "A Functional Calculus of First Order Based on Strict Implication", *Journal of Symbolic Logic* 11 (1946), pp. 1–16.

—— *Modalities* (Oxford: Oxford University Press, 1993).

Margalit, A., ed. *Meaning and Use* (Dordrecht: Reidel, 1979).

Moore, G. E. "Russell's Theory of Descriptions", in *The Philosophy of Bertrand Russell*, ed. P. A. Schilpp (Evanston IL: The Library of the Living Philosophers, 1946), pp. 175–225.

Mounce, H. O. *Wittgenstein's Tractatus* (Chicago: The University of Chicago Press, 1981).

Neale, Stephen *Facing Facts* (Oxford: Oxford University Press, 2002).

Neurath, Otto "Protokollsätze", *Erkenntniss* 3 (1932–33); trans. as "Protocol Sentence" by George Schick in *Logical Positivism*, ed. A. J. Ayer (New York: Free Press, 1959), pp. 199–208.

Nozick, Robert "Experience, Theory and Language", in *The Philosophy of W. V. Quine*, eds E. Hahn and P. A. Schilpp (Peru IL: Open Court, 1986; 2nd, expanded edn, 1998), pp. 339–63.

Orenstein, Alex and Petr Kotatko *Knowledge, Language and Logic* (Dordrecht: Kluwer Academic, 2000).

Pakaluk, Michael "Quine's 1946 Lectures on Hume", *Journal of the History of Philosophy* 27 (1989), pp. 445–59.

Patterson, James T. *Grand Expectations: The United States, 1945–1974* (Oxford: Oxford University Press, 1996).

Peacocke, Christopher "The Philosophy of Language", in *Philosophy 2: Further through the Subject*, ed. A. C. Grayling (Oxford: Oxford University Press, 1995), pp. 72–121.

Pike, Kenneth "Into the Unknown", *Pike on Language*, program 5, on 3.4-inch videocassettes (NTSC standard) and 16mm kinescopes (Ann Arbor: University of Michigan Television Center, 1977).

Pinker, Stephen *The Language Instinct* (New York: William Morrow and Company, 1994).

Putnam, Hilary *Mathematics, Matter and Method: Philosophical Papers, Volume 1* (Cambridge: Cambridge University Press, 1975).

—— *Mind, Language and Reality: Philosophical Papers, Volume 2* (Cambridge: Cambridge University Press, 1975).

—— "The Analytic and the Synthetic", in *Minnesota Studies in the Philosophy of Science* III, eds Herbert Feigl and Grover Maxwell (Minneapolis: University of Minnesota Press, 1962); reprinted in Putnam, *Mind, Language and Reality* (Cambridge: Cambridge University Press, 1975), pp. 33–69.

——"The Logic of Quantum Mechanics", first published under the title "Is Logic Empirical?" in *Boston Studies in the Philosophy of Science*, 5, eds R. Cohen and M. Wartofsky (Dordrecht: Reidel, 1968); reprinted in Putnam, *Mathematics, Matter and Method: Philosophical Papers, Volume I* (Cambridge: Cambridge University Press, 1975), pp. 174–97.

Ramsey, Frank P. *The Foundations of Mathematics and Other Logical Essays*, ed. R. B. Braithwaite (London: Routledge and Kegan Paul, 1931).

—— "Theories", in *The Foundations of Mathematics and Other Logical Essays*, ed. R. B. Braithwaite (London: Routledge and Kegan Paul, 1931), pp. 212–36.

Resnik, Michael D. *Mathematics as a Science of Patterns* (New York: Oxford University Press, 1997).

Richardson, Alan *Carnap's Construction of the World* (Cambridge: Cambridge University Press, 1998).

de Rouilhan, Philippe "On What There Are", *Proceedings of the Aristotelian Society* (2002), pp. 183–200.

Russell, Bertrand *The Problems of Philosophy* (London: Williams & Norgate, 1912; 2nd edn, Oxford: Oxford University Press, 1946).

—— *Our Knowledge of the External World as a Field for Scientific Method in Philosophy*, 2nd edn (London: George Allen and Unwin, 1926).

—— *Introduction to Mathematical Philosophy* (London: George Allen and Unwin, 1919).

—— *Inquiry into Meaning and Truth* (London: George Allen and Unwin, 1940).

—— *The Collected Papers of Bertrand Russell, vol. 4, Foundations of Logic, 1903–5*, ed. Alistair Urquhart, with the assistance of Albert Lewis (London: Routledge, 1994).

—— *The Collected Papers of Bertrand Russell, vol. 8, The Philosophy of Logical Atomism and Other Essays, 1914–19*, ed. John G. Slater (London: George Allen and Unwin, 1986).

—— "Lectures on the Philosophy of Logical Atomism", *Monist* 28, 29 (1918–19); reprinted in *Logic and Knowledge*, ed. R. C. Marsh (London: George Allen and Unwin, 1956), pp. 177–281.

—— "On Denoting", *Mind* 14 (1905); reprinted in *The Collected Papers of Bertrand Russell, vol. 4, Foundations of Logic, 1903–5*, ed. Alistair Urquhart, with the assistance of Albert Lewis (London: Routledge, 1994), pp. 415–27, and very many other places.

—— "The Relation of Sense-Data to Physics", *Scientia* (1914); reprinted in *The Collected Papers of Bertrand Russell, vol. 8, The Philosophy of Logical Atomism and Other Essays, 1914–19*, ed. John G. Slater (London: George Allen and Unwin, 1986), pp. 5–26.

Schilpp, P. A., ed. *The Philosophy of Bertrand Russell* (Evanston IL: The Library of the Living Philosophers, 1946).

—— *The Philosophy of Rudolf Carnap* (La Salle IL: Open Court, 1963).

Searle, John "Indeterminacy, Empiricism, and the First Person", *Journal of Philosophy* LXXXXIV (1987), pp. 123–46.

Sleigh, Robert C. "On a Proposed System of Epistemic Logic", *Nous* 2 (1968), pp. 391–98.

Smullyan, Arthur "Modality and Description", *Journal of Symbolic Logic* XIII (1948), pp. 31–37.

Soames, Scott *Philosophical Analysis in the Twentieth Century* (Princeton NJ: Princeton University Press, 2003), vol. II.

Solovay, R. M. "Provability Interpretation of Modal Logic", *Israel Journal of Mathematics* 25 (1976), pp. 287–304.

Spelke, Elizabeth S. and Gretchen A. Van de Walle, "Perceiving and Reasoning about Objects: Insights from Infants", in *Spatial Representation*, eds Naomi Eilen, Rosaleen McCarthy and Bill Brewer (Oxford: Oxford University Press, 1993).

van Straaten, Z., ed. *Philosophical Subjects: Essays on the Work of P. F. Strawson* (Oxford: Oxford University Press, 1980).

Strawson, P. F. *Introduction to Logical Theory* (London: Methuen, 1952).

—— *Individuals* (London: Methuen, 1959).

—— *Logico-Linguistic Papers* (London: Methuen, 1971).

—— *Subject and Predicate in Logic and Grammar* (London: Methuen, 1974).

——"On Referring", *Mind* n.s., 59 (1950), pp. 320–44; reprinted in Strawson, *Logico-Linguistic Papers* (London: Methuen, 1971), pp. 1–27.

—— "Particular and General", *Proceedings of the Aristotelian Society* (1953–54); reprinted in Strawson, *Logico-Linguistic Papers* (London: Methuen, 1971), pp. 28–52.

—— "Singular Terms and Predication", first published in *The Journal of Philosophy* LVIII (1961); reprinted in Strawson, *Logico-Linguistic Papers* (London: Methuen, 1971), pp. 53–74.

—— "Reference and Its Roots", in *The Philosophy of W. V. Quine*, eds E. Hahn and P. A. Schilpp (Peru IL: Open Court, 1986; 2nd, expanded edn, 1998), pp. 519–32.

Tarski, A. *Logic, Semantics, and Metamathematics* (Oxford: Oxford University Press, 1956; 2nd edn Hackett Publishing Company, 1983).

—— *Pojęcie prawdy wjęzykach nauk dedukcyjnych* (Warsaw, 1933); trans. by J. H. Woodger as "The Concept of Truth in Formalized Languages", in Tarski, *Logic, Semantics, and Metamathematics* (Oxford: Oxford University Press, 1956; 2nd edn, Hackett Publishing Company, 1983), pp. 152–278.

Ullian, Joseph S. "Quine and the Field of Mathematical Logic", in *The Philosophy of W. V. Quine*, eds E. Hahn and P. A. Schilpp (Peru IL: Open Court, 1986; 2nd, expanded edn, 1998), pp. 569–89.

Unwin, Nicholas "The Individuation of Events", *Mind* 105 (1996), pp. 316–30.

Watson, John B. *Psychology from the Standpoint of a Behaviourist* (Philadelphia: 1919).

Whitehead, Alfred North and Bertrand Russell *Principia Mathematica*, 3 vols (Cambridge: Cambridge University Press, 1910–13; 2nd edn, 1925–27).

Williams, Bernard *Descartes: The Project of Pure Inquiry* (London: Pelican Books, 1978).

Wittgenstein, Ludwig *Tractatus Logico-Philosophicus*, with a translation by C. K. Ogden (London: Routledge and Kegan Paul, 1922; corrected edn, 1933).

—— *Philosophical Investigations* (Oxford: Blackwell, 1953; 2nd edn, 1958).

—— *Blue and Brown Books* (Oxford: Blackwell, 1958).

—— *Notebooks 1914–16* (Oxford: Blackwell, 1961).

Wright, Crispin *Frege's Conception of Numbers as Objects* (Aberdeen: Aberdeen University Press, 1983).

INDEX

abstract objects: demanded by theory 303–4; no separate sense of existence 258–59; and naturalism 175; reification of 174–75; resistance to in 1940s 303–4; sets as the only 305

"Analytic and the Synthetic, The" (Putnam) 66–67

analytic–synthetic distinction: 51 passim; and a priori 9, 75; Carnap and 48–50; and convention 73–74; no epistemological distinction 74; and holism 71–72; and internal and external revisions 69–71; not a philosophically useful distinction 9, 52–53, 66–67; and pragmatism 70–71

analyticity 9, 64; and acquisition of language 67, 68–9; analytic intuitions 63–64; and artificial languages 60, 62–63, 64–65; Carnap and 48–50; contrast with significance 63–64; and convention 73–4; and definition 59–60; epistemological significance of 68–74; general syntax and semantics and 60–62; and inference patterns 67–68; Lewis and 51; of logic 49; of mathematics 49, 68; and meaning 65–66, 68; scope of 53; and single criterion concepts 67; and synonymy 55–56; special syntax and semantics and 60–61; and use of language 64

anomalous monism 313; and propositional attitudes 328–29; see also physicalism

Antony, Louise 376n15

a priori and a posteriori 9, 10; and analytic and synthetic distinction 75; and

analyticity 68, 74–5; Carnap and 74–75; no distinction between 9, 10; and internal and external questions 75; and logic and mathematics 74–75; and set theory 75–6

artificial languages 60–65; general syntax and semantics and 60–62; and meaning, synonymy, and analyticity 60; special syntax and semantics and 60–61

attributes see properties

Ayer, A. J. 377n2

Barcan (Marcus), Ruth 386–87n6

beliefs 17; there are no 333–34; see also de dicto propositional attitudes

behavioural similarity 117

behaviourism 102–3, 106–7

Bergström, Lars 377n4, 377–78n5

Berkeley, George 92

Birkhoff, Garrett 373n18, 382n13

bivalence 259–63; and ambiguity 262; determinate truth-values 260–61; and quantum mechanics 263–64; and simplicity 260–61, 263; and vagueness 261–62

Blackburn, Simon 379n12, 14, 385–86n6

bodies 300–302; identity criteria for 301; as physical objects 302; see also objects, physical

Boolos, George: on ontological assumptions of second-order logic 268–69, 382n16, 383n22; on quantified modal logic (QML) 387n7

Bradley, F. H. 383n24

397

with de dicto propositional attitudes 343–44, 347, 348–49; early account of 344–46; exportation 346–48; failure of extensionality for 344; later exclusion of in scientific languages 346–49; semantics of 345–46; syntax of 345; as relation between person and open sentence 345; as relation between person and proposition 345

de Rouilhan, Philippe 383n23

Descartes, René 370n7

dispositions 103–5; and innate mechanisms 106–7; and language 106–8; and truth-conditions 111- 13

Dreben, Burton 38

Duhem, Pierre 33–34, 220, 371n4

Dummett, Michael 260, 382n10, 11

Ebbs, Gary 372n8, 380n19

Einstein, Albert 238

emotions 328

empirical content 186; no criterion for 187–88; and holism 188–89; lack of for logic and mathematics 186–87; and Logical Positivists 187–88; as matter of degree 187; and progress of science 188

empiricism 13, 15; and Carnap's use of analytic–synthetic distinction 49–50; and language 56, 102–3, 106–7, 204; and naturalism 90; and regimentation 233, 244

"Empiricism, Semantics and Ontology" (Carnap) 39

Epicurus 385n6

epistemology 6–7, 26, 81 passim, 114 passim, 149 passim; Cartesian 83; and cognitive language 81–82; criteria of success for Quine's 363–65; and evidence 88–89; as genetic project 26–27, 95–96, 363; as justification 83–84; and metaphysics 22, 26, 363–66; naturalized 82–113; nature of 81–85; normativity of 84; and observation 88; philosophical significance of Quine's 364–65; and physical objects 87–88; reciprocal containment with science 22; and relation between evidence and theory 95–96; and scepticism 91–95; as semantics 96; and sensory evidence 89; and sensory experience 85; and sensory stimulation 88–89

essentialism see modality

eternal sentences 112–13; as bearers of truth-values 270–71, 274; compared to propositions 273–74; and regimented language 272–73, 274; as replacing context-dependent sentences 271–72

evidence: and epistemology 88–89; implied by theory 177–78; relation to theory 27–28, 71; and logic 28–29; and meaning 56–57; and observation categoricals 181–82, 190; and observation conditionals 180–81; and observation sentences 178, 179–80; and pegged observations sentences 180; and theory 91, 177–96

experience 11

existence: univocal criterion for 258–59

explication and elimination 62, 249–50; and convenience 247–48; and convention 73–74; and modality 354, 355

extensional contexts 288; non- and failure of referentiality 293–96

extensionality 288–97; and contrast between extension and intension 288; failure of 326, 344, 351–52, 356–57; and failure of referentiality 292–93; importance of 289–91; of logic 289–90; and reference 292–96; as single condition 289, 291, 296–97; see also causality; de re propositional attitudes; modality; propositional attitudes

Feigl, Herbert 386n7

Feyerabend, Paul 141

fictionalism see instrumentalism

first-order logic (quantification theory): advantages over second-order logic 265–69; completeness of 265–66; contrasted with second-order logic 263–65; and ontology 267–69; and ordinary language 268–69; soundness of 265–66; see also logic

Fodor, J. A. 375n11

Fogelin, Robert 373n2

Føllesdal, Dagfinn 375–76n7, 379n12, 387n9, 10

Frank, Philip 371n4

Frege, Gottlob 34, 111, 226–27, 233, 264, 305, 371n8, 373n17, 380n1, 384n10

Friedman, Michael 372n13, 378n6

Geach, Peter T. 169, 382n16

Gibson, Roger 370n1, 370n3, 371n10, 374n8, 378n6, 386n10

Gödel, Kurt 383n18; incompleteness
  theorem of 61; 383n19
Goodman, Nelson 385n2
Gregory, Paul 377n1
Grice, Paul 372n4, 373n10, 378n4
Grünbaum, Adolf 378n7

Hanson, N. R. 141
Harding, S. G. 378n7
Harman, Gilbert 370n5
Hart, W. D. 382n12
Hegel, Georg Wilhelm Friedrich 34
Heidegger, Martin 34
Hempel, Carl G. 371n4, 377n2
higher-order logic see second-order logic
Hintikka, Jaakko 201
Hobbes, Thomas 385n6
Holbach, Paul-Henri Thiry, Baron d'
  385n6
holism 14; and a priori and empirical
  distinction 76; and knowledge 13; and
  learning of relation 155; and logic and
  mathematics 76–78; and Principle of
  Tolerance 72–73; and relation of theory
  to evidence 154–55; and revision 76;
  and sensory stimulation 13; and
  observation sentences 13
Hookway, Christopher 371n10, 373–74n2;
  on indeterminacy of translation 223–24
Hughes, G. E. 386–87n6
Hume, David 83, 92, 373n2, 387n13; on
  necessity 359
Humphries, B. M. 194
Huxley, T. H. 385n6
hyper-Pythagoreanism 306–7; and realism
  319; see also physical objects, elimination of
hypothetico-deductive method 177–78

identity: and ontological commitments
  258; and reference 168, 172–75
indeterminacy of translation 59, 109, 197–
  200, 197 passim; and agnosticism about
  meaning 59; and dispositions 204, 228;
  and criterion for successful translation
  202, 215; as holophrastic indeterminacy
  197–98; and analytical hypotheses 216–
  17; arguments against 221–25; arguments
  for 215–21; and neurology 221–23; as
  conjecture 215, 219, 220–21; and
  holism 219–21; and meaning(s) 226–29;
  and propositions 226–30; significance of
  225–30; and stimulus meaning 216; and

synonymous expressions 226–27;
  synonymy 230; and underdetermination
  of theory 217–19; and incompatible
  translations 201; as indeterminacy of
  reference 197–98, 205–9; and
  observation sentences 205–6; as
  demonstrated by proxy functions 207–8;
  and ontological reduction 208–9; and
  reference 205, 207; and science 223–25;
  and semantic primacy of sentences 205–
  7; and translation 208; as ontological
  rather than epistemological 201–4, 212–
  13, 225; and solipsism of meaning 210–
  12; and synonymy 201; threatened
  incoherence of 209–14; and underdetermination of theory 202–3; and use
  of language 213–14; see also radical
  translation
Individuals (Strawson) 237
induction 83; instinct for 126–27; and
  observation categoricals 183
instrumentalism 19–20
intensionality: and non-referentiality 293–
  96
Introduction to Mathematical Philosophy
  (Russell) 33
Introduction to Semantics (Carnap): and
  analyticity 61–62

James, William 33
justification 75; of knowledge 83–84

Kant, Immanuel 33, 34, 383n24
Kaplan, David 382n16; on exportation
  346–47, 386n4
Katz, Jerrold 374n8
knowledge 8; as biological 15–17, 24;
  clarifying (re-formulating) our system of
  7–8, 13–14, 15, 29–30, 233, 236, 240,
  see also regimentation; and dispositions
  111; distinguished from brain states 23–
  24; as genetic project 94–99; as given
  83, 88, 89; and holism 13, 14; justification
  of 83–84; and language 23–24, 27, 30,
  98–99; and naturalism 19–20; and
  observation sentences 13–14; and
  philosophy 11; possibility of 26; as
  public 24; as seamless 11; and sensory
  stimulations 15–16, 27, 91; survival
  value of see knowledge as biological; and
  theory 8, 9–10, 25; theory of see also
  epistemology; theory

physical objects: contrasted with bodies 301–2; elimination of 306–8; identity criteria for 302; as portions of space-time 306

physicalism 310; challenges to 316–17; clarifies behaviourism 317; as constraint on physical vocabulary 312; empirical assumptions of 315–16; mentalist challenge to 314–15; and minds and mental 310–11; as non-reductive 312–14; as ontological doctrine 310; and physics 313–14; as principle of no difference without physical difference 312–15, 316; and propositional attitudes 328–29; semantic facts against 316–17; and theory 310–11

physics: full coverage of 313–16

Pike, Kenneth 374n10

Pinker, Stephen 376n9

Poe, Edgar Allen 33

posits 19, 20–21; as real 21; and theory 21, 85; existence of 85–87

pragmatism 33–34, 70–71; distinction between cognitive and non-cognitive 23

predications: eternal 162–63, 182; and general terms 163; learning of 158, 162–64, 167–68; occasional 162; physical 306–7, 314; and universal categoricals 163

predictions: and observations sentences 14; and theory 18

Principia Mathematica (Whitehead and Russell) 33, 35; influence on Quine 36–38, 290–91; and logicism 35

Principle of Tolerance 45–48, 87; and ontology 234; Quine's rejection of 53, 72, 235–36, 237, 373n12

Principles of Mathematics (Russell) 33

properties 259

propositional attitudes 325; and behaviour 328–29; and extensionality 326; not understood as attributions of neural states 328–29; *see also* de dicto propositional attitudes; de re propositional attitudes

propositions 270; and eternal sentences 273–74; have unclear identity-conditions 273; as timelessly true or false 270

proxy functions 207–8, 308; and realism 319–20

Putnam, Hilary 339, 341, 378n7; on analytic truths 66–67; on quantum logic 373n18

quantification: objectual 169, 256; and ontological commitment 256–59; and non-extensional contexts 295–96; substitutional 169, 256 radical translation 108–9, 197–98; and analytical hypotheses 203; and empirical approach to language 199, 203–4; and evidence 203–4; *see also* indeterminacy of translation

Ramsey, F. P. 378–79n8, 381n6

realism: epistemology does not threaten 318–19; indeterminacy of reference does not threaten 319–20; and scepticism 318–19; underdetermination of theory does not threaten 320–23; underpinned by naturalism 18–23, 317–18, 323

receptual similarity 117, 119

reference: and abstract objects 174–75; apparatus of 166; and identity 168, 172–75; and individuative general terms 167; learning the ability for 164–75; logic (quantification theory) 171–72, 176; and names 170–71; and objects (bodies) 172–76; and objectual quantification 169; and observation categoricals 170; and observation sentences 144–47; and predications 167; and pronouns 169–72; and regimentation 280; and relative clauses 167–69; and singular terms 170–71; and substitutional quantification 169, 255; and theory 148, 171, 176; and variables 171–72

regimentation 238–45; as avoiding philosophical problems 243–44; contrast between Quine and Carnap over 239–41; and inference 244–45; and ontology 236–38, 245–51, *see also* logic and ontological commitments; and ordinary language 239–41; as paraphrase of theory 242–43; as suited to particular purposes 241–42, 251–52; of theory 232–33; *see also* logic

Reichenbach, Hans 44

reification: of abstract objects 174–75; full versus perceptual 145–48; and perceptual similarity 146–47; and reference 147

Resnik, Michael D. 373n19

Richardson, Alan 372n13

Russell, Bertrand 33, 34, 39, 226–27, 234, 305, 371n8, 373n1, 377n5, 380n1–2,